MARRIAGE LAW AND PRACTICE IN THE LONG EIGHTEENTH CENTURY

This book uses a wide range of primary sources – legal, literary and demographic – to provide a radical reassessment of eighteenth-century marriage. It disproves the widespread assumption that couples married simply by exchanging consent, demonstrating that such exchanges were regarded merely as contracts to marry and that marriage in church was almost universal outside London. It shows how the Clandestine Marriages Act of 1753 was primarily intended to prevent clergymen operating out of London's Fleet prison from conducting marriages, and that it was successful in so doing. It also refutes the idea that the 1753 Act was harsh or strictly interpreted, illustrating the courts' pragmatic approach. Finally, it establishes that only a few non-Anglicans married according to their own rites before the Act; while afterwards most (save the exempted Quakers and Jews) similarly married in church. In short, eighteenth-century couples complied with whatever the law required for a valid marriage.

REBECCA PROBERT is an Associate Professor at the University of Warwick, teaching family law and child law. She has published widely on both modern family law and its history.

CAMBRIDGE STUDIES IN ENGLISH LEGAL HISTORY

Edited by
J. H. BAKER
Fellow of St Catharine's College, Cambridge

Recent series titles include

Marriage Law and Practice in the Long Eighteenth Century
A Reassessment
REBECCA PROBERT

The Rise and Fall of the English Ecclesiastical Courts, 1500–1860
R. B. OUTHWAITE

Law Courts and Lawyers in the City of London, 1300–1550
PENNY TUCKER

Legal Foundations of Tribunals in Nineteenth-Century England
CHANTAL STEBBINGS

Pettyfoggers and Vipers of the Commonwealth
The 'Lower Branch' of the Legal Profession In Early Modern England
C. W. BROOKS

Roman Canon Law in Reformation England
R. H. HELMHOLZ

Sir Henry Maine
A Study in Victorian Jurisprudence
R. C. J. COCKS

Sir William Scott, Lord Stowell
Judge of the High Court of Admiralty, 1798–1828
HENRY J. BOURGUIGNON

The Early History of the Law of Bills and Notes
A Study of the Origins of Anglo-American Commercial Law
JAMES STEVEN ROGERS

The Law of Treason in England in the Later Middle Ages
J. G. BELLAMY

William Sheppard, Cromwell's Law Reformer
NANCY L. MATTHEWS

MARRIAGE LAW AND PRACTICE IN THE LONG EIGHTEENTH CENTURY

A Reassessment

REBECCA PROBERT

CAMBRIDGE
UNIVERSITY PRESS

CAMBRIDGE UNIVERSITY PRESS
Cambridge, New York, Melbourne, Madrid, Cape Town,
Singapore, São Paulo, Delhi, Mexico City

Cambridge University Press
The Edinburgh Building, Cambridge CB2 8RU, UK

Published in the United States of America by Cambridge University Press, New York

www.cambridge.org
Information on this title: www.cambridge.org/9780521516150

First published 2009

A catalogue record for this publication is available from the British Library

ISBN 978-0-521-51615-0 Hardback

FOR LIAM

CONTENTS

PREFACE

This book has taken shape over many years and has benefited in different ways from conversations with numerous people, including Stephen Cretney, Judith Masson, Anne Barlow, Brian Dempsey, Steve Hindle, John Snape, and Gary Watt. Gren Hatton provided invaluable context on Kilsby, while Gwen Wilkins kindly let me consult her Warwickshire marriage index. My wonderful mother-in-law Rachel Brown was always willing to provide accommodation in London when I needed to use the libraries there, and made sure that I was well fed. Emma Watt provided both the first reference in the book and, indirectly, the last, and Ruth Foster-Smith provided encouragement throughout.

The research for this book has also entailed visiting numerous archives and libraries, and I would like to thank all the helpful staff at Denbighshire Record Office, Northamptonshire Record Office, Bedfordshire and Luton Archives and Records Service, Warwickshire County Record Office, the Record Office for Leicestershire, Leicester and Rutland, Carlisle Record Office, Wiltshire and Swindon Record Office, Somerset Record Office, Gloucestershire Record Office, Canterbury Cathedral Library, the Borthwick Institute at York University, Lambeth Palace Library, the City of Westminster Archives Centre, the Family Records Centre, the London Metropolitan Archives, the Guildhall Library, the Quaker Library, Dr Williams's Library, the Society of Genealogists' Library, the Institute for Historical Research, the University of London Library, the Wellcome Library, the Bodleian Library, the British Library, and Rothesay Library on the Isle of Bute. I would also like to thank Phillip Chancellor of the Queen's Chapel of the Savoy, for making its registers available for examination. Other institutions and individuals responded to my requests for information, including the Berkshire Record Office, Kendal Record Office, the County Record

Office Huntingdon, the Cobh Genealogical Project, Michael Snape, Martin MacGregor and Rosemary Harden of the Fashion Museum in Bath. Since the Exeter archive holding the Devon marriage index was unfortunately closed when I visited, Heather Holmes kindly agreed to act as a research assistant and checked the index for the marital status of the final few couples that I had been unable to trace. Tony Foster-Smith provided valuable information about life in eighteenth-century Anglesey, incidentally confirming my suspicion that Lewis Morris was not a source to be relied upon (see pp. 98–9). And I would also like to thank Helen Riley of the University of Warwick library for always informing me of the latest electronic resources available from my desk.

But, above all, I would like to thank my husband Liam, not only for his patience and forbearance, but also for his diligence as a research assistant, his willingness to engage with the arguments in the book, and his meticulous proof-reading. If he had not discovered that the marriage register of Llansantffraid Glyn Ceiriog not only existed, but was available to order as a transcript, I might never have developed the case studies that form so important a part of this book (and we would certainly have had fewer holidays located by local record offices). This book is dedicated to him, with all my love.

1

INTRODUCTION

It is a scene we are all familiar with: another country church; another bride in incongruously virginal white walks up the aisle, to be given away by a father under whose roof she has not resided for over a decade. The minister asks whether there are any impediments to their union, and members of the congregation look round furtively, perhaps half hoping that an unknown previous spouse will stand up and object. The parties exchange their vows and are declared to be husband and wife.

Many of the components of the supposedly 'traditional' wedding – the diamond engagement ring, the white dress, the morning suits, the late-afternoon ceremony followed by dinner and dancing – are innovations of the nineteenth and twentieth centuries.[1] But celebration in church can trace a longer pedigree, and the scene above would have been recognisable to our forbears. While the words of the marriage service have been periodically updated, all the fundamentals currently required by law for a marriage according to the rites of the Church of England – banns or licence, celebration in church, and registration – were in place by the mid-sixteenth century. Today, a Church of England wedding is merely one of a number of permissible routes to legal marriage and only a minority of couples choose to marry in this way. In the sixteenth century, however, a ceremony conducted according to the rites of the Church of England was prescribed as the only method for tying the knot, and the majority of couples observed its rules. Long before the Clandestine Marriages Act of 1753 made certain formalities essential to the creation of a valid marriage in England and Wales, the

[1] See e.g., L.-C. Windle, 'Forever and a Day: the Life of the English Wedding Dress, 1860–1906' (unpublished MA dissertation, Winchester School of Art, 2005). I am grateful to Emma Watt for this reference.

practice of celebrating a marriage in a church, or at least before an Anglican clergyman, had become virtually universal.

Yet this is not the impression of eighteenth-century marriage practices conveyed by modern commentators. Instead, stories of high-profile clandestine marriages, non-marital cohabitation and various esoteric ceremonies such as jumping over a broomstick abound.[2] Some scholars have gone so far as to suggest that marriage in church was in fact the practice of a minority, and that those without property had no need to observe legal rites and rules.[3] Others depict a system in chaos: according to one commentator, 'before 1753, marriage was to a considerable extent out of the control of either church or state'.[4] From this perspective the 1753 Act has been seen as a watershed in the history of the legal regulation of marriage, marking the change from a pluralistic system, in which multiple forms of marriage were accepted, to a more restrictive, prescriptive approach.[5] According to this interpretation the Act

[2] Most notably in the work of J. Gillis, whose work *For Better, For Worse: British Marriages 1600 to the Present Day* (Oxford University Press, 1985) is the mainstay of many subsequent accounts. For an analysis of the extent to which subsequent commentators have relied on his account, see R. Probert, 'Chinese Whispers and Welsh Weddings' (2005) 20 *Continuity and Change* 211.

[3] S. Parker, *Informal Marriage, Cohabitation and the Law, 1754–1989* (Basingstoke: Macmillan, 1990), p. 4; J. Schellekens, 'Courtship, the Clandestine Marriage Act, and Illegitimate Fertility in England' (1995) 25 *Journal of Interdisciplinary History* 433; A. Laurence, *Women in England 1500–1760: a Social History* (London: Weidenfeld & Nicolson, 1994), p. 51; W. Mansell, B. Meteyard, and A. Thomson, *A Critical Introduction to Law*, 2nd edn (London: Cavendish, 1999), p. 92; M. E. Rodgers, *Understanding Family Law* (London: Cavendish, 2004), p. 1; A. Diduck and F. Kaganas, *Family Law, Gender and the State: Text, Cases and Materials*, 2nd edn (Oxford: Hart Publishing, 2005).

[4] L. Stone, *Road to Divorce: a History of the Making and Breaking of Marriage in England* (Oxford University Press, 1990), p. 11. See also W. Cornish and G. N. de Clark, *Law and Society in England, 1750–1950* (London: Sweet & Maxwell, 1989), p. 361: 'control by church and state ... arrives only as our period begins, and even then has considerable headway still to make'.

[5] See e.g., C. Hill, *Liberty Against the Law: Some Seventeenth Century Controversies* (London: Penguin, 1996), p. 205: 'Hardwicke's Marriage Act of 1753 was resented, among other reasons, because it made illegal practices which were still tacitly accepted in some areas: it posed law and property against customary liberties'; see also Parker, *Informal Marriage*, p. 27; C. Gibson, *Dissolving Wedlock* (London: Routledge, 1994), p. 47; R. B. Outhwaite, *Clandestine Marriage in England, 1500–1850* (London: Hambledon Press, 1995), ch. 3; C. Flint, *Family Fictions: Narrative and Domestic Relations in Britain, 1688–1798* (Stanford University Press, 1998), p. 12.

'was designed to regularise state control over marriage and ... echoes ... the triumph of law over custom'.[6]

Academic opinions tend to be divided over the pros and cons of most aspects of modernisation, but the 1753 Act seems to have attracted nothing but adverse criticism. It has been perceived as a patrician measure, designed to serve the interests of the ruling classes whose aim was to increase their control over the marriages of their children rather than to benefit the majority of the population.[7] Others have seen it as a means of imposing 'middle-class' notions upon the rest of society, identifying it as 'part of a more general movement to discipline the lower orders'.[8] It is taken as a given that the freedom of choice of those intending to marry was circumscribed by the Act.[9] It has even been claimed that the Act fundamentally altered the very meaning of marriage for the participants,[10] transforming marriage from a private and meaningful rite to a bureaucratic transaction.[11] The fact that a Church of England ceremony was required – with exceptions only for Jews and Quakers – has led to accusations of intolerance and discrimination on the part of the legislature.[12] And it has been criticised as being prejudicial to women in particular: when the Bill was debated,

[6] D. Hay and N. Rogers, *Eighteenth-Century English Society* (Oxford University Press, 1997), p. 37; see also K. O'Donovan, *Sexual Divisions in Law* (London: Weidenfeld & Nicholson, 1985), p. 44; Mansell *et al.*, *Critical Introduction*, p. 92.

[7] See e.g., Cornish and de Clark, *Law and Society in England*, p. 362: '[t]he Act displayed a myopic preoccupation with the affairs of those who passed it'; see also B. Meteyard, 'Illegitimacy in Eighteenth-Century England: a Reply' (1981) 11 *Journal of Interdisciplinary History* 511; E. Harth, 'The Virtue of Love: Lord Hardwicke's Marriage Act' (1988) 9 *Cultural Critique* 123, 130; S. Parker, 'The Marriage Act 1753: a Case Study in Family Law-Making' (1987) 1 *International Journal of Law and the Family* 133; Gibson, *Dissolving Wedlock*, p. 46.

[8] C. Lasch, 'The Suppression of Clandestine Marriage in England: the Marriage Act of 1753' (1974) 26 *Salmagundi* 90, 104.

[9] G. E. Howard, *A History of Matrimonial Institutions* (New York: Humanities Press, 1964; original edn 1904), p. 463; R. Trumbach, *The Rise of the Egalitarian Family: Aristocratic Kinship and Domestic Relations in Eighteenth-Century England* (New York: Academic Press, 1978), p. 71; A. Macfarlane, *Marriage and Love in England: Modes of Reproduction 1300–1840* (Oxford: Basil Blackwood Ltd, 1986), p. 127; M. Vermillion, 'Clarissa and the Marriage Act' (1997) *Eighteenth-Century Fiction* 395.

[10] L. O'Connell, 'Marriage Acts: Stages in the Transformation of Modern Nuptial Culture' (1999) *Journal of Feminist Cultural Studies* 68.

[11] Gibson, *Dissolving Wedlock*, p. 47; Flint, *Family Fictions*, p. 54; S. Emsley, 'Radical Marriage' (1999) 11 *Eighteenth-Century Fiction* 477, 480.

[12] Howard, *History of Matrimonial Institutions*, p. 460.

it was claimed by one of its opponents that it would be 'of the most dangerous consequence to the female sex',[13] as a woman would no longer be able to enforce a promise of marriage. A number of later commentators have adopted the view that the Act did indeed cause hardship to women and led to a rise in the number of those who were debauched under a promise of marriage and then abandoned, thereby contributing to the rise in illegitimacy.[14]

The operation of the Act has attracted just as much criticism as the motivations of the legislators. It has been described as 'draconian',[15] 'stringent',[16] and 'in many instances productive of great hardship and injustice'.[17] It has also been assumed that it was strictly interpreted: commentators have claimed that a marriage might be annulled on the basis of trivial or accidental non-compliance with the formalities.[18] Finally, it has been seen as a failure: persuaded by purported evidence of cohabitation in the late eighteenth century, Hay and Rogers conclude that the attempt to regularise plebeian marriage did not succeed, and that in the end custom triumphed over law.[19]

So the Act is generally depicted as harsh, biased, and ultimately ineffective. But how far are such criticisms justified? The evidence

[13] *Hansard's Parliamentary History*, vol. XV, col. 69 (Henry Fox).

[14] See e.g., E. Tavor Bannet, 'The Marriage Act of 1753: "A Most Cruel Law for the Fair Sex"' (1997) 30 *Eighteenth Century Studies* 233. V. Duff, 'Early English Women Novelists Testify to the Law's Manifest Cruelties Against Women Before the Marriage Act of 1753' (2000) 29 *Women's Studies* 583, points out the deficiencies of the earlier law but agrees that the 1753 Act operated to the detriment of women.

[15] O. M. Stone, *Family Law* (London: Macmillan Press, 1977), p. 30; W. Holland, *Unmarried Couples: Legal Aspects of Cohabitation* (Toronto: Carswell Company Ltd, 1982), p. 17; J. Hall, 'Common Law Marriage' (1987) 46 *Cambridge Law Journal* 106, 107; D. Lemmings, 'Marriage and the Law in the Eighteenth Century: Hardwicke's Marriage Act of 1753' (1996) 39 *Historical Journal* 339, 346.

[16] N. Lowe and G. Douglas, *Bromley's Family Law*, 10th edn (Oxford University Press, 2007), p. 53.

[17] J. F. MacQueen, *A Practical Treatise on the Law of Marriage, Divorce and Legitimacy, as administered in the Divorce Court and in the House of Lords*, 2nd edn (London: Maxwell, Sweet, Stevens & Sons, 1860); W. P. Eversley, *The Law of the Domestic Relations* (London: Stevens & Haynes, 1885), p. 26.

[18] Howard, *History of Matrimonial Institutions*, p. 463; A. H. Manchester, *A Modern Legal History of England and Wales 1750–1950* (London: Butterworths, 1980), p. 365; Stone, *Road to Divorce*, p. 132; Parker, *Informal Marriage*, p. 61.

[19] Hay and Rogers, *Eighteenth-Century English Society*, p. 50. See also Cornish and de Clark, *Law and Society in England*, p. 363; L. Davidoff, 'The Family in Britain' in F. M. L. Thompson (ed.), *The Cambridge Social History of Britain 1750–1950*, vol. II, *People and their Environment* (Cambridge University Press,

on which they are based is often deficient. Basic errors about the terms of the Act crop up with alarming frequency.[20] No modern commentator has explored the case law on the interpretation of the Act in any depth.[21] And there is very little information about the way in which ordinary people experienced the law: few parish-level studies have been devoted to the specific issue of conformity. When I began to look at the operation of the law of marriage in the eighteenth century I was constantly surprised by the disjunction between the claims made by secondary sources and the evidence of the primary sources. At regular intervals throughout the research and writing of this book I have convinced myself that I must have misunderstood something.[22] But every time I have returned to the original sources – whether the Act itself, legal texts, contemporary cases on marriage law, the fiction of the time, or the parish registers that form the mainstay of a number of case studies used in this book – I have been reassured. In particular, I have drawn comfort from the fact that other scholars have had to explain away much evidence that does not fit with their arguments. It is of course entirely possible that some eighteenth-century individuals were confused about their legal status, but the more evidence that has to be explained away on the questionable basis of the confusions of contemporaries, the more any such theory should be regarded with suspicion. Occasional confusions could occur, but mass delusion seems unlikely. On the basis of such primary evidence, I have come to the conclusion that the 1753 Act did not constitute such a radical break with the past as has been claimed, was almost universally observed, and was not subject to harsh interpretation by the courts.

1990), p. 90; O. Hufton, *The Prospect Before Her: a History of Women in Western Europe*, vol. I, *1500–1800* (London: HarperCollins, 1995), p. 135; Mansell *et al.*, *Critical Introduction*, p. 92.

20 The two most common errors are that the marriage of a minor would be invalid in the absence of parental consent, and that a failure to comply with any requirement of the legislation rendered the marriage void: on the actual requirements of the Act see further Chapter 6.

21 Parker, *Informal Marriage*, p. 61 cites only a single case when discussing the impact of the Act, while the discussion of post-1754 cases in Stone's *Road to Divorce* and Outhwaite's *Clandestine Marriage* is relatively brief.

22 Indeed, in earlier publications I followed the standard view that a contract *per verba de praesenti* constituted a valid marriage: see e.g., 'The Impact of the Marriage Act of 1753: Was it Really "A Most Cruel Law for the Fair Sex"?' (2005) 38 *Eighteenth-Century Studies* 247. It took a considerable amount of primary evidence to persuade me otherwise and to give me the confidence to challenge this view.

But this is to anticipate. Two preliminary issues need to be considered before I can begin to substantiate these arguments: first, the definition of certain basic concepts that will recur throughout the book, and, secondly, the nature of the evidence on which I have relied.

DEFINING REGULAR MARRIAGE AND ITS ALTERNATIVES

In order to demonstrate that the 1753 Act did not constitute a radical break with the past it is necessary to consider law and practice both before and after the Act. The focus will be on the decades immediately before and after 1754, when the Act came into force:[23] too often in other accounts, as we shall see, evidence from the sixteenth, seventeenth, or nineteenth centuries is pressed into service as 'evidence' of trends in the eighteenth. The extent to which the 1753 Act was an innovation, and the impact that it had, can only be judged by examining law and practice as it stood in the eighteenth century.

It is appropriate to start with what was required for a regular marriage before 1754, as a basis for evaluating how far practice in the early eighteenth century departed from these prescriptions and how far the 1753 Act built on existing requirements. Christian marriages had long been celebrated with due ceremony, and the canon law that governed marriage prior to 1754 made it clear that marriages should be celebrated according to a prescribed form. The canons – as revised in 1604 – stipulated that the marriage should be preceded by the calling of banns in the church of the parish or parishes where the parties resided, or by the obtaining of a licence from the appropriate authorities. Further detailed prescriptions required minors to obtain parental consent and stipulated the hours and even days when marriages could take place. The canons also stated that the marriage should be celebrated by a minister, in the church of the parties' parish of residence, before at least two witnesses, and recorded in the church register.[24] Before 1754,

[23] Specifically, on 25 March, which under the old calendar had marked the start of the new year. In 1752 the Julian calendar was adopted, and henceforth the new year began on 1 January. Throughout the book I have used the modern style of dating: i.e., 1 January 1733 rather than 1 January 1732/3.

[24] On the details of the canonical requirements, see Chapter 6.

a marriage was only 'regular' if it complied with *all* of the requirements of the canon law; the same exacting definition will be used in this book.

The very existence of such rules inevitably necessitated a legal category to describe those marriages that failed to comply. There has been some debate among modern scholars as to whether non-compliant marriages should be described as 'clandestine', 'irregular', or 'informal': some use different terms to denote different forms of non-compliance,[25] while others encompass all deviations from the required norm within a single term.[26] Such modern classifications are, however, unsatisfactory in that they do not reflect eighteenth-century usage. I have not found the term 'informal marriage' in any eighteenth-century text, and the term 'irregular marriage' but rarely;[27] by contrast the term 'clandestine marriage', widely used in the eighteenth century, had a specific meaning, and one that is crucial for the correct interpretation of contemporary legal texts and cases. Although to modern readers the term 'clandestine marriage' might suggest secrecy and romantic elopements, in the eighteenth century[28] it would have been understood simply as a marriage celebrated before a clergyman of the Church of England otherwise than

[25] T. Benton, *Irregular Marriages in London Before 1754*, 2nd edn (London: Society of Genealogists, 2000), for example, reserves the term 'clandestine' for marriages that were not preceded by banns and did not take place in the parties' parish of residence, and uses the term 'irregular' either to denote marriages that took place in the parties' parish of residence but without banns or licence, or marriages that were preceded by banns or licence but did not take place in the parties' parish of residence.

[26] See e.g., Outhwaite, *Clandestine Marriage*, p. xiv, who uses the term 'clandestine' to describe all those marriages that did not comply with the canon law; and Parker, *Informal Marriage*, who employs the term 'informal marriage' in a similar fashion.

[27] At least in England and Wales, in contrast to the position in Scotland: see e.g., T. C. Smout, 'Scottish Marriage, Regular and Irregular, 1500–1940', ch. 9 in R. Outhwaite (ed.), *Marriage and Society* (London: Europa Publications Ltd, 1981), and, on the differing terminology of the Bill that dealt with Scottish marriage law, B. Dempsey, 'The Marriage (Scotland) Bill 1755: Lord Hardwicke's Attempt to Abolish Clandestine and Irregular Marriage in Scotland' (2009) *Stair Society Miscellany* (forthcoming).

[28] That it was used in a less specific sense in the medieval period and again in the nineteenth century, after the decision in *Dalrymple* v. *Dalrymple* (1811) 2 Hag. Con. 54; 161 ER 665 (see further Chapter 2), should not be taken as evidence of its meaning in the eighteenth century, any more than the Gothic revival of the early nineteenth century should lead an outsider to assume architectural continuity from the Middle Ages.

in strict accordance with the requirements of canon law.[29] Both the negative and the positive aspects of this should be stressed: the failure to comply with the law was not the sole defining feature of such a marriage, since exchanges that did not involve an Anglican clergyman[30] were not described as clandestine marriages.[31]

The term 'clandestine marriage' will therefore be used in this book in the way in which it would have been understood in the eighteenth century. This usage also has the advantage of drawing a sharp distinction between marriages that were celebrated before a clergyman – whether regularly or clandestinely – and the contract *per verba de praesenti*. The latter simply comprised an exchange of vows between the parties in words of the present tense; for example 'I take thee for my wife/husband'. It was binding on the parties (assuming it could be proved to the satisfaction of the ecclesiastical courts: no easy task, as Chapter 2 will show), but it was not, by itself, a complete marriage. Maintaining the distinction between a clandestine marriage and the contract *per verba de praesenti* is essential to an understanding of law and practice prior to 1754, since too often the evidence of one form of non-compliance has been mistaken for evidence of another.[32] Since it is a fundamental contention of this book that it is misleading to describe a contract *per verba de praesenti* as a marriage, it will be referred to as a contract, in line with eighteenth-century usage.[33]

Of course, to say that the contract *per verba de praesenti* was not the same as a marriage inevitably poses the question: by what criteria is this being assessed? This leads on to a final definitional point. It is commonly claimed that there were numerous alternatives to a

[29] This is also the meaning ascribed to it by Stone: see *Road to Divorce*, p. 96.
[30] On marriages celebrated by *non*-Anglican ministers, see Chapter 4.
[31] The reason for this was that such exchanges were not regarded as *marriages*, rather than because they were not regarded as clandestine. One could, for example, have a clandestine *contract*: see e.g., M.N., *A letter to a Friend Concerning Marriage Contracts, occasioned by a late Appeal from the Dean of Arches to a Court of Delegates* (London, 1740), p. 29. The ample evidence demonstrating the necessity of an Anglican clergyman to preside over the ceremony will appear in the course of the following chapters.
[32] As noted by D. Cressy, *Birth, Marriage and Death: Ritual, Religion and the Life-Cycle in Tudor and Stuart England* (Oxford University Press, 1997), p. 317.
[33] Stone, *Road to Divorce*, p. 46, suggested that the terminology of 'contract marriage' was used in the eighteenth century but there is no support for this in the primary sources: see further Chapter 2.

regular marriage prior to 1754.[34] One major problem with such accounts is that the status and function of the practices described is not always made clear. This leads to a number of practices (such as, for example, that attributed to the inhabitants of the Isle of Portland of not marrying until the woman was pregnant) being described as marriages or alternatives to marriage.[35] Pre-marital sex, by itself, hardly seems to merit the description of an alternative marriage practice. It is therefore important to determine what is actually meant by an 'alternative' to marriage.

A practice may be an 'alternative' to a regular marriage in two different ways. First, it may offer a different way of achieving the same end, i.e., a different route to all the same rights that would usually attach to a regular marriage. Secondly, the term 'alternative' may be used in a more radical sense to denote a different type of marriage that does not carry the same rights or legal status. In considering the prevalence of, and motivation for, alternative marriage practices, it is important to be certain which of these two types of alternative is meant.

From the first perspective, if a particular practice or ceremony did not give rise to a legally valid marriage, it would not be appropriate to regard it as a genuine alternative to a regular marriage. After all, a modern client seeking legal advice would be unimpressed by a legal advisor who expounded on all of the possible options but then admitted that none of them would be valid in the eyes of the law. With this in mind, some basic criteria for assessing whether a particular practice can really be described as an alternative to a regular marriage in the first sense will be suggested. First, a marriage may be defined as a relationship that is at least *intended* to be permanent: it is binding on the parties in a way that mere cohabitation is not, and exit from the relationship is regulated by law. A second criterion is that the relationship is recognised by the law, which accords a defined package of legal rights to the parties. Finally, marriage may be defined as a relationship that is accepted as legitimate by both law and society. The parties are regarded as a unit and would be allowed to set up home together with neither legal punishment nor social disapproval. The term 'full alternative' will

34 See e.g., Parker, *Informal Marriage*, p. 27; Outhwaite, *Clandestine Marriage*, ch. 2, who identifies no fewer than seven types of what he terms 'clandestine marriages'.
35 See e.g., Parker, *Informal Marriage*, p. 26, who describes it as a 'trial marriage'.

be used to denote practices other than regular marriage that meet all these criteria.

From the second perspective, a less legalistic definition of marriage should be applied, but it is still important to make sure that like is being compared with like. A particular practice could hardly be considered as a real alternative to a regular marriage if it did not fulfil broadly the same functions. If a couple were not actually living together, could they really be regarded as engaging in an 'alternative marriage practice'? It may be objected that not all eighteenth-century spouses lived under the same roof, but the fact that some did not does not mean that co-residence should not be a basic criterion for assessing whether a practice resembles a marriage. But at the same time co-residence might be explained by convenience rather than an emotional relationship: our concern is with couples, and therefore with those who were in a sexual relationship. A third potential element – namely the way in which a couple defined themselves – does not lend itself so easily to objective evidence, but on occasion we do have surviving statements from individuals that can throw light on their own perception of their status. Thus, the term 'functional alternative' will be used to denote a relationship that involved co-residence, sex, and, where this can be ascertained, some recognition by the parties themselves that the relationship was felt to be equivalent to a marriage.

These different meanings of 'alternative' will be used to analyse different practices for which the status of marriage (or of an alternative to marriage) has been claimed, both before and after 1754. After the 1753 Act, there was no question of any alternative form of marriage being a *full* alternative (at least if it took place within England and Wales and did not comply with those terms of the Act that were mandatory), but the question remains as to whether *functional* alternatives existed, as well as whether various evasive measures resulted in valid marriages.

Within this conceptual framework, a further question arises regarding the nature of the evidence used to determine whether any particular practice was a full or functional alternative to regular marriage.

VARIETIES OF EVIDENCE

The devil, it is said, has all the best tunes. It could also be said that those who argue that the 1753 Act was an imposition on ancient customs have all the best stories. When I first read the works of Gillis and Parker I was fascinated by their accounts of 'broomstick weddings', so much so that I told all my friends and acquaintances. On walking through Waterloo station one evening, a pair of us espied a broom lying invitingly on the floor, left there by a cleaner. We jumped over it (and, since neither of us wished to marry the other, even in play, jumped back again). So, in jest or in earnest, we may replicate what we believe to be tradition. Little did I realise then that the only actual examples of couples jumping a broom derived from a similar misunderstanding that this had once been possible.[36]

But even if a particular story does have a basis in fact, there is a danger in relating dramatic tales of elopements and infractions of the law: the memorable may be all that is remembered,[37] thereby giving a wholly misleading impression. The point is well made by Shorter:

> The easiest way to tell ... a story is to string together anecdotes from literary sources ... [However] [b]ecause one peasant couple exchanged affectionate greetings, does it necessarily follow that all did so? This is the old fallacy of confusing illustration with verification. Representing a general point with an example is not at all the same as establishing the generalization's validity.[38]

Conformity, by its very nature, does not lend itself to exciting stories. This affects certain types of sources more than others. Some diarists, no doubt, recorded every event they witnessed with exactness, but for most it would have been the exceptional that was worthy of note, and the quotidian that was left unrecorded. Novelists rarely concerned themselves with precise legal details, preferring to depict the form of marriage that offered the most drama and interest (or, where the wedding takes place at the end of the book, hurrying the parties to the altar to provide a speedy resolution to the narrative). Even weightier commentators are prone to reliance on exceptional instances: the eighteenth century had no equivalent of the social scientist engaged in empirical research. But since one would not assert that there was universal compliance with the Act

36 See further Chapter 3.

37 History 'is what you can remember': W. C. Sellar and R. J. Yeatman, *1066 and All That: a Memorable History of England* (New York: E.P. Dutton & Co. Inc., 1931), p. vii.

38 E. Shorter, *The Making of the Modern Family* (London: Collins, 1976), pp. 9–10.

solely on the basis of evidence that any given individual observed its requirements, so too any single example of non-compliance should not be accorded any greater weight in the opposite direction.

This is not to say that such evidence should be disregarded. Any source will provide evidence of *something*. The challenge for those attempting to decipher the past is to decide exactly what it is evidence of. Statements by contemporaries may only be evidence of scare-mongering, smear campaigns, or simple misunderstandings rather than proof of the practices they purport to describe. Travellers' tales may owe as much to what they have read in the comfort of their armchairs as to their observations on the road. No source should be taken at face value, and no theory should hang on the slender thread of a single piece of evidence. The need for caution may perhaps be illustrated by examining the oft-quoted[39] statement of a French visitor to England, M. Misson, who claimed confidently that '[t]o proclaim Ban[n]s is a Thing no Body now cares to have done; very few are willing to have their Affairs declar'd to all the World in a publick Place, when for a Guinea they may do it Snug, and without Noise'.[40] Less often quoted are the self-confessed limitations of his account of marriage practices: he warns the reader 'what I shall say here therefore is ordinarily practis'd only among those of the Church of England, and amongst People of a middle Condition: To which we may add, that live in or near London'.[41] And we know from other evidence that the majority of the population married by banns at this time.[42] Misson's observation may have held good for those of a certain social level, but were hardly accurate as a description of general practice.[43] In every case, the evidence should be considered as a whole; and we should be wary of attaching undue weight to vague and speculative claims that are not supported by other evidence.

39 See e.g., Outhwaite, *Clandestine Marriage*, pp. 60, 129; B. Hill, *Eighteenth-Century Women: an Anthology* (London: Allen & Unwin, 1984), pp. 182–4.

40 M. Misson, *Memoirs and Observations in his Travels over England, with some account of Scotland and Ireland* (London, 1719), p. 183.

41 Misson, *Memoirs*, p. 349. 42 See further Chapter 3.

43 Similarly, one might note that one commentator was fulminating about 'numerous Divorces' – in 1739: Philogamous, *The Present State of Matrimony, Or, The Real Causes of Conjugal Infidelity and Unhappy Marriages* (London, 1739), p. 36. No one would cite this as evidence that there *were* numerous divorces (as we today would understand the term) in the early eighteenth century, since it is apparent from other sources that there were not.

It is clear that different types of evidence are needed to answer different questions. For example, in determining whether a particular practice was a full alternative to a regular marriage, we need to know what its status was in the eyes of the law; in examining how far the 1753 Act was an innovation we need to be able to situate each of its nineteen provisions in the legal context of the time; and in assessing how far the courts' interpretation of the Act was harsh, there is no substitute for a careful reading of the case law. But, of course, it would not be legitimate to infer the prevalence of a particular social practice from a single case, or even a series of cases, any more than it would be to infer social practice from a single novel or contemporary statement. In considering whether a particular practice was a *functional* alternative to a regular marriage, or whether alternative practices sprang up in the wake of the Act, we need to know how people actually behaved. In the absence of any national census or reliable social statistics for the relevant period, the process of piecing together evidence about social trends must start from the very bottom, by examining how individuals within particular cohorts lived their lives. Parish registers and the listings that survive for some parishes provide cohorts whose marital status can be checked; while settlement examinations, whereby paupers were examined as to their place of settlement in order to determine which parish would be responsible for them, offer unrivalled insights into the lives of the poor. Each type of evidence does need to be considered in the light of the other: a bare account of the statute and the case law would tell us little about actual practice, while a particular practice might be inexplicable without a knowledge of the underpinning legal framework. This book is thus an attempt to fuse two forms of legal history that are often divided: what have been termed 'internal' and 'external' legal history.[44]

Of course, none of these forms of evidence are without their problems. The value of case law as a historical source has been much debated by historians,[45] but certain claims can be made for it. Cases do, for example, deepen our knowledge of the way people

[44] D. Ibbetson, 'Historical Research in Law', ch. 38 in P. Cane and M. Tushnet, *The Oxford Handbook of Legal Studies* (Oxford University Press, 2003).

[45] See e.g., Stone, *Road to Divorce*, pp. 27–33; J. Bailey, 'Voices in Court: Lawyers or Litigants?' (2001) 74 *Historical Research* 382; R. Probert, 'Control over Marriage in England and Wales, 1753–1823: the Clandestine Marriages Act of 1753 in Context' (2009) 27 *Law and History Review* (forthcoming).

behaved by providing rich details of individual examples. Nor are they confined to a particular social class: disputes relating to settlement offer an insight into the lives of the poorest members of society, those dependent on the parish, while rich and poor alike might be tried for bigamy. The law had ways of impinging on the lives of those who had no means (or intention) of invoking it themselves. Moreover, unlike novels and plays, there is at least the certainty that the characters existed and were embroiled in a particular dispute. For the lawyer, of course, matters are much simpler: cases provide essential evidence of how the law was interpreted and applied. The reasoning of the judge is of particular importance, since the lawyer needs to know how the decision was reached – and therefore how it can be applied to the next case[46] – rather than the objective truth of the facts alleged or the bare result. In addition, the pronouncements of judges were just as much a part of the social discourse of the day as were the diaries and fictional sources upon which the historians of the 'sentiments' school rely.[47] Legal cases are, therefore, a legitimate and rich source both for the lawyer and for the historian.

So too are the textbooks and treatises written by eighteenth-century lawyers. The early textbooks written by common lawyers have attracted considerable (and indeed entirely justified) criticism. All too often they consist of no more than a random assemblage of cases on particular topics (arranged, dictionary-style, in alphabetical order),[48] but even these may be of use in identifying and commenting on relevant precedents. The literature of the ecclesiastical

[46] Although it was not until the later part of the nineteenth century that a strict view of the binding force of precedent emerged, it is clear that judges did rely on earlier precedents when deciding cases, even if such cases were regarded as evidence of the law rather than as a source of law: see Manchester, *Modern Legal History*, p. 28; J. H. Baker, *An Introduction to English Legal History*, 4th edn (London: Butterworths, 2002), p. 199. On the nature of legal reasoning in the eighteenth century generally, see M. Lobban, *The Common Law and English Jurisprudence 1760–1850* (Oxford: Clarendon Press, 1991).

[47] M. Anderson, *Approaches to the History of the Western Family, 1500–1914* (London: Macmillan, 1980), ch. 3. On the extent to which law formed part of the general education of the educated elite in this period see W. Twining, *Blackstone's Tower* (London: Sweet & Maxwell, 1994). Even further down the social scale knowledge of the law was disseminated: see e.g., P. Griffiths, A. Fox and S. Hindle (eds.), *The Experience of Authority in Early Modern England* (Basingstoke: Macmillan Press Ltd, 1996), p. 3.

[48] See Lobban, *The Common Law*, p. 12; Baker, *Introduction to English Legal History*, p. 186.

lawyers was rather more sophisticated, perhaps because there was a longer history of learned treatises to draw on,[49] and forms an important source of information about law and practice.

Similarly, novels and other literary sources can provide useful insights – if used with due caution. We cannot assume that characters in novels are representative, or that the events portrayed ever happened outside their pages, or even that anyone at any time went through similar experiences. But novels both reflect and influence their social context, and it is thus legitimate to draw on literary sources to *illustrate* ideas that were current at the time: always bearing in mind, of course, the fact that the author may put words into the mouth of a character to illustrate the nature and disposition of that character rather than to provide legally or socially accurate information.

But for evidence of practice we must turn to other sources. Although parish registers are far from perfect as a tool for reconstituting the population,[50] they do provide certain basic evidence about the way in which people married, and a number of studies based on such material have been carried out for this book. Since reference will be made to them at various points throughout the book, it is convenient to set out their scope, and their various advantages and disadvantages, at this stage. To date, most demographic work has focused on single parishes (or an accumulation of single parishes).[51] Such reconstructions provide valuable evidence, but are open to the objection that they capture only the 'reconstitutable minority' who were baptised, married, and buried in the same parish.[52] The studies carried out for this book focus instead on specific cohorts of couples, drawn from baptismal registers,[53]

[49] See e.g., J. Baker, 'Famous English Canonists V: Henry Swinburne, B.C.L.' (1993–5) 3 *Ecclesiastical Law Journal* 5, 9.

[50] See e.g., E. A. Wrigley and R. S. Schofield, *The Population History of England, 1541–1871* (Cambridge University Press, 1981), Part 1, ch. 1.

[51] See e.g., Wrigley and Schofield, *The Population History of England*; S. Watts, 'Demographic Facts as Experienced by a Group of Families in Eighteenth-Century Shifnal, Shropshire' (1984) 32 *Local Population Studies* 34.

[52] See e.g., P. Sharpe, *Population and Society in an East Devon Parish: Reproducing Colyton, 1540–1840* (University of Exeter Press, 2002), ch. 1.

[53] Kilsby, Northamptonshire (1706–1836); St Mary, the Scilly Isles (1734–54); Holy Trinity Goodramgate, City of York (1735–52); Llansantffraid Glyn Ceiriog, Denbighshire (now in Wrexham County Borough) (1768–99); Colyton, Devon (1765–77); St Olave, City of York (1770–85).

settlement examinations,[54] and a rare parish listing.[55] The practices of non-Anglicans were also subject to scrutiny through baptismal and marriage records:[56] one might imagine that the very existence of a non-Anglican marriage register is proof enough of alternative practices, but care must be taken in ascertaining what such registers actually recorded, and whether the ceremony in question was supplemented by an Anglican marriage.

This comparison of different types of test groups allows two questions to be addressed: first, did these couples actually comply with the law, and, secondly, what techniques need to be employed, and what information is necessary, to answer this question? A few years ago tracing the marriages of those who married outside their parish of origin would have been an immense task; today, however, the surge of interest in genealogy has made much material available and, crucially, searchable electronically. The Internet-based International Genealogical Index is a boon to the researcher in identifying possible matches, while county-wide electronic indexes mean that searches can be extended over a much wider area than was previously practicable. Of course, the fact that one finds an apparent match is not a guarantee that it is the *right* match. If one has a John Smith and a Mary, it is usually impossible to determine which, if any, of the hundreds of possible matches is correct, and therefore all matches outside the actual parish being studied generally have to be excluded unless there is other evidence to confirm which is the correct one.[57] If, by contrast, one has a Malby Beckwith and an Alice (one couple who baptised their children in Holy Trinity Goodramgate in York in the 1730s)[58] one can be fairly sure that there will only be one couple with that combination of names. Propinquity also plays a part in determining whether any given match is a likely one: one cannot assume, without further evidence, that a couple baptising their children in York may have married

[54] P. Hembry (ed.), *Calendar of Bradford-on-Avon Settlement Examinations and Removal Orders, 1725–98* (Trowbridge: Wiltshire Record Society, 1990).

[55] D. Baker, *The Inhabitants of Cardington in 1782* (Bedfordshire Historical Record Society vol. 52, 1973).

[56] See further Chapters 4 and 9.

[57] For example, that the bride or groom is stated as being from the parish studied, or the use of the mother's surname as a Christian name for a child.

[58] Borthwick Institute, PR/Y/HTG.

in Cornwall, even if one finds an apparent match. Yet the mobility of eighteenth-century couples is a constant surprise: one would not, for example, usually make a link between a marriage in Berwick-upon-Tweed on the Scottish border and a couple claiming settlement in the Wiltshire town of Bradford-on-Avon. Yet this is where one such couple claimed to have married, and the marriage register verifies their claim. In not taking account of matches where there are multiple plausible options, or options that do not, on the face of it, appear plausible, I sometimes risk understating the extent of conformity, but it is better to do so if this inspires greater confidence in the results actually obtained.

Without giving away the ending, it is worth making the (somewhat obvious) point that the ability to ascertain that a particular marriage occurred depends on the information available, both about the couples in question and in the archives. Searching for a marriage is far easier if (as in the case of the settlement examinations) the parties have given evidence as to where it took place; similarly, if one searches electronic indexes, it is useful to have the additional confirmatory detail of the wife's maiden name, since the vagaries of eighteenth-century spelling[59] and the decisions of modern transcribers may mean that one spends fruitless hours searching for a husband with the surname Fitcomb only to find, when searching by the wife's maiden name, that it has been recorded as Titcomb. The mistakes of those who recorded the information in the first place are even more difficult to detect, but, since marriages were, in general, not registered contemporaneously prior to 1754, all too common.[60] Even more fundamentally, the record of the marriage may simply not exist. It is frustrating when one learns that the registers for a particular parish have been lost (or even, in one instance, stolen). Even if the register does survive, it may not be complete, as the candid response of the parish officers of Newbury to a request for information illustrates:

[59] See e.g., P. Sharpe, 'The Total Reconstitution Method: a Tool for Class-Specific Study' (1990) 44 *Local Population Studies* 41, 46–7.

[60] See e.g., the illuminating study by D. Ashurst, 'St Mary's Church, Worsbrough, South Yorkshire: a Review of the Accuracy of a Parish Register' (1995) 55 *Local Population Studies* 46, who compared different sources of information and detected misspellings of names in 10 per cent of the entries, different forenames in 0.6 per cent, and different surnames in 0.4 per cent.

Several couple as been married at our church during that clerk's time which was not entered in the Redgester, owing to his negligence, he being a very Drinking Man.[61]

The simple fact that the percentage of marriages traced rises in direct proportion to the information available indicates that researchers should not automatically infer non-compliance from a seeming absence of evidence. Given an eternity and infinite patience one could try to reconstitute the entire population of England and Wales, although, given the prevalence of missing and badly-kept registers,[62] omniscience would also be required for such an enterprise to succeed. In the absence of such powers, the researcher can only hope to make a useful contribution rather than to provide a definitive answer.

THE SCHEME OF THIS BOOK

In studies of this kind, there is always a question of how far back one should go:[63] should one begin in 1688, the conventional date for studies of the long eighteenth century, or in 1604, the year in which new canons regulating marriage were promulgated, or perhaps even in 1215, when the fourth Lateran council prescribed how marriages should be celebrated?[64] Given that the purpose of the book is to provide a reassessment of the impact of the 1753 Act, it is inappropriate to draw evidence of practice from earlier

61 B. Berryman (ed.), *Mitcham Settlement Examinations* (Guildford: Surrey Record Society vol. 27, 1973), p. 54. See also H. Tapley-Soper (ed.), *Topsham Parish Register* (Exeter: Devon and Cornwall Record Society, 1938), p. 318, and, more generally, *Report from the Select Committee on Parochial Registration*, 15 August 1833, Paper No. 669 in *Reports of Select Committees* 1801–52 (House of Commons, 1853), vol. 14, p. 25.

62 See generally N. J. G. Pounds, *A History of the English Parish* (Cambridge University Press, 2000), p. 290; Wrigley and Schofield, *The Population History of England*, pp. 23–4.

63 One has to draw the line somewhere, else one begins to resemble the character of Camel in David Lodge's novel *The British Museum is Falling Down* (London: Penguin, 1983; original edn 1965), p. 40, whose preparatory reading for his thesis on 'Sanitation in Victorian Fiction' 'spread out in wider and wider circles . . . [I]t often seemed that he was bent on exhausting the entire resources of the Museum library before commencing composition. Some time ago a wild rumour had swept through Bloomsbury to the effect that Camel had written his first chapter, on the hygiene of Neanderthal Man; but Camel had wistfully denied it.'

64 J. Brundage, *Law, Sex and Christian Society in Medieval Europe* (University of Chicago Press, 1987), p. 363; C. McCarthy (ed.), *Love, Sex and Marriage in the Middle Ages: a Sourcebook* (London: Routledge, 2004), p. 70.

centuries: the focus, therefore, will for the most part be on the period between the Marriage Duty Act of 1695 (which, as Chapter 5 will show, had a significant impact on the way people married) and the Marriage Act of 1836 (which introduced, for the first time, a number of equally legitimate routes to a valid marriage). Sometimes the history leading up to that period will need to be sketched in, in order to make sense of subsequent developments, but the core evidence presented will relate to the long eighteenth century.

Occasional forays are made into other jurisdictions where this is necessary to explain a certain legal development or to put wider trends in context,[65] but I have avoided relying on evidence of practice elsewhere, even by way of analogy, since there are obvious dangers in transposing evidence to a different social and legal context.[66] Some of the characters in the chapters that follow ventured north over the border to Scotland, but I have been hesitant to follow suit, save when demonstrating how the myth of 'handfasting' developed[67] or when describing how English couples eloped to Gretna Green in the late eighteenth century.[68] Differences between the law of Scotland and that of England and Wales existed both before and after the 1753 Act,[69] and the complexities of Scottish marriage law will need to be unravelled at a later date.

The scheme of the book is both thematic and (broadly) chronological. The first half considers different aspects of law and practice prior to the 1753 Act: contracts *per verba de praesenti*, non-Anglican marriages, and clandestine marriages. In relation to each the same questions are posed: given the law and practice of the time, what would the impact of the 1753 Act have been? Was each of these practices a full and/or functional alternative to a regular marriage in church? Chapter 6 then examines the reasons for the

65 Such as the Europe-wide increase in illegitimacy in the second half of the eighteenth century despite the lack of legislative change to the laws of marriage elsewhere: see Chapter 7.

66 See e.g., A. Thornton, *Reading History Sideways: the Fallacy and Enduring Impact of the Developmental Paradigm on Family Life* (University of Chicago Press, 2005).

67 See further Chapter 3.

68 See further Chapter 7.

69 See Smout, 'Scottish Marriage, Regular and Irregular'; L. Leneman and R. Mitchison, 'Clandestine Marriage in the Scottish Cities 1660–1780' (1993) 26 *Journal of Social History* 845; W. D. H. Sellar, 'Marriage, Divorce and the Prohibited Degrees: Canon Law and Scots Law' in W. N. Osborough (ed.), *Explorations in Law and History: Irish Legal History Society Discourses, 1988–1994* (Dublin: Irish Academic Press, 1995).

passage of the Act, how its provisions built on existing rules, and how the courts interpreted those provisions.

Chapter 7 considers the reaction to the Act, which came into force on 25 March 1754, and the extent to which its provisions were observed in practice. The way in which judges interpreted the terms of the Act is discussed in Chapter 8, which also traces the eventual replacement of the 1753 Act – after a good innings of almost seventy years – in the 1820s. Chapter 9 focuses on the marriage practices of non-Anglicans after 1754. This aspect of conformity merits a separate chapter, as the sheer diversity of religious practice in the late eighteenth century requires separate consideration of each sect. And the story of conformity was not a static one: the extent and nature of dissent changed over the period under consideration. The position of non-Anglicans also forms the backdrop to the passage of the 1836 Marriage Act, which did constitute a fundamental change to the law of marriage, and which provides an appropriate point at which to close the story of the 1753 Act. Of course, both history and law are continuing stories, and the concluding chapter considers the significance of this re-evaluation of the Act for our understanding of our past, present, and future.

2

THE MISUNDERSTOOD CONTRACT *PER VERBA DE PRAESENTI*

The prevailing view that the 1753 Act marked a radical shift in the regulation of marriage is based in large part on the hypothesis that prior to 1754 all that was required to create a marriage was the exchange of consent by the individuals concerned,[1] and that as a consequence couples had no need or desire to marry in church.[2] This chapter, by contrast, will show that an exchange of consent was not a full alternative to regular marriage – in that it did not carry the same legal rights as one celebrated before an Anglican minister – and that it was not regarded by contemporaries in the same way as such a marriage. As a result, couples had no option but to observe the rites and rules demanded by the law.

But if this was the case, then why has such a different view been advanced by other commentators? As with many myths, there is an underlying substratum of facts that are not in dispute. Lawyers today may point to the fact that it is still (technically) possible to enter into a marriage by a simple exchange of consent in certain

[1] R. B. Outhwaite, *Clandestine Marriage in England, 1500–1850* (London: Hambledon Press, 1995), p. 2, 'consent ... was the touchstone. Nothing else was strictly speaking necessary'; see also L. Stone, *Road to Divorce: a History of the Making and Breaking of Marriage in England* (Oxford University Press, 1990), p. 52; J. Jackson, *The Formation and Annulment of Marriage*, 2nd edn (London: Sweet & Maxwell, 1969), p. 16; N. Lowe and G. Douglas, *Bromley's Family Law*, 10th edn (Oxford University Press, 2007), p. 53.

[2] See e.g., E. Tavor Bannet, 'The Marriage Act of 1753: "A Most Cruel Law for the Fair Sex"' (1997) 30 *Eighteenth-Century Studies* 233, 234, who suggests that it was 'perfectly acceptable in many classes for a couple to exchange promises, go to bed and start a family before going to church, even to skip the Church ceremony altogether'; see also K. O'Donovan, *Sexual Divisions in Law* (London: Weidenfeld & Nicholson, 1985), p. 43; W. Mansell, B. Meteyard, and A. Thomson, *A Critical Introduction to Law*, 2nd edn (London: Cavendish, 1999), p. 92.

limited circumstances[3] as evidence that this was possible prior to the 1753 Act. But reading history backwards is a dangerous matter. The very fact that *Dalrymple* v. *Dalrymple*,[4] the case most often cited as authority for the proposition that before the 1753 Act marriage could be created by a simple exchange of consent,[5] was decided almost sixty years *after* the Act was passed indicates the need for caution. Leading cases like *Dalrymple* attain their status precisely because they establish a new point or settle what was before doubtful, and this chapter will show that *Dalrymple* did effect a change in the way a contract *per verba de praesenti* was regarded. The lengthy judgment of Sir William Scott in *Dalrymple* has been held in high esteem, but the learning that he displayed so abundantly related to the theory of the general canon law of Europe prior to the Council of Trent in the sixteenth century,[6] which he assumed to be the law of Scotland, where the events at the heart of the case had taken place, and which he also assumed represented the law of England and Wales prior to 1754.[7] Whether his comments were accurate in relation to Scotland is an issue requiring separate consideration;[8] whether they represented the law of England will be addressed in the course of this chapter.

But what of the canon law itself? Was not the English law of marriage based on the canon law, and did not medieval canonists

[3] Basically, in overseas jurisdictions where it is not possible to comply with the local law of marriage, or where there is no local form of marriage: see Jackson, *The Formation and Annulment of Marriage*, ch. 5; L. Collins, *Dicey and Morris on the Conflict of Laws*, 13th edn (London: Sweet & Maxwell, 2000), ch. 17. Of course, on the evidence presented in this chapter, the possibility of such a marriage is based on a misunderstanding of the legal position prior to 1754.

[4] (1811) 2 Hag. Con. 54; 161 ER 665.

[5] See e.g., Outhwaite, *Clandestine Marriage*, p. 2; R. H. Helmholz, *Marriage Litigation in Medieval England* (Cambridge University Press, 1975), p. 26; H. Elphinstone, 'Notes on the English Law of Marriage' (1889) 5 *Law Quarterly Review* 48.

[6] The 'Tametsi' decree of the Council reformed marriage law across Catholic Europe, requiring marriages to be solemnised in a certain form (see J. Brundage, *Law, Sex and Christian Society in Medieval Europe* (University of Chicago Press, 1987), p. 563). Since it occurred after England and Wales had broken with Rome, it had no effect on marriage law in this jurisdiction, although similar reforms were debated at the time (see e.g., Outhwaite, *Clandestine Marriage*, p. 7).

[7] This view was not, however, universally accepted by his contemporaries and was challenged in *R* v. *Millis* (1843) 10 Cl. & F 534; 8 ER 844: see further below.

[8] Certainly some commentators regarded *Dalrymple* as based on a mistaken assumption: see Lord Patrick Fraser, *A Treatise on the Law of Scotland, as applicable to the personal and domestic relations* (Edinburgh: T. & T. Clark, 1846), p. 110; *Report of the Royal Commission on the Laws of Marriage* (1868) PP vol. 32, p. xviii.

teach that an exchange of vows in words of the present tense – *per verba de praesenti* – created a marriage? The answer is a qualified yes; the caveats, central to this chapter, being that the writings of medieval canonists should be located as part of a theological debate rather than as part of a discussion about the practical regulation of marriage,[9] and that when theory was put into practice matters became rather more complicated.[10] Exactly what was required for a marriage to exist had been a matter of debate for centuries.[11] The key issue was whether a marriage had to be perfected by consummation or whether consent alone was needed.[12] The debate was not, therefore, concerned with the validity of a bare exchange of consent as opposed to a marriage formally celebrated in church.[13] To require consummation was theologically problematic, because so to hold would cast doubt on the validity of the marriage between Mary and Joseph at the time of Jesus' birth. Eventually, the view that consent alone was necessary prevailed, and '[c]onsent in the present tense was almost universally accepted by canonists after the late 1180s as the critical test of whether a marriage existed or not'.[14]

But this theologically inspired debate did not take place in a vacuum. The celebration of marriage had long been regulated by the Church.[15] And the acceptance of consent as the key criterion for a marriage led to a proliferation of twelfth-century legislation stressing that marriages should be celebrated with a due formality which allowed the public expression of that consent, precisely to avoid the problems that might ensue from a private exchange of

9 See e.g., F. Pedersen, *Marriage Disputes in Medieval England* (London: Hambledon Press, 2000), p. 2, describing Gratian's *Decretum* as 'a text intended more for the classroom than for the actual practice of law'.

10 See e.g., E. J. Carlson, *Marriage and the English Reformation* (Oxford: Blackwell, 1994), p. 15.

11 See e.g., Brundage, *Law, Sex and Christian Society*; C. Brooke, *The Medieval Idea of Marriage* (Oxford University Press, 1989).

12 See e.g., Thomas Aquinas, *Summa Theologiae*, quoted in C. McCarthy (ed.), *Love, Sex and Marriage in the Middle Ages: a Sourcebook* (London: Routledge, 2004).

13 See e.g., Carlson, *Marriage and the English Reformation*, p. 24, noting that theologians had little option but to prioritise consent, given the lack of any scriptural warrant for specific formalities.

14 Brundage, *Law, Sex and Christian Society*, pp. 268–9.

15 K. Stevenson, *Nuptial Blessing: a Study of Christian Marriage Rites* (London: SPCK, 1982), discusses the evolution of the church ceremony in detail, providing evidence of rituals dating back to Anglo-Saxon England, see pp. 42–3, 63.

consent.[16] An emphasis on consent was not incompatible with a relatively formal mode of marrying, such as that which existed at the time. It did, however, lead to changes in the actual wording of the service: Stevenson, in his study of the development of Christian marriage rites, noted the twelfth-century innovation whereby each party was asked by the priest if they consented to the marriage, commenting that '[a]s the canon lawyers exert influence on marital consent ... the man and wife have to express their desire to marry each other publicly, and no longer assume it as an implicit aspect of the rite, or part of a rite of betrothal not under the Church's influence'.[17] It is clear that consent was an aspect of a broader ceremony, not a factor rendering it redundant.

It may be objected that this emphasis on formal celebration was merely an attempt by the Church to extend its control over the populace[18] and that marriages based on private consent may have co-existed alongside formal marriages. This leads on to a second point: it cannot be assumed that canonical theories devised in the twelfth century by continental jurists automatically translated into legal and social practice in early eighteenth-century England (or indeed into social practice in twelfth-century England).[19] In order to understand the position in England and Wales prior to the 1753 Act it is essential to examine just how far theory corresponded to reality. We need evidence, not inferences.

[16] See Brundage, *Law, Sex and Christian Society*, p. 362, who notes that while consent made a marriage 'the popes also insisted that marriages should be public and made secret marriages illegal'; McCarthy, *Love, Sex and Marriage*, who sets out the twelfth-century English provisions requiring certain formalities.

[17] Stevenson, *Nuptial Blessing*, p. 68.

[18] On the acceptance of the ecclesiastical courts' jurisdiction, see Pedersen, *Marriage Disputes*, p. 208.

[19] Stone, *Road to Divorce*, p. 53, suggests that in the Middle Ages there were 'two culturally acceptable forms of marriage in England', the 'official mode' involving marriage in church, which was practised by the elite, and 'the popular mode of verbal contract or spousals, accompanied by folk rituals'. Those who have examined medieval records are more cautious in their assessment of the extent to which a verbal contract did act as a functional alternative to marriage: the argument advanced by Helmholz, *Marriage Litigation*, p. 51, that people believed in their 'freedom to regulate their own matrimonial arrangements' related to the disregard of contracts, not their use as an alternative to formal marriage. Indeed, he suggests that laymen did not share the Church's view that a contract *per verba de praesenti* constituted a marriage but regarded it as merely a contract: '[w]hat counted in the mind of many people was the formal solemnization and the consummation of the union' (p. 32). The prevalence of solemnisation in church is also evident in Pedersen, *Marriage Disputes*, pp. 36, 60, 80, 114, 173.

The legal and social practice of medieval England lies outside the scope of this book;[20] given that the impact of the 1753 Act on law and customs would have been conditioned by the situation as it stood at mid-century, rather than by the practices of earlier generations, it is important to focus on the period immediately prior to the passage of the Act. Earlier developments will, however, be noted where they confirm the longevity of a particular rule or practice. I will look first at how contracts were proved in court, in order to illustrate the distinction between an exchange of vows that was binding in conscience and one that could be proved to the satisfaction of the courts and thereby show the difficulties in establishing a contract. I will then go on to examine the legal consequences of such a contract, demonstrating that it did not carry full legal rights.[21] Of course, it could be argued that legal status does not necessarily accord with popular understandings, and in the third section I accordingly consider the ways in which a contract *per verba de praesenti* was perceived by contemporaries, including those who debated the 1753 Act in Parliament, individual litigants who sought to enforce such contracts, and those novelists and playwrights whose fictional characters experienced legal as well as emotional obstacles in their progress to the happy ending. Finally, I trace the process by which a different understanding of the contract *per verba de praesenti* emerged, in order to show why the modern conception of it is so different from the way in which it was understood in the past.

PROOF

Seeing secret contracts cannot be proved, it is all one in effect as if they were not.[22]

[20] For a recent account see C. Donahue, *Law, Marriage, and Society in the Later Middle Ages: Arguments about Marriage in Five Courts* (Cambridge University Press, 2007), who notes that 'going from the evidence of the patterns of the cases to conclusions about marriages that were not disputed is . . . highly risky' (p. 216).

[21] For ease of exposition, I focus on the status of the contract *per verba de praesenti*, since the same principles applied to a contract *per verba de futuro* (or indeed a conditional contract) that was followed by sexual intercourse.

[22] H. Swinburne, *A Treatise of Spousals, or Matrimonial Contracts*, 2nd edn (London, 1711), p. 194. Henry Swinburne (c. 1551–1624) was an ecclesiastical lawyer who held a number of judicial posts in the York courts. His treatise was published posthumously in 1686, with a second updated edition appearing in 1711.

The quotation from Swinburne illustrates how a contract might have taken place and yet not be accorded any recognition by the law. According to the theory expounded by the canon lawyers, no formalities were necessary, nor was the presence of a priest or any witnesses required, to make a contract *per verba de praesenti* binding – at least *in foro interno* or before God.[23] Indeed, Swinburne was of the opinion that individuals should be guided by conscience, and adhere to their contracts even if they could not be proved. But it is clear that this was a standpoint motivated by religious considerations rather than a statement of the law. Morally, whether or not a contract could be proved was irrelevant;[24] legally, it was crucial: a contract that was morally binding was not necessarily enforceable in the ecclesiastical courts that had jurisdiction over such contracts.

Before examining the way in which contracts were dealt with by the church courts, it is necessary to set out what exactly had to be proved for a court to be satisfied that a contract existed. The promises of the parties had to be mutual: as Ayliffe put it, 'if the man says to the woman, I promise that I will marry thee, and the woman does not promise the like to the man, this is a contract that walks upon one leg; and, consequently, not of any force in law'.[25] But the reciprocating promise did not need to be made in the same words, or in any words at all: if, for example, the man added 'if thou wilt marry me, then kiss me or give me thy hand', and the woman complied, this would be sufficient indication of her consent.[26] The law did not insist that a set phrase be used to signify consent to marriage: any words or other means[27] that signified the

23 Swinburne, *A Treatise of Spousals*, p. 196.

24 As Baker notes, a man who had entered into an unwitnessed contract *per verba de praesenti* with one woman and then publicly married another would be required by the church courts to live with the second, but '[t]heologians were forced into the position that such a man ought in conscience to disobey the Church and suffer excommunication on earth, safe in the knowledge that he would be absolved at the last judgment': J. H. Baker, *An Introduction to English Legal History*, 4th edn (London: Butterworths, 2002), p. 548. See also Helmholz, *Marriage Litigation*, p. 63, and Swinburne, *A Treatise of Spousals*, p. 228.

25 J. Ayliffe, *Parergon Juris Canonici Anglicani* (London, 1726), p. 246; see also T. Salmon, *A Critical Essay concerning Marriage* (London, 1724), p. 181; Swinburne, *A Treatise of Spousals*, p. 107.

26 Swinburne, *A Treatise of Spousals*, p. 205.

27 Swinburne devoted an entire chapter of *A Treatise of Spousals* to the issue of whether a contract could be made by signs: clearly this was possible if the parties were unable to speak, but in other cases the potential for ambiguity was a reason for caution. Thus, the giving and receiving of a ring might, Swinburne suggested, be

parties' consent would suffice.[28] However, given the importance of marriage it had to be very clear that this was what was intended: words spoken in jest were 'said not to be obligatory in so serious a matter'.[29] The main issue was the tense used by the parties: the exchange of words such as 'I do take thee to my wife/husband' constituted a contract *per verba de praesenti*,[30] but 'I will marry thee' or 'I will take thee to my wife/husband' was only a contract *per verba de futuro*,[31] and therefore not binding on the parties unless they subsequently had sex, which was deemed to represent their present consent to marriage.[32] Whether any condition had been stipulated was also relevant: if the parties agreed to marry subject to a stipulated condition being fulfilled, the contract was binding either if the condition was fulfilled, or if sexual intercourse took place, the latter being taken as evidence that the condition was no longer operative.[33]

After a contract *per verba de praesenti* had been entered into, either party could bring an action in the ecclesiastical courts[34] to compel

sufficient to establish the necessary consent to marriage, but only if it was delivered 'in solemn form, and put on the Woman's fourth finger, by the Party himself, and she willingly, not only accept the same, but wear it accordingly': *A Treatise of Spousals*, p. 211. Significantly, this contention rested on the fact that it was customary for a ring to be given during the marriage ceremony, but not when parties exchanged consent *per verba de praesenti*. For a contrary view, see Ayliffe, *Parergon Juris Canonici Anglicani*, p. 249, and see Helmholz, *Marriage Litigation*, pp. 45–6.

28 Ayliffe, *Parergon Juris Canonici Anglicani*, p. 247.

29 Salmon, *Critical Essay*, p. 187; Swinburne, *A Treatise of Spousals*, p. 105. Internal reservations, however, were irrelevant in the eyes of the law: Swinburne, *A Treatise of Spousals*, p. 84.

30 See Swinburne, *A Treatise of Spousals*, ch. 11 on the variety of ways in which this could be phrased.

31 See e.g., Swinburne, *A Treatise of Spousals*, p. 56.

32 A contract *per verba de futuro* that was *not* followed by sexual intercourse was not binding on the parties, although from the late seventeenth century backing out of such a promise was rendered more difficult by the availability of a remedy for damages in the common-law courts: see e.g., *Baker* v. *Smith* (1651) Style 295; 82 ER 722; *Rutter* v. *Hebden* (1664) 1 Lev. 147; 83 ER 341; *Mills* v. *Middleton* (1670) 1 Keble 866; 83 ER 1289; *Burrell* v. *Strong* (1672) 1 Freem. 65; 89 ER 50.

33 Ayliffe, *Parergon Juris Canonici Anglicani*, p. 248; Swinburne, *A Treatise of Spousals*, p. 147.

34 The existence of a contract *per verba de praesenti* was not a matter for the common-law courts, since such a contract conferred no rights on the parties at common law: see further below. Cf. Outhwaite, *Clandestine Marriage*, p. 2, who suggested that written proof of a contract was required by common lawyers, citing the Statute of Frauds, 29 Car. 2 c. 3. The common-law courts did deal with *future* promises of marriage, awarding damages for breach, but the roles of the two courts were clearly demarcated (see e.g., *Collins* v. *Jessot* (1705) 6 Mod. 155;

solemnisation in church: '[i]f any doth contract Marriage, but doth not solemnise it in the Face of the Church; and if [either] doth deny this contract; the [other] may Institute an Action in a Cause of Contract'.[35] This particular cause was the *only* way of enforcing a contract *per verba de praesenti*;[36] there was no English equivalent to the Scottish declarator of marriage. It was also distinct from the form of action used to bring back a reluctant spouse once a marriage had been solemnised in church: in this context the appropriate remedy was an action for restitution of conjugal rights.[37]

The proof that would be required in a cause of contract was regulated by the canon law, as revised in 1604.[38] If both parties to the contract agreed that they had entered into a contract in words of the present tense, and no third parties were involved, then no further evidence was required.[39] Of course, few, if any, cases were this easy, since there would be little need for legal enforcement if the parties were in agreement.[40]

87 ER 913), and by the start of the eighteenth century it had been established that s. 4 of the Statute of Frauds only required contracts *in consideration of* marriage to be in writing, not contracts *for* marriage (see e.g., *Cork* v. *Baker* (1717) 1 Str. 34; 93 ER 367; *Atkins* v. *Far* (1738) West T Hard. 589; 25 ER 1100, cf. the earlier decision in *Philpott* v. *Wallet* (1682) 3 Lev. 65; 83 ER 579).

35 H. Consett, *The Practice of the Spiritual or Ecclesiastical Courts* (London, 1708), p. 253. See also P. Floyer, *The Proctor's Practice in the Ecclesiastical Courts* (London, 1744), p. 78, and the precedent provided in *The Clerk's Instructor in the Ecclesiastical Courts* (London, 1740), p. 308.

36 See e.g., the arguments advanced by Henry Fox in the debates on the Clandestine Marriages Bill. He spoke passionately about those unfortunate women debauched under a promise of marriage: 'by this Bill you are going to take from them the *only remedy they have*, the *only method in which they can sue for the performance of such a promise*'. *Hansard's Parliamentary Debates*, vol. XV, col. 68 (emphasis added). In such a case it would not matter whether the promise was in the present or future tense, since the subsequent debauching would render the tense used irrelevant.

37 Consett, *Practice of the Spiritual ... Courts*, p. 253; Helmholz, *Marriage Litigation*, p. 67. This distinction is not appreciated by Stone, who incorrectly describes the case of *Moseley* v. *Collier*, an action to enforce a contract, as a case of restitution of conjugal rights: *Uncertain Unions, and Broken Lives: Intimate and Revealing Accounts of Marriage and Divorce in England* (Oxford University Press, 1995) p. 96.

38 It should be noted, however, that the 1604 canons largely codified existing practice. Indeed, as early as the twelfth century the Council of Westminster stipulated that an unwitnessed promise of marriage would be null if denied by either party: see M. Sheehan, *Marriage, Family and the Law in Medieval Europe: Collected Studies* (J. Farge and J. Rosenthal (eds.), Cardiff: University of Wales Press, 1996), ch. 8.

39 Salmon, *Critical Essay*, p. 200.

40 This should not be taken as implying that most couples took no further action after contracting: see further Chapter 3.

If a third party was involved in the case, the issues became much more complex. Take, for example, a case in which one of the parties to a private exchange of consent had subsequently gone through a public ceremony of marriage with another person, or had contracted to another before witnesses. In this situation, the consensus of opinion was that the public ceremony or the witnessed contract would prevail over the private exchange of vows unless there was other proof of the first contract. The canon law explicitly stated that the sole confession of the parties themselves was not sufficient in this situation: canon 105 of the redrafted 1604 code advised caution in cases 'wherein Matrimony, having been in the Church duly solemnised, is required upon any Suggestion or Pretext whatsoever to be dissolved or annulled' and stipulated that 'credit be not given to the sole confession of the Parties themselves, howsoever taken upon Oath'.[41] As one early eighteenth-century writer explained:

> altho', before God, the secret Precontract never published, is to be preferr'd before the like subsequent Contract, how publick soever; yet before Judges Ecclesiastical it is otherwise, and the Confession of both Parties, pretending themselves precontracted, without other Proof, shall not be credited, in Prejudice of a Contract sufficiently testify'd and prov'd by Witnesses; because then it would be a very easy Matter for such as were duly contracted, under Pretence of a Precontract, at their Pleasure, when they were weary of one another, to undo the most undoubted Contract, by suborning those whom they lik'd better, to affirm a former secret Contract with them.[42]

Thus, quite sensibly, it was not possible to undo a marriage by claiming a prior, unwitnessed exchange with a third party.[43] The law, after all, had to deal with practicalities, and it made sense that a prior unwitnessed exchange should not have the effect of dissolving a later marriage or contract. Even if there had been *one* witness to the first contract, it would not usually prevail as against a later

[41] *A collection of articles, canons, injunctions, &c. Together with several Acts of Parliament concerning ecclesiastical matters* (London, 1713), p. 70.

[42] Salmon, *Critical Essay*, pp. 199–200. See also Swinburne, *A Treatise of Spousals*, p. 199.

[43] M. Ingram, *Church Courts, Sex and Marriage in England, 1570–1640* (Cambridge University Press, 1987), p. 177, notes that annulments were sometimes granted on the unsupported testimony of the parties but that this became much less common after it was expressly forbidden by the canons of 1604.

marriage or even a subsequent contract supported by two witnesses, even if the first contract was also supported by 'common Fame'.[44]

At the same time, it was recognised that a strict application of this rule would allow an individual to renege on an earlier unwitnessed contract by entering into a marriage or a second, public contract. Steps could therefore be taken to prevent a marriage or second contract while the first was being litigated: the defendant would be forbidden to contract or solemnise marriage with any other person while the case was being decided,[45] while parties marrying by licence were obliged to swear that there was no impediment to the marriage, and 'no Controversy of Suit depending in any Court, before any Ecclesiastical Judge, concerning such Precontract'.[46] If these measures failed, 'the former Contract, prov'd by one Witness, and common Fame, of the Precontract, is preferr'd before the second Contract, prov'd by two Witnesses'.[47] This meant that the proof required for the first contract was lessened if there had been a fraudulent attempt to avoid it by entering into a second one.[48] The first contract would also be preferred if the second contract had been made upon the condition that there was no precontract, or if the second contract took the form of a promise of future marriage 'or there be other Circumstances to induce the Judge to give Sentence for the former Contract'.[49] A second marriage may in any case have deterred the plaintiff from pursuing the matter: as one commentator noted, a woman might enter into a second contract and have

44. Salmon, *Critical Essay*, p. 200; see also R. H. Helmholz, *The Oxford History of the Laws of England*, vol. I, *The Canon Law and Ecclesiastical Jurisdiction from 597 to the 1640s* (Oxford University Press, 2004), p. 531. However, in such a case the ecclesiastical courts could, if they saw fit, administer a suppletory oath to allow the claimant to swear to the truth of the matters alleged. It was explained that '[t]he accepting this oath ... lies in *arbitrio judicis* and is only used where there is but what the civilians esteem a *semiplena probatio*', i.e., 'that degree of evidence which would incline a reasonable man to either side of the question': Sir J. Strange, *Reports of Adjudged Cases in the Courts of Chancery, King's Bench, Common Pleas and Exchequer* (London, 1755), vol. I, pp. 80, 82, discussing *Williams* v. *Lady Bridget Osborne* (1717).

45 Floyer, *The Proctor's Practice*, pp. 78–9; '[i]f a person so inhibited from marrying do marry pending Suit, he or she may be cited to answer Articles of Contempt'. See also Consett, *Practice of the Spiritual Courts*, pp. 253, 257.

46 R. Grey, *A System of English Ecclesiastical Law*, 4th edn (London, 1743), p. 144.

47 Salmon, *Critical Essay*, p. 201. See also Consett, *Practice of the Spiritual Courts*, pp. 268–9.

48 Consett, *Practice of the Spiritual Courts*, p. 269.

49 Salmon, *Critical Essay*, p. 201.

the marriage solemnised in the belief that 'her Adversary will not (willingly however) obtain an adjudicatory Sentence for a Woman who (in his opinion) is known by another Man; and upon this supposition, that he will willingly compound, or desist from the Sute'.[50] One jilted suitor, the Rev. John Goole, put it more sourly: 'a Woman who has broke a Secret Contract of the present Time by entring into a Second Marriage, cannot be worthy of the Desires and Affections of any Man of Honour and Virtue'.[51]

Goole's case, heard by the Court of Arches in 1732, in fact provides a telling illustration of the difficulties in proving a contract.[52] He had paid his addresses to the nineteen-year-old Miss Hudson, and proposed to her. After some time she accepted: 'I think 'tis time for me to engage myself to you',[53] and they contracted themselves according to the words of the Prayer Book, in words of the present tense. Yet not long afterwards she went through a ceremony of marriage in church with a Mr Boyce, son of one Sir John Boyce and presumably a more socially advantageous match. The Rev. Goole thereupon brought an action in the ecclesiastical court to establish whether his contract with her was binding. The Court of Arches ruled that the contract was of no force in law, and that the marriage between Miss Hudson and Mr Boyce was therefore perfectly valid. Yet Mrs Boyce (as she now was) had admitted the crucial details of her earlier contract *per verba de praesenti* in court. Why, then, was it not upheld? The answer, of course, lies in canon 105: even her word was not sufficient in the circumstances. The problem for the Rev. Goole was that his contract with Miss Hudson had been made privately, without any witnesses being present. Thus, the decision of the court was far from being patently illegal, as Stone suggests,[54] but rather was in exact accordance with the canon law. The means by which the church courts sought to prevent marriages where one of

50 Consett, *Practice of the Spiritual Courts*, p. 268.

51 J. Goole, *The Contract Violated, or the Hasty Marriage* (London, 1733), p. xiii.

52 While the following account is based on his own somewhat self-serving account of their courtship, the supporting documents show that Miss Hudson herself confessed the truth of the key elements.

53 Goole, *The Contract Violated*, p. 11.

54 *Road to Divorce*, p. 79. Stone was perhaps misled by the pamphleteer who used Goole's case as an opportunity for a general rant against the ecclesiastical courts: see *Dr Johnstoun's Dissertation against Ecclesiastical Courts: a Judicial Dissertation concerning the Scripture Doctrine of Marriage Contracts* (London, 1734).

the parties was contracted to another were of no avail in this case: as the Rev. Goole had not suspected Miss Hudson's plans to marry Mr Boyce, he had had no reason to instigate a legal case to establish his contract with Miss Hudson. The 'hasty marriage' solemnised between Miss Hudson and Mr Boyce may have been attended by certain irregularities, but it had not been solemnised in defiance of an inhibition. And even if the court had decided that the marriage between Mr Boyce and Miss Hudson had been intended to defeat the latter's contract with the Rev. Goole, it would still have proved impossible to prove that contract, given the lack of any witnesses or 'common fame'. The Rev. Goole, baulked of success in this world, had to satisfy himself by hinting darkly at divine retribution in the next:

> If a contract of the present Time can never be dissolved ... if (though an Ecclesiastical Judge is obliged to pass Sentence according to Evidence) no Sentence upon Earth can make that good, which is in itself evil; then all these Particulars may deserve the most serious Consideration of Mr and Mrs Boyce; their eternal Happiness or Misery may depend upon it.[55]

As the judge of the Court of Arches noted in *Goole* v. *Hudson*, '[h]ad she not been married [i.e., to Mr Boyce], the Case would have been otherwise'.[56] This, of course, was based on the assumption that Miss Hudson would still have admitted the contract with the Rev. Goole in this situation. This brings us on to the rules that were applied if there were no third party, but where the two parties disputed the existence of the contract. Even in this context, the court's task was not simply a matter of assessing the veracity of the opposing parties. Supporting evidence was again required, for example, a written document, or at least two witnesses of good character.[57] In the absence of such evidence it would not be possible to prove that consent had been exchanged. Since witnesses might be bribed not to give evidence, there is considerable force in Addy's suggestion that '[t]he only real security a girl had was to have the promise recorded in a formally witnessed contract so

[55] Goole, *The Contract Violated*, p. 75. [56] *Ibid.*, p. 72.

[57] See e.g., Floyer, *The Proctor's Practice*, p. 85. Again, a suppletory oath could be administered if deemed appropriate, but this was not automatic: see e.g., *Observations on the case of the Right Honourable the Lord Fitzmaurice, and Mrs Elizabeth Leeson, concerning a pretended contract of marriage* (London, 1733), p. 58.

that she could rely upon a legal enforcement'.[58] Insisting on this might pose its own problems: one can hear the apologetic note struck when Catharine Imbert asked Stephen Bourget to enter into a written contract confirming their exchange of vows, assuring him that 'altho' she did not mistrust his sincerity and love and affection or his solemnizing the contract he had entered into yet it would be a great satisfaction to her' if he would do so.[59] Most, of course, did not have such evidence, and, as Lord Hardwicke noted in *Priest* v. *Parrot*, there were often promises of marriage 'which it is almost impossible to give evidence of'.

It is generally agreed that by the eighteenth century it had become more difficult to prove a contract than before.[60] This was linked to changes in the nature of such contracts: in previous centuries the very act of contracting had been a formal and public event, carried out before witnesses; an independently important stage in the process that culminated in the church ceremony.[61] If either party subsequently tried to renege on the contract, there would be ample evidence to satisfy the ecclesiastical courts of its existence. The decline in such publicly-celebrated contracts apparently occurred in the early seventeenth century,[62] and thereafter disputed contracts coming before the courts were very different in nature – less formal and more private.[63] For this very reason they were less likely to meet the standards of proof demanded by

58 J. Addy, *Sin and Society in the Seventeenth Century* (London: Routledge, 1989), pp. 170–1. Of the cases reviewed by Stone, the one contract to be upheld against a later (unconsummated) marriage was that evidenced in a formal written contract: see *Brace* v. *Cudworth* (1680) in *Uncertain Unions*, p. 98. One doctor of civil law went so far as to claim that no case had succeeded on the basis of parole evidence alone during his thirty years of practice in the ecclesiastical courts: M.N., *A Letter to a Friend Concerning Marriage Contracts, occasioned by a late Appeal from the Dean of Arches to a Court of Delegates* (London, 1740), p. 4.

59 *Bourget* v. *Imbert* (1744) Lambeth Palace Library (LPL) E33/120.

60 See Ingram, *Church Courts*, p. 209; Stone, *Road to Divorce*, p. 69.

61 See e.g., D. Cressy, *Birth, Marriage and Death: Ritual, Religion and the Life-Cycle in Tudor and Stuart England* (Oxford University Press, 1997), ch. 11; D. O'Hara, *Courtship and Constraints: Rethinking the Making of Marriage in Tudor England* (Manchester University Press, 2002), p. 38; M. Ingram, 'Spousals Litigation in the English Ecclesiastical Courts c. 1350-c. 1640' in R. Outhwaite (ed.) *Marriage and Society: Studies in the Social History of Marriage* (London: Europa, 1981), p. 46.

62 See e.g., Cressy, *Birth, Marriage and Death*, p. 267; L. Gowing, *Domestic Dangers: Women, Words, and Sex in Early Modern London* (Oxford: Clarendon Press, 1998), pp. 143–4.

63 See e.g., the case studies collected in Stone, *Uncertain Unions*.

the canon law.[64] Stone is premature when he suggests that three cases in the 1730s 'seem to have made legal history as the last of their kind',[65] since there are later examples of contracts being upheld[66] (or indeed dismissed). The point remains, however, that fewer contracts were litigated[67] and, of these, fewer were upheld.[68] Throughout the debates on what was to become the Clandestine Marriages Act, those on both sides referred to the difficulties of enforcing such a contract,[69] and it was implicit in the accounts of many that while promises were morally binding, not all were legally enforceable.[70]

Overall, then, the need to operate a workable legal system meant that the canonists' theory that a marriage was made by consent was heavily modified in practice by the requirement that such consent be proved to the satisfaction of the court before a contract *per verba de praesenti* could be enforced.[71] Hasty words breathed in a moment of private passion might create a marriage 'in the sight of God' but if either reneged on the contract it would be impossible to prove it as a matter of law, as many women seduced

64 Gowing, *Domestic Dangers*, p. 144.

65 Stone, *Road to Divorce*, p. 79. He is also inaccurate in suggesting that '[a]ll three were cases of women who gave birth as a result of sexual relations entered into on the basis of an alleged contract with a suitor which was later repudiated' (*ibid.*). *Mendez da Costa* v. *Da Costa Villa Real* (1731) LPCA E 30/4 in fact involved a widow who contracted to marry her cousin once a year had elapsed from the death of her husband. Her parents objected and prevented the couple from meeting. The frustrated suitor sought to enforce the contract. *Goole* v. *Hudson* also involved a jilted male suitor: see Goole, *The Contract Violated*. The third case, *Fitzmaurice* v. *Fitzmaurice*, did involve a woman seeking to enforce a promise of marriage, but, contrary to Stone's suggestion, she succeeded in doing so.

66 See e.g., *Baxtar* v. *Buckley* (1752) 1 Lee 42; 161 ER 17.

67 Ingram, *Church Courts*, p. 192; Gowing, *Domestic Dangers*, p. 178; Stone, *Road to Divorce*, p. 35, fig. 1.2.

68 Ingram, *Church Courts*, p. 209; and see generally Stone, *Uncertain Unions*.

69 'As the law stands at present, a young woman may trust to a promise of marriage, because she may have some hopes of being able to compel the man to fulfil his promise, though such hopes generally prove abortive' (Mr Murray, Solicitor-General, *Hansard's Parliamentary Debates*, vol. XV, col. 76).

70 'A young woman is but too apt by nature to trust to the honour of the man she loves, and to admit him to her bed on a solemn promise to marry her. Surely the moral obligation is as binding as if they had been actually married' (Mr Nugent, *Hansard's Parliamentary Debates*, vol. XV, col. 21).

71 See e.g., J. Boyce, *Studies in History and Jurisprudence* (Oxford: Clarendon Press, 1901), p. 422, who notes that the strict rules of evidence applied by the ecclesiastical court 'practically withdrew much of the liberty that had been granted by the lax theory of what constituted a marriage'.

under a promise of marriage found to their cost.[72] The system clearly had its problems – as Donahue has noted, the insistence on witnesses 'created a highly undesirable tension between the external and internal *fora*'[73] – but it was arguably more convenient than the alternatives.

But what happened once the existence of a contract *per verba de praesenti* had been established?

LEGAL CONSEQUENCES

[L]e marriage doit estre solmnize devant que ils seront complete baron & feme.[74]

The most significant legal consequence of a contract *per verba de praesenti* was that it gave each party the right to insist on performance of the contract,[75] i.e., to require that the marriage be celebrated in church.[76] Solemnisation would be ordered whether the recalcitrant party was still single or had married another in defiance of the contract.[77] In the well-timed case of *Baxtar* v. *Buckley*,[78] for example, Susanna Baxtar managed to establish that she had exchanged vows with Millington Buckley, and he was ordered to solemnise marriage in church with her within sixty days of being

72 See e.g., B. Hill, *Eighteenth-Century Women: an Anthology* (London: Allen & Unwin, 1984), p. 35; Charlotte Lennox, *The Female Quixote* (London, 1752; Oxford University Press, 1998), pp. 75–6.

73 C. Donahue, 'The Canon Law on the Formation of Marriage and Social Practice in the Later Middle Ages' (1983) 8 *Journal of Family History* 144, 146. Equally, a marriage upheld by the law might not be a marriage in the sight of God if there were an undiscovered impediment: see e.g., Swinburne, *A Treatise of Spousals*, p. 227; G. Booth, *Considerations upon the Institution of Marriage, with Some Thoughts Concerning the Force and Obligation of the Matrimonial Contract* (London, 1739), p. 76.

74 *Sir Robert Paine's Case* (1661) 1 Sid. 13; 82 ER 941, per Twisden J.

75 This had been the case for centuries: see L. Bryan, 'Marriage and Morals in the Fourteenth Century: the Evidence of Bishop Hamo's Register' (2006) CXXI *English Historical Review* 467; L. R. Poos, 'The Heavy-Handed Marriage Counsellor: Regulating Marriage in Some Later-Medieval English Local Ecclesiastical Court Jurisdictions' (1995) 39 *American Journal of Legal History* 291; Helmholz, *Marriage Litigation*, p. 25; Cressy, *Birth, Marriage and Death*, ch. 11.

76 Swinburne, *A Treatise of Spousals*, p. 222; Ayliffe, *Parergon Juris Canonici Anglicani*, p. 248, noting that a contract *per verba de praesenti* could in this sense be described as 'a Promise of future marriage'.

77 Grey, *System of English Ecclesiastical Law*, p. 146, and see further below.

78 (1752) 1 Lee 42; 161 ER 17.

served with the monition to this effect. After the church ceremony, the parties would be expected to live together and conform to the law's requirements of a husband and wife.[79]

For those who still proved reluctant to honour their promises, there were various legal mechanisms to reinforce such orders: in ascending order of severity, these were admonition,[80] excommunication, and imprisonment. Thus:

> if they refuse, after lawful admonition given them, he or she refusing, may, for his or her Contumacy or Disobedience therein, be excommunicated: And if the Party excommunicate do still persevere in that State, by the Space of forty Days, the Ordinary may, by a *Significavit*, or Certificate under his Seal, certify into the Chancery the Contempt of the Party, and craving the Aid of the secular Power thereupon, a Writ *de excommunicato capiendo* is to be directed to the Sheriff, for the Apprehension of the Body of the same Party excommunicated, who being apprehended by vertue thereof, is to be kept in Prison without Bail or Mainprize, until he or she have humbled themselves, and obey'd the Monition of the Ordinary.[81]

In short, solemnisation was insisted upon by the church courts.

But there is an important distinction between being bound to perform an act, and being entitled to all the same rights as if that act had been performed – between what one might term, borrowing the terminology of conveyancing,[82] contract and completion. In the conveyancing process, the contract signed by the parties binds them to the sale. If either party attempts to renege on the contract, the other may seek specific performance, but it is only upon completion that the buyer acquires the rights of an owner.[83] So it

[79] An Act for the repeal of a Statute touching Precontract 1548, 2 & 3 Edw. 6 c. 23, noted that once a precontract was proved the judge could give sentence 'commanding solemnization, cohabitation, consummation and tractation [i.e., treatment] as becometh man and wife to have' (s. 1).

[80] As Floyer, *The Proctor's Practice*, p. 78, explained, 'a Monition goes out against the Defendant to cause him to solemnize the Marriage with the Plaintiff before such a Day *sub poena* etc.'.

[81] Salmon, *Critical Essay*, p. 202; see also Swinburne, *A Treatise of Spousals*, p. 231. Absolution from excommunication could be achieved by giving security to comply with the court's order: Floyer, *The Proctor's Practice*, p. 36.

[82] An analogy used by contemporaries: see *Burrell* v. *Strong* (1672) 1 Freem. 66; 89 ER 50; C. Wheatly, *A Rational Illustration of the Book of Common Prayer of the Church of England* (London, 1722), p. 435.

[83] See e.g., M. P. Thompson, *Modern Land Law*, 3rd edn (Oxford University Press, 2006), p. 193.

was with marriage: as one legal commentator noted, 'neither the Contract nor the Sentence makes a compleat Marriage'.[84] Thus, it is necessary to ask: what was the effect of a contract *per verba de praesenti* before the marriage was solemnised in church?

Sex was forbidden

Just as the purchaser is not entitled to take possession of the property in advance of completion, so too contracted couples were not meant to anticipate the church ceremony by having sex,[85] and those who did incurred the censure of the ecclesiastical courts. To engage in sexual intercourse before the marriage had been solemnised in church was a sin, and the parties, if detected, might be required to do penance in church.[86] Public penance was still being exacted in Yorkshire dioceses in the seventeenth century, although practice appears to have varied: sometimes the fact that the parties had entered into a contract was seen as a full defence, sometimes it justified a modified penance being awarded, and sometimes 'the full rigour of public penance' was exacted.[87] Prosecutions for fornication continued in some places well into the eighteenth century.[88] And had the existence of a contract constituted a defence to a charge of fornication, the ecclesiastical courts would hardly have prosecuted those who had gone through a non-Anglican ceremony for the offence.[89]

84 M. Bacon, *A New Abridgment of the Law* (London, 1736), vol. I, p. 284.

85 See also E. Haywood, *The History of Miss Betsy Thoughtless* (London, 1751), p. 223, in which the heroine rebuffs an attempt by her affianced husband to embrace her, telling him 'you have yet no right to liberties of this nature'.

86 See e.g., Bryan, 'Marriage and Morals' on the position in the fourteenth century; R. Wunderli, *London Church Courts and Society on the Eve of the Reformation* (Cambridge Mass.: Medieval Academy of America, 1981) on the sixteenth century, and Ingram, 'Spousals Litigation', p. 55 on the seventeenth century. See also P. Hair (ed.), *Before the Bawdy Court: Selections from Church Court and Other Records relating to the Correction of Moral Offences in England, Scotland and New England, 1300–1800* (London: Elek Books, 1972).

87 R. A. Marchant, *The Church under the Law: Justice, Administration and Discipline in the Diocese of York, 1560–1640* (Cambridge University Press, 1969), p. 137.

88 See e.g., Rev. M. G. Smith, *Pastoral Discipline and the Church Courts: the Hexham Court 1680–1730* (York: Borthwick Papers No. 62, 1982), pp. 29–30; M. Kinnear, 'The Correction Court in the Diocese of Carlisle, 1704–1756' (1990) 59 *Church History* 191, and see further Chapter 3.

89 See e.g., *Hilliard* v. *Phaly* (1723) 8 Mod. 180; 88 ER 132; Quaker Library, Book of Cases, vol. II, p. 1.

It is true that the offence for which contracted couples were cited was contempt rather than fornication,[90] and that the common-law courts proved willing to issue prohibitions to prevent the ecclesiastical courts from so prosecuting couples who had not married according to the rites of the Church of England.[91] Yet the common-law courts did not deny the power of the ecclesiastical courts to punish contracted parties for contempt.[92] They were not treated in the same way as couples not bound by any contract (who would have been punished for fornication),[93] but neither were they treated in the same way as couples who had solemnised their marriage in church.

Subsequent marriage with another was forbidden

Similarly, just as the vendor is not meant to sell the property to anyone else once contracts have been exchanged, a person who had contracted *per verba de praesenti* was not meant to marry any other person.[94] In theological terms this was the case whether or not the contract could be proved, as shown by the Rev. Goole's prognostications of eternal damnation. Legally, of course, it depended on the contract being established: once it had been, it was not releasable by either party,[95] and formed an impediment to a subsequent marriage with a third party. A proven contract had the effect of annulling the later marriage and bastardising any children born during it.[96] Yet this simply reflected the fact that the contract was binding, rather than indicating that it was regarded as a full marriage. One commentator spelt out this distinction:

[90] See e.g., *Bunting's Case* (1580) Moo. KB 170; 72 ER 510: 'contempt encounter un edict del Esglise, que avoit phibite carnal copulacõn devant espousals solemnised in facie Ecclesiae'.

[91] See e.g., *Hutchinson* v. *Brookbanke* (1693) 3 Lev. 376; 83 ER 738 and *Wigmore's Case* (1707) Holt KB 460; 90 ER 1153. Cf. *R* v. *Paty* (1705) 2 Ld. Raym. 1105; 92 ER 232.

[92] See e.g., *Collins* v. *Jessot* (1705) 6 Mod. 155; 87 ER 913.

[93] And note also that if either of the contracted parties had sex with another, this was regarded as adultery: see e.g., C. Wheatly, *The Church of England Man's Companion, or a Rational Illustration of the Harmony, Excellency and Usefulness of the Book of Common Prayer* (Oxford, 1710), p. 152.

[94] Salmon, *Critical Essay*, p. 181; Grey, *System of English Ecclesiastical Law*, p. 139.

[95] Grey, *System of English Ecclesiastical Law*, pp. 139–46.

[96] *Robertson* v. *Stallage* (1609) Cro. Jac. 186; 79 ER 162.

if they were solemnly contracted to any other, it ought to be confess'd as an impediment to this Marriage; for though such Contracts *be not properly Marriage* (because they do not give the Persons contracted power to use the Freedom of Marriage towards each other) yet it binds them so fast, that it takes from them all possibility of being married to any body else, and makes it no less than Adultery for them to join themselves to any other Person.[97]

Similarly, although a contract rendered a later marriage voidable,[98] it did not have the same effect on it as a marriage celebrated in church would have done. A marriage could not be set aside on the ground of a precontract after the death of either party.[99] If it was not challenged, any children would be legitimate in the eyes of the law,[100] and the wife would be entitled to dower.[101] By contrast, if there had been a marriage in church, or before an Anglican priest, any second marriage was *ipso facto* void, and could be challenged even after the death of the parties.[102] As Holt CJ noted in *Hemming* v. *Price*,[103] when faced with an allegation that the 'wife' had a previous husband still living, '[t]he meaning of the saying, that one shall not be bastardised after the death of either of his parents,

97 Wheatly, *The Church of England Man's Companion*, p. 152 (emphasis added).

98 See e.g., *Bunting's Case* (1580) Moo. KB 170; 72 ER 510. On the distinction between void and voidable marriages, which emerged after the Reformation, see Jackson, *The Formation and Annulment of Marriage*, p. 54; J. Masson, R. Bailey-Harris, and R. Probert, *Cretney's Principles of Family Law*, 8th edn (London: Sweet & Maxwell, 2008), pp. 44–5.

99 See e.g., Salmon, *Critical Essay*, p. 210.

100 See e.g., W. Nelson, *The Rights of the Clergy of that part of Great-Britain, call'd England*, 2nd edn (London, 1715), p. 269: 'if a Man marrieth a Woman, who is precontracted to another, and hath Children by her, they are his Children till the Divorce, and then they are Bastards'. The 'divorce' in this case was of course *divortium quoad vinculum*, a declaration of nullity: see e.g., Jackson, *The Formation and Annulment of Marriage*, p. 29.

101 See e.g., E. Coke, *The First Part of the Institutes of the Laws of England, or, a Commentary on Littleton*, 10th edn (London, 1703), lib. 1, cap. v, sec. 36, p. 33, who noted that 'if a marriage *de facto* be voidable by divorce in respect of consanguinity, affinity, precontract or such like, whereby the marriage might have been dissolved and the parties freed *à vinculo matrimonii*, yet if the husband die before any divorce, then, for that it cannot now be avoided, the wife *de facto* shall be endowed, for this is *legitimum matrimonium*'. In contemporary usage, a marriage *de facto* was one in which the parties had gone through a ceremony of marriage, but to which some impediment might exist.

102 See e.g., *Pride* v. *The Earls of Bath and Montague* (1694) 1 Salk. 120; 91 ER 113, at 121: '[i]f H. marries a woman, and that woman marries again, living H., the last marriage is void without any divorce, and the jury shall try the fact which proves it no marriage'.

103 (1701) 12 Mod. 432; 88 ER 1430.

is that the Spiritual Court shall not proceed to dissolve a marriage de facto after the death of either parties, as in case of consanguinity, *precontract* etc., but in this case, if the republication below be true, the marriage was ipso facto void'.[104]

The fact that the impact of a contract *per verba de praesenti* on a later marriage was different from that of a previous marriage celebrated in church is also evident if one examines the law of bigamy. Some historians have used the term 'bigamous' to refer to marriages invalidated by a contract *per verba de praesenti*,[105] but this reflects twentieth-century misunderstandings rather than contemporary language.[106] As Lord Lyndhurst pointed out in *R* v. *Millis*, 'it seems never to have occurred to any one, in suits to annul a marriage by reason of precontract, to suggest that the party had been guilty of bigamy. There is no trace of any such intimation.'[107] If a precontract had rendered a later marriage to a third party bigamous, then one would expect such contracts to feature in bigamy trials. Yet in not one of the 168 bigamy trials heard at the Old Bailey between 1715 and 1755 was such a contract alleged.[108] Nor did any eighteenth-century commentators suggest that a contract *per verba de praesenti* rendered a later marriage bigamous: while one noted that a man might be guilty of bigamy if he went through a second ceremony of marriage, even if the first marriage was voidable because of a previous contract *per verba de praesenti*, he clearly did not envisage that this first marriage was itself bigamous by virtue of that precontract.[109]

In cases where a subsequent formal marriage was challenged on the basis of a precontract, a decision in favour of the contract *per verba de praesenti* would result in the parties to the contract being required to marry each other:[110] while the sentence automatically annulled the later marriage with a third party without the

[104] *Ibid.*, p. 432, per Holt CJ (emphasis added).

[105] See e.g., Cressy, *Birth, Marriage and Death*, p. 307, although his use of quotation marks indicates some doubt about the appropriateness of the term; Stone, *Road to Divorce*, p. 53.

[106] See further R. Probert, '*R* v. *Millis* Reconsidered: Binding Contracts and Bigamous Marriages' (2008) 28 *Legal Studies* 337.

[107] (1843–44) 10 Cl. & F 534; 8 ER 844, at 871.

[108] Probert, '*R* v. *Millis* Reconsidered', 346.

[109] E. Gibson, *Codex juris ecclesiastici Anglicani* (London, 1713), p. 508.

[110] See e.g., Grey, *System of English Ecclesiastical Law*, p. 146.

need for a divorce,[111] it did not automatically make the contracted parties husband and wife. This may be illustrated by the decision in *Sir Robert Paine's Case.*[112] Here, the ecclesiastical court had pronounced in favour of the first contract, but when the question of the parties' status was raised in the common-law courts, Twisden J insisted, in the words quoted at the start of this section, that the marriage would have to be solemnised before the parties would be accounted 'baron & feme'.[113]

Solemnisation was necessary for full legal rights and responsibilities to arise

It followed from this that a contract *per verba de praesenti* did not confer the same rights as a ceremony of marriage. While marriage made the parties one in the eyes of the law, a contract did not.[114] Some early writers had suggested that if a man and woman had contracted, any enfeoffment[115] between them was void, but by the sixteenth century the law had changed on this point: 'whereas long ago, they did seem to hold that the Feoffment was not good, as being made to his own wife, now they do hold that it is good, as being made not unto his Wife, but unto a single Woman, and another Person in Law'.[116] More generally, as one writer explained:

> The common law does not esteem a Couple who are betroth'd or espous'd, even by Words of present Time, to be so far Man and Wife, as to give

111 See e.g., *Bunting* v. *Lepingwell* (1585) 4 Co. Rep. 29a; 76 ER 950. However, a divorce *praecontractus* might be required to establish the parties' status in other contexts: see e.g., *Foster* v. *Norclif* (1664) 1 Keble 552; 83 ER 1107, a case of ejectment.

112 (1661) 1 Sid. 13; 82 ER 941.

113 A contrary view had been expressed in a lecture by Noy, then Attorney-General, in 1632, and was followed by some (see e.g., Anon, *Baron and Feme: A Treatise of Law and Equity concerning Husband and Wives* (London: T. Waller, 1738)), but as a matter of both authority and consistency the view of Twisden J must be accorded more weight (and see e.g., Nelson, *The Rights of the Clergy*, p. 269).

114 Ayliffe, *Parergon Juris Canonici Anglicani*, p. 245.

115 A grant in fee simple: see Baker, *Introduction to English Legal History*, p. 249.

116 Swinburne, *A Treatise of Spousals*, p. 234. See also W. Sheppard, *An Epitome of all the Common & Statute Law of this Nation now in force* (London, 1656), p. 720; *A Profitable Book of Mr John Perkins, treating of the Laws of England* (London, 1657), pp. 74–5, s. 194: 'if a contract of marriage be between a man and a woman, yet one of them may enfeoff the other. For yet they are not one person in law.' John Perkins, who died in 1545, had been a fellow of the Inner Temple; this edition of his book was translated from the original French 'for the benefit of young students and others'.

either Party any Interest or Property in the other's Lands or Goods, or to Legitimate their Issue, until the Marriage be solemniz'd according to the Rites of the Church of England.[117]

And if either died before such solemnisation, the survivor did not enjoy the rights of a widow or widower. This meant that the woman would not be entitled to dower:[118] as one early legal writer bluntly put it: 'if a man seized of land in fee make a contract of Matrimonie with I.S. and he die before the marriage solemnized between them, she shall not have dower, *for she never was his wife*'.[119] Similarly, a contracted woman retained the right to make a will[120] (for which she would have needed permission had she been regarded as married), while the man to whom she was contracted acquired no right to her goods upon her death.[121] Given that women were likely to own less property than men, the advantages to a contracted woman of retaining her own property,[122] and the ability to make a will, were probably outweighed for most by the disadvantage of not being entitled to any of the man's property.

And it was not only at common law that a contract *per verba de praesenti* did not entitle the parties to the rights enjoyed by spouses. The ecclesiastical courts, too, made the enjoyment of certain rights dependent on a regular marriage.[123] In *Haydon* v. *Gould*,[124] for example, a husband was refused the administration of his deceased wife's estate on the basis that he had not been married by a clergyman. The court noted that he was 'demanding a right due to him as a husband by the ecclesiastical law and must prove himself a husband according to that law'.[125] Nor was a woman who had

117 Salmon, *Critical Essay*, p. 180. See also Swinburne, *A Treatise of Spousals*, p. 235: 'neither Spousals *de praesenti*, neither Spousals *de futuro* consummate, do make her Goods his, or his Goods hers'.

118 See e.g., Swinburne, *A Treatise of Spousals*, pp. 233–4; Ayliffe, *Parergon Juris Canonici Anglicani*, p. 245.

119 *Perkins*, p. 117, s. 306 (emphasis added).

120 *Perkins*, pp. 74–5, s. 194; Swinburne, *A Treatise of Spousals*, p. 235.

121 Sheppard, *Epitome*, p. 720; *Perkins*, p. 75, s. 194.

122 On the disabilities of coverture, see W. Blackstone, *Commentaries on the Laws of England* (Oxford, 1766), vol. II, pp. 433–6.

123 As the seventeenth-century clergyman and poet John Donne put it, '[i]n a marriage without the benediction of the Priest they cannot claim any benefit of the Church': G. Potter and E. Simpson (eds.), *The Sermons of John Donne* (University of California Press, 1957), vol. III, p. 243.

124 (1711) 1 Salk. 119; 91 ER 113.

125 At p. 120. The parties had in fact been married by a Sabbatarian ceremony: see further Chapter 4.

been contracted to a man in any better position:[126] 'the Man dying intestate before Celebration of the Marriage, the Woman to whom he was betroathed surviving, cannot obtain the Administration of his Goods, as his Widow, which otherwise, the Marriage being solemnized, she might do'.[127]

What about the status of children born to a couple who had contracted marriage but who had not solemnised their marriage in church? Contemporary texts offer little guidance on this point, although much was written on the differing approaches of the canon law and the common law to the possibility of legitimation by a subsequent marriage, on the different types of bastardy, and on the status of children born within a marriage that was subsequently held to be invalid.[128] When one finds discussion of the (presumably rather rare) situation in which a man marries his sister in the face of the church and has children by her but the marriage is not questioned in his lifetime,[129] the absence of any equivalent discussion of children born to a couple who have contracted *per verba de praesenti* is quite striking.[130] But if one reflects on the context it is hardly surprising. In the vast majority of cases couples who agreed to marry would do so within a relatively short period of time;[131] and if one party reneged on the contract after engaging in sexual relations with the other, a provable contract could be enforced and the marriage solemnised, while an unprovable one would simply not exist in the eyes of the law. There was thus no

[126] Cf. the suggestion in the report of *Haydon* v. *Gould* that the result would have been different had a surviving widow or the children claimed administration. It appears that this was mere speculation on the part of the reporter, as noted by a contemporary commentator who disagreed with the suggestion: *Baron and Feme: a Treatise of the Common Law concerning Husbands and Wives*, 2nd edn (London, 1719), p. 5.

[127] Swinburne, *A Treatise of Spousals*, p. 235.

[128] See e.g., J. Brydall, *Lex Spuriorum: or, the Law relating to Bastardy* (London, 1703); Ayliffe, *Parergon Juris Canonici Anglicani*, pp. 106–10. On the latter point, common law and canon law again disagreed: see e.g., Helmholz, *Oxford History*, p. 558.

[129] See e.g., Bacon, *Abridgment*, p. 311; C. Viner, *A General Abridgment of Law and Equity* (Aldershot, 1748), vol. IV, p. 215.

[130] Although there was some discussion of the status of children born within a marriage that was voidable for a precontract: see e.g., Sir J. Comyns, *A Digest of the Laws of England* (London, 1762–7), vol. I, tit. Baron and Feme, p. 585. This work was compiled before Comyns' death in 1740 but was not printed until much later.

[131] See further Chapter 3.

need to discuss the status of a child born after a contract *per verba de praesenti* whose parents did not go on to marry: as one legal writer noted, 'by a Contract of Marriage, it is no Marriage, if Espousals do not afterwards ensue'.[132] And since the canon law regarded as legitimate children whose parents had married after the birth, there would be no need to differentiate the status of a child born between a contract *per verba de praesenti* and solemnisation in church from any other child born before solemnisation. This explains the rather vague statement by Swinburne to the effect that any children born to a contracted couple would be legitimate in the eyes of the canon law:[133] he was referring, as the context makes clear, to children 'begotten before Celebration of the Marriage, betwixt those which have contracted Spousals', the assumption being that solemnisation would follow.

But such legitimation by the canon law had limited implications for the rights of the children in question. In contrast to the canon law, the common-law courts denied the possibility of legitimation by a subsequent marriage.[134] And the ecclesiastical courts were not entitled to issue a free-standing declaration as to the legitimacy of a child: only when a writ was issued from the common-law courts could bastardy be tried by the bishop.[135] Such a writ would only be issued if the question of bastardy was relevant to a case before the common-law courts,[136] as for example if the individual's right to inherit property was disputed.[137] And the terms in which it was phrased required the bishop to supply certain information, such as whether the individual in question had been born before or after

132 Comyns, *Digest*, p. 550, citing *Bunting's Case* (1580) Moo. KB 170; 72 ER 510.

133 Swinburne, *A Treatise of Spousals*, p. 233.

134 Viner, *Abridgment*, p. 216, and see generally W. Blackstone, *Commentaries on the Laws of England* (Oxford, 1765), vol. I, pp. 442–4; R.H. Helmholz, 'Bastardy Litigation in Medieval England' (1969) XIII *American Journal of Legal History* 360.

135 Bacon, *Abridgment*, p. 313: 'If the Ordinary certify or try Bastardy without a writ from the King's Temporal Courts, it is void, for the Spiritual Jurisdiction within these Kingdoms is derived from the King, and therefore it must be exercised in the Manner the King hath appointed; for it would be injurious if they should declare Legitimation where the Rights of Inheritance are so nearly concerned, without an apparent Necessity.' See also Brydall, *Lex Spuriorum*, p. 58.

136 Bacon, *Abridgment*, p. 312; Ayliffe, *Parergon Juris Canonici Anglicani*, p. 108.

137 And as Baker notes, 'in all except the old real actions a party could plead "special bastardy" (that is, birth out of wedlock), which was a question of fact triable by a jury': Baker, *Introduction to English Legal History*, p. 490; see also Sir S. Eure, *Trials per pais*, 5th edn (London, 1718).

the parents' marriage, and whether the parents' marriage was valid,[138] rather than simply giving an opinion as to the legitimacy of the individual in question. Thus, as Swinburne noted, children born to those who had contracted to marry were not lawful 'by the Laws of this Realm', even if their parents had later solemnised their marriage in church.[139]

In expounding the rights that were denied to contracted couples, it has been necessary to rely for the most part on the statements of writers rather than judicial decisions, simply because there are practically no cases in which the legal consequences of a contract – other than its enforceability – were tested.[140] It is telling that these legal writers assumed that celebration would in the normal course of events follow the contract: they were not commenting on the rights of couples who set up home after a contract but rather those of couples whose progress to matrimony had been interrupted. And the absence of cases strongly suggests the truth of their assumption: if it had been common practice for couples to live together after a simple exchange of vows one would expect such cases to have generated no little amount of litigation. Even if those without property had little reason to resort to the courts themselves, their marital arrangements might well come under the scrutiny of the courts when deciding on issues such as settlement for the purpose of entitlement to parish relief. In actual fact, the handful of cases in which the courts commented on the legal rights that flowed from the mere exchange of consent largely involved ceremonies presided over by a non-Anglican celebrant rather than a bare exchange of consent. The status of non-Anglican ceremonies is considered in more detail in Chapter 4; for present purposes it is sufficient to note the contemporary consensus that such ceremonies were not accorded the same legal recognition as a marriage before a minister of the Established Church.

The evidence reviewed in this section gives a rather different impression of contracts *per verba de praesenti* from that usually

138 Ayliffe, *Parergon Juris Canonici Anglicani*, p. 109.

139 Swinburne, *A Treatise of Spousals*, p. 233.

140 *Bunting* v. *Lepingwell* (1585) 4 Co. Rep. 29a; 76 ER 950 is often cited as one example, but in this case the ecclesiastical court had ordered the contracted couple to marry, which they did before the birth of the child whose legitimacy was in question. That *Bunting* is so often quoted in eighteenth-century texts is itself an illustration of the dearth of other examples.

presented. Accounts that focus solely on those cases dealing with the enforcement of such contracts may lead to too much weight being placed on their binding force. By contrast, in every context examined above – the form of action, whether a sexual relationship had legal sanction, the impact on a subsequent marriage with a third party, the rights enjoyed by the contracted parties themselves, and the status of their children – we have seen that a distinction was drawn between a contract *per verba de praesenti* and a marriage celebrated in church. Marriage in early modern England may well have been a process rather than an event, but the final stage – that of solemnisation – cannot be assumed to be optional, any more than it is optional for the sale of a house to be completed by formal transfer. A contract was both binding *and* incomplete, requiring the final formalities to be observed. Only when a couple married before an Anglican minister were full legal rights and responsibilities conferred upon them.

CONTEMPORARY PERCEPTIONS OF THE CONTRACT *PER VERBA DE PRAESENTI*

> [C]ontracted persons are in a middle degree betwixt single persons and married persons; they are neither simply single nor actually married.[141]

But, it may be objected, even if a contract did not have the same legal consequences as a regular marriage, it might nevertheless be regarded as a full marriage by contemporaries, in the absence of litigation to the contrary. The evidence (from judicial dicta, parliamentary debates, pamphlets and novels)[142] suggests that it was not. But at the same time it is easy to see how other scholars have come to a different conclusion: statements that consent was of the 'essence' of matrimony, and contracted couples describing themselves as 'man and wife before God' might seem, at first sight, to suggest that a contract *per verba de praesenti* was indeed thought to be the same as a marriage celebrated in church. When examined in context, however, such apparently unambiguous statements turn out to be no more than an acknowledgement of the binding nature

141 W. Gouge, *Of Domesticall Duties: Eight Treatises* (London, 1622), p. 199.

142 A more detailed review of the literary evidence may be found in R. Probert, 'Examining Law through the Lens of Literature: the Formation of Marriage in Eighteenth-Century England' (2008) *Law and Humanities* 29.

of a contract, as the following discussion will show. Not only was there a widespread perception that a contract *per verba de praesenti* was inchoate, but there was also an equally strong assumption that the presence of a clergyman was necessary for the celebration of a marriage.

The 'essence' of matrimony?

Consent was the basis of marriage. On that all eighteenth-century writers agreed. So too would their twenty-first-century counterparts: but that marriage in the Western world is based on the free and full consent of both parties does not mean that it is the only requirement for a marriage to come into existence. And when eighteenth-century commentators spoke of the 'essence' or 'substance' of marriage, they did not necessarily have in mind legal validity. As one pamphleteer wrote:

> Suppose a Man and Woman liking each other, do make a verbal Agreement to live with conjugal Intercourse together ... This is the essence of a matrimonial Contract, and perhaps the Parties might think themselves bound to fulfil their respective stipulations: *yet the Law does not look upon their Contract to be binding.*[143]

A similar example was given by the Solicitor-General, in the course of the debates over the Bill that became the Clandestine Marriages Act, to illustrate the distinction between, on the one hand, a marriage 'in the sight of God' or according to 'the law of nature', and, on the other, one that would be regarded as a marriage in the eyes of law and society:

> I believe it will be allowed, that if a man and woman seriously and sincerely enter into a marriage contract, without the interposition of a clergyman, or any religious ceremony whatever, it will be a good marriage both by the law of God and the law of nature, yet the law of this society, and, I believe, of every Christian society, has declared it not to be a good marriage.[144]

Of course neither example establishes that a *proven* contract *per verba de praesenti* was not regarded as a good marriage, but both do

[143] *A Letter to the Public: Containing the Substance of what hath been offered in the late Debates upon the Subject of the Act of Parliament for the better preventing of Clandestine Marriages* (London, 1753), p. 36 (emphasis added). See also Salmon, *Critical Essay*, p. 186, and Swinburne, *A Treatise of Spousals*, p. 87: 'proof is not of the essence of Matrimony'.

[144] *Hansard's Parliamentary Debates*, vol. XV, p. 78.

illustrate the care that must be taken in interpreting phrases such as the 'essence' of matrimony or marriage 'before God', 'in nature' or 'in conscience'. The very need for the use of such qualifying terms is an indication that the contract in question was *not* a full marriage in the eyes of law and society.[145]

Moreover, when we turn to texts dealing with established contracts *per verba de praesenti* we find similar shades of meaning. Such a contract was often described as *ipsum matrimonium*, or 'very matrimony'.[146] This was, after all, in accordance with the teachings of the canon law. But a case decided in 1752 on the status of a marriage celebrated by a Roman Catholic priest[147] made a clear distinction between *ipsum matrimonium* and what was described as 'legal marriage': as the judge put it, '[u]pon what reason or foundation then should a contract of marriage entered into by the intervention of the Popish priest, not in the form prescribed by law, be deemed a legal marriage in this country, more than any other contract that is considered by the canon law as *ipsum matrimonium*?'[148]

With all such evidence, the context is crucial: what looks like a declaration that a contract *per verba de praesenti* was a marriage may read very differently if one looks at other statements in the same text. One eighteenth-century treatise, for example, stated that a contracted couple were 'Man and Wife before God' before qualifying this by explaining that even a marriage celebrated in a conventicle did not entitle the parties to the same legal rights as one celebrated in church.[149] Swinburne appears to be even more explicit in stating that 'it is a present and perfect consent, the which alone maketh matrimony, without either public solemnization or carnal copulation, for neither is the one nor the other the essence

[145] See also Daniel Defoe, *Moll Flanders* (London: Penguin Classics, 1989; original edn 1722), p. 80, in which the eponymous heroine claims that she is 'effectually' a wife – having engaged in sexual relations after a contract of marriage – but acknowledges that this is not the case 'in the Eye of the World'.

[146] Swinburne, *A Treatise of Spousals*, p. 75; M.N., *A Letter to a Friend concerning Marriage Contracts, occasioned by a late Appeal from the Dean of Arches to a Court of Delegates* (London, 1740), p. 18.

[147] The marriage in question took place in France, but the judge devoted a considerable part of his judgment to the question of what status such a marriage would have had if celebrated in England.

[148] *Scrimshire* v. *Scrimshire* (1752) 2 Hag. Con. 395; 161 ER 782, at 401.

[149] Anon, *Baron and Feme: a Treatise of Law and Equity concerning Husband and Wives* (London, 1738), pp. 4–7.

of matrimony, but consent only'.[150] In context, however, it must be understood that he was simply referring to the fact that a contract *per verba de praesenti* (as distinct from a contract *per verba de futuro*, which he discussed on the preceding page) was binding on the parties, and he went on to explain that the principal effect of such a contract was that the parties were 'bound by the Laws Ecclesiastical of this Realm, to perform their promise, and to celebrate Matrimony together accordingly'.[151] The way in which promise and performance were intertwined was clarified by Comyns: 'the contract makes the Marriage, *if Espousals afterwards ensue*; for they have Relation to the first Contract, and avoid all mesne Acts'.[152] And by the same token: 'it is no Marriage, if Espousals do not afterwards ensue'.[153]

Context is particularly important in understanding the widely-quoted[154] statement of Holt CJ in *Collins* v. *Jessot* to the effect that 'if a contract be *per verba de praesenti*, it amounts to an actual marriage, which the very parties themselves cannot dissolve or release by mutual agreement; for it is as much a marriage in the sight of God as if it had been in *facie ecclesiae*'.[155] But the actual question before the court in *Collins* v. *Jessot* was which court – ecclesiastical or secular – should try the question of whether there had been a contract. If there had been an exchange of vows *per verba de praesenti* the matter was one for the ecclesiastical court to resolve by ordering the parties to solemnise their marriage; if, by contrast, there had been a contract *per verba de futuro*, the matter could be dealt with in either court.[156] Holt CJ refused to prevent the ecclesiastical court from hearing the case: the mere fact that the contract might turn out to be *de futuro* rather than *de praesenti* did not justify a prohibition as the ecclesiastical court had jurisdiction

150 Swinburne, *A Treatise of Spousals*, p. 28. 151 *Ibid*. p. 222.
152 Comyns, *Digest*, p. 500 (emphasis added). 153 *Ibid*.
154 See e.g., *Fenton* v. *Reed* 4 Johns (NY) 52 (1809); *Dalrymple* v. *Dalrymple* (1811) 2 Hag. Con. 54; 161 ER 665; Outhwaite, *Clandestine Marriage*, p. 2.
155 (1705) 6 Mod. 155; 87 ER 913, at 913.
156 A party could elect between their remedy in the common-law courts (damages for breach of contract) and that in the ecclesiastical court (an order that the parties should perform their contract by marrying in church). The powers available to the ecclesiastical court to enforce a contract *per verba de futuro* were considerably weaker than those available to enforce a contract *per verba de praesenti*: the parties would be admonished rather than compelled, see Swinburne, *A Treatise of Spousals*, p. 232.

in either case. He was, therefore, simply abdicating the decision in favour of the proper forum rather than declaring the status of a contract. His description of the contract *per verba de praesenti* as an 'actual' marriage represented the theory of that forum; his qualification that it was a 'marriage in the sight of God' indicates that he was not declaring it to be a marriage in the eyes of the law. And that a contract did not have all the same consequences as a marriage in church is clear from his very next words, in which he identified a key difference between those who were married and those who were merely contracted: if the latter 'cohabit before marriage *in facie ecclesiae*, they are for that punishable by ecclesiastical censures'.[157] The fact that this important qualification did not appear in some reports[158] may have contributed to subsequent misunderstandings of the case.

And it would seem that Holt's contemporaries interpreted his words as merely denoting that a contract was binding. Most legal authors of this period, of course, simply summarised the decisions of cases without any attempt at analysis or synthesis. But we do have the arguments of one lawyer, who in puzzling over Holt's further statement in *Wigmore's Case*,[159] two years later, that 'i[f] the contract be executed, and he does take her, 'tis a marriage, and the Spiritual Court cannot punish for fornication',[160] opined that 'he can only mean what he here [i.e., in *Collins* v. *Jessot*] explicitly says with Respect to the very Parties themselves, that they could not release one another, or dissolve their own mutual Agreement'.[161] All these phrases that might at first sight seem to prove that a contract *per verba de praesenti* was regarded as a marriage simply denoted the binding force (whether legal or moral, depending on the proof available) of such a contract.

157 At p. 155. Further, it is clear from Holt's comments in *Hemming* v. *Price* (1701) 12 Mod. 432; 88 ER 1430 (discussed above) that he was fully aware of the distinction between a contract *per verba de praesenti* and a marriage.

158 See e.g., 2 Salk. 437; 91 ER 380 where it appears under the name *Jesson* v. *Collins*.

159 *Wigmore's Case* (1707) Holt KB 459; 90 ER 1153. This case, which involved a ceremony conducted by a non-conformist minister, is considered further in Chapter 4.

160 It could, of course, punish them for contempt, as Holt had himself noted in *Collins* v. *Jessot*.

161 *R* v. *The Inhabitants of Luffington* (1744), in Sir J. Burrow, *A Series of the Decisions of the Court of King's Bench upon Settlement Cases* (London, 1768), p. 234.

'Man and wife before God'

The same is true of phrases such as 'we are man and wife before God'. It is easy to find contracted couples referring to each other in this way, but once again such references need to be read with care. This is a situation in which the use of a word masks different understandings of that word. The same couple may define themselves, without contradiction, as married in one sense (being bound to each other, and married before God) but not yet married in another sense (in that the law would not regard them as married, nor grant them full legal rights). There was no contradiction in claiming to be 'man and wife before God' and announcing that one intended to marry.[162]

The case of *Bourget* v. *Imbert* in 1744 provides a good illustration of this. According to the depositions in the case, Stephen Bourget and Catharine Imbert had contracted before witnesses in words of the present tense: 'I do take you Madam from this time for my lawful wife'.[163] Catharine subsequently declared that she would never depart from her word but expressed her anxiety that Stephen might not love her as much as she loved him, and that if he did not 'she should be very unhappy for that they were contracted and were Man and Wife before God as much as possible without Solemnization'.[164] Later, however, when asked whether she was married to Stephen Bourget, she replied that she was not, 'but that there was a Contract of Marriage passed between them and that they were married before God'.[165] Their inchoate status as contracted couples is further illustrated by the fact that Catharine remained living with her family after the contract, and a date was set for their marriage in church.

In a similar vein, in *Evers* v. *Michell*,[166] John Evers was alleged to have declared that 'he and ... Elizabeth Michell ... were married or mutually contracted in marriage to each other and that by means of such contract he the said John Evers looked upon ... himself and the said Elizabeth Michell to be lawful Man and Wife'. However, it was only when he was settled in business that he wrote

[162] Cf. B. Capp, *When Gossips Meet: Women, Family, and Neighbourhood in Early Modern England* (Oxford University Press, 2003), p. 344.
[163] Lambeth Palace Library (LPL), Eee 14/262b. [164] *Ibid.*
[165] *Ibid.* [166] (1744), LPL, E35/25.

to her to request that she 'would carry the Contract of Marriage between them ... into Execution by Publicly marrying each other in the Church and then to come and live with him'.[167]

And it is clear that the use of such terms did not depend on the parties' perceptions that they had entered into a legally binding contract. When the Rev. Goole entered into a contract *per verba de praesenti* with Miss Hudson he could say 'you are my Wife, as much as ever you can be, in the Presence of God',[168] yet at the same time profess ignorance of the legal distinction between a contract *per verba de praesenti* and one *de futuro*.[169] Similarly, even those who had only exchanged vows *de futuro* might describe themselves as husband and wife. Such was the case in *Mendez da Costa* v. *Da Costa Villa Real*.[170] In this case Philip Mendez da Costa and Catharine Da Costa Villa Real agreed to marry after a year had elapsed from the death of Catharine's husband: the day after so contracting, Catharine sent Philip a letter 'subscribing herself his wife' and in his reply he described himself as her 'affectionate husband'. In this case the parties had not begun to live together, or even engaged in sexual relations, and the contract would not have been binding in legal *or* theological terms.

But it was not universal practice for those who had contracted in words of the present tense to describe themselves as 'husband' and 'wife'. Joanna Sleeze, for example, described herself as a 'spinster' at the time that the events in her deposition took place, even though she acknowledged that she was then contracted to the man who subsequently became her husband.[171] All the evidence suggests that individuals simply used the terminology that best fitted the context: the word 'husband' or 'wife' might be used to convey the emotional link between the parties, and to convey the binding nature of the vows that had been exchanged, while describing oneself as a spinster emphasised that one was living the life of a single woman under the parental roof, as Joanna was. We should not be too hasty to assume that contemporaries were confused about their marital status, but should rather consider what they actually meant.

Nor did divine omniscience mean that it was *sufficient* to be man and wife 'before God'. God, it was thought, had a decided preference for regular marriage before an Anglican clergyman.

[167] *Ibid.* [168] Goole, *The Contract Violated*, p. 11. [169] *Ibid.* p. 19.
[170] (1731) LPL, E30/4. [171] London Metropolitan Archives, DL/C/201/1.

Even those who suggested that consent was all that was necessary from a divine point of view acknowledged the legal necessity of solemnisation.[172] As one eighteenth-century clergyman argued, 'God cannot be said to join two Persons in Marriage, but when this is done by certain legal means.'[173] When one pamphleteer tried to justify marriages that were not celebrated according to the rites of the Established Church, demanding 'may not God joyn together Man and Woman in Marriage, without the Consent of the Clergy, and Ceremonies of the Church?',[174] he was met with a tart response:

> If God descends Miraculously, to Marry any Man or Woman, he Supersedes the Laws ... but if not, then God has Ordain'd all Persons to be Married, as the Legal Christian Forms of their Country appoint.[175]

An even harsher rebuke is meted out by Mr Allworthy in Fielding's *Tom Jones*, when the amoral Jenny Jones declares that:

> in the eye of heaven I was married to him; for, after much reading on the subject, I am convinced that particular ceremonies are only requisite to give a legal sanction to marriage, and have only a worldly use in giving the woman the status of a wife; but that she who lives constant to one man, after a solemn private affiance, whatever the world may call her, has little to charge on her own conscience.[176]

Mr Allworthy quickly scotches this idea: 'I am sorry, madam ... [that] you made so ill a use of your learning. Indeed, it would have been well that you had been possessed of much more, or had remained in a state of ignorance.'[177]

172 Anon, *The Lady's Law or, a Treatise of Feme Coverts*, 2nd edn (London, 1737), p. 25: 'Marriage is of Divine Institution, to which only the Consent of the Parties is necessary, though the Solemnizing of it is a Civil Right, regulated by the Laws and Customs of Nations.'

173 H. Gally, *Some Considerations upon Clandestine Marriages* (London, 1750), p. 124.

174 J. MacBride, *A Vindication of Marriage, as Solemnized by Presbyterians in the North of Ireland* (Dublin, 1702), p. iv.

175 R. Lambert, *An Answer to a late pamphlet, entitl'd A Vindication of Marriage, as Solemnized by Presbyterians in the North of Ireland* (Dublin, 1704), p. 10. See also Wheatly, *The Church of England Man's Companion*, pp. 148–9.

176 H. Fielding, *Tom Jones* (London, 1749; Oxford: World Classics, 1998), p. 837. See further Probert, 'Examining Law through the Lens of Literature'.

177 Fielding, *Tom Jones*, p. 837. It is significant that Fielding puts these words in the mouth of this particular character, who personifies justice both in the narrow sense of the law (he is the local magistrate) and in the broader sense of fairness, as indicated by his name.

Inchoate and incomplete

The inchoate status of a contract *per verba de praesenti* is further illustrated by those cases in which there was some disruption to the process. I suggested above that too much weight has been attached to the fact that the ecclesiastical courts regarded such contracts as binding; the cases in which contracts were litigated could also be seen as demonstrating that at least one of the parties to the contract did not. In *Bourget* v. *Imbert*, for example, it was Catharine's friends and relations who took steps to prevent the marriage going ahead, detaining Catharine at the home of her guardian and denying even the evidence of the written contract, arguing that she had been made 'to subscribe her name to some paper but is ignorant of the contents'.[178] When Stephen begged Catharine to tell the truth about what had passed between them, she told him that her relations did not approve and she 'was frightened of disobliging them if she proceeded any further & thereupon fell a crying'.[179] Considerable moral pressure was brought to bear on Catharine: she was told that she 'should commit a great sin if she married without the consent of her friends & she should never be happy & God would never bless her'.[180] Clearly it was felt that it was still possible to break off the match between the parties, even if the law would have regarded such a contract as binding. Similarly, in the case of *Collier* v. *Moseley*, it was alleged that Elizabeth Moseley and Arthur Collier had 'solemnly contracted in words of the present tense', after which she said 'now you are my own are you not' and he replied 'I am'.[181] Yet when Elizabeth's father refused to consent to the match she told Arthur that the marriage could not take place, and that he was not to think of her.

A similar disregard for a contract – in this case a promise followed by sex – is evident in Fielding's *Tom Jones*. Tom's friend Nightingale promises to marry his landlady's daughter, but despite the sexual relationship between them they are not regarded as married by any of their friends or relations. Indeed, Nightingale's

[178] (1744), LPL, E35/25. [179] *Ibid.*

[180] *Ibid.* For another case of parental interference, see *Mendez da Costa* v. *Da Costa Villa Real* (1731) LPL, E30/4.

[181] LPL, E37/31.

uncle urges Nightingale to break off the relationship in order to make a more socially advantageous match:

'*If you had been married* I should have assisted you as much as was in my power to have made the best of a bad matter; but there is a great difference between considering a thing which is already done and irrecoverable, and that which is yet to do ...' 'How, sir!' replies young Nightingale, 'is there this difference between having already done an act, and being in honour engaged to do it?' ... 'Pugh', said the uncle, '... you well know how trivial these breaches of contract are thought; even the grossest make but the wonder and conversation of a day'.[182]

That the contract was viewed as incomplete is also clear from the steps taken by those who *did* wish to marry. In *Baxtar* v. *Buckley*, following an exchange of vows in an inn, Millington Buckley promised to marry Susanna in church as soon as he could.[183] Diarists recorded their progress to matrimony, from courtship to consent to ceremony.[184] Novelists hustled their characters off to church.[185] In Smollett's *Peregrine Pickle*, for example, the hero finally wins the favour of his beloved Emilia, who consents to be his wife:

'You are willing, then, to take me for better for worse, in presence of heaven and these witnesses?' cried Peregrine ... 'Why – ay – and heaven grant me patience to bear the humours of such a yoke-fellow.'[186]

One might regard this as a straightforward contract *per verba de praesenti* (or, if *de futuro*, one that could be converted by the consummation that Peregrine has been panting after for most of the 700-plus pages of the novel). But it is to church, rather than to the bedroom, that Peregrine begs 'immediate recourse be had', and, when Emilia prevaricates, the extravagance of his response does not suggest that he regards himself as already married.

Peregrine, maddening with desire, assaulted her with the most earnest entreaties ... He fell at her feet, in all the agony of impatience; swore

182 Fielding, *Tom Jones*, p. 683 (emphasis added).

183 *Baxtar* v. *Buckley* (1752) 1 Lee 42; 161 ER 17.

184 See e.g., M. Hunter and A. Gregory (eds.), *An Astrological Diary of the Seventeenth Century: Samuel Jeake of Rye* (Oxford: Clarendon Press, 1988), pp. 153–4; R. Houlbrooke (ed.), *English Family Life, 1576–1716: an Anthology from Diaries* (Oxford: Basil Blackwell Ltd, 1989), pp. 32–3.

185 See e.g., S. Fielding, *The Adventures of David Simple* (London: Penguin Classics, 2002; original edn 1744), p. 279.

186 T. Smollett, *The Adventures of Peregrine Pickle* (Oxford University Press, 1964; original edn 1751), p. 775.

> that his life and intellects would actually be in jeopardy by her refusal; and when she attempted to argue him out of his demand, began to rave with such extravagance, that ... the amiable Emilia was teized into compliance.[187]

Time and time again, in both literary and non-literary sources, we find this distinction between the promise and the performance of it.[188] But here it is necessary to draw a distinction between what was desirable and what was essential for such performance.

The essential ingredient

The canon law, as we know, prescribed when and where marriages should take place,[189] and the Book of Common Prayer set out the form to be used. Yet it did not state that a marriage celebrated without such rites would be void, and, as several authors noted, if a man and woman were married by a clergyman, without any such solemnity, the marriage was still good.[190] The crucial element in this should not, however, be overlooked: as another commentator noted, 'a private Contract without the Priest's Blessing will make no Marriage'.[191]

The assumption that an ordained clergyman was necessary pervades eighteenth-century discussions of marriage.[192] Throughout the debates in Parliament on the Bill that became the Clandestine Marriages Act, no-one, not even the most vehement opponents of the Bill, ever suggested that a contract *per verba de praesenti*

187 *Ibid.*

188 See e.g., *The L – d's Protest Against the Marriage Contract* (London, 1733), p. 4; *Love without Artifice: or, the Disappointed Peer: a History of the Amour between Lord Mauritio and Emilia, being the Case of Elizabeth Fitz-Maurice, alias Leeson, and the Lord William Fitz-Maurice, relating to a Marriage-Contract between Them* (London, 1733), pp. 27–8; E. Haywood, *The History of Miss Betsy Thoughtless* (London, 1751), p. 451.

189 See further Wheatly, *The Church of England Man's Companion*, ch. 9.

190 See e.g., H. Rolle, *Un abridgment des plusiers cases et resolutions del common ley alphabeticalment digest desouth severall titles* (London, 1668), p. 341; Viner, *Abridgment*, p. 30.

191 Bacon, *Abridgment*, p. 284. See also A. MacDowall Bankton, *An Institute of the Laws of Scotland in Civil Rights, with Observations on the Agreement or Diversity between Them and the Laws of England* (Edinburgh, 1751–3), vol. I, p. 141, noting that there was no complete marriage without the priest's blessing.

192 A deacon could celebrate a marriage, but by this period such men themselves had to be ordained: see W. Watson, *The Clergy-man's Law; or the Complete Incumbent* (London, 1701), p. 99.

constituted an actual marriage. The fact that the Bill would render promises of marriage unenforceable was criticised by its opponents, but it was assumed by every speaker that the clandestine marriage needed the presence of a clergyman. Thus, one argued that 'if there were no such public marriage shops kept, a young gentleman or lady would find it very difficult to get married to any low or infamous person, because the settled clergyman would have some regard to his character'.[193] Another commented that if all clergymen were of good character 'there would be no infamous marriages'.[194] And Lord Barrington, scoffing at the objection that the state could not prescribe that a marriage not duly celebrated would be void, commented that '[g]entlemen may as well argue, that if a ploughman should take it upon him to marry people in a neighbouring barn, the law ought not to declare such marriages void'.[195] The moral obligation, he acknowledged, was the same wherever and however the vows had been exchanged; the legal force, by contrast, was not.

Similarly, however hasty,[196] secret,[197] or scandalous[198] the marriage, literary characters invariably procure the services of a clergyman to preside.[199] Richardson's Pamela was not being over-cautious when she checked the credentials of the priest who was to perform her wedding ceremony. The predatory Mr B acknowledged that it had originally been his intention to have an attorney to impersonate a parson and read as little of the marriage ceremony as possible. 'And I did not in Haste intend you the Mortification of being undeceived, so that we might have liv'd for years, perhaps, very lovingly together; and I had, at the same time been at Liberty

[193] *Hansard's Parliamentary Debates*, vol. XV, col. 40.

[194] *Hansard's Parliamentary Debates*, vol. XV, col. 43.

[195] *Hansard's Parliamentary History*, vol. XV, col. 26.

[196] Smollett, *Peregrine Pickle*, p. 776.

[197] See Smollett, *Peregrine Pickle*, pp. 42 and 359; F. Sheridan, *The Memoirs of Miss Sidney Biddulph* (Oxford University Press, 1999; original edn 1761), p. 323; Probert, 'Examining Law through the Lens of Literature'.

[198] See e.g., the projected forced marriage in S. Richardson, *Clarissa, or, The History of a Young Lady* (London: Penguin, 1985; original edn 1747–8), pp. 239, 364, and the attempt to deceive Betsy Thoughtless into marrying Sir Frederick Fineer in *The History of Betsy Thoughtless*.

[199] If they cannot procure the services of a clergyman, they do not marry: see e.g., J. Gay, *The Beggar's Opera* (London: William Heinemann, 1921; original edn 1728), p. 49.

to confirm or abrogate it, as I pleas'd.'[200] A clergyman is both necessary and sufficient: in *Clarissa*, Lovelace notes the advantage that the formal requirements offer a cooling-off period,[201] but ruefully declared that 'had a parson been there, I had certainly been a gone man'.[202]

There are, in addition, a number of cases demonstrating that the status of the person celebrating the disputed marriage was thought to be relevant by the courts.[203] In *Weld* v. *Chamberlaine*, for example, the ceremony in question had taken place before an ordained minister who had been ejected from his living. Pemberton CJ inclined to the view that 'words of contract *per verba de praesenti* repeated after a parson in orders' created a good marriage; this was challenged but the point was not resolved.[204] In *R* v. *The Inhabitants of Luffington*,[205] the settlement of the pauper in question rested on whether she had been validly married – and *this* turned on whether her supposed husband's first marriage had been valid. There was evidence that the first ceremony had taken place according to the rites of the Church of England, but in a private house, conducted 'by a Person in a black Coat and Band'.[206] The bride assumed that he was a clergyman but 'has since been informed that he was a layman'.[207] After much discussion as to the status of a marriage not celebrated by a clergyman, the court quashed the order of removal on the basis that the case had been so imperfectly

[200] S. Richardson, *Pamela, or Virtue Rewarded* (London, 1740; Oxford: World Classics, 2001), p. 269. See also G. S. Alleman, *Matrimonial Law and the Materials of Restoration Comedy* (Wallingford, Pa.: 1942), p. 74, who notes the assumption among Restoration dramatists that a false clergyman would invalidate the ceremony.

[201] Richardson, *Clarissa*, p. 915. See also *The L – d's Protest Against the Marriage Contract* (London, 1733), p. 4.

[202] Richardson, *Clarissa*, p. 492. See also pp. 513, 730, 914, 934, 1169.

[203] The earlier case of *Costard* v. *Winder* (1599) Cro. Eliz. 775; 78 ER 1005, which might suggest the contrary, predated the stricter requirement that a clergyman be ordained, which was not introduced until the Act of Uniformity 1662, 14 Car. 2 c. 4, s. 10. The change is reflected in the dismay occasioned in 1681 when it was discovered that a man who had been celebrating marriages on Barbados for the previous twenty-four years was not actually ordained: the Governor, Sir Richard Dutton, wrote to the Board of Trade that 'he has married so many persons the legitimacy of whose children will be questioned that I am solicited to pass a bill for the confirmation of those marriages to prevent suits at law': quoted in Alleman, *Matrimonial Law*, p. 78.

[204] (1684) 2 Shower KB 301; 89 ER 952. [205] (1744) Burr. Sett. Cas. 232, No. 79.

[206] *Ibid*. p. 232. [207] *Ibid*.

stated, but confirmed the significance of clerical marriage by stating that the sessions should have determined whether the marriage was by a person in holy orders or not.[208] Of course, had a contract *per verba de praesenti* constituted a marriage, there would have been no need for any such debate.

Confusion or an appreciation of ambiguity?

Each of the sources examined in this section is open to objection by itself. Individuals may be confused as to the law, as indeed may their more literate contemporaries. Those involved in the administration or formulation of laws may be out of touch with real life. There is an obvious danger in relying on single sources. But there is also a danger in trying to explain away an entire body of evidence on the basis that contemporaries must have been mistaken or confused.[209] Rather than indicating confusion, the various sources discussed in this section perfectly illustrate the distinction between a promise that was binding, whether in conscience alone or at law, and a marriage that was celebrated with due formality in church. While eighteenth-century men and women may not have had a detailed knowledge of the law, it is highly probable that there was general awareness of its broad principles.[210] As one contemporary commentator noted, 'I presume there is not a marriageable couple in the kingdom so absolutely uninformed as not to know a clergyman to be a necessary instrument in matrimony'.[211]

208 *Ibid.* p. 235. See also *Haydon* v. *Gould* (1711) 1 Salk. 119; 91 ER 113, at 120: 'it appeared that the minister was a mere layman, and not in orders; upon which the letters of administration were repealed'.

209 A number of modern authors attribute contemporary statements about marriage to confusion: see e.g., Stone, *Road to Divorce*, p. 77; Alleman, *Matrimonial Law*; S. Dwyer Amussen, *An Ordered Society: Gender and Class in Early Modern England* (Oxford: Basil Blackwell Ltd, 1988), p. 110.

210 This was no doubt fostered by the requirement that the canons be publicly read 'once every Year, upon some Sunday or Holiday in the afternoon before Divine Service': see J. Shaw, *Parish Law*, 7th edn (London, 1750), p. 62.

211 *A Letter to the Public: Concerning the Substance of what hath been offered in the late Debates upon the subject of the Act of Parliament for the better preventing of clandestine marriages* (London: Charles March, 1753), p. 40. See also L. Stone, *The Family, Sex and Marriage in England 1500–1800* (London: Weidenfeld & Nicolson, 1977), p. 34.

HOW THE EVIDENCE WAS MISUNDERSTOOD

[T]he judgment of Sir William Scott has cleared the present case of all the difficulty which might, at a former time, have belonged to it.[212]

So how did we arrive at the modern misunderstanding that a bare exchange of vows would suffice? In order to understand how later authorities came to take a different view of the contract *per verba de praesenti*, it is necessary to jump both forward in time and across the Atlantic. The point at which a contract *per verba de praesenti* began to be referred to as a valid marriage, rather than as a binding contract, can be dated quite precisely, to the nineteenth-century Supreme Court of New York in *Fenton* v. *Reed*.[213] The judgment paraphrased the words of Holt CJ in *Collins* v. *Jessot*, that we read above, stating that:

[a] contract of marriage made *per verba de presenti* amounts to an actual marriage, and is as valid as if made *in facie ecclesiae*.

The key word here is 'valid'; a word that does not appear in *Collins* v. *Jessot*. The mistake of the court in *Fenton* v. *Reed* was to assume that if a contract was as *binding* as if the parties had married in church, it was therefore as *valid* as if the parties had married in church. By holding that marriages could be validly created with so little formality, the decision paved the way for the development of the distinctive American concept of 'common-law marriage'.[214]

Two years after *Fenton* v. *Reed*, the English ecclesiastical judge Sir William Scott came to a similar conclusion as to the status of a contract *per verba de praesenti* in the case of *Dalrymple* v. *Dalrymple*.[215] The question in *Dalrymple* was actually whether

[212] *Latour* v. *Teesdale* (1816) 8 Taunt. 829; 129 ER 606, at 837.
[213] 4 Johns (NY) 52 (1809).
[214] See O. E. Koegel, *Common Law Marriage and its Development in the United States* (Washington, DC: John Byrne & Co, 1922), ch. 7; M. Grossberg, *Governing the Hearth: Law and the Family in Nineteenth-Century America* (Chapel Hill: University of North Carolina Press, 1985); R. Probert, 'Common-Law Marriage: Myths and Misunderstandings' (2008) 20 *Child and Family Law Quarterly* 1. The concept of 'common-law marriage' is discussed further in Chapter 3.
[215] (1811) 2 Hag. Con. 54; 161 ER 665.

an exchange of vows created a marriage in nineteenth-century *Scotland*, where the events at the heart of the case had taken place.[216] Sir William frankly admitted his 'inferior qualifications'[217] to decide the matter, but then took the view that the Scottish law of marriage could be assumed to be the same as the canon law of marriage that had been applied across Europe until the Council of Trent in the mid-sixteenth century unless the contrary could be proved, remarking airily that '[i]t is not for me to attempt to trace the descent of the matrimonial law of Scotland since the time of the Reformation'.[218] His judgment does, however, contain detailed discussion of the law of Scotland: there is a lengthy analysis of case law, evidence from experts, and consideration of key legal texts. By contrast, his discussion of English law as it stood prior to 1754 is rather more perfunctory: a mere four cases are cited in an attempt to demonstrate that a contract *per verba de praesenti* had been regarded as a marriage there prior to 1754. Of these, the ambiguities of *Collins* v. *Jessot* and *Wigmore's Case* have already been noted,[219] while *Bunting* v. *Lepingwell*[220] and the unreported decision in *Fitzmaurice* v. *Fitzmaurice*,[221] decided in 1732, merely established that a contract *per verba de praesenti* was binding on the parties. Whatever the law of Scotland was, there was nothing in the English authorities to justify Scott's

216 The case originated in a suit for restitution of conjugal rights brought by Johanna Gordon, a Scotswoman, in the London Consistory Court. She claimed to have married John Dalrymple, an Englishman, when he was quartered in Scotland with his regiment several years earlier. Young Dalrymple (only nineteen when he ventured north of the border) had subsequently been required to leave Scotland. Initially he wrote passionate letters to the woman he termed his wife, but his affections waned and then became fastened on a new object. It was when he went through a ceremony of marriage with Miss Laura Manners that the spurned Johanna brought her claim.

217 At p. 59.

218 At p. 70. He made some attempt to trace the law of England from the Reformation to the 1753 Act, but his analysis of the law occupies less than a page in the English Reports.

219 It is also significant that the reports of these cases cited by Scott are noticeably less full than others that have survived.

220 (1585) 4 Co. Rep. 29a; 76 ER 950.

221 For an account of the case, see *Love without Artifice: or, the Disappointed Peer: a History of the Amour between Lord Mauritio and Emilia, being the Case of Elizabeth Fitz-Maurice, alias Leeson, and the Lord William Fitz-Maurice, relating to a Marriage-Contract between Them* (London, 1733).

assumption that such a contract had ever constituted a legal marriage there.[222]

And the idea that the law had flowed in an unbroken stream since the sixteenth century is rather difficult to reconcile with the fact that *Dalrymple* clearly effected a shift in the way that a contract *per verba de praesenti* was regarded in the English courts. Only three years before the decision in *Dalrymple*, the court had struggled to determine this issue in *R* v. *Brampton*.[223] The case required the court to determine the validity of a marriage celebrated by an English couple in St Domingo. They had gone through a public ceremony of marriage in a chapel in the town, conducted by a person they had reason to suppose was a priest, and according to what they assumed was the marriage service of the Church of England (read in French and interpreted for the parties by a person officiating as a clerk); a complicating factor was that it was not clear whether the priest was an Anglican or a Roman Catholic. It was decided by the court that, in default of evidence to the contrary, this was a good marriage by the law of St Domingo, and, more tentatively, that it would also have been good by the law of England prior to 1754. Lord Ellenborough, while noting that a contract *per verba de praesenti* would have been *binding* on the parties, attached importance to the status of the celebrant,[224] rather desperately reasoning that a Roman Catholic priest 'would be recognized by our Church as a priest capable of officiating as [an Anglican clergyman], upon his mere renunciation of the errors of the Church of Rome, without any new ordination'.[225] But had the

[222] In arguing that Scott misunderstood the law of England and Wales as it stood prior to 1754, it is not my intention to suggest that the actual outcome of *Dalrymple* would have been different had it been heard in that jurisdiction in the first part of the eighteenth century. Johanna Gordon would have brought a case in contract, rather than one for restitution of conjugal rights, but John Dalrymple's marriage to Laura Manners could have been set aside on the basis of the written evidence of the contract that Johanna produced. Dalrymple would then have been ordered to marry Johanna. The point is that Johanna would have succeeded on the basis that the contract was binding, rather than on the basis that there was a valid marriage.

[223] (1808) 10 East 282; 103 ER 782.

[224] As did Le Blanc and Bayley JJ, but it is not entirely clear whether this was in the context of English law or the law of St Domingo. Similarly, Grose J was more confident that it would constitute a valid marriage by the law of St Domingo than he was regarding its status in English law.

[225] At p. 288.

court been of the opinion that a contract *per verba de praesenti* constituted a marriage in and of itself, the issue could have been quite simply decided, since it was clear that the parties had, at the very least, exchanged vows.

The uncertainties expressed by the judges in *Brampton* reflect the fact that it was a long time since the courts had been called on to answer this question: the contract *per verba de praesenti* had been of no effect in England and Wales since the coming into force of the Clandestine Marriages Act in 1754, while marriage across the empire was generally governed by legislation. However, by the time that *Latour* v. *Teesdale*[226] was decided, a mere eight years later, the status of a contract *per verba de praesenti* was regarded as settled. The facts of the case were very similar: British subjects living in Madras had gone through a Roman Catholic ceremony of marriage there. The reasoning of the court, however, was very different. Counsel for the plaintiffs, arguing that the marriage was valid, noted confidently that the subject had received exhaustive treatment in *Dalrymple* v. *Dalrymple*; counsel for the defendants did not even attempt to challenge the authority of *Dalrymple* but tried to argue that it was not applicable as the canon law has been displaced by local regulations. The court decided that the canon law was applicable, and that as the parties had exchanged vows *per verba de praesenti* they had been validly married in Madras. But Gibbs CJ acknowledged the uncertainty that had existed prior to *Dalrymple*,[227] and throughout his judgment all his remarks on the applicable law were supported by reference to that case.

Indeed, it is clear from Scott's earlier decision in *Lindo* v. *Belisario*[228] that his own views on the status of such a contract had changed. *Lindo* concerned the validity of a Jewish ceremony of marriage, and Scott contrasted the situation of the parties before him, having gone through such a ceremony, with that of a couple who had exchanged vows in words of the present tense:

> There is then, on this state of the parties, *more than the mere* contract *per verba de praesenti* in the Christian Church, which was a perfect contract of marriage law, though public celebration was afterwards required by the rules and ordinances of the canon law.[229]

[226] (1816) 8 Taunt. 830; 129 ER 606. [227] At 837.
[228] (1795) 1 Hag. Con. 216; 161 ER 530. [229] At 242 (emphasis added).

Elsewhere in *Lindo*, Scott referred to such a contract as being 'a good marriage ... according to the law of nature'.[230] Had he regarded it as good under the law as it stood prior to the 1753 Act, much of his lengthy judgment would have been unnecessary.

Given that Scott does not refer to *Fenton* v. *Reed* in the course of his judgment in *Dalrymple*, the suggestion that it influenced his decision must rest on circumstantial evidence. A brief review of this evidence shows that the dates all fit: in 1795 Scott describes a contract *per verba de praesenti* as a contract rather than an actual marriage; in 1808 this is still the prevailing view in *R* v. *Brampton*; in 1809 there was a clear assertion in *Fenton* v. *Reed* that a contract *per verba de praesenti* was an actual marriage, it being assumed that this was the case in English law prior to 1754; two years later, in 1811, there is an equally clear assertion by Scott in *Dalrymple* to the same effect. It is possible that this is no more than a coincidence, but to attribute at least some influence to *Fenton* would explain both why Scott changed his views and also why he did so when he did. The timing of these cases is also significant for another reason: it was only after those who had practised as lawyers under the old system had died out that uncertainty about the earlier law could develop. Scott, Ellenborough, and Gibbs had all begun their legal careers in the 1770s and 1780s,[231] and would not have had any practical knowledge of the way in which the theory of the canon law was modified in practice.

It is clear that the decision in *Dalrymple* effected some subtle but significant changes: it was thereafter common for an exchange of vows *per verba de praesenti* to be described as a 'valid marriage' rather than a binding contract.[232] It is only in the wake of *Dalrymple* that the term 'marriage *per verba de praesenti*' is regularly used, the earlier practice being generally to refer to 'a *contract* of

[230] At p. 232.

[231] See M. Lobban, 'Law, Edward, first Baron Ellenborough (1750–1818)', R. A. Melikan, 'Gibbs, Sir Vicary (1751–1820)', and 'Scott, William, Baron Stowell (1745–1836)' in *Oxford Dictionary of National Biography* (Oxford University Press, 2004).

[232] It is true that Blackstone at one point refers to a contract *per verba de praesenti* as a 'valid marriage' but this is instantly followed by the words 'for many purposes' and the fact that the parties would be compelled to solemnise the marriage in church: Blackstone, *Commentaries*, p. 427.

marriage *per verba de praesenti*'.[233] Scott's judgment also blurred the eighteenth-century distinction between the clandestine marriage (i.e., a marriage celebrated before an Anglican minister otherwise than in accordance with the canon law) and a contract *per verba de praesenti*, since he described the contract in the case as a form of clandestine marriage.[234] And, in practical terms, it led to a number of individuals being successfully prosecuted for bigamy in cases where they had gone through a ceremony of marriage with one person after having married another according to rites other than those of the Established Church.[235]

The House of Lords had the opportunity to check Scott's misunderstanding in *R* v. *Millis*,[236] in which Millis, who had gone through a Presbyterian ceremony of marriage in Ireland with one woman before marrying another in England, was prosecuted for bigamy. The fact that he was acquitted might suggest that the mistake in *Dalrymple* was corrected; in fact, their Lordships were equally divided, with Millis escaping conviction solely because of the presumption in favour of innocence.[237] The fact that the result in *Millis* has been widely derided as wrongly decided[238] is indicative of the influence of *Dalrymple*. But in the light of the law as it stood before the 1753 Act it was correct, as this chapter has shown.

233 The fact that much material is now available in electronic form makes the task of establishing the point at which a particular term emerged much easier than in the past, although care must be exercised as the search tools are far from perfect. The absence of a particular term does at least raise a *presumption* that it was not generally used by contemporaries. A search of the electronic version of the English Reports, for example, yielded no mention of the term 'marriage *per verba de praesenti*' before the decision in *Dalrymple* in the nineteenth century, while only one clear example of the concept appears in the electronic database Eighteenth-Century Collections Online – which contains the full text of all the 150,000-or-so books published in England in the eighteenth century, and this related to the marriage law of Holland, not England.

234 This was inevitable once he had decided that it was a marriage, since it was clearly not a regular marriage. It also reflected the way in which the case was argued before him: counsel had argued that the marriage was clandestine, using that word in the more popular sense of private, surreptitious, or nefarious.

235 The first, the case of Lathroppe Murray in 1815, had been heard at the Old Bailey; others had been decided by Irish judges at assizes: see *R* v. *Millis* (1843–44) 10 Cl. & F 534; 8 ER 844, at 933.

236 (1843–44) 10 Cl. & F 534; 8 ER 844.

237 See further Probert, '*R v. Millis* Reconsidered'.

238 Pollock and Maitland, *History of English Law*, p. 372; W. Holdsworth, *A History of English Law* (London: Methuen & Co, 1903), p. 622.

CONCLUSION

This rather explodes the Dalrymple theory.[239]

By unpacking the meanings of a contract *per verba de praesenti*, and focusing on all the ways in which such contracts were *not* regarded as marriages, it is possible to build up a more accurate picture of law and practice in the eighteenth century. The true nature of a contract *per verba de praesenti* has been obscured by the modern tendency to describe it as a marriage, and the assumption that it was therefore equivalent to a marriage solemnised in church.[240] While it is true that a contract *per verba de praesenti* was binding on the parties, what it bound them to do was to marry each other – and to refrain from marrying anyone else. This chapter has shown how the strict requirements of proof created a difference between an agreement that was only morally binding and one that was legally enforceable; how the lack of legal consequences attached to a proven contract expose the difference between a contract to do something and the completion of that act; and how discussions of the nature of a contract bridged the gap between theory and practice.

An unwitnessed and unacknowledged contract was morally but not legally binding; a contract that had been established to the satisfaction of the ecclesiastical courts required the parties to marry in church; and the canonical theory that consent was central to marriage does not mean that it was the only thing necessary for a marriage in eighteenth-century England and Wales. Stone describes contracts *per verba de praesenti* as 'contract marriages'[241]

[239] P. G. Wodehouse, *Money in the Bank* (Harmondsworth: Penguin Books Ltd, 1964), p. 165.

[240] The strength of the consensus among modern academic commentators that a contract *per verba de praesenti* constituted a valid marriage has meant that even those whose evidence suggests otherwise have not challenged it. For example, Cressy's review of marriage contracts in the sixteenth and seventeenth centuries supports the argument presented in this chapter that a contract was binding on the parties but not in itself regarded as a marriage, but he still states that vows *per verba de praesenti* created a valid marriage. This statement is, however, hedged around with phrases such as 'in principle' and 'technically' and he is more confident in his claim that '[i]n practice . . . simple, private secular commitments were treated as seriously deficient': Cressy, *Birth, Marriage and Death*, p. 317. See also Helmholz, *Oxford History*, p. 527; and Ingram, *Church Courts*, p. 132, who suggests that the 'practical significance' of the theory that an informal declaration constituted a marriage 'should not be exaggerated'.

[241] Stone, *Road to Divorce*, ch. 3.

(a term that I have not found in any of the sources here examined) but it is as a contract to marry, rather than as a marriage, that such exchanges of vows should be understood. As the examples quoted in this chapter show, this is the way in which it was understood in the eighteenth century, and it was only after the decisions in *Fenton* v. *Reed* and *Dalrymple* v. *Dalrymple* that this view transmuted into the current misunderstanding that a contract *per verba de praesenti* was a marriage for all purposes.

This chapter has demonstrated that a contract *per verba de praesenti* cannot be regarded as a full alternative to a regular marriage, as it did not carry the same legal rights as one celebrated in church. But it may be objected that not all couples were concerned with legal rights. To test whether the contract *per verba de praesenti* constituted a *functional* alternative to a regular marriage it is necessary to look at the issue from a different angle and ask whether there is any evidence that couples who were living together were bound merely by informal vows rather than by a formal ceremony of marriage. But this is a task for the next chapter.

3

THE MYTHS OF 'INFORMAL' AND 'COMMON-LAW' MARRIAGE

The argument advanced in the previous chapter was that a contract *per verba de praesenti* was not a full alternative to a regular marriage in that it did not carry the same legal rights as a marriage celebrated in church. This chapter asks whether, despite this, such contracts did in fact operate as a *functional* alternative to a regular marriage, as a number of commentators have claimed.[1] This brings us back to the definitions of marriage and alternatives to marriage set out in the introductory chapter. It was there suggested that a 'functional alternative' would entail co-residence, a sexual relationship, and some recognition by the parties themselves, and by the wider community, that their relationship was equivalent to a formal marriage.

It is, of course, the combination of such elements that is important. In order to make a convincing case that a contract *per verba de praesenti* was the functional equivalent of a marriage in church, it would not be enough to show that some contracted couples engaged in sexual relations. There is a wide gulf between snatched moments of illicit passion and stable cohabitation.[2] The evidence that some couples began sexual relations after entering into a

[1] See e.g., K. O'Donovan, *Sexual Divisions in Law* (London: Weidenfeld & Nicholson, 1985), p. 46: '[s]pousals, or common law marriage, was the traditional form of marriage of the people'; S. Parker, *Informal Marriage, Cohabitation and the Law, 1754–1989* (Basingstoke: Macmillan, 1990), pp. 14–27; W. Mansell, B. Meteyard, and A. Thomson, *A Critical Introduction to Law*, 3rd edn (London: Cavendish, 2004); A. Diduck and F. Kaganas, *Family Law, Gender and the State: Text, Cases and Materials*, 2nd edn (Oxford: Hart Publishing, 2005), pp. 58–60.

[2] See e.g., R. Adair, *Courtship, Illegitimacy and Marriage in Early Modern England* (Manchester University Press, 1996), p. 147, and J. Addy, *Sin and Society in the Seventeenth Century* (London: Routledge, 1989), pp. 130–1, noting that locations such as lanes and ditches were often specified in prosecutions for fornication. Similar evidence relating to the eighteenth century is discussed further below.

contract to marry reflects the fact that such contracts, if witnessed, were legally binding, and that the woman had the security that she would be able to enforce it if she became pregnant;[3] it does not indicate that the contract was regarded as the end of the process.[4] Nor is the use of terms such as 'husband' and 'wife' sufficient. As noted in the previous chapter, a couple might use those terms simply to reflect their contracted status, even if they had only exchanged vows *de futuro*. Some might object that excluding such evidence pays too little heed to the perceptions of the individuals involved,[5] but in assessing whether a contract *per verba de praesenti* constituted a functional alternative to a regular marriage the focus must be on the *behaviour* of the parties, rather than their unreconstructable emotions. It is co-residence, therefore, that is the most crucial element: setting up home together was a public act (and therefore one that might depend on public approval or at least acquiescence). Evidence that it was commonplace for contracted couples to live together would go some way to showing that the contract was regarded as the final stage in the road to a marriage, rather than simply a preliminary.

It has, of course, been claimed that some individuals valued less formal varieties of marriage precisely because they were not the same as a regular marriage:[6] specifically because they did not carry full legal rights and because (it is claimed) they allowed the possibility of self-divorce. It is suggested that these elements were present in 'handfasting' (presented as a marriage for a year and a day, with the possibility of separation if the union did not result in the conception of a child in that period) and the 'broomstick

[3] Although an enforceable promise was not a *sine qua non* of sexual activity: see e.g., R. Trumbach, *Sex and the Gender Revolution*, vol. I, *Heterosexuality and the Third Gender in Enlightenment London* (University of Chicago, 1998), p. 234.

[4] Contrast R. B. Outhwaite, *Clandestine Marriage in England, 1500–1850* (London: Hambledon Press, 1995), p. 38, who suggests that many people saw the 'troth-plight' as 'the vital event that legitimated sexual activity and thus brought a marriage into existence'. The first part of the claim does not justify the inference in the second. Similarly L. Stone, *Road to Divorce: a History of the Making and Breaking of Marriage in England* (Oxford University Press, 1990), p. 65, rather tenuously infers at least 'temporary concubinage' from pre-marital pregnancy. That sex cannot be equated with cohabitation is evident from studies of mothers who bore illegitimate children: see further below.

[5] See e.g., Parker, *Informal Marriage*, p. 4.

[6] See e.g., J. Gillis, *For Better, For Worse: British Marriages 1600 to the Present* (Oxford University Press, 1985), p. 99; Mansell *et al.*, *Critical Introduction*, p. 96.

wedding' (the assumption being that couples could marry by jumping over a broom, and could separate by jumping backwards over it).[7] Given the popularity of these ideas, it is important not to prejudge the issue and to stress at the outset that the criteria outlined above – co-residence, sexual relations, and reputation – would not exclude such forms of marriage. A functional alternative to marriage need not, therefore, be a *permanent* union.

As we shall see, however, the idea that 'handfasting' and 'broomstick weddings' were popular has to be discounted for other reasons – basically, that modern ideas about them are based on misunderstandings and that the practices never occurred in the form claimed. It is tempting to skip from the lack of evidence that contracted couples lived together (discussed in the second section) to the indisputable evidence that the majority of couples married in church (discussed in the fourth section), and consider the case closed. But so much has been written on this subject, and so many different ideas need to be disentangled, that rather more explanation is required, to reassure the reader that no angle has been overlooked.

First, it may be helpful to explain the varying terminology used in the literature. Stone, for example, used the concept of 'contract marriage';[8] other writers have referred variously to 'consensual',[9] 'common-law',[10] 'irregular',[11] 'formless',[12] or 'informal' marriage.[13] While neither the terminology nor the definitions offered by

[7] See e.g., O'Donovan, *Sexual Divisions*, p. 49.

[8] Stone, *Road to Divorce*, ch. 3.

[9] B. Meteyard, 'Illegitimacy in Eighteenth-Century England: a Reply' (1981) 11 *Journal of Interdisciplinary History* 507, 514; R. Porter, *English Society in the Eighteenth Century* (London: Allen Lane, 1982), p. 164; Mansell *et al.*, *Critical Introduction*, p. 92.

[10] See e.g., E. A. Wrigley, 'Clandestine Marriage in Tetbury in the Late 17th Century' (1973) 10 *Local Population Studies* 15, 16; A. Macfarlane, *Marriage and Love in England: Modes of Reproduction 1300–1840* (Oxford: Basil Blackwood Ltd, 1986), pp. 226, 310; O'Donovan, *Sexual Divisions*, p. 43; A. Laurence, *Women in England 1500–1760: a Social History* (London: Phoenix, 1996), p. 50; S. M. Cretney, J. M. Masson, and R. Bailey-Harris, *Principles of Family Law*, 7th edn (London: Sweet & Maxwell, 2002), p. 10; M. E. Rodgers, *Understanding Family Law* (London: Cavendish Publishing Ltd, 2004), p. 1.

[11] O'Donovan, *Sexual Divisions*, p. 43.

[12] Mansell *et al.*, *Critical Introduction*, p. 92; O'Donovan, *Sexual Divisions*, p. 43.

[13] S. Parker, 'The Marriage Act 1753: a Case Study in Family Law-Making' (1987) 1 *International Journal of Law and the Family* 133, 138; *Informal Marriage*, p. 5.

commentators in this area are entirely consistent,[14] all are, in essence, referring to the same idea: an explicit exchange of consent between two individuals otherwise than before an Anglican clergyman. Some refer to such exchanges being presided over by a third party, or involving some kind of 'folk' ceremony or community involvement;[15] others are concerned only with the bare exchange of consent. The key point for present purposes is that such consent is portrayed as being articulated. This needs to be emphasised to differentiate it from a second idea, namely that in certain circumstances an exchange of consent could be inferred. This is what in America became known as a 'common-law marriage',[16] although rather confusingly that term has also been applied to a variety of different practices.[17] Of course, once it has been shown that an *actual* exchange of consent without the presence of a clergyman did not carry the same rights as a regular marriage, there is no discernable advantage to a cohabiting couple in being presumed to have exchanged such consent: it is self-evident that one cannot gain more rights upon being presumed to have exchanged consent than one would gain upon proof of an explicit exchange of consent. But because ideas about 'common-law marriage' have been intertwined with ideas about informal marriage it is useful to dispose of both myths together. And both, of course, are crucial in assessing the impact of the 1753 Act.

[14] See e.g., Parker, *Informal Marriage*, who notes that his concern is mainly with 'those marriage forms ... which might not have counted as marriage at all under ecclesiastical or civil law' (p. 17). It is difficult to see how such practices fall within his definition of 'informal marriage' as 'that which before 1754 carried some religious and legal consequences' (p. 5). Later still he claims that for certain groups a simple exchange of consent 'before a credible witness was sufficient and, if it mattered, had some recognition in civil law' (p. 24).

[15] Diduck and Kaganas, *Family Law*, p. 59.

[16] See e.g., O. E. Koegel, *Common Law Marriage and its Development in the United States* (Washington, DC: John Byrne & Co, 1922), ch. 7; M. Grossberg, *Governing the Hearth: Law and the Family in Nineteenth-Century America* (Chapel Hill: University of North Carolina Press, 1985); R. Probert, 'Common-Law Marriage: Myths and Misunderstandings' (2008) 20 *Child and Family Law Quarterly* 1.

[17] See e.g., J. M. Thomson, 'Irregular Marriages' (1974) 90 *Law Quarterly Review* 28, 28–9, referring to both an exchange of consents before an episcopally ordained priest and, 'as adapted for the colonies', a bare exchange of consents; and A. Barlow, S. Duncan, G. James, and A. Park, *Cohabitation, Marriage and the Law: Social Change and Legal Reform in the 21st Century* (Oxford: Hart, 2005), p. 27, who imply that living together constituted a common-law marriage.

This (necessarily somewhat lengthy) chapter accordingly approaches from a number of different angles the question as to whether an exchange of vows formed a functional alternative to a regular marriage. The first section shows that current beliefs as to the extent of 'informal marriage' are based on a series of misunderstandings, as are both 'handfasting' and 'broomstick weddings'. I then go on to examine whether there is any evidence that contracted couples lived together, or any evidence that couples known to be cohabiting regarded themselves as married. The third section then dispels the myth that cohabitants would have been regarded as living in a 'common-law marriage' prior to 1754, and the fourth draws on a number of case studies to show the overwhelming popularity of regular marriage. Finally, I discuss the reasons that have been put forward to justify the hypothesis that couples married by consent alone, and show that they are unconvincing. In short, it will be argued that there was no reason for couples to marry informally, no evidence that they did so, and widespread evidence of conformity.

CHINESE WHISPERS

What I got was – at least I think it was – 'Miss Dene was on the stairs and she was a cannibal!'[18]

There certainly appears to be a widespread belief among modern academics[19] and commentators[20] that many, perhaps even most, couples married informally, i.e., by exchanging consent without the intervention of a clergyman, prior to the 1753 Act. Parker, for example, suggested that many couples entered into domestic

[18] The headmistress reporting the outcome of a game of Chinese whispers: E. M. Brent-Dyer, *The New Mistress at the Chalet School* (Bath: Girls Gone By Publishers, 2006; original edn 1957), p. 151. See also T. Smollett, *The Adventures of Peregrine Pickle* (Oxford University Press, 1964; original edn 1751), pp. 559–60, for another example of the garbled transmission of ideas.

[19] See e.g., L. Davidoff, 'The Family in Britain', ch. 2 in F. M. L. Thompson (ed.), *The Cambridge Social History of Britain 1750–1950*, vol. II, *People and their Environment* (Cambridge University Press, 1990), p. 90: 'it is estimated that at least half of all unions were sealed in a simple folk ceremony, exchanging rings or in rituals such as jumping over a broomstick before a few witnesses'; O'Donovan, *Sexual Divisions*, p. 44; Mansell *et al.*, *Critical Introduction*, p. 92; Diduck and Kaganas, *Family Law*, p. 59.

[20] G. Stewart, 'The Swinging 1700s were so Like Today', *The Times*, 24 February 2007, p. 23.

arrangements that had the blessing of the local community, if not the sanction of the law or the church, and that in the eighteenth century 'local practices meant that many, *if not most*, adults in an area might not be recognised by the civil law as married'.[21] This section will investigate the truth of the two key elements underpinning these claims: first, the high estimate of the extent of informal marriage; secondly, the idea that marriages were celebrated with some kind of 'folk' ceremony deriving from local custom.[22] Two supposed forms of local custom will be considered, namely 'handfasting' and the 'broomstick wedding'. It will be shown that, like the garbled sentence that heads this section, both elements of this claim are the product of 'Chinese whispers', based on accumulated errors and bearing little or no relation to their sources.

The supposed extent of 'informal marriage'[23]

Our starting point is the claim that 'informal marriage' accounted for at least half of all marriages before 1754. While Parker appears to have been the first person to make this specific claim about the prevalence of 'informal marriage'[24] he did not regard himself as an innovator in this respect. Indeed, he stated that other scholars had also uncovered evidence of 'informal marriage', and that '[s]ome historians have settled for a figure of one fifth while others have put it as high as one-half'.[25] In fact, the debate in the academic literature concerned the prevalence of *clandestine* marriages, i.e., marriages celebrated before an Anglican minister that did not comply with the canon law, rather than pure exchanges of consent. And it is difficult to see how Parker could derive the idea that half of marriages were informal from Stone's tentative suggestion that '[p]erhaps not much more than half the population were being

21 Parker, *Informal Marriage*, p. 4, emphasis added.

22 See also C. Hill, *Liberty Against the Law: Some Seventeenth Century Controversies* (London: Penguin, 1996), p. 205, and W. Cornish and G. N. de Clark, *Law and Society in England, 1750–1950* (London: Sweet & Maxwell, 1989), p. 361, who claim that 'pure folk-practices ... were widespread'.

23 This section draws on Probert, 'Common-Law Marriage'.

24 Parker, 'The Marriage Act 1753', 138–9.

25 Parker, *Informal Marriage*, p. 17; 'The Marriage Act 1753', 139.

married strictly according to the rules of canon law',[26] especially since it is clear that Stone was including marriages celebrated in church as examples of the minority that flouted the law.

But Gillis may have been seen as providing some support for the myth when he suggested that up to half of all weddings may have been celebrated with some element of privacy:[27] in this category he included marriages preceded by a licence as well as clandestine marriages and a further category of what he (anachronistically)[28] termed 'common law arrangements'. Given that Gillis was estimating the proportion of clandestine marriages to be between one-quarter and one-third of all marriages, and that marriages by licence would account for a further one-fifth, even by his own account the balance being attributed to other forms of marriage could only be very small. Similarly, Gillis' own sources focus on the prevalence of clandestine marriages and provide little support for the existence of other alternatives.[29]

However, in *Road to Divorce* Stone specifically challenged the argument that large swathes of the population were living in customary unions that had some degree of social recognition. Although Stone's arguments are not entirely consistent (he is willing to assume that such practices occurred 'in remote areas such as Wales',[30] and precisely the same arguments that he marshals against 'concubinage' could be used to negate the existence of what he termed 'contract marriages'), he does make a number of telling points, rightly noting the 'combined pressure by community, church, and state ... to regularise sexual and marital behaviour and punish deviants' which 'undoubtedly reduced the amount of bastardy and pre-nuptial conceptions to an astonishingly low level, and must have made concubinage by folk custom uncomfortable and fairly rare'.[31] He also

[26] L. Stone, *The Family, Sex and Marriage in England 1500–1800* (Harmondsworth: Penguin, 1979), pp. 34–5. In 'Common-Law Marriage', I overlooked this specific source, largely because Stone had later explicitly suggested that clandestine marriages accounted for one-fifth of the total in mid-eighteenth-century England without acknowledging his earlier work: see Stone, *Road to Divorce*, p. 115.

[27] Gillis, *For Better, For Worse*, p. 84.

[28] The term was not used in the eighteenth century: see further Probert, 'Common-Law Marriage'.

[29] One source cited by Gillis, Wrigley, 'Clandestine Marriage in Tetbury', does mention 'common-law marriage' but only on the erroneous supposition that the contemporary term 'clandestine marriage' may have included less formal arrangements: for a reinterpretation of his data see further Chapter 5.

[30] Stone, *Road to Divorce*, p. 64. [31] *Ibid.* p. 64.

correctly points to 'the absence of any obvious large deficit in the figures for marriages taken from parish registers'.[32]

I shall return to the evidence from the parish registers later: for now, the key point to make is that the idea that up to half of couples married informally is based not on empirical evidence of the behaviour of real people but rather on a speculation by one academic about the extent of exact compliance and another's hypothesis that up to half may have preferred privacy. Of course, the fact that this specific claim can so easily be shown to be baseless does not prove that couples did not engage in informal marriage practices. So, let us turn to the evidence that has been put forward to support the idea that they did.

Handfasting

'Handfasting' has been described as a Scottish form of marriage whereby the parties lived together for a year and a day and at the end of that period could choose either to remain together or to part.[33] It has been claimed that this practice also occurred in England before 1754, in particular in 'remoter areas'.[34] The fact that modern scholars still claim that this occurred[35] is somewhat surprising given that an article published fifty years ago pointed out that there was no foundation for such a practice, either in England *or* Scotland.[36] The author, Anton, suggested that the early sources for the idea of handfasting as a form of temporary marriage could be reduced to three: two of which involved claims by outsiders that such unions used to occur in the distant past, without any evidence, and the third of which related to a single union and was contradicted in relation to that same union by other sources. Of course, the very existence of such evidence, however vague, might lead some to believe that there must be *some* foundation

[32] *Ibid.* p. 65.

[33] M. Baker, *Wedding Customs and Folklore* (Newton Abbot: David & Charles Publishers Ltd, 1977), p. 22.

[34] Parker, *Informal Marriage*, p. 18. He suggests that it was particularly prevalent in border counties, Wales, and the extreme south-west; it has also been claimed that it was practised in the Lake District (see Gillis, *For Better, For Worse*, p. 50), and the Isle of Man (C. R. Chapman, *Marriage Laws, Rites, Records and Customs: Was Your Ancestor Really Married?* (Dursley: Lochin Publishing, 1996), p. 32).

[35] For a recent example, see M. Bennett, 'Courtship and Marriage' in M. Lynch (ed.), *The Oxford Companion to Scottish History* (Oxford University Press, 2007).

[36] A. E. Anton, '"Handfasting" in Scotland' (1958) 37 *Scottish Historical Review* 89.

for the idea. It is therefore important to look carefully at the evidence and to trace the process by which the idea that one could be handfasted for a year and a day actually emerged. This Anton failed to do, simply referring to various sources without establishing their chronology; moreover, his assumption that consent alone made a permanent marriage led him to overlook certain significant developments that would explain the emergence of the idea.

The changing claims can be illustrated by three key sources, dating from the last years of the seventeenth century to the first year of Victoria's reign. The earliest source, Martin's *Description of the Western Islands of Scotland*, claimed that:

> It was an Ancient Custom in the Islands, that a Man should take a Maid to his Wife and keep her the space of a Year *without marrying her*, and if she pleased him all the while, he married her at the end of the Year, and legitimated these Children, but if he did not love Her, he return'd her to her Parents and her Portion also, and if there happened to be any Children, they were kept by the father.[37]

No mention here of 'handfasting', and a very clear indication that such a trial was not, in itself, regarded as a marriage. Moreover, Martin added that 'this unreasonable Custom was long ago brought into disuse'.[38]

Eighty years later another traveller, Thomas Pennant, gave an account of a similar, if apparently more egalitarian, tradition in Eskdale,[39] 'in use about a century past'[40] and linked to the annual fair:

> The unmarried looked out for mates, made their engagement by joining hands, or by handfisting, went off in pairs, cohabited till the next annual return of the fair, appeared there again, and then were at liberty to declare their approbation or dislike of each other. If each party continued constant, the handfisting was renewed for life: but if either party dissented, the engagement was void, and both were at full liberty to make a new choice;

37 M. Martin, *Description of the Western Islands of Scotland* (London, 1703), p. 114 (emphasis added). Martin's tour took place a few years prior to publication, in 1695.

38 *Ibid.*

39 The place Pennant is describing is located some miles north of Lockerbie, 'at the confluence of the white and the black Esk' (T. Pennant, *A Tour in Scotland, and Voyage to the Hebrides* (Chester: John Monk, 1774), p. 91), and is not Eskdale in the Lake District.

40 Pennant, *A Tour in Scotland*, p. 92.

but with this proviso, that the inconstant was to take the charge of the offspring of the year of probation.[41]

By the 1830s, a subtle but significant shift has occurred in the way the supposed practice is described. The historian William Skene attributes the practice of handfasting to the Highlanders, and describes it as a contract between the parents, rather than the parties themselves, but for present purposes the most important change is his suggestion that:

> If in that time the lady became a mother, or proved to be with child, *the marriage became good in law*, even although no priest had performed the marriage ceremony in due form.[42]

Four separate developments need to be teased out from these three accounts. First, there is the idea of a trial lasting a year and a day; secondly, there is the application of the term 'handfasting' to such an arrangement; thirdly, there is the idea that having a child makes the union binding; and, finally, the assumption that such unions were a form of marriage that was complete in itself, and did not require the intervention of a priest.

The idea of 'a year and a day' is one that appears in various legal (and non-legal)[43] contexts on both sides of the border.[44] This is perhaps unsurprising: it has a certain resonance, and, in practical terms, is a means of obviating disputes as to whether a full year has passed. But we cannot automatically assume the truth of the reports by Martin and Pennant; after all, would we accept such statements at face value if they were written by a contemporary

41 *Ibid.* pp. 91–2.

42 W. F. Skene, *The Highlanders of Scotland: their Origin, History, and Antiquities, with a Sketch of their Manners and Customs* (London: John Murray, 1837), vol. I, p. 166 (emphasis added).

43 See e.g., the story of the Dunmow Flitch as told by Daniel Defoe: only a married man who 'did not Repent of being marry'd, or Quarrel, or Differ or Dispute with his Wife within a Year and a Day after his Marriage' may claim the flitch of bacon: *Curious and Diverting Journies, thro the whole island of Great-Britain* (London, 1734).

44 Under Scottish law, if a marriage was dissolved by death within a year and a day of solemnisation, 'all things done in contemplation of the marriage become void, and return to the condition wherein they were before the same': Viscount Stair, *The Institutions of the Law of Scotland* (University Presses of Edinburgh and Glasgow, 1981; original edn 1693), p. 120; for other examples of 'a year and a day' within Scottish law see pp. 141, 302, 349, 365, 405, 428–32, 436, 558, 600. See also R. Burn, *Ecclesiastical Law* (London, 1763), vol. II, pp. 173, 178, 444 for a number of examples in the English context.

travel writer about events that occurred a century ago?[45] The differences between the accounts should also give us pause: in one the trial lasts a year and a day, it is the man who chooses whether or not to end the relationship, and care of any children is regarded as a paternal right; in the other, cohabitation is for a year, being tied to the annual fair, either may make the choice to end the relationship, and care of the children seems to be regarded as a punishment rather than a right. At best these accounts would support the idea that pre-marital cohabitation may have been practised in certain areas of Scotland at some earlier date, but the truth of this is beyond the scope of the present work.[46]

In any case, there are a number of reasons why it would be unsafe to infer that practices in eighteenth-century England echoed those of Scotland in (at the latest) the early seventeenth century. Quite apart from the fact that both Martin and Pennant describe the practices as long obsolete, there is a lack of any equivalent (even equivocal) evidence for England. Indeed, there is one piece of evidence that positively suggests that the idea was unknown at this time in England: in Richardson's *Clarissa*, the rake Lovelace expresses his wish that couples could marry for a year at a time but gives no indication that this might be possible anywhere in Great Britain – as indeed it was not.[47] In addition, there was a key difference between Scottish law and English law: Scottish law, unlike English law, allowed children to be legitimated by the subsequent marriage of their parents. Whether or not this encouraged pre-marital cohabitation as a means of testing a potential spouse's fertility must be mere speculation, but the rule did at least mean that there was a

45 And see e.g., J. Black, *Eighteenth-Century Britain, 1688–1783* (Basingstoke: Palgrave, 2001), p. 177 on the invention of much Welsh folklore in the late eighteenth century.

46 For the view that medieval Scotland did have various peculiar customs of marriage see W. D. H. Sellar, 'Marriage, Divorce and Concubinage in Gaelic Scotland' (1978–80) 51 *Transactions of the Gaelic Society of Inverness* 464. Sellar attributes such practices to the influence of Celtic law, which 'declined in lowland Scotland from the twelfth century onwards' and only survived into the seventeenth century in the Highlands and Islands. Such practices would explain the reference in the Statutes of Iona of 1609 to 'marriageis contractit for certaine yeairis'; their disappearance would also accord with the declaration that henceforth such marriages are 'simpliciter dischairgit and the commitaris thereof haddin, reput and punist as fornicatouris'.

47 Samuel Richardson, *Clarissa, or, the History of a Young Lady* (London: Penguin Classics, 1985; original edn 1747–8), pp. 872–4.

means of rescuing the status of a child born before the marriage in Scotland, in stark contrast to the position in England.

The second key development in the sources is the application of the term 'handfasting' to such unions. Pennant's 1774 account noted the joining of hands, which he termed 'handfisting'; by contrast, an almost identical account, published in the 1790s, changes this to handfasting.[48] The problem was that the term already existed, in England as well as in Scotland, but bore a different meaning. In the seventeenth century a betrothed woman would regularly be referred to as a 'handfast wyf *per verba de praesenti*' in legal documents,[49] but this simply denoted that there had been a contract to marry, rather than any special form of marriage.[50] The use of the same term meant that it was all too easy for the two ideas to be elided, and for evidence of English betrothals to be interpreted as evidence of the practice of living together for a year and a day.

The third development is the idea that having a child made the union binding. This does not appear in the accounts of Martin and Pennant, and it is clear from the rules for the care of the children after separation that it was not an element of the practices they described. The eighteenth-century writer Millar may have inadvertently fostered the idea that a union for a year and a day could be rendered binding by the birth of a child by his coupling of two very distinct practices. He claimed that among the Kalmuck Tartars 'it is usual for a young pair to retire, and live together as man and wife for one year; and if, during this time, the woman has produced a child, their marriage is understood to be completed; but if not, they either separate at pleasure, or agree to make another year's trial'.[51] Millar then went on to draw a parallel with Scotland:

[48] Sir J. Sinclair, *The Statistical Account of Scotland* (Edinburgh, 1791–99), vol. XII, p. 615.

[49] See e.g., D. Cressy, *Birth, Marriage and Death: Ritual, Religion and the Life-Cycle in Tudor and Stuart England* (Oxford University Press, 1997), pp. 268–9.

[50] See e.g., R. Helmholz, *The Oxford History of the Laws of England*, vol. I, *The Canon Law and Ecclesiastical Jurisdiction from 597 to the 1640s* (Oxford University Press, 2004), p. 527, who cites a sixteenth-century case in which the issue was the appropriate construction of the words 'I, John, take thee, Agnes, to my handfast wife'. The contract was construed as being one of future consent only, and since the parties had not engaged in sexual relations the man was absolved from solemnising the marriage.

[51] J. Millar, *The Origin of the Distinction of Ranks*, 3rd edn (London, 1781), p. 25. The discussion as to the Tartars and the supposed parallels with Scottish practices

Traces of this primitive custom may still be discovered in the law of Scotland, according to which, a marriage dissolved within a year and a day, and without a child, has no legal consequences, but restores the property of either party to the same situation as if no such alliance had ever existed.[52]

It is clear from the context that Millar was referring to the Scottish law of inheritance whereby the wife's right to terce (the Scottish equivalent of dower) depended either on the marriage having subsisted for a year and a day before the death of the husband or on the birth of a child.[53] This, of course, was a rule applied to formal marriages, rather than being a means of entering into a trial union. In suggesting that the custom ever prevailed in Scotland on the basis of custom among the Tartars, Millar can be seen to be 'reading history sideways' in the manner practised by many eighteenth-century scholars.[54] But his account may well have misled readers not well-versed in Scottish law, who might have failed to appreciate that the rule described only applied where the marriage was dissolved by death.

The final development is the mutation of the practice into a full marriage that did not require any further form of solemnisation.[55] As described in the previous chapter, the origin of the assumption within English law that a contract *per verba de praesenti* had amounted to a full marriage can be dated to *Dalrymple* in 1811. By the late 1830s, this had become accepted (although not without criticism)[56] as the definitive statement of the law, and it was therefore natural for historians to reconceptualise earlier exchanges of consent as actual marriages. Some, indeed, rewrote such exchanges using the terminology of handfasting: we may

did not appear in the earlier editions of this work, published under the title of *Observations concerning the Distinction of Ranks in Society* in 1771 and 1773, so one might infer that the later edition was influenced by Pennant's 1774 claims.

52 *Ibid.*

53 W. M. Gloag and R. C. Henderson, *Introduction to the Law of Scotland* (Edinburgh: W. Green & Son Ltd, 1927), p. 449.

54 See A. Thornton, *Reading History Sideways: the Fallacy and Enduring Impact of the Developmental Paradigm on Family Life* (University of Chicago Press, 2005).

55 See e.g., Skene, *The Highlanders of Scotland*, p. 166; Rev. A. MacDonald and Rev. A. MacDonald, *The Clan Donald* (Inverness: Northern Counties Publishing Company Ltd, 1896), vol. I, p. 432. Not all writers followed suit, since some were following earlier sources that indicated the necessity of church solemnisation.

56 For contemporary criticism of the decision in *Dalrymple*, see P. Irvine, *Considerations on the Inexpediency of the Law of Marriage in Scotland* (Edinburgh: Thomas Clark, 1828), p. 46.

contrast the account written by one 'seneachie', or historian, in 1838, with an earlier description of the very same couple, compiled in the early 1760s. The Victorian historian states that the fourth laird of Ardgour 'had handfasted (as it was called) with a daughter of Mac-Ian of Ardnamurchan';[57] the details in the eighteenth-century manuscript source are identical but there is no mention of handfasting.[58] One finds a similar pattern in other works: while historians writing after the early years of the nineteenth century regularly refer to handfasting as a form of marriage,[59] sources compiled prior to the late eighteenth century either do not mention it, or only as a form of betrothal.[60] And for some nineteenth-century historians, it followed that if handfasting constituted a valid marriage, then any children born during it were legitimate,[61] rather than needing to be legitimated by a later church marriage.[62] The myth of handfasting was complete.

[57] 'A Seneachie', *An Historical and Genealogical Account of the Clan Maclean* (London: Smith, Elder and Co., 1838), p. 105.

[58] The relevant part of the manuscript is quoted by Rev. A. Maclean Sinclair, *The Clan Gillean* (Charlottetown: Haszard and Moore, 1899), pp. 521–2, who takes issue with a number of the Seneachie's claims, in particular the suggestion that the children of the union were legitimate. Sinclair's own interpretation is that the children were *not* reputed to be legitimate, but rather that they held as good a social position as if they were legitimate, as a result of being acknowledged by their father.

[59] For a recent example, see C. Nicholl, *The Lodger: Shakespeare on Silver Street* (London: Allen Lane, 2007), ch. 27, which is headed 'A Handfasting' despite the fact that this word does not appear in the sources quoted.

[60] See e.g., the original sources quoted by A. MacBain and Rev. J. Kennedy (eds.), *Reliquiae Celticae* (Inverness, 1894), vol. II, p. 159; MacDonald and MacDonald, *The Clan Donald*, pp. 127, 570; Robert Lindesay of Pitscottie, *The Historie and Chronicles of Scotland* (Edinburgh: Scottish Text Society, 1899), vol. I, p. 64: 'Issobel was hand fast with him and deceissit *befor the marieage*' (emphasis added); Sir R. Gordon, *A Genealogical History of the Earldom of Sutherland from its Origin to the Year 1630* (Edinburgh, 1813), p. 95: 'his mother was handfasted *and affianced* to his father' (emphasis added).

[61] See e.g., Skene, *The Highlanders of Scotland*, p. 167; D. Gregory, *History of the Western Highlands and Isles of Scotland* (Edinburgh: William Tait, 1836), p. 41; MacDonald and MacDonald, *The Clan Donald*, p. 433. This view was not unanimously held: see e.g., J. Cameron, *Celtic Law* (London: William Hodge & Co. Ltd, 1937), p. 196, who suggests that although 'Highland custom' regarded the children of a handfast marriage as entitled to succeed, 'Lowland law' did not; see also Sinclair, *The Clan Gillean*, p. 521.

[62] Cf. Gordon, *A Genealogical History of the Earldom of Sutherland*, p. 95. This, published in 1813, unequivocally describes the son of the alleged handfast union as 'the bastart'.

Of course, the fact that a new idea has emerged does not mean that all subsequent authors necessarily adopt it. Some later writers relied on earlier sources rather than those of their contemporaries.[63] But while adoption of these ideas was uneven, the process of evolution is clear. One might also note how tentative interpretations (Skene's account, part of which is quoted above, is riddled with terms such as 'more probable supposition', 'must have been', and 'perhaps not improbable')[64] evolve into definite facts, and how single examples mutate into general practice.[65] This is all the more likely to occur when the 'facts' not only make for a good story but also fit with commonly-held perceptions. The purportedly ancient poems of 'Ossian' may have been unmasked as an invention,[66] but Victorian audiences, weaned on the romances of Sir Walter Scott,[67] were receptive to the image of the wild, untamed Highlander, and the stranger the marriage practice the more it resonated with that image.[68] The new concept of handfasting was also linked to the claims made by Roman historians that North Britons had held their wives in common: the possibility of a woman having several 'handfast' husbands in succession might, it was opined, give rise to such a rumour.[69] It was clearly more reassuring to assume that the

63 See e.g., J. Graham Dalyell, *The Darker Superstitions of Scotland* (Glasgow: Richard Griffin & Co., 1835), p. 283; Rev. C. Rogers, *Scotland: Social and Domestic* (London: Grampian Club, 1869), p. 109.

64 Skene, *The Highlanders of Scotland*, pp. 165–6.

65 For example, Pennant's suggestion that handfasting took place at the public fair in Eskdale seems to have caught the imagination of some authors who imply this was the standard practice: see e.g. Rogers, *Scotland: Social and Domestic*, p. 109; Bennett, 'Courtship and Marriage'.

66 See e.g., P. Langford, *A Polite and Commercial People: England 1727–1783* (Oxford: Clarendon Press, 1998), p. 475.

67 Scott had himself made reference to handfasting in *The Monastery* (Boston: Estes and Lauriat, 1893; original edn 1822), vol. II, pp. 97–8: 'We Bordermen ... take our wives, like our horses, upon trial. When we are handfasted, as we term it, we are man and wife for a year and a day; that space gone by, each may choose another mate, or at their pleasure, may call the priest to marry them for life.'

68 The fact that the supposed practice of handfasting *was* perceived as strange in these early accounts is further evidence that it found no echoes in England: Skene, for example, suggests that '[i]t is manifest that the practice of so peculiar species of marriage must have been in terms of the original law among the Highlanders, otherwise it would be difficult to conceive how such a custom could have originated': *The Highlanders of Scotland*, p. 166.

69 See e.g., MacDonald and MacDonald, *The Clan Donald*, p. 432. Others tried to link Scottish practices to Roman law: see e.g., Sinclair, *The Statistical Account of Scotland*, p. 615; Sir P. Vinogradoff, *Outlines of Historical Jurisprudence* (Oxford

Romans had misunderstood Scottish practices than to envisage the possibility of past promiscuity. It might, however, have been more pertinent had such writers pondered whether similar misunderstandings might taint the claims made by other travellers north of the Border, such as Martin and Pennant.

The final task is to show how these ideas percolated into new jurisdictions and contexts. Once the key elements – the language of 'handfasting', the assumption that a child made the union binding, and the idea that it was a marriage without the need for any further ceremony – were in place, it is understandable how later scholars made the leap from a supposed Scottish practice that was obsolete by the eighteenth century to an English or Welsh one that was thriving at the time of the 1753 Act. Any references to 'handfasting' south of the border could be construed as a reference to a special form of marriage, rather than to a bare exchange of consent that created only a binding contract;[70] any intimation of pre-marital trials of fertility could be regarded as part of the same practice.[71] In addition, the Scottish Eskdale described by Pennant might have been confused with the English Eskdale, located in the Lake District. This possible geographical drift was matched by a temporal one: in Scotland, historians tended to assume that either the Reformation[72] or the 1609 Statutes of Iona had put an end to the practice,[73] but once 'handfasting' for a year and a day was claimed as an English practice, then it was naturally assumed that it must have continued there until stamped out by Parliament.

University Press, 1920), p. 244, but cf. H. F. Jolowicz and B. Nicholas, *Historical Introduction to the Study of Roman Law*, 3rd edn (Cambridge University Press, 1972), pp. 116–17.

70 See e.g., Vinogradoff, *Outlines of Historical Jurisprudence*, p. 246.

71 See e.g., D. A. Mackenzie, *Scottish Folk-Lore and Folk Life* (London: Blackie & Son Ltd, 1935), p. 34, who links the custom to Wales on this basis.

72 Rev. C. Rogers, *Scotland: Social and Domestic* (London: Grampian Club, 1869), pp. 109–10: '[e]xcept in Highland districts where it lingered, hand-fasting ceased within twenty years after the Reformation'.

73 See e.g., A. Lang, *A History of Scotland* (Edinburgh: William Blackwood & Sons, 1902), vol. II, p. 530; see also Gregory, *History of the Western Highlands and Isles of Scotland*, p. 331; MacDonald and MacDonald, *The Clan Donald*, vol. III, p. 132; Cameron, *Celtic Law*, p. 196.

Jumping the broomstick

At first sight the evidence that couples once married by jumping over a broomstick appears to be strong. According to one historian, 60 per cent of births in one Welsh village were attributed to such unions in the late eighteenth century;[74] other historians have projected such evidence back into the first part of the century on the assumption that if such practices occurred after 1754, when they could have had no legal status, they must perforce have occurred before that date.[75] The *Oxford English Dictionary* lists four references for the term 'broomstick marriage', the first dating from the late eighteenth century.[76] And there are even pictures that would appear to depict such an event.[77]

If the 60 per cent figure were correct, then it would be fair to assume that this was a significant social practice. Upon examination, however, it is clear that the figure is based on a gross misreading of the evidence.[78] The original estimate was made by Gillis in relation to the parish of Llansantffraid Glyn Ceiriog,[79] being based on the work of a Welsh folklorist writing in the 1920s under the name of Gwenith Gwynn.[80] Gwynn had examined the parish baptism register for the period between 1768 and 1799. He noted that there were variations in the recording of baptisms: of the 608 entries made in this period, in 199 the mother was described as the father's wife, and in a further 6 she was said to be his 'lawful' wife; however in 257 cases both parents were described by name without any further description, 112 entries recorded only the father, and 34 noted that the child was illegitimate.

74 Gillis, *For Better, For Worse*, p. 198.

75 See e.g., Cornish and de Clark, *Law and Society in England*, p. 361; Parker, *Informal Marriage*, p. 19; D. Howell, *The Rural Poor in Eighteenth Century Wales* (Cardiff: University of Wales Press, 2000), p. 147.

76 *Oxford English Dictionary* (Oxford University Press, 1971), vol. I, p. 1130.

77 See e.g., 'The Scotch Wedding' in G. Paston, *Social Caricature in the Eighteenth Century* (London: Methuen & Co., 1905), p. 29; and 'Marrying over the Broomstick' in *The New Marriage Act* (London, 1822).

78 The case study of Llansantffraid Glyn Ceiriog draws on material previously published in 'Chinese Whispers and Welsh Weddings' (2005) 20 *Continuity and Change* 211.

79 This lies on the river Ceiriog, three miles from Llangollen, and during the eighteenth century was located in Denbighshire.

80 G. Gwynn (W. Rhys Jones), 'Besom Wedding in the Ceiriog Valley' (1928) 39 *Folklore* 149.

Gwynn suggested that these apparent discrepancies represented a tripartite distinction between children of parents whose marriage was recognised by the church (these mothers being described as wives or lawful wives); children of parents whose marriage was not recognised by the church but who for some reason could not be classified as illegitimate (those parents, or only the father, being simply named without further description); and children who were illegitimate (those who were actually described as such). He then linked this speculation to rumours that he had heard of 'broomstick weddings' in the past, suggesting that this may have been the form adopted by 'many'[81] of those in his second category, those whose marriage had some social recognition. Gillis' figure of 60 per cent was based on the premise that *all* of those in the second category were the offspring of couples who had married this way.

In fact, my examination of the original baptism register[82] revealed that Gwynn's hypothesis was simply mistaken. The method of recording baptisms varied over time rather than between different categories of parents. From 1768, when the register begins, to 1777, mothers are almost invariably described as 'wife of', apart from a handful whose children are designated as 'base' or 'illegitimate'. After 1777 they are only rarely described as wives, and in some years few are named at all. At this point the curate, David Jones, had begun to confine entries of baptisms to a single line. Thereafter, the only instances of mothers being described as wives generally occur when the names of the parents are short enough for this additional information to be added. There was simply no such system for distinguishing between different types of unions: many couples were recorded differently at different times. In this the baptism register for Llansantffraid was in no way out of the ordinary.[83]

The next task was to check the names of parents against the marriage register of Llansantffraid,[84] a task that Gwynn failed to carry out, claiming that the marriage register had not survived. It soon became clear that most couples, however described in the

[81] Gwynn, 'Besom Wedding', 151.

[82] Denbighshire Record Office (DRO), PD/75/1/1.

[83] See further D. Ashurst, 'St Mary's Church, Worsbrough, South Yorkshire: a Review of the Accuracy of a Parish Register' (1995) 55 *Local Population Studies* 46, 54.

[84] DRO PD/75/1/4.

baptism register, could be shown to have married in church. Marriages were traced for 126 couples (accounting for 390 of the 608 entries);[85] in addition, all but 20 of the remaining 67 mothers were described as wives somewhere in the baptism register.[86] It is clear, therefore, that the registers were used as evidence on a false premise. If we adopt Gwynn's reasoning that being described as a wife signifies that the parties had married in church, then nearly 90 per cent of the mothers in the register definitely did so, based on the numbers who were described as 'wife' or who were known to have married. All but thirty-eight of the children who were not described as base can be linked either to a marriage, or to a description of the mother as 'wife' elsewhere in the register. The idea that 60 per cent of the baptisms in Llansantffraid were the offspring of alternative unions is completely untenable.

But, of course, the fact that one can disprove a claim that a specific proportion married in this way does not mean that broomstick weddings did not occur at all. Gwynn relied on interviews with local villagers and a number of secondary sources in making the claim that such practices had been widespread. But none of his interviewees had ever seen such a wedding. 'It must have disappeared before I was born, and I am seventy-three', said one old man.[87] Two others had heard of the practice, but all three were somewhat hazy on the details of such celebrations, their evidence being peppered with phrases such as 'it must have' and 'I should think'. Others interviewed by Gwynn had never heard of the practice.[88] The dangers in relying on such evidence are obvious: while one would not expect individuals deliberately to invent traditions of this kind, it is all too easy for stories to change as they

[85] Sixty-nine had married in Llansantffraid itself and fifty-seven in a different parish. This figure is likely to be an underestimate, since linking marriages to baptisms was rendered more difficult by the lack of detail at certain points in the baptism register and the fact that the names of the parents were hardly distinctive. For example, trying to trace the Thomas Jones whose first child by Mary was baptised in Glyn Ceiriog in 1797, I found marriages in the parish of Llangollen between persons of those names in 1756, 1758, 1761 (two), 1772, 1774, 1775, 1788, 1790 (another two) and 1796. The last would fit best, but the sheer number of possibilities made the link too tenuous, and this possible match was therefore excluded, as were others.

[86] Even this twenty may have married elsewhere: forty-four mothers whose marriages have been traced are nowhere described as wives in the baptism record.

[87] Gwynn, 'Besom Wedding', 153.

[88] *Ibid.* 152, who seemed to attribute this to deliberate withholding of information.

are passed down the generations, and for the original meaning of actions to be lost in transmission. As Fox has noted, '[a]s studies of diachronic verbal communication reveal, imperceptible alterations in narrative, and the practices which structure it, gradually take place, adding up to substantial changes in the long run'.[89] Even suggestions that others have seen certain practices should be treated with caution, as this conversation held by another traveller in the very same Ceiriog valley will illustrate:

> 'Do the Tylwyth Teg ever pay you visits?'
> 'The Tylwyth Teg, sir?'
> 'Yes; the fairies. Do they never come to have a dance on the green sward in this neighbourhood?'
> 'Very rarely sir: indeed, I do not know how long it is since they have been seen.'
> 'You have never seen them?'
> 'I have not, sir, but I believe there are people living who have.'[90]

Similarly, the evidence that Gwynn assembles to prove the existence of past broomstick weddings in other areas is equivocal, to say the least. A secondary source quoting a woman as saying 'she thought no more of marriage in the Register's office than of marriage by jumping over a besom'[91] seems derogatory rather than confirming that it was a widespread and respected practice. Moreover, the woman in question did not have any clear idea of the practice: '[q]uestioned about the expression she said she had heard in olden times people could be married by jumping over a broomstick'.[92] Another source referred to the evidence of one woman that, in Anglesey, couples were described as having jumped over the broom whether they had married in a church or registry office.[93] This was interpreted by Gwynn as showing that '[t]he expression "jumping over the besom" had exactly the same meaning, therefore, as the word "marriage" in the nineteenth century in Anglesey'.[94] And, this, in his view, 'goes far to prove that, at one time, the Besom Wedding was the *only* form of marriage known

[89] A. Fox, 'Custom, Memory and the Authority of Writing', ch. 3 in P. Griffiths, A. Fox, and S. Hindle (eds.), *The Experience of Authority in Early Modern England* (Basingstoke, 1996), p. 99.
[90] G. Borrow, *Wild Wales* (London: John Murray, 1901; original edn 1862), p. 62.
[91] Gwynn, 'Besom Wedding', 160, quoting Rev. E. Owen, *Old Stone Crosses of the Vale of Clywd* (London: B. Quaritch, 1886).
[92] Gwynn, 'Besom Wedding', 160. [93] *Ibid.* 160–1. [94] *Ibid.* 161.

on that island'.[95] It hardly needs to be pointed out that this is an almost comically broad inference from the most limited of evidence.

Again, the fact that those interviewed in the 1920s had never seen a couple marrying by jumping over a broomstick does not prove that eighteenth-century couples did not tie the knot in this way. We therefore need to turn to the evidence that actually dates from this period. While there are a few examples of couples actually jumping over a broomstick in the *nineteenth* century, such evidence is conspicuous by its absence for the preceding century. Rather than actual accounts, all we have are references that are either figurative or foreign, and sometimes both.

Thus, for example, we find the English translation of letters written by a seventeenth-century French noblewoman referring to a marriage that apparently took place in France in 1689 between an illegitimate daughter of Louis XIV and a prince of the house of Condé: according to this source the two had 'performed the marriage ceremony by leaping over a broomstick'.[96] The original text, however, simply referred to the marriage being celebrated 'sur la croix de l'épée',[97] or 'on the cross of the sword'. We need not trouble ourselves with the meaning of the French phrase: our concern is with the reasons for the very free English translation. Given that the original made no mention of broomsticks or jumping, it would seem that the phrase was understood as denoting an irregular marriage ceremony rather than that the couple in question had actually jumped over a physical broomstick.[98] This is even clearer in the teasing allusion to the invalid Catholic ceremony of marriage between the Prince of Wales and Mrs Fitzherbert[99] that appeared in the *Evening Mail*:

95 *Ibid.* (emphasis added).

96 *Letters from the Marchioness de Sévigné, to her daughter the Countess de Grignan. Translated from the French of the last Paris edition*, 2nd edn (London, 1763–8), vol. IX, p. 152.

97 *Recueil des Lettres de Madame la Marquise de Sévigné* (Paris, 1738), vol. VI, p. 120, lettre DXXXIV, 25 Mars 1689.

98 See also *Loyola: A Novel* (London, 1784), p. 85: 'Let the married couple only now and then jump over a broom and imagine themselves sinners, and they will be happy.'

99 The ceremony had taken place in 1785, but by 1791 the relationship was coming under strain: see J. Munson, *Maria Fitzherbert: the Secret Wife of George IV* (London: Constable & Robinson Ltd, 2001), pp. 147, 255.

The Royal Broomstick, over which a certain couple leaped some few years ago, is now a laughing stick among the Brothers.[100]

A third example of the phrase being used in a figurative sense comes from the account of the elopement of Robert Morris with his ward, the twelve-year-old Frances Harford. In 1774 the pair travelled to the Continent together to marry, but once in France found that marriage there was hedged around with as many restrictions as at home. It was suggested to Morris that a sexton could simply read over the marriage service to them, but he 'plainly told him, he had no inclination for a Broomstick-marriage'.[101] Again, this can only be understood in a figurative sense: no mention had been made of jumping a broomstick, and all that was being offered was a marriage that had no legal validity. Finally, there is Gillray's caricature of the hastily-arranged marriage of Charles Lennox to Charlotte Gordon at Gordon Castle in 1789, showing them leaping over a broomstick in a bedroom.[102] The marriage certainly appears to have been irregular (in the Scottish sense of a marriage otherwise than before a priest),[103] but no accounts mention a broomstick.[104] But then again, how exactly would one depict an irregular marriage in a cartoon, if no priest were present to signify the nature of the event?[105] The broomstick operates as visual shorthand for irregularity, just as the pipes held by the beaming mother of the bride indicate the Scottish context.

But, of course, one must ask *why* jumping over a broomstick would be used as a synonym for an irregular marriage, given that there is no obvious connection between the two. One interpretation

100 *Evening Mail*, 19 December 1791.

101 (1774) 2 *Westminster Magazine* 16. See also *Harford* v. *Morris* (1776) 2 Hag. Con. 422; 161 ER 792.

102 'The Scotch Wedding': Paston, *Social Caricature*, p. 29.

103 See e.g., T. C. Smout, 'Scottish Marriage, Regular and Irregular, 1500–1940', ch. 9 in R. Outhwaite (ed.), *Marriage and Society* (London: Europa Publications Ltd, 1981).

104 R. Baird, *Goodwood: Art and Architecture, Sport and Family* (London: Frances Lincoln Ltd, 2007), p. 158, notes that Lennox, the future Duke of Richmond, 'had been in the house for five days when they were married, at no notice, in the Duchess's dressing room, with two maids as witnesses'. See also *St James' Chronicle*, 19 September 1789.

105 On the use of symbols to convey meanings in eighteenth-century satires and caricatures, see S. O'Connell, *London 1753* (London: British Museum Press, 2003), pp. 40–1; V. Gatrell, *City of Laughter: Sex and Satire in Eighteenth-Century London* (London: Atlantic Books, 2007), ch. 7.

might be that marrying by jumping over a broomstick was the best-known form of irregular marriage and so was used as a synonym for any other irregular marriage. But it is difficult to square this with the lack of any actual evidence of the practice. Indeed, there is one source that explicitly denies that such a practice occurred in England, a pamphlet published in 1753, which noted that:

> [i]n some countries the same Convention between Males and Females is accompanied with the Ceremonial of jumping over a Stick;[106] but if in *England* a Couple were to interchange Promises of perpetual Fidelity, Cohabitation, and good Offices ratified by the like Ceremony, and then going to Bed together, were gravely to expect to be called Husband and Wife by their Acquaintance, they would be looked upon as People out of their Wits.[107]

However, a second and more plausible explanation for the phrase emerges if one examines the use of the term 'broomstick' in other eighteenth-century sources. Along with all the references one might expect – domestic uses or witches flying – there are a significant number in which a broomstick is used to symbolise something ersatz, or lacking the authority that its true equivalent might possess.[108] If one could have 'broomstick bail',[109] why not a

[106] Whether this was true must be a matter of speculation, although if one could trace the chain of evidence, we might find that this claim had no foundation in reality either. After all, we have seen in this chapter how misunderstandings may occur even when one academic reads the work of another: extend the chain of evidence and throw in the complication of a foreign tongue and who knows what bizarre ideas might ensue. And no mention of jumping over a stick in any form appears in the contemporaneous translation of L. de Gaya's *Matrimonial Ceremonies Displayed* (London, 1748), which ranges across most of the globe.

[107] *A Letter to the Public: Containing the Substance of what hath been offered in the late Debates upon the Subject of the Act of Parliament for the better preventing of Clandestine Marriages* (London: Charles March, 1753), p. 37, emphasis in original.

[108] See e.g., F. Douglas, *Familiar Letters, on a Variety of Important and Interesting Subjects, from Lady Harriet Morley, and others* (London, 1773), p. 219: 'takes no more notice of a private man than of a broomstick'; *Amusements in High Life: or, Conjugal Infidelities in 1786* (London, 1786), p. 75: 'He has no more a commission than a broom-stick'; A. Dullass, *The Rights of Asses, a Poem* (Edinburgh, 1792), p. 10: 'The former speaker talks of Bruns'ick/But who for him now cares a broom-stick?'; S. Drew, *Observations (in behalf of the Methodists) on a pamphlet lately published by the Rev. R. Polwhele, entitled 'Anecdotes of Methodism'* (Falmouth, 1800), p. 31: '[An oath] whether taken before a magistrate, or a broom-stick.'

[109] See e.g., *The Bow-Street Opera, in three Acts. Written on the plan of The Beggar's Opera: all the most celebrated songs of which are parodied; and the whole piece adopted to modern times, manners and characters*, 4th edn (London, 1773, 1776), p. 7.

'broomstick' – i.e., sham – marriage? Add to this the fact that many synonyms for marriage, past and present, invoke the idea of a leap of some kind,[110] and one can begin to understand how the phrase may have evolved.

That the figurative sense of 'jumping the broomstick' predated the more literal interpretation is also suggested by one further piece of evidence. In these early references there is no mention of jumping *back* over the broom to divorce: this was only to be expected if the phrase denoted a marriage that lacked legal validity, since in this case there would be no need for a divorce should the relationship prove unsatisfactory. There were, of course, non-legal expedients such as separation or desertion that were resorted to by the unhappily married, but by definition these expedients were only necessary if the marriage had been valid in the first place. It was only when post-Revolutionary France introduced both civil marriage and divorce that we find a disapproving link being made between the form of marriage and the form of divorce:

> It is remarked, that the matrimonial system in France is perfectly a-la-Hottentot: the new system of divorce is extremely convenient for the dissolute; it is merely jumping and rejumping over the broom.[111]

Of course, this description of French law was purely figurative;[112] one presumes that the writer had even less knowledge of 'Hottentot' practices.

In the early years of the nineteenth century references to 'broomstick' weddings were similarly figurative.[113] It can reasonably be argued that the woodcut in the 1822 broadside 'The New Marriage

110 For example 'to take the plunge'. See also P. G. Wodehouse, *Heavy Weather* (London: Penguin Classics, 2001; original edn 1933), p. 54: 'By which time, I take it, you will be an old married woman. When do you and Ronnie plan to leap off the dock?'

111 *Oracle and Daily Publisher*, 21 September 1799.

112 On the introduction of divorce and civil marriage in France in 1792, see R. Phillips, *Putting Asunder* (Cambridge University Press, 1988), pp. 178–80.

113 See e.g., *The Times*, 13 August 1824, p. 3, in which an irregular Jewish marriage was said by a parish beadle to amount 'to nothing more than a broomstick marriage, which the parties had in their power to dissolve at will'. The 1836 Marriage Act, which introduced civil marriage, was similarly described as the 'Broomstick Marriage Act': *Jackson's Oxford Journal*, 12 September 1840, p. 1; J. Gossamer, 'Saint Valentine: or, Thoughts on the Evil of Love in Mercantile Community: the Galanti Show' (1843) 13 *Bentley's Miscellany* 151.

Act' was employing the same figurative tradition:[114] the broomstick appears to be floating in mid-air, while an old crone with a black cat on her shoulder looks on, while in another woodcut a devil dances on the roof of the church. Yet it would seem that by the mid-nineteenth century it had begun to be assumed that a physical leap was required: after all, the shape and domestic nature of a broomstick made it an ideal prop in threshold rites,[115] and many wedding customs have been said to involve a leap of some kind.[116] In 1850 the *Daily News* reported the case of an Irish servant-girl who had been promised marriage and was 'induced to jump over a broom, and go through other mock ceremonies of marriage'.[117] The practice was also attributed to gypsies,[118] and appeared in slave communities across the Atlantic,[119] as well as in a number of literary

[114] If, indeed, the original woodcut was depicting a wedding at all: only the woman is jumping in this picture. Given that it was published by James Catnach, whose output was often recycled, plagiarised, and even fabricated (see C. Hindley, *The Life and Times of James Catnach (Late of Seven Dials), Ballad Monger* (London: Reeves and Turner, 1878), pp. 75–6), its reliability as a historical document must be open to doubt. The heading and doggerel verse (which names four couples rather than the three in the picture) may have been added for the purposes of this particular publication.

[115] See e.g., B. Picart, *Ceremonies & Religious Customs of the Various Nations of the Known World* (London, 1733–9), vol. V, p. 441, claiming in Friesland there was a custom in which the husband's relatives would block up the door with a pole or a broomstick as though to prevent the bride entering and would have to be bribed to stand aside. See also Gillis, *For Better, For Worse*, p. 75.

[116] See e.g., R. E. Bosanquet (ed.), *In the Troublesome Times* (Stockfield: Spreddon Press, 1989; original edn 1929), pp. 36, 37 (jumping 'the petting stool'). See also J. G. Georgi, *Russia: or a Complete Historical Account of all the Nations which compose that Empire* (London, 1780–3), vol. I, p. 26, who referred to various games that accompanied weddings among the Laplanders, including wrestling and jumping over a stick.

[117] *Taylor* v. *Sullivan*, *Daily News*, 25 February 1850, p. 7.

[118] See e.g., *Notes and Queries* 4th Series vol. III (1869), pp. 461–2; Rev. J. Hudson Barker, 'The Gipsy-Life of Northumberland' in *Bygone Northumberland* (London: William Andrews & Co., 1899), p. 229. There is some evidence that gypsy couples were not averse to playing up to popular stereotypes: E. A. Jones, *Yorkshire Gypsy Fairs, Customs and Caravans 1886–1985* (Beverley: Hutton Press, 1985), p. 15.

[119] See e.g., the account by M. A. Livermore, *The Story of My Life, or the Sunshine and Shadow of Seventy Years* (Hartford, Conn.: A.D. Worthington & Co., 1897), p. 256. Interestingly, there have been attempts by some writers to claim an African origin for the practice: see A. Dundes, '"Jumping the Broom": On the Origin and Meaning of an African American Wedding Custom' (1996) 109 *Journal of American Folklore* 324 for a review and rebuttal of such claims.

sources of the period.[120] No wonder, then, that in the early years of the twentieth century Gwynn was able to find individuals who believed that it had once been possible to marry in this way. As Marshall has demonstrated in another context, supposedly 'oral' traditions 'can often be shown to have their origins in printed sources'.[121] But Victorian references to broomstick marriages should be interpreted in the context of their times;[122] they should not be projected back to the eighteenth century.

Custom or consistency?

Since 'handfasting' and 'broomstick weddings' form the mainstay of the claim that before 1754 marriage was a matter of local custom, we should by now be sceptical as to how far this was in fact the case. Of course, there were local customs associated with courtship and marriage, but this does not mean that marriage formation was itself dictated by custom. In particular, the unifying force of the Church of England should not be overlooked.[123] It is difficult today to appreciate just how significant a force the Church was in this period:[124] while examples of neglect by incumbents and non-observance by parishioners can be found, there is also a considerable body of evidence emphasising the deep-rooted attachment of the populace to

[120] C. Dickens, *Great Expectations* (Ware: Worthsworth Editions Ltd, 1992; original edn 1861), p. 336; *The Miscellaneous Writings of Lord Macaulay* (London: Longman, Green, Longman and Roberts, 1860), vol. I, p. 95; J. Hawthorne, 'Fortune's Fool' (1881–2) 45 *Macmillan's Magazine* 81, 99.

[121] P. Marshall, *Mother Leakey and the Bishop: a Ghost Story* (Oxford University Press, 2007), p. 244.

[122] See e.g., H. Mayhew, *London Labour and the London Poor*, vol. I, *The London Street-Folk* (London, 1851), p. 353.

[123] See e.g., J. Gregory and J. Chamberlain, 'National and Local Perspectives on the Church of England in the Long Eighteenth Century' in J. Gregory and J. Chamberlain (eds.), *The National Church in Local Perspective: the Church of England and the Regions, 1660–1800* (Woodbridge: Boydell Press, 2003), p. 15. At the same time, local sensitivities were recognised: Parker's suggestion that Welsh monoglots might have favoured informal marriages because of the language barrier (*Informal Marriage*, p. 23) overlooks the fact that services would often have been conducted in Welsh in the early eighteenth century – it was a condition of appointment that the incumbent was either able to speak Welsh or appointed a curate who could do so: P. Jenkins, 'Church, Nation and Language: the Welsh Church, 1660–1800' in Gregory and Chamberlain.

[124] Black, *Eighteenth-Century Britain*, pp. 22–4 and ch. 8; and see C. Steedman, *Master and Servant: Love and Labour in the English Industrial Age* (Cambridge University Press, 2007), pp. 4–6, for an attempt to make an imaginative leap in the mindset of the time.

the established Church.[125] Non-belief does not necessarily preclude couples from marrying in church, but faith in the Church's teachings (not least in the threat of eternal damnation for sinners)[126] would make the populace more willing to accept the Church's prescription that marriages should take place in church.[127]

It has been suggested, however, that some clergyman were in fact willing to record informal arrangements, thereby indicating their tolerance of them.[128] Yet once again the evidence is inferential and fades away on closer inspection. The case study of Llansantffraid has powerfully demonstrated the dangers of interpreting discrepancies in a register as evidence of alternative practices, and the rather haphazardly-kept register of Tetbury in the 1690s, examined by Wrigley and cited by Parker, suggests haste rather than any deliberate classification of marriages.[129] Similar problems infect Newman's inferences (from the baptism register of Ash-next-Sandwich) that discrepancies in the recording of children of certain couples indicated occasional tolerance of 'stable unions':[130] it cannot be inferred that a particular couple did not marry simply because no record of the marriage was found in Ash itself (this being Newman's methodology), and modern technology allows it to be ascertained that many of those given as examples of irregularity by Newman had in fact married in a different parish.[131] As for Parker's suggestion that 'some' clergy were prepared to notarise informal arrangements after the 1753 Act, which in his view 'must support' the view that they did so before, the 'some' turns out to be just one – the incumbent of

125 See e.g., W. M. Jacob, *Lay People and Religion in the Early Eighteenth Century* (Cambridge University Press, 1996); D. Spaeth, *The Church in an Age of Danger: Parsons and Parishioners 1660–1740* (Cambridge University Press, 2000), pp. 3, 106; and more generally A. Gilbert, *Religion and Society in Industrial England: Church, Chapel and Social Change, 1740–1914* (London: Longman, 1976).

126 See e.g., R. Porter, *Flesh in the Age of Reason: How the Enlightenment Transformed the Way We See our Bodies and Souls* (London: Penguin, 2004), p. 212.

127 And if faith did not, pragmatism might: see M. R. Watts, *The Dissenters: from the Reformation to the French Revolution* (Oxford: Clarendon Press, 1978), p. 288 on the pressure to conform, and see further below.

128 A. Newman, 'An Evaluation of Bastardy Recordings in an East Kent Parish', ch. 4 in P. Laslett, K. Oosterveen, and R. Smith, *Bastardy and its Comparative History* (London: Edward Arnold, 1980), pp. 145–8; Parker, *Informal Marriage*, p. 20.

129 And see further Chapter 5.

130 Newman, 'An Evaluation of Bastardy Recordings', 145.

131 For example, Christopher Renalles married Ealse Solly in Staple in 1690; Thomas Hodgeman married Ann in Canterbury in 1732; Henry Saffery married Hannah Marsh in 1797, at St Mary Dover.

Llansantffraid,[132] about which parish nothing more need be said. Far from notarising stable unions as if they were marriages, what is in fact recorded in parish registers (and then but rarely) is the occasional suspicion that a particular couple were *not* married.[133]

Given that the claims that have been made in relation to 'informal marriage' can be shown to be without foundation, we now need to start afresh in considering whether contracts *per verba de praesenti* constituted a functional alternative to regular marriage in the eighteenth century.

DID CONTRACTED COUPLES COHABIT?

If an exchange of vows was regarded as the final stage on the road to marriage, one would expect to find that large numbers of those litigating over contracts had in fact been living together. But this is not the case: the cases that came before the courts generally involved individuals either trying to enforce a contract or to undo an existing marriage on the basis of a precontract.[134] These were, in short, cases in which the 'marriage' created by vows *per verba de praesenti* had never existed in any practical sense. In fact, it is extremely hard to find *any* evidence of contracted parties cohabiting. Although eighteenth-century litigants might refer to the existence of a 'common fame' that they were husband and wife to support the evidence that a contract *per verba de praesenti* had been made between them, this did not necessarily denote cohabitation. It referred rather to the circumstantial evidence that might be provided by friends and acquaintances who, even if they had not been present at the contract, had learnt of it by other means. And it should be seen in the context of the theory that consent made a marriage 'before God'. As Gowing has pointed out, 'the phrase "man and wife" that some contracted couples used to describe their relationship did not necessarily imply the sexual relations of marriage',[135] and it would be even more tenuous to infer from the use of that phrase that the couple were in fact living together.

132 Parker, *Informal Marriage*, p. 66. 133 See further below.

134 See e.g., *Bourget* v. *Imbert* (1744), LPL, Eee 14/262b; *Evers* v. *Michell* (1744), LPL, E35/25; and *Baxtar* v. *Buckley* (1752) 1 Lee 42; 161 ER 17, discussed in Chapter 2.

135 L. Gowing, *Domestic Dangers: Women, Words, and Sex in Early Modern London* (Oxford: Clarendon Press, 1998), p. 165.

Specific evidence that contracted parties lived together is virtually non-existent. In Stone's case studies, which he presents as evidence of the flexibility of marriage prior to 1754, none of the parties to the disputed contracts had ever lived together.[136] Outhwaite's examples of marriages 'without Church or Priest' appear more in the form of betrothals: the couples in question initially planned to marry but problems arose to frustrate this, and there is no suggestion that they lived together without marrying.[137] Gillis, by contrast, does at least supply one example of a couple living under the same roof after entering into a contract,[138] but this is far from being a clear-cut illustration of a widespread practice in the period before the 1753 Act. First, it dates from the 1560s – almost two hundred years earlier. Secondly, at least one of the parties did not regard the contract as binding: the case only came to court because George Johnson had reneged on his contract with Anne Yate and had married another. Thirdly, the account is riddled with ambiguities. One witness gave evidence that 'the neighboures thereabout did take them as man and wife, in somuche that they have Laine together in bed, and so used them selfes as man & wife'.[139] Another, however, gave a rather different account of their sleeping arrangements, noting that 'they did lye in one house, and nothinge betwix them but a broken wall and a paintid cloth'.[140] Occasionally residing under the same roof was not necessarily the same as setting up home together, let alone having sex. Perhaps it was the fact that Anne kept 'a vittaylinge house' that had induced George to 'daylie and howrely use the house, and ... nightly Lye ther'.[141] Perhaps this also explained why she had the room to accommodate the livestock that George had brought to Anne's house: the same witness noted that he 'brought his dogges, his horse, and his hawkes thither'.[142] Such detail could be seen as suggesting that George had moved in lock, stock, and barrel.

[136] L. Stone, *Uncertain Unions and Broken Lives: Intimate and Revealing Accounts of Marriage and Divorce in England* (Oxford University Press, 1995), pp. 57–102.

[137] Outhwaite, *Clandestine Marriage*, pp. 21–22.

[138] Gillis, *For Better, For Worse*, p. 46. His source for this is F. J. Furnivall, *Child-Marriages, Divorce and Ratifications, etc., in the Diocese of Chester, AD 1561–6* (London: Kegan Paul, Trench, Trübner & Co., 1897).

[139] Furnivall, *Child-Marriages*, pp. 58–9.

[140] *Ibid.* p. 58. [141] *Ibid.* [142] *Ibid.*

But it might better suggest that George had not moved any other belongings into Anne's house. One final little puzzle in the account is the evidence that George had over 40 shillings out of Anne's purse, 'which the said Anne did Lend unto the said George'.[143] The first part of this might lead the reader to draw parallels with modern pooling systems of money-management. But the reference to Anne *lending* George the money should give us pause: at a time when a woman's property passed to her husband on marriage, could a wife be said to lend her husband money that was regarded as his?

Other examples are similarly unconvincing. Outhwaite cites a deposition that it was the practice for a man to stay the night in the woman's house after entering into the contract,[144] but this too dates from the sixteenth century,[145] and if a contract itself was regarded as the marriage, the fact that it was usual for the man to stay the night would hardly be worthy of comment. A longer period of cohabitation appears in the case of a Terling labourer who was presented for incontinency in Terling in 1617: his defence, however, was not merely that he was 'contracted in matrimonie', since he pointed out that the banns had been called but 'the parishe would not suffer them to marry else they had bin marryed ere now'.[146] He thus appears to have been a most unwilling cohabitant, who would have married if he had been allowed to do so by the parish.[147] The fact that both this example and that cited by Outhwaite are also cited by a number of other scholars raises the suspicion that even such ambiguous examples may be thin on the ground.[148] If these are the best examples of contracted couples

[143] *Ibid.* [144] Outhwaite, *Clandestine Marriage*, p. xix.

[145] It originates in a secondary source: A. P. Moore, 'Marriage Contracts or Espousals in the Reign of Queen Elizabeth' (1909) 30 *Associated Architectural Societies' Reports and Papers* 291.

[146] K. Wrightson and D. Levine, *Poverty and Piety in an English Village: Terling, 1525–1700* (Oxford: Clarendon Press, 1995), p. 133.

[147] For a discussion of attempts by parish officials to prevent the marriages of the poor for fear that any children would have to be supported by the parish, see S. Hindle, *On the Parish? The Micro-Politics of Poor Relief in Rural England, c. 1550–1750* (Oxford University Press, 2004), pp. 339–42.

[148] See P. Laslett, *The World We Have Lost* (London, 1965), pp. 141–2; M. Ingram, *Church Courts, Sex and Marriage in England, 1570–1640* (Cambridge University Press, 1987), p. 227.

setting up home together in the two hundred years preceding the Act that these scholars could uncover, it hardly inspires confidence in the ubiquity of such practices.

There is, however, one source that has been cited as an example of practices *after* 1754[149] that deserves consideration.[150] The Welsh land surveyor Lewis Morris[151] wrote of the 'little wedding' practised by 'some couples', particularly miners, in the parish of Llanbadarn Fawr in Cardiganshire at the time that the 1753 Act was passed.[152] This was contrasted to the 'great wedding in church',[153] which, as Morris' earlier writings had made clear, was the standard method of marrying across all classes of society in this area.[154] But the nature of the 'little wedding' is not clear from his account, which describes the practice as being to 'procure a man to wed them privately, which will not cost above two or three mugs of ale'.[155] Morris may simply have meant that a clergyman performed the ceremony clandestinely. But this is a little difficult to square with his subsequent claim that this was an arrangement that 'does not bind them so effectually but that after a month's trial they may part by consent'.[156] It is possible that this was an exaggeration:[157] his description of the 'wedding for trial' as 'too ludicrous' and 'arbitrary'[158] does rather suggest that he had scant regard for them. If this detail was an embellishment it casts doubt on the veracity of Morris' other claims; if couples could and did part after a month, then, even accepting (as discussed above) that an alternative to marriage need not be a *permanent* union, this seems too short to count as a functional alternative to marriage. In any case, we should

149 See e.g., Gillis, *For Better, For Worse*, p. 190; Parker, *Informal Marriage*, p. 68.

150 The evidence, as discussed in Chapter 7, suggests that the practices referred to, if true, occurred before the Act.

151 D. Wyn William, 'Lewis Morris (1701–65)' in *Oxford Dictionary of National Biography* (Oxford University Press, 2004).

152 'Cardigan Weddings' (1792) 62 *Gentleman's Magazine* 325. These accounts were published posthumously, Morris having died in 1765.

153 As to which see 'Cardigan Weddings' (1792) 62 *Gentleman's Magazine* 111.

154 Specifically, 'among the mechanicks, farmers and common people' in his parish of Llanbadarn Fawr in Cardiganshire: 'Cardigan Weddings' (1791) 61 *Gentleman's Magazine* 1103.

155 'Cardigan Weddings' (1792) 62 *Gentleman's Magazine* 325.

156 *Ibid.*

157 To which Morris was all too prone: see G. Nesta Evans, *Religion and Politics in Mid Eighteenth Century Anglesey* (University of Wales Press, 1953), p. 86.

158 'Morrisian Miscellany' (1791) 61 *Gentleman's Magazine* 13; 'Cardigan Weddings' (1792) 62 *Gentleman's Magazine* 325.

beware, as ever, of taking the exceptional example[159] as proof of a general trend.[160]

This uncertain example aside, scholars have singularly failed to provide contemporary evidence that it was common for couples to live together after entering into a contract in the eighteenth century. The few examples that have been cited are ambiguous and generally relate to much earlier periods. However, it may be objected that the absence of evidence of cohabitation in examples derived from contracts disputed in the ecclesiastical courts are not representative of the majority, and that if a couple had indeed lived together happily ever after there would have been no need to litigate.[161] To test this, it is necessary to look at the issue from a different angle, and ask whether there is any evidence that couples who were *known* to be living together regarded themselves as married on the basis of an informal exchange of consent.

DID COHABITING COUPLES REGARD THEMSELVES AS MARRIED BY CONSENT?

The first challenge in answering this question is finding a cohort of cohabiting couples. This is rendered more problematic by the ambiguity of terms such as 'cohabit' or 'live together' in eighteenth-century England: they might denote that a couple lived under the same roof, but equally might simply be euphemisms for sexual relations.[162] Care must therefore be taken to verify whether any

159 Even in Morris' own account, it is only '[s]ome couples' who choose this form of marriage, being those who do not have sufficient friends to make the more public wedding, with its gifts, worthwhile. On the extent of gift-giving, see further below.

160 Morris' posthumous editor appended a note to the final extract, stating that 'Mr Morris styles this account Cardigan weddings, but the custom is, or was till lately, general through Dimetia, and old people remember it in parts of North Wales; therefore we may suppose it prevailed formerly over all Wales' ('Cardigan Weddings' (1792) 62 *Gentleman's Magazine* 325). The degree of supposition in this should indicate the need for caution; moreover, it is worth noting that the entire series in which wedding ceremonies are discussed (including the account of the 'great wedding') is entitled 'Cardigan Weddings' and it is therefore possible that one of the other customs was intended by this reference. This is supported by the fact that Morris explicitly identifies the ceremonies surrounding the *public* wedding as being 'peculiar ... to this country, and its borders': 'Cardigan Weddings' (1791) 61 *Gentleman's Magazine* 1103.

161 See e.g., Outhwaite, *Clandestine Marriage*, p. 22.

162 See e.g., S. Johnson, *A Dictionary of the English Language* (London, 1756), which defines 'to bed' as 'to cohabit'. See also H. Rubenhold, *The Covent*

given source constitutes evidence of co-residence or merely of sexual intercourse.

One potential source of evidence is the bastardy examinations that survive for a number of eighteenth-century parishes: one might assume that at least some mothers would have been living under the same roof as the fathers. But studies of such sources have come to the conclusion that only a minority of these illegitimate children were the products of co-residential relationships, and that if such relationships did exist they were usually of short duration.[163] In the parish of Chelsea, for example, of the seventy-four women who had given birth to, or were pregnant with, a bastard child,[164] only two had definitely been living in a cohabiting relationship,[165] and one of them, Susanna Jones, explicitly disclaimed any marital ties, declaring 'that she was never married to the said Benjamin Smith, though they lived and cohabited together as man and wife'.[166] Indeed, in this particular cohort there are more examples of relationships in stables than there are of stable relationships.[167] Similarly, in the 377 settlement examinations for Bradford-upon-Avon, only one contains evidence of a cohabiting relationship: in 1757 Elizabeth Pope, 'singlewoman' told the authorities that for many years she had 'kept company with Thomas Hilliar ... who died about three years ago and by whom she had two children still alive'.[168] She made no claim that she had been married to the said Thomas, by consent or otherwise. The fact that the justices recorded the nature of the relationship in these cases does at least indicate that there was no official policy of suppressing any mention of cohabiting unions. It is thus more

Garden Ladies: Pimp General Jack and the Extraordinary Story of Harris's List (Stroud: Tempus, 2006), p. 161; S. Richardson, *Clarissa, or, the Story of a Young Lady* (Penguin Classics 1985; original edn 1747–8), p. 615.

163 See e.g., N. Rogers, 'Carnal Knowledge: Illegitimacy in Eighteenth-Century Westminster' (1989) 23 *Journal of Social History* 355; Trumbach, *Sex and the Gender Revolution*, pp. 245, 261.

164 T. Hitchcock and J. Black, *Chelsea Settlement and Bastardy Examinations, 1733–1766* (London Record Society, 1999).

165 There were a further seven cases where the evidence was ambiguous but in the remaining sixty-five it is clear that the parties were not living together, either at the time of the conception or at the time of the examination.

166 Hitchcock and Black, *Chelsea Settlement and Bastardy Examinations*, p. 65.

167 *Ibid.* pp. 6–7, 23, 30, 94.

168 P. Hembry (ed.), *Calendar of Bradford-on-Avon Settlement Examinations and Removal Orders, 1725–98* (Trowbridge: Wiltshire Record Society, 1990), p. 15.

likely that the paucity of evidence of cohabiting unions reflects low levels of cohabitation rather than official reluctance to record them.

Thus, just as contracted couples were, almost invariably, not living together, if one examines the records of those few couples who were cohabiting, one finds no reference to any exchange of consent between the parties. But, it might be objected, the above records only relate to those cohabitants who declared that they were *not* married. What about those who tried to pass themselves off as married?

There is strong evidence to suggest that claims to be married were not automatically accepted by the community. It is worth bearing in mind that the poor laws created an incentive for the community to ascertain the marital status of any newcomers: after all, if a couple were not married, any children would be settled in the parish of their birth, at the expense of the neighbours. As a result, women and men 'subjected their neighbours to a level of scrutiny that appears to us both intrusive and obsessive, prompted by a combination of curiosity, moral principle, and self-interest'.[169]

Newcomers might expect to face questions about their marital status.[170] Moreover, establishing a settlement without public knowledge was difficult: an act of 1692 required newcomers to a parish to give public notice of their arrival – 'their forty-day trial period began only after their presence was announced in church to give everyone the chance to object and to brand them as undesirables'.[171] Since much migration was over relatively short distances,[172] it would be an easy matter to check the marital status of new arrivals. That parish authorities *did* check is clear: Kenilworth overseers of the poor recorded in their accounts 'our charges going to Fillongley to know if Ruth Shuttleworth was married' and '[c]harges sending to

169 B. Capp, *When Gossips Meet: Women, Family and Neighbourhood in Early Modern England* (Oxford University Press, 2003), p. 268. See also Trumbach, *Sex and the Gender Revolution*, p. 248.

170 L. Hollen Lees, *The Solidarities of Strangers: the English Poor Laws and the People, 1700–1948* (Cambridge University Press, 1998), p. 29.

171 Hollen Lees, *The Solidarities of Strangers*, p. 29 and S. Peyton (ed.), *The Churchwardens' Presentments in the Oxfordshire Peculiars of Dorchester, Thame and Banbury* (Oxfordshire Record Society, 1928), p. xxxv.

172 D. Levine, *Family Formation in an Age of Nascent Capitalism* (London: Academic Press, 1977), ch. 3.

Hanbury for Mr Burden to prove Martha Green's marriage before we could have an order'.[173]

Nor did cohabitation and reputation create a marriage in the eyes of the community.[174] The settlement examinations for the parish of Chelsea provide a number of examples: in the case of Sarah Norton in 1733, a woman who was present at the birth was able to give details of Sarah's parents, but stated that she did not know whether they were married, even though the mother went by the father's name;[175] similarly, in 1742 the godfather of John Bell gave evidence that the child's parents 'lived and cohabited together ... as man and wife' but added that '[he] cannot say that the said Sarah Bell, alias Morgan, was ever married to the said John Bell, though she went always by his name and was reputed to be his wife'.[176]

But such suspicion was not confined to the case in which an individual or couple was making a claim against the parish funds. Those recording the baptism of a child sometimes noted their doubts as to the marital status of the parents, using terms such as 'supposed wife'[177] or stating, with evident scepticism, that an individual claimed to be married.[178] The records of the church courts when exercising their office jurisdiction reinforce this evidence of suspicion. It was once thought that the church courts failed to resume their regulatory role after their restoration in 1660,[179] but in

[173] Warwick Record Office, DR 296/46, 29 December 1733, 9 July 1735.

[174] Cf. Stone, *Road to Divorce*, p. 52, who claims that cohabitation, using the same surname, and the baptism of children created 'a *socially* acceptable presumption of marriage' (my emphasis). Stone may have been thinking of the legal presumption in favour of marriage: see further below.

[175] Hitchcock and Black, *Chelsea Settlement and Bastardy Examinations*, p. 1.

[176] *Ibid.* p. 36.

[177] East Farndon, 16 April 1716, baptism of son of George Bayley of Slipton, deceased, and 'Unica his supposed wife'.

[178] See e.g., Flore, 20 March 1720, baptism of daughter of Susannah Bitten, 'who declared herself wife of William Carrington', and 19 February 1725, baptism of son of 'a vagrant woman, who saith she is the wife of one Christopher Rose an Irish man'; Bozeat, 20 May 1733, baptism of son of Sarah Somerlyn 'married she declares to James Grimeshaw in the Guards'; Byfield, 3 April 1738, baptism of daughter of James Riddel and Ann Garner 'whom he calls his wife', and 2 February 1739, baptism of daughter of Henry Bradford and Ann Maud 'whom he owned for his wife' (this appears as 'who he called his wife' in the Bishop's Transcripts).

[179] On their earlier role see e.g., Cressy, *Birth, Marriage and Death*, p. 280 and M. Ingram, 'Spousals Litigation in the English Ecclesiastical Courts c. 1350–c.1640' in R. B. Outhwaite (ed.), *Marriage and Society: Studies in the Social History of Marriage* (London: Europa, 1981).

some areas there is evidence of such courts continuing to exercise close supervision over the morals of the local population well into the eighteenth century.[180] As Outhwaite has noted, prosecutions for sexual immorality 'appear to have survived longest, and in greatest number, in jurisdictions where economic change was least evident, where small village and modest urban communities prevailed, in those face-to-face communities where reputation clearly mattered'.[181] If it was uncertain whether a particular couple were married, they might be cited before the ecclesiastical courts for living 'suspiciously' together as husband and wife without being married.[182] In such cases the onus was on the parties themselves to prove that they had in fact gone through a ceremony of marriage. Those who could not might be required to do penance before the congregation, which involved 'an appearance in church, clad in a white sheet, and an expression of contrition'.[183]

The correction court books for the Diocese of Carlisle provide a number of examples of such accusations – of 'living and cohabiting scandalously and suspiciously as man and wife without lawful marriage'[184] – and the responses of the couples themselves. The first point to note is that the number of such cases is low: only 38 couples being presented for the period 1731 to 1740, in contrast to the 195 men and 299 women presented for fornication in the first half of this period (with a further 214 individuals cited for ante-nuptial fornication).[185] The second, and more important point for present purposes, is that none of those cited for living 'scandalously and suspiciously together' claimed that they had contracted together. A few informed the court that they had in fact married, but it is clear that the marriages in question involved the presence of an

180 S. L. Ollard and P. C. Walker (eds.), *Archbishop Herring's Visitation Returns, 1743* (Yorkshire Archaeological Society Record Series, 1927), vol. 71; A. Warne, *Church and Society in Eighteenth Century Devon* (Newton Abbot: David and Charles, 1969), ch. 6; Rev. M. G. Smith, *Pastoral Discipline and the Church Courts: the Hexham Court 1680–1730* (York: Borthwick Papers No. 62, 1982), pp. 29–30; M. Kinnear, 'The Correction Court in the Diocese of Carlisle, 1704–1756' (1990) 59 *Church History* 191; Jacob, *Lay People and Religion*, ch. 5.

181 R. B. Outhwaite, *The Rise and Fall of the English Ecclesiastical Courts, 1500–1860* (Cambridge University Press, 2006), p. 95.

182 See e.g., *Matingley* v. *Martyn* (1632) Jones, W. 257; 82 ER 134.

183 N. J. G. Pounds, *A History of the English Parish* (Cambridge University Press, 2000), p. 297.

184 Carlisle Record Office (CRO), DRC/5/7.

185 Kinnear, 'The Correction Court', Table 1.

Anglican clergyman, even if some were clandestine.[186] There is no reason why couples who had simply exchanged consent before setting up home would have escaped such scrutiny if those who had actually married did not.

But were there any circumstances in which a cohabiting couple *would* be presumed to have married?

PRESUMED MARRIED?

At this time English law *did* have (and indeed still has)[187] a presumption in favour of marriage based on the cohabitation and reputation of the parties. However, this was a legal presumption born out of the difficulties of proving a marriage[188] rather than a social assumption equating those living together with those legally married. In an era before systematic registration of baptisms, marriages, and burials, even if a marriage had been regularly celebrated in church it was possible that no documentary evidence would exist, either because no entry of the event had been made, or because the registers were carelessly kept or had not survived;[189] and even if a record did exist the court might require evidence to link the names to the parties in the case.[190] Moreover, it is important to note exactly when and how the presumption operated. It was, like so many legal rules in the early modern period, highly dependent on the context of the case.

First, a distinction should be drawn between cases in which evidence of cohabitation and reputation was relied upon to support the evidence of a marriage ceremony, and those in which evidence of cohabitation and reputation alone would suffice. If either or both

[186] CRO, DRC/5/7, 2 November 1733. See also the case of John Wilkinson and Sarah Weathersall, Patterdale, 7 October 1735.

[187] Although modern cases are a poor guide to the way in which the doctrine operated in this period: see e.g., R. Probert, 'When are We Married? Void, Non-existent and Presumed Marriages' (2002) 22 *Legal Studies* 398.

[188] See also *Revel* v. *Fox* (1751) 2 Ves. Sen. 269; 28 ER 174.

[189] Numerous writers have testified to the poor state of early registers: see e.g., J. Burn, *The History of the Parish Registers in England* (London: John Russell Smith, 1862), pp. 42–3; W. E. Tate, *The Parish Chest* (Chichester: Phillimore & Co. Ltd, 1983; original edn 1946), p. 49.

[190] See e.g., *Draycott* v. *Talbot* (1718) 3 Brown 564; 1 ER 1501. The insistence that there be some evidence to link the entry in the register with the couple whose marriage was in dispute might seem unduly demanding, but bearing in mind the limited range of names and the possibility of forgery it was a necessary precaution against spurious claims.

of the parties were still alive, the ecclesiastical courts would usually require evidence of some kind of ceremony to be produced. As one commentator explained: 'Where one party after the Death of the other, insists upon a marriage once had between them, or where one party alledges a marriage with another, who denies the fact, the additional solemnisation of the marriage, *with the necessary ceremonies*, must be made out in proof.'[191] It was, after all, reasonable to expect individuals to recall at least some details of their marriage.[192] How strictly this requirement of proof was insisted upon might depend on the facts of the case: in *Bond* v. *Bond*,[193] for example, the supposed widow had given details of the marriage but failed to provide a witness or prove that the clergyman who had celebrated it was dead and no longer available to give evidence. The court held that she had failed in her proof as to the fact of the marriage, but held that the evidence of reputable cohabitation, the baptism of the children as legitimate, and, significantly, the fact that she was acknowledged as the wife of the deceased by the step-son who was now challenging her right, was sufficient evidence of the marriage. The step-son was condemned in costs.

By contrast, if both parties were dead the ecclesiastical courts were much more willing to hold that evidence of cohabitation and reputation alone would suffice, for example, if the issue of the alleged marriage were seeking to prove the validity of their parents' (or remoter ancestors') union in order to claim under a will.[194] This made sense, since the children might well be unable to produce either written documentation or witnesses; indeed, they might even be ignorant of the time or place of the marriage. In *Lady Mayo* v. *Brown*, for example, Sir George Lee took the view that 'it might easily happen that [a claimant] might not be able to find out the time or place of her father and mother's marriage, and therefore that circumstantial evidence and public owning might

[191] *A Letter to the Public: Containing the Substance of what hath been offered in the late Debates upon the Subject of the Act of Parliament for the better preventing of Clandestine Marriages* (London: Charles March, 1753), p. 52 (emphasis added).

[192] See e.g., *Alfray* v. *Alfray* (1758) 2 Lee 547; 161 ER 435, at 548.

[193] (1754) 2 Lee 46n; 161 ER 258.

[194] Although not necessarily: in *Taylor* v. *Taylor* (1756) 2 Lee 274; 161 ER 339 the court had to decide which of a man's alleged three marriages was valid: proof of the first rested on cohabitation alone and it could thereby not prevail over a later proven ceremony.

be sufficient to establish the marriage';[195] in this case the fact that the parents had lived in Jamaica as well as in London illustrates the potential problem of proving such a marriage. In another case the *latest* of the marriages in question in the case was thought to have taken place sixty years earlier.[196] The Prerogative Court accordingly held in such cases that evidence that the parents or remoter ancestors had lived together as man and wife and had been reputed as such would be sufficient proof.[197] Account was also taken of the status of the parties: it was noted in *Shand* v. *Gardiner* that the pedigree in question related to 'persons in low rank, who could not be supposed to have any writings, &c, to exhibit'.[198]

It is important to emphasise precisely what was being presumed in these cases. It was *not* the case that cohabitation and reputation created a valid marriage. Nor was it presumed that the parties had simply exchanged vows *per verba de praesenti*,[199] as in the American form of common-law marriage.[200] Rather, the fact that the parties had lived together and had been reputed to be married created the presumption that the parties had gone through a valid ceremony of marriage. The difference between the two is that a presumption can be rebutted by contrary evidence that the parties had not in fact married, or, if the case rested on the legitimacy of the claimant, had married after the birth of the child making a

195 *Lady Mayo* v. *Brown* (1753) 1 Lee 271; 161 ER 100, at 271.

196 *Fownes* v. *Ettricke* (1756) 2 Lee 257; 161 ER 333.

197 *Ibid.* 257: 'common reputation of relationship in such a certain degree, legitimacy, and public ownings were fully pleaded, and also declarations of persons now dead, who were conversant in the families of the parties, were admitted as proof of public reputation of relationship in the degree alleged'. See also *Eaton* v. *Bright* (1755) 2 Lee 85; 161 ER 272 (held to be unnecessary to provide evidence of marriage between grandfather and grandmother: 'in a case of interest, it was sufficient to prove owning and acknowledging').

198 (1754) 1 Lee 529; 161 ER 195, per Sir George Lee.

199 Cf. Stone, *Road to Divorce*, p. 77, who suggests that '[r]ight up to the passage of the new Marriage Act of 1753, some lawyers and clergy continued to advance the theory that "habit and repute, with cohabitation of man and wife, is in general good evidence that the parties at some time or other exchanged the matrimonial consent"'. The individual quoted by Stone is in fact a late-nineteenth-century barrister giving evidence to the Royal Commission on Marriage in the 1860s (*Report of the Royal Commission on the State and Operation of Laws of Marriage* (1867–8), House of Commons Sessional Papers, vol. XXXII, p. 1), whose views are hardly a safe guide to the views held over a hundred years earlier, and who would inevitably have been influenced by the decision in *Dalrymple*.

200 See e.g., Koegel, *Common Law Marriage*; Grossberg, *Governing the Hearth*.

claim.[201] The evidence of cohabitation and reputation simply placed the onus on the person opposing the claim to provide such contrary evidence.[202]

Far from equating cohabitation and marriage, these cases were in fact premised on the assumption that there was a sharp distinction between the two. It was expected that a couple would not cohabit unless they were married: as Sir George Lee explained in *Conran* v. *Lowe*,[203] 'cohabitation created a very strong presumption in favour of marriage, where the woman's character was unblemished, because the law would not suppose a woman whose character, in general, was virtuous, would live with a man as her husband who was not so'.[204] Similarly, it was assumed that a couple would not enjoy the reputation of married persons without good reason. This should be viewed in the context of the evidence of suspicion levelled at couples who were not known to be married; the very fact that a particular couple were reputed to be married suggested local knowledge that there had been a ceremony of marriage.

The common-law courts did not have the task of deciding on the validity of a marriage; if the validity of a marriage was crucial to the case, then the issue was referred to the Bishop for determination.[205] Moreover, if in any case the ecclesiastical court had decided that there was no marriage, this decision was binding on the common-law courts.[206] In other contexts, however, the fact of the marriage

[201] See e.g., *R* v. *Inhabitants of St Peter's in Worcestershire* (1735) Burr. Sett. Cas. 25 No. 9, in which a man gave evidence that he had never been married to the mother of his child, even though they had been reputed to be married and their children had been registered as legitimate.

[202] See e.g., *Lady Mayo* v. *Brown* (1757) 2 Lee 391; 161 ER 380, at 381, in which 'the full proof Lady Mayo had made of her being reputed to be legitimate, and of the constant owning of her as such by her father and mother, threw the proof on Brown that she was not legitimate, and obliged him to shew that she was born before her parents' marriage, by shewing the precise time of her birth, and of their marriage subsequent to it'.

[203] (1754) 1 Lee 630; 161 ER 630.

[204] *Ibid.* 638–9. Although in that particular case no such presumption could be made as the woman 'appeared from her own witnesses to be a common prostitute'.

[205] See e.g., Sir S. Eure, *Trials per pais*, 5th edn (London, 1718), p. 8.

[206] See e.g., *Blackham's Case* (1709) 1 Salk. 290; 91 ER 258; *Clews* v. *Bathurst* (1734) 2 Strange 960; 93 ER 968; *Brownsword* v. *Edwards* (1750–1) 2 Ves. Sen. 243; 28 ER 157.

(i.e., whether the parties had gone through a ceremony of marriage) would be sufficient,[207] and this was something that the common-law courts could determine.[208] The evidence required of a marriage would depend very much on the facts of the case: if a man and a woman pleaded coverture to avoid a bond, the marriage had to be 'well proved';[209] by contrast, if a woman who would forfeit certain property if she remarried denied having remarried, her cohabitation with a man could be taken into account.[210] As the judge pointed out, in that type of case the marriage 'is probably clandestine; if therefore the court was to say, such circumstances were not evidence, it would be impossible to prove it'.[211] Similarly, given the legal disabilities that attached to illegitimacy, there was a strong presumption in favour of a child's legitimacy:[212] cohabitation and reputation could therefore be taken into account after the death of the principal parties.[213] But in none of these cases, ecclesiastical or common-law, is there any indication that cohabitation *outside* marriage was regarded with anything but disfavour.[214]

THE EVIDENCE OF CONFORMITY

For now they're fairly in for Life
The Priest declares them Man and Wife.[215]

[207] As in, for example, a husband's liability for his wife's debts: *Alleyne* v. *Grey* (1689) 2 Salk. 437; 91 ER 380. In *Norwood* v. *Stevenson* (1738) Andrews 227; 95 ER 374, the court gave short shrift to the attempt of the husband to argue that he and his wife 'were never joined in lawful matrimony'.

[208] Eure, *Trials per pais*, pp. 12, 18.

[209] J. Clayton, *Reports and Pleas of Assizes at York* (Dublin, 1741), pp. 61–2. See also *Dry* v. *Sutton* (1721): J. Strange, *A Collection of Select Cases relating to Evidence* (London, 1754), p. 79.

[210] See e.g., *Revel* v. *Fox* (1751) 2 Ves. Sen. 269; 28 ER 174. A woman could not be compelled to provide evidence of her marriage if this would lead to a forfeiture: see e.g., *Chauncey* v. *Tahourden* (1742) 2 Atk. 392; 26 ER 637.

[211] *Revel* v. *Fox* (1751) 2 Ves. Sen. 269.

[212] See e.g., *Franklin's Case* (1725) 2 P Wms. 299; 24 ER 739; *Stapylton* v. *Stapylton* (1736) West T Hard. 12; 25 ER 794.

[213] See e.g., *May* v. *May* (1743), cited in Sir F. Buller, *An Institute of the Law relative to Trials at Nisi Prius* (London, 1789), p. 105.

[214] See e.g., *Chetwynd* v. *Lindon* (1752) 2 Ves. Sen. 450; 28 ER 288; *Finch* v. *Finch* (1752) 2 Ves. Sen. 491; 28 ER 315.

[215] E. Chicken, *The Collier's Wedding* (Newcastle, 1764). Chicken's poem was probably written in 1729, although it was not published until after his death in 1746. It contains a precise account of the marriage formalities: though not regular churchgoers, the couple concerned marry in church.

Having disentangled these various myths, we can now turn to the question of whether there is any positive evidence that couples complied with the law and married in church. Three types of evidence were used in drawing up cohorts whose marital status could be tested, namely baptism registers, settlement examinations, and listings. Each form of evidence has its own advantages and disadvantages. Baptism registers survive in abundance for the eighteenth century, and so it is possible to choose cohorts of parents from a range of areas and different types of communities. Yet such registers pose problems in determining the overall extent of conformity, since the cohort is self-defining, being limited to those who brought their children to be baptised in the parish church. Settlement examinations offer an unparalleled insight into the lives of the poor: this is of particular importance in this context, since it has been claimed that informal marriage practices were widespread among the poor. Unfortunately, they are much rarer than baptism registers, which means that one's choice is more limited. Listings of those residing in the parish are, in the decades before the first census, rarer still, but are perhaps our best hope of obtaining a sample that provides a genuine cross-section of all the community.

For each couple within the test groups the same question was asked: could a marriage be traced in the Anglican parish registers? Of course, it may be objected that this does not tell us whether *all* of the requirements of the canon law were observed, an issue that is impossible to determine for many marriages so long after the event, especially when parish registers do not always record whether the marriage was by banns or by licence. But it is worth noting that the standard assumption that the calling of banns was 'bitterly resented'[216] is difficult to square with the fact that most marriages were preceded by banns.[217] The extent to which couples may have married in the wrong church will be considered in

[216] See e.g., R. L. Brown, 'The Rise and Fall of the Fleet Marriage', ch. 6 in R. B. Outhwaite, *Marriage and Society* (London: Europa, 1981), p. 124.

[217] See e.g., D. J. Steel, *National Index of Parish Registers*, vol. I, *Sources of Births, Marriages and Deaths Before 1837* (London: Society of Genealogists), p. 54; see also V. Elliott, 'Marriage Licences and the Local Historian' (1973) 10 *Local Historian* 282, noting that licences accounted for only one-fifth of marriages in one Warwickshire parish in the eighteenth century.

a later chapter; for now, the question is whether couples married in *any* church.

Although the following discussion will, of necessity, be couched in terms of numbers and percentages, the individual stories that lie behind the statistics should not be forgotten. For each marriage traced, the reader is invited to conjure up an image of quiet country churches, or of the impressive structure of York Minster, where many of those in the York samples married. Conformity does not preclude romance or intriguing stories. Some eighteenth-century registers do give the reader some hints as to the appearance of the bride and bridegroom: Mary Steed, for example, was described by the self-styled 'Archbishop of Seasalter'[218] as 'a doleful, forbidding saturnine damsel', while John Housdon and Hannah Matthews fared still worse, the former being dismissed as a '[y]oung gape-mouth lazy fellow' and the latter, more cruelly still, as 'an old toothless wriggling Hagg'.[219] Sadly, the registers with vivid descriptions of this kind tend not to display the carefulness in recording essential to any case study, and so we must simply rely on our imagination for such matters.

Baptism registers

The Northamptonshire village of Kilsby was, in the mid-eighteenth century, a parish of some 650 to 700 inhabitants, many of whom were engaged in weaving and wool-combing.[220] At the start of the project, there was nothing to suggest how Kilsby couples may have lived their lives: it was chosen because it was where I grew up, rather than because it was expected to yield a particular result. The register of baptisms and marriages commences in 1706; the cohort chosen for study consisted of parents bringing their children to be baptised in the twenty years before the implementation of the 1753 Act, in order to maximise the possibility of there being a record of those who married in Kilsby itself.

Of the 70 combinations of parents that made up this cohort, who between them accounted for 201 entries in the baptism register

[218] See R. H. Goodsall, *Whitstable, Seasalter and Swalecliffe: the History of Three Kent Parishes* (Canterbury: Cross & Jackman Ltd, 1938).
[219] Marriage register of St Alphege, Seasalter: Kent Record Office, U3/137/1/2.
[220] G. Hatton, *Kilsby: the Story of a Village* (Rugby, 1989), p. 66.

in this period,[221] marriages in church[222] have been traced for 80 per cent.[223] This should not, however, be taken as evidence that the remaining 20 per cent (made up of 14 couples) did *not* marry in church. It would be fair to assume that Mary Smith, 'traveller', was unaccompanied by any husband, since he does not appear in the register. But five of the mothers were described as the wife of the father in the baptism register, and in another case this was inscribed on her tombstone. Potential marriages have been traced for Robert and Mary Hall, and for Thomas and Elizabeth Matthew: the problem is rather that their names are so common that more than one match has been traced. There is also the potential for the misrecording of data: Richard Barnet married Mary York in Kilsby in 1748, but the mother of his son, born in 1750, is recorded as Jane. It cannot be assumed that this is the right person, but it cannot be ruled out.[224] Potential mistranscriptions of this kind are particularly difficult to detect when there is only one entry relating to the couple in the register, as was the case for six of the fourteen whose marriage remains untraced. If in such cases there is no other family in the parish with the same surname, as with John and Ann Else, it is plausible that their stay in Kilsby was a brief one.[225] Even if it was not possible to trace a marriage for the entirety of this cohort, therefore, there are at least plausible reasons why this was the case, and indications that a substantial proportion were definitely regarded as married by the incumbent who recorded the birth.[226]

221 A further seventy-four had further children baptised outside the period under consideration.

222 Although not necessarily the right church: see further Chapter 5.

223 See Table 3.1 for the location of such marriages.

224 The potential for mistakes was increased by the fact that events were not recorded in the register as they occurred: rather, as Wrigley has described, the registers 'were usually made up periodically from information recorded by the minister or his parish clerk in notebooks or on scraps of paper': E. A. Wrigley, 'How Reliable is Our Knowledge of the Demographic Characteristics of the English Population in the Early Modern Period?' (1997) 40 *Historical Journal* 571, 576.

225 See further below on the reasons why a child might be baptised in a parish to which the parties did not belong.

226 As the case study of Llansantffraid indicates, no adverse inferences should be drawn from discrepancies in the register: there were simply periods when mothers were described as wives and periods when they were not.

Table 3.1 *Proportion and location of marriages traced*

	Parish studied	*Adjacent parishes**	*Same county*	*Different county*	*Number traced*
Kilsby, Northamptonshire, 1734–54	17 (24%)	9 (13%)	28 (40%)	2 (3%)	56 (80%)
St Mary, Scilly Isles, 1734–54	137	n/a	10	2	149
– all cases	(76%)		(6%)	(1%)	(83%)
– excluding illegitimate births	(79%)		(6%)	(1%)	(86%)
HTG, York, 1735–52	25	100	40	3	168
– all cases	(11%)	(45%)	(18%)	(1%)	(76%)
– excluding illegitimate births	(12%)	(49%)	(20%)	(1%)	(82%)
Bradford-on-Avon pre-1754 settlement examinations	26 (37%)	10 (14%)	2 (3%)	6 (9%)	44 (63%)
Cardington, baptism cohort 1734–54	81	25	39	3	148
– all cases	(45%)	(14%)	(22%)	(2%)	(83%)
– excluding illegitimate births	(47%)	(15%)	(23%)	(2%)	(86%)
Cardington pre-1754 (from 1782 listing)	25 (38%)	15 (23%)	22 (33%)	–	62 (94%)

* Kilsby: Barby, Ashby St Ledgers, Watford, Crick, and Hillmorton

Bradford: taken as including the chapelries of Limpley Stoke, Winsley, South Wraxall, and Holt, and the adjacent parishes of Westwood, Winkfield, North Bradley, Trowbridge (including Staverton), Whaddon, Broughton Gifford, Atworth (including Chalfield Magna), Box (including Ditteridge), Monkton Farleigh, Freshford, Bathford, Claverton, South Stoke, Hinton Charterhouse, and Monkton Combe.

Holy Trinity Goodramgate: taken as all parishes in the City of York for current purposes.

Cardington: Cople, Old Warden, Southill, Haynes, Willhamstead, Elstow, Bedford St Mary, Bedford St John, Goldington.

The first lesson learned from the study of Kilsby was the importance of location – Kilsby parents had proved to be frustratingly mobile and the village's location on the Warwickshire border and close to Leicestershire made tracing their marriages even more difficult.[227] Of course, in central England, nowhere is very far from anywhere. For the majority of couples many months would elapse between their marriage and the birth of their first child, and they would not necessarily remain in the same parish for the convenience of later historians. Thinking that a small island might provide a more static population, I examined the baptism registers of St Mary, the parish comprising the largest of the Scilly Isles. This study clearly showed that where the mobility of couples was limited by external constraints, a far higher proportion of those whose children were baptised on the islands had themselves married there. Of the 180 couples whose children were baptised in the twenty years before the Act came into force,[228] 76 per cent had married at St Mary. Of course, once under sail it would be possible to travel longer distances more quickly than would be the case inland (Cesar Sapp, for example, had married in a parish on the Kentish coast) and it only proved possible to be certain of a further 7 per cent of marriages traced to other churches away from the Scilly Isles. A further complicating factor was the transient population of the Scilly Isles: among the fathers whose marriages have not been traced were a captain and an ensign in the Company of Invalids, and eight sets of parents had only one child baptised on the island. Two marriages were likely to prove untraceable because the first child was baptised in 1726, the same year that the marriage register began. Finally, seven mothers (four from the Barrisfield family) gave birth to children who were unequivocally described as 'base' in the register. Overall, however, the overwhelming impression is one of conformity.

The second lesson learned from Kilsby was the need for registers that recorded more than the bare names of the parents. Here

[227] There is an electronic index of marriages celebrated in Northamptonshire, compiled by Alan Clarke and Marilyn Ponting (*The Northamptonshire Marriage Index, 1700–1837*, 2004), but the electronic version of the Warwickshire Marriage Index is as yet unfinished, and no such index exists for Leicestershire.

[228] Six hundred and nine children were baptised between 25 March 1734 and 24 March 1754, and a further sixty-nine children were baptised outside this period.

there was rather more choice, although no one register included all the information one would regard as desirable. But the number of baptism registers does mean that researchers can afford to choose those that allow particular questions to be answered. Between 1735 and 1752, for example, the parish of Holy Trinity Goodramgate in York recorded whether a child was baptised publicly or privately, and often noted the occupation of the father.[229] This therefore made it possible to test whether those who preferred privacy for the rite of baptism were more or less likely to marry in church than those whose children were baptised publicly. Of the 217 sets of parents who brought their children to be baptised there during this period, marriages have been traced for between 75 and 81 per cent (the lower figure representing clear matches, the higher figure including less clear-cut ones).[230] Almost two-thirds of these parents chose to baptise their children privately; the remainder were evenly split between those who baptised all their children publicly,[231] and those who baptised some privately and some publicly. At first sight it would appear that the proportion of marriages traced is lowest for those who baptised their children privately, but this is largely due to the fact that almost all of the children in this sample who were directly described as 'base' were baptised privately: once these are excluded then the proportion of marriages traced is more or less consistent across each group.[232]

This raised a further question about the behaviour of those who had children outside marriage. If the parents of illegitimate children shared a home they would fulfil at least two of the criteria for a functional alternative to marriage outlined in the introduction, namely co-residence and a sexual relationship. Since the numbers of illegitimate children in any given parish is small, a cohort was drawn up from an electronic index of births and baptisms for the whole of Northamptonshire for the period 1730 to 1751.[233] This

[229] Borthwick Institute, PR/Y/HTG.

[230] However, given the evidence of the distances travelled by urban migrants (see e.g., P. Clark, 'Migration in England During the Late Seventeenth and Early Eighteenth Centuries' (1979) 83 *Past and Present* 57, Table 4), it would be reasonable to extend the geographical area within which a match is regarded as plausible.

[231] This included children who were first baptised privately and then publicly.

[232] See further Table 3.1.

[233] A. Clarke and K. Lyman-Clarke, *Northamptonshire Birth and Baptism Index* (2007).

had the advantage not only of providing a substantial cohort but also of providing a means of tracking children who were baptised in different parishes. In total, 847 instances of children being described as 'bastard', 'base', 'illegitimate', 'spurious', 'natural', 'reputed', 'supposed', 'misbegotten', or 'fathered out of wedlock' were traced. In 623 cases only the mother's name appeared, or neither parent was named at all. Given that any expenditure by the parish on an illegitimate child could be recouped from the father, one would not expect the authorities to deliberately omit the father's name if it were known to them: the implication, therefore, is that the fathers were unknown in three-quarters of the cases and were therefore unlikely to be living with the mother. Of the 221 couples whose names are known to us, a mere six (2.7 per cent of this sub-sample or 0.7 per cent of the larger cohort) had brought a subsequent illegitimate child to be baptised. This is in sharp contrast to the samples drawn from the general population of parents: in Kilsby, for example, 80 per cent brought more than one child to be baptised in the parish. The conclusion must be that only a tiny proportion of the bastard-bearers and begetters in this sample had an ongoing non-marital sexual relationship. Often there is further evidence that the parties were not living in a co-residential relationship: thirty of the fathers are identified as being from a different parish, a further fourteen were soldiers, at least two were already married to other women, and one had died.

Similarly, it would appear that only a very small number went on to marry. Marriages were traced for only 21 of the 221 couples, in percentage terms, 9.5 per cent of the sub-sample and a mere 2.5 per cent of the larger sample. This included one of the couples who had brought more than one child to be baptised, which would seem to indicate that they did not regard their relationship as equivalent to a regular marriage despite its lengthy duration and the baptism of two children. But the gap of eleven years between the baptism of the first child and the eventual marriage in this case was unusual: those who did marry after bearing an illegitimate child tended to do so quickly, sometimes within days of the baptism.

To check whether or not any of the bastard-bearing couples for whom no subsequent marriage could be traced did in fact marry in a ceremony which has not left a record, the index was also examined for subsequent *non*-illegitimate children baptised in the same parish as the other(s) or in parishes mentioned as being the residences of either parent. In five cases, or 2.5 per cent of those for whom no marriage has been traced, it would appear that the couple went on to have subsequent children who were not described as illegitimate. The most plausible explanation of this is that the record of the marriage has not survived, rather than that the community accepted the couple as married on the basis of continued cohabitation. Overall, the cohort of known bastard-bearers and begetters is very distinct from that of other couples. This is not to say that other couples rigidly observed the church's prohibition on sex before marriage (there is plenty of evidence of pre-marital pregnancy),[234] but it was clearly deemed important to marry before a child was born.

Settlement examinations

Settlement examinations capture the lives of the very poorest members of society, those claiming relief from the parish authorities. The laws of settlement meant that each parish was financially responsible only for those who were settled within its bounds, and so each applicant was closely examined. A wife took her husband's settlement, and legitimate children took their father's settlement, so whether or not a couple had validly married was a vital question for the justices who carried out the examinations.

The parish of Bradford-on-Avon in Wiltshire was chosen as a test-case because of the level of detail in the settlement examinations, of which 377 survive for the period 1725 to 1798.[235] This produced a cohort of 268 couples,[236] of whom 70 either claimed that they had married before 1754 or gave evidence (for example,

[234] As officiously noted in some registers: see e.g., Orlingbury, 27 July 1707, baptism of James Hanners, son of John and Rachel 'who were married on Easter Monday'; Wappenham, 28 December 1716, baptism of George Roberts, 'born ten weeks after marrying', 4 March 1731, baptism of George Broomall, 'born about nine or ten weeks after marriage', 21 December 1746, baptism of Thomas Isham '17 weeks after marriage'.

[235] Hembry, *Calendar of Bradford-on-Avon Settlement Examinations*. It is also worthy of note that since the settlement examinations do include references to clandestine ceremonies (pp. 19, 28, and see further Chapter 5), and (once) to cohabitation (p. 15, quoted above), if any distinctive marriage practices did occur one would expect to find mention of them here, but one does not.

[236] Five cases were omitted as no details of the spouse were given, making it impossible to trace the marriage. For further information on the cohort see R. Probert and L. D'Arcy Brown, 'The Impact of the Clandestine Marriages Act: Three Case-Studies in Conformity' (2008) 23 *Continuity and Change* 309.

relating to the age of their children) suggesting that this was the case. Unfortunately, although comprehensive details are included in some examinations (the wife's maiden name, the location of the marriage and the approximate date of the marriage), this was by no means the case for all. Most recorded only the place and approximate date of the marriage, and some not even this.[237] The proportion of marriages traced varied, as one would expect, in direct proportion to the information available: marriages were traced for 78 per cent of cases where all three pieces of information were provided, but for only 55 per cent of cases where there was no information beyond the names of parties and the approximate date of the marriage.[238]

One might imagine that if there is evidence as to where the marriage took place there would be no difficulty in tracing it. However, such evidence varied from the specific (e.g., 'Bradford parish church') to the less helpful ('Dublin'). The advantage of having such evidence was that it allowed *untraceable* marriages to be identified, for example, where the register for the parish in question was missing or incomplete.[239] In addition, four marriages were specifically identified as clandestine, having taken place before a clergyman outside any church.[240] A further advantage is that it revealed a geographical spread that explained why marriages in other samples may have proved impossible to trace: of the thirty-nine individuals whose place of marriage had been recorded, 36 per cent had married in Bradford parish church, 23 per cent in one of its chapelries or an adjacent parish, but 33 per cent in another county,[241] and one overseas.

237 Such discrepancies simply reflect the lack of any standard form and the fact that the examinations were recorded over three-quarters of a century: there is a tendency for information to be recorded in a certain way for a few entries, and then for a different system to be adopted.

238 See further Probert and D'Arcy Brown, 'The Impact of the Clandestine Marriages Act', Table 2.

239 Mary Isick, for example, married in Walcott in 1719, but the marriage register does not begin until 1728, and the register for Limpley Stoke, where another examinant claimed to have married, is clearly incomplete. It was further inferred that in five cases apparently complete registers contained errors or omissions: a couple claiming settlement in Bradford would hardly claim to have married in the parish if this was not the case, since their claim could all too easily be proved false.

240 See further Chapter 5.

241 Including the four clandestine marriages that took place in Bath and London.

Parish listing

The final cohort is based on a list of the inhabitants of Cardington in Bedfordshire.[242] This list, drawn up in 1782 by the local schoolmaster, takes the form of a house-to-house survey, giving the names (including wives' maiden names), occupations, and ages of the occupants of each household. While the list may not be *perfect* as a tool for identifying the total number of inhabitants of Cardington, omissions tend to be of single persons – servants and widows – rather than couples.[243] In any case, the important point for present purposes is that inclusion on the list was not dependent on compliance with the rites of the Church of England.[244] It is also noticeable that the list is at its most detailed when discussing the poorer inhabitants of the parish, the very persons who some commentators have claimed eschewed formal marriage. A final advantage of the list is that it enables practice both before and after the 1753 Act to be tested: even upon a preliminary examination it was obvious, judging from the age of the parties and their children, that around one-quarter of those named must have married (if indeed they did so) before the Act came into force.

Of the sixty-six couples who are known, or can be inferred, to have married before 1754, a marriage has been traced for sixty-two, a success rate of 94 per cent. The missing marriages are those of the widowed Mary Beckels, whose husband's first name was not recorded; Samuel Redman, whose wife is recorded as Sarah in the marriage register but Hannah in the baptism register (which may simply be a mistake); Richard and Ann Haynes, neither of whom were born in the parish and whose first three children do not appear to have been baptised there; and Samuel and Judith Butcher, of whom we know little save that their children were baptised in Cardington in the 1730s[245] and that Judith was described as

[242] This section draws on the discussion in Probert and D'Arcy Brown, 'The Impact of the Clandestine Marriages Act'.

[243] D. Baker, *The Inhabitants of Cardington in 1782* (Bedfordshire Historical Record Society vol. 52, 1973), p. 12.

[244] See Baker, *Inhabitants of Cardington*, p. 5 on the likely way in which the list was drawn up.

[245] It was unclear from the listing when this marriage might have taken place (see Probert and D'Arcy Brown, 'The Impact of the Clandestine Marriages Act'), but carrying out a further study of the baptism register clarified the time period within which to search for a marriage: see further below.

Samuel's wife in the burial register.[246] A more appropriate inference might be that the conformity rate in fact approached 100 per cent, given that there is no positive evidence of cohabitation among these older couples,[247] and the fact that the failure to trace the remaining marriages can plausibly be attributed to defective information.

Must we conclude that Cardington was an aberration, and that couples there were more likely to marry in church than those living in other areas? I would argue that this would be a misinterpretation of the evidence. The reasons why it was possible to trace such a high percentage of marriages for the Cardington cohort are threefold: first, the level of detail provided in the listing; secondly, the survival of registers from surrounding parishes; and, thirdly, the fact that the listing focuses on households. Having the wife's maiden name can be crucial in tracing or confirming marriages: the results from Bradford-on-Avon show that a higher percentage of marriages were traced where this information was available.[248] In addition, the Cardington listing often includes details as to the parties' parish of origin, which is useful in identifying possible parishes to search for a marriage or in confirming a potential match. But having such information is of little use if the marriage registers have not survived. Crucially, Bedfordshire has the best collection of transcribed registers in England and Wales, which means that if a Cardington couple did marry in Bedfordshire (which is likely, given its location in the centre of the county), then it is likely that their marriage can be traced. In the case of Bradford-on-Avon, by contrast, we know that some relevant marriage registers have not survived, while the task of tracing marriages of those baptising their children in Kilsby is rendered more difficult by its location on the border with Warwickshire and not far from Leicestershire, and by the fact that the information for these counties is both less complete and less accessible than that for Bedfordshire.[249] And the advantage

246 Baker, *Inhabitants of Cardington*, p. 81.

247 In contrast to the cohort of younger couples, one of which is clearly identified in the listing as non-marital: see Chapter 7.

248 See Probert and D'Arcy Brown, 'The Impact of the Clandestine Marriages Act', Table 2.

249 As noted above, many Northamptonshire registers do not begin until well into the eighteenth century, and as yet there is no equivalent of the electronic index for Warwickshire and Leicestershire.

of the fact that the listing focuses on households is that it automatically excludes a number of difficult cases, namely those who are not resident in the parish. A separate but equally important point is that there are virtually no households containing illegitimate children and their parents in the Cardington listing, reflecting the findings above to the effect that child-rearing outside marriage was in general a solitary affair that did not involve a co-residential relationship with the child's father.[250] Given that our concern is with those in co-residential relationships, and that there is in general no evidence that the parents of illegitimate children were living together, it would be appropriate to exclude children identified as illegitimate from the study altogether. Once this is done, the proportion of couples whose marriage has been traced rises accordingly: to 86 per cent for the cohort from the Scilly Isles, and to 82 per cent for those baptised at Holy Trinity Goodramgate.[251]

In order to determine which of the above reasons for the high success rate in the case of the Cardington listing might be the most significant, a blind test was carried out, whereby the marital status of those who baptised children in Cardington in the twenty-year period before 25 March 1754 was checked without reference to the findings of the earlier study.[252] Excluding the 6 whose children were illegitimate, marriages were traced for 148 of the 178 combinations of parents that made up this cohort, or 86 per cent – a result very little different from that achieved for other cohorts based on baptism registers. In a few cases, a possible match could not be confirmed because of multiple possibilities within Bedfordshire – as, unsurprisingly, in the case of John and Mary White. But more significant was the fact that there were other plausible matches that had taken place further afield, that could not be linked explicitly to the couple baptising their children in Cardington. And a comparison of the two Cardington cohorts showed that the main reason for the different success rates was not the level of detail in the listing as opposed to the baptism register (although this was significant

250 Of course, it is likely that the children of those who married before 1754 would themselves have attained adulthood by the time the listing was drawn up in 1782 and would therefore not be described as 'illegitimate children'. But it is still significant that the only illegitimate children identified in the listing are living with their mothers – either in the workhouse or with maternal grandparents.

251 The records for Kilsby do not record any children as base in this period.

252 *Bedfordshire Parish Registers*, vol. 8, SOG BE/R 8.

in two cases), but rather the fact that the 1782 listing relates to permanent residents: of the forty couples who appeared in *both* the listing and the baptism register, marriages were traced for all but one.

This does not mean that those who had a less secure connection to the parish did not marry, simply that they may have married further afield and cannot be linked to the parish in question. The problem is essentially that baptism registers may include individuals who had the most fleeting connection with the parish. Sometimes the registers explicitly identify this: for example, when Mary Macknulling was baptised in Daventry in 1721 it was noted that she was a child of 'a foot soldier's wife [that] lay in upon the march'.[253] More often such explanations are not provided, and we have to draw inferences from the fact that a couple have only a single child baptised in the parish, from the occupations of the fathers, where given,[254] or that their surname is one that does not appear elsewhere in the registers for that parish.

The study of Cardington, therefore, simply illustrates the results that can be achieved when one has adequate information about couples who are actually resident in a parish with excellent records that is situated in the middle of a county with similarly good registers. Were these conditions to be replicated for the other case studies one would expect the proportion of marriages traced to rise to the same levels. In the absence of such conditions, it must simply be noted that the fact that a marriage has not been traced does not mean that it did not take place: we cannot assume that the missing few were engaging in alternative practices for which no evidence survives rather than, like their peers, marrying in church.

Table 3.1 summarises the findings of the case studies discussed above, showing in particular the importance of looking beyond the immediately adjacent parishes in order to find where couples

253 Daventry, 12 February 1721. See also Cottingham, 16 May 1707, noting the baptism of the son of John Reynolds of Great Easton, 'his wife being delivered at her mothers, Widow Newman of this parish'; and Castle Ashby, 22 January 1718, noting the baptism of the 'son of a travailing woman who says that her name is Anne Lee, and her husband Charles Lee was settled in ... London, but ... buried at Gillmorton in Leicestershire Dec 10 1717'.

254 In Holy Trinity Goodramgate the small number for whom no marriage has been traced included four soldiers, two players and a sailor, who each appear only once in the baptism register.

actually married. It shows whether the marriage took place in their own parish, an adjacent parish, another parish in the same county, or a different county. It also calculates the proportion traced to each location both as a percentage of each cohort and as a percentage of the cohort excluding those whose children were baptised as illegitimate and who do not appear to be living as a couple.[255]

Taken as a whole, therefore, these case studies provide overwhelming evidence that marriage in church was the norm, which leaves little room for any alternative practice of marriage by consent alone. Add to this the fact that there is virtually no evidence of contracted couples living together, or of cohabiting couples who claimed to be contracted, and the conclusion that the contract *per verba de praesenti* was not a functional alternative to regular marriage seems inevitable.

WHY WOULD COUPLES WANT TO MARRY INFORMALLY?

If there are any readers that remain unconvinced, perhaps one last set of arguments will persuade them. A number of reasons have been advanced by other commentators as to why couples might have preferred to marry by consent alone. Can it be inferred that if there are good reasons for a practice to occur, it must have done so? My instinctive answer would be 'not without evidence': if the evidential basis for a particular practice has been removed, the reasons advanced to explain that practice cannot be relied upon as independent evidence of that practice's existence. But in any case, such an inference would depend on the reasons advanced being sound – and the remainder of the chapter will demonstrate that this is simply not the case.

Some commentators have, for example, suggested that marriage by consent was popular because such unions were easy to dissolve.[256] This allows them to bring forward examples of informal

[255] Percentages are rounded to the nearest whole number, with the result that the two different calculations may produce the same percentage where the numbers are small.

[256] Mansell *et al.*, *Critical Introduction*, p. 96: '[c]ouples felt able to form and dissolve their unions in their own way'.

divorce – of which evidence *does* exist[257] – as evidence of informal marriage.[258] While Trumbach has suggested that self-marriage created an assumption that self-divorce was possible,[259] it seems that among academic commentators the influence works the other way: the evidence of self-divorce creates an assumption that self-marriage occurred.[260] Yet there is no reason why such informal methods of separation as abandonment or agreed separation should be linked to the degree of formality with which the marriage was originally celebrated. Indeed, such informal methods of separation continued long after the 1753 Act had clarified the boundaries of marriage,[261] and even today they are not unknown. The only supposed practice which was thought to involve a link between the mode of entry and the mode of exit is the broomstick wedding;[262] but, as noted above, the idea that one could marry in this way is based on a series of misunderstandings.

Besides, the linkage of informal divorce with informal marriage would seem to undermine the claim of such commentators that an informal marriage was the equivalent of one formally celebrated: if informal unions based solely on the consent of the parties had been regarded as full marriages, then it would have been necessary for the parties to end the union in a way recognised by the law, namely by annulment or the expensive and rare procedure of parliamentary divorce. Indeed, the argument that self-divorce was an option where the union was based on consent alone would seem to deny the exchange of consent the binding force that it *did* have.[263] And one has to wonder whether greater ease of separation would have been so attractive to eighteenth-century couples as modern academics assume: would women, in particular, embrace an arrangement that left them vulnerable to the possibility of desertion

257 Of course, the fact that there *is* contemporary documentary evidence of practices such as wife-sale (see Pounds, *History of the English Parish*, p. 315 for an example from 1486, and E. C. Cawte, 'Precise Records of Some Marriage Customs' (1985) 96 *Folklore* 254, for an example from 1696) renders the absence of evidence of informal marriage all the more striking.

258 See e.g., Parker, 'The Marriage Act 1753', 140; *Informal Marriage*, p. 27.

259 Trumbach, *Sex and the Gender Revolution*, p. 377.

260 Parker, *Informal Marriage*, p. 27.

261 Stone, *Road to Divorce*, chs. 6 and 7.

262 Discussed above, and see further S. P. Menefee, *Wives for Sale* (Oxford: Basil Blackwell, 1981), p. 20.

263 See further Chapter 2.

without legal redress?[264] The fate of the woman with children left dependent on the parish was not an enviable one.[265]

Modern preoccupations are also evident in the suggestion that women preferred 'informal marriages' because they retained control of their property in such arrangements.[266] This argument tends to be advanced by the same commentators who suggest that women were disadvantaged in other ways:[267] both in their ability to acquire property and in their relations with their husbands. The flaws in the argument are easy to spot: if women were less able to acquire property, might they not prefer an arrangement that gave them a secure claim on their husband's property? And if the society of the time was as patriarchal as has been portrayed by feminist historians, one might wonder how those with property managed to obtain sufficient clout in courtship negotiations to insist on a form of marriage that was to their advantage.

These first two reasons projected modern preoccupations into the past; by contrast, the third reason commonly advanced to explain the supposed popularity of informal marriage assumes a very different set of values. It has been suggested that practices such as handfasting and 'trial marriage' were ways by which each party could test the other's fertility at a time when children were an important economic asset.[268] Yet once again such arguments are at odds with the fact that a contract *per verba de praesenti* (or a contract *per verba de futuro* followed by sexual intercourse) was, if nothing else, legally binding[269] regardless of whether pregnancy followed. If they did not exchange any form of promise before embarking on sexual relations then they were not bound to each other, and it is difficult to see how this could be described as any

264 See e.g., J. Bailey, *Unquiet Lives: Marriage and Marriage Breakdown in England, 1660–1800* (Cambridge University Press, 2003), p. 178.

265 In 'Cardigan Weddings' (1792) 62 *Gentleman's Magazine* 325, Morris does state that the 'wedding for trial' can be ended by consent, but since in the next sentence he refers to the man leaving his 'mistress' and moving 'to a minework in some distant county', one is forced to wonder just how consensual such partings were.

266 O'Donovan, *Sexual Divisions*, p. 47; Parker, 'The Marriage Act 1753', 143 and *Informal Marriage*, p. 24; Diduck and Kaganas, *Family Law*, p. 61.

267 O'Donovan, *Sexual Divisions*.

268 Parker, 'The Marriage Act 1753', 141. Fertility does not, however, seem to be the point of the trial in Morris' account: see 'Cardigan Weddings' (1792) 62 *Gentleman's Magazine* 325, discussed above.

269 Assuming, of course, that it could be proved: see Chapter 2.

form of trial marriage.[270] The only way of testing fertility without incurring legal ties was thus to ensure that no promises were made. Such sexual experimentation, assuming that the woman was willing to yield without any promise of security, did not require the parties to share a home. If either party wished to test the other's fertility in advance of a binding commitment,[271] surreptitious sex would serve the purpose just as well as cohabitation – in fact, far better, since it would be far easier to deny the relationship if it did not turn out as desired. Of course, all this assumes that parties contemplating marriage *did* wish to test each other's fertility. One imagines that most would be aware of the difficulties in doing so. Pregnancy was no guarantee that a child would be born alive; still less, in an era of high infant mortality, did it ensure that the couple would have children to support them in their declining years.[272]

A final argument is that marriage was only important to those with property, and that therefore the poor had no reason to marry.[273] The argument, if articulated, would run something like this: couples had to marry according to the rites of the Church of England in order for the husband to be entitled to the wife's property and for the wife to be entitled to dower; but the majority of people did not own

[270] Indeed, the contemporary accounts of the alleged practice on the Isle of Portland of delaying marriage until the woman was pregnant did not use this terminology: see Smeaton's *History of the Eddystone Lighthouse Book*, quoted by J. Hutchins, *The History and Antiquities of the County of Dorset*, 3rd edn (Westminster, 1864), p. 811.

[271] This in itself remains a moot point: G. Wyatt, 'Bastardy and Prenuptial Pregnancy in a Cheshire Town during the Eighteenth Century' (1992) 49 *Local Population Studies* 49 notes that the pattern of prenuptial pregnancies does not suggest that couples were waiting for evidence of fertility before marrying; see also the discussion in P. E. H. Hair, 'Bridal Pregnancy in Earlier Rural England Further Examined' (1970) 24 *Population Studies* 59, 65–6, and B. Reay, *Popular Cultures in England 1550–1750* (London: Longman, 1998), p. 9.

[272] Even at the highest levels of society this could not be guaranteed: Queen Anne, for example, became pregnant seventeen times in seventeen years, but her only living child predeceased her, dying shortly after his eleventh birthday: M. Waller, *Ungrateful Daughters: the Stuart Princesses who Stole their Father's Crown* (London: Hodder & Stoughton, 2002), pp. 352–5.

[273] Wrigley, 'Clandestine Marriage in Tetbury', 19: 'couples of low status were more likely to have disregarded the church ceremony'. See also Parker, 'The Marriage Act 1753', 138; Stone, *Road to Divorce*, p. 69; Mansell *et al.*, *Critical Introduction*, pp. 92, 96; Diduck and Kaganas, *Family Law*, p. 59; J. Schellekens, 'Courtship, the Clandestine Marriage Act, and Illegitimate Fertility in England' (1995) 25 *Journal of Interdisciplinary History* 433.

property, therefore it can be inferred that the majority of people had no need to marry in church and did not do so. Evidence that should lead us to question whether a contract *per verba de praesenti* was actually a marriage at all is thereby turned on its head and used to argue for its popularity as a social practice. No thought is given to the other consequences of marriage, spiritual and social, and how they might affect the poor; nor is any evidence of actual practice adduced. Most spouses, then as now, would be surprised if told that marriage had no significance beyond its economic consequences.

In any case, it is important to have a more nuanced concept of poverty in the eighteenth century. There is an important distinction between the very poor – vagrants and others who lived on the fringes of society – and those who were simply poor in relative terms. The fact that the majority of the population did not belong to the 'property-owning-mortgaged-to-a-building-society democracy' of the late twentieth and twenty-first centuries does not mean that they were completely lacking in assets.[274] Even paupers might possess personal property, and the transmission of such items was an important consideration at a time when narrow margins might mean the difference between 'making shift' and absolute destitution.

But could the poor afford to marry? There were few indeed who were so poor that they could not afford the cost of a marriage by banns. Gough, writing at the end of the seventeenth century, noted that such a marriage would cost only a few shillings.[275] Some vicars exempted the poor from the payment of duties on marriages,[276] or even from the marriage fee,[277] and charities were set up to assist with marriage portions. In any case, marriage among the poorer classes was usually delayed until the parties had reached their late twenties, and both parties would have been saving their wages for a considerable period of time. Snell estimates that 'the average sum saved in the late eighteenth century between the two marrieds was

[274] The litigation over relatively small amounts of money bequeathed in wills provides another illustration of the importance of such sums for those who had little: see e.g., J. Addy, *Death, Money and the Vultures: Inheritance and Avarice, 1660–1750* (London: Routledge, 1992), ch. 7.

[275] 1s. for banns (plus extra 1s. for certificate), and 2s. 6d. for the marriage itself: R. Gough, *The History of Myddle* (D. Hey (ed.), Harmondsworth: Penguin, 1981), p. 46.

[276] S. King, 'Reconstructing Lives: the Poor, the Poor Law and Welfare in Calverly, 1650–1820' (1997) 22 *Social History* 318.

[277] Cressy, *Birth, Marriage and Death*, p. 366.

probably about £50–60'.[278] The expense of marrying was unlikely to be a deterrent: eighteenth-century weddings were celebrated far more modestly than modern extravaganzas. Moreover, since marriage would often be a trigger for financial assistance and gifts,[279] the modest outlay on the formalities would have paid dividends. Lewis Morris described the role of the bidder in his parish of Llanbadarn Fawr, which was to invite guests to the church wedding while hinting strongly that they should not come empty-handed: 'bring current money ... with cheese and butter'.[280] According to Morris, '[s]ometimes 30l. or 40l. is collected this way in money, cheese, and butter',[281] a haul sufficiently lucrative (assuming one liked cheese) as to provide an incentive to marry publicly. In any case, it was setting up home that constituted the major expense: if a couple could not afford to marry it was unlikely that they could afford to cohabit.

It might be more relevant to ask whether the lower classes could afford *not* to marry. It is important to remember that parish control permeated many aspects of daily life. A good reputation within the community was essential: as Tate has noted, the minister's 'certificate of good character [was] needed by a parishioner desiring to perform any one of a wide variety of actions, from leaving his employment in husbandry for labour in another parish, to opening an alehouse, or even a slaughterhouse'.[282] Those who lacked property also lacked independence: if one does not own the roof over one's head (security of tenure for tenants being some centuries away) one does not have the liberty to behave as one might wish.[283] It has

278 K. D. M. Snell, *Annals of the Labouring Poor: Social Change and Agrarian England, 1660–1900* (Cambridge University Press, 1985), p. 347.

279 Cressy, *Birth, Marriage and Death*, pp. 365–6. See also *The Annual Register, or a View of the History, Politicks, and Literature for the Year 1768* (London, 1768), p. 156, which reported ten marriages in Hendon: 'To each of the brides was given a wedding ring of ten shillings value; to each couple ten shillings more for their wedding dinner; for the purchase of some useful necessaries towards housekeeping, forty shillings; and the expences of the marriage fees defrayed for them.'

280 'Cardigan Weddings' (1791) 61 *Gentleman's Magazine* 1103.

281 'Cardigan Weddings' (1792) 62 *Gentleman's Magazine* 110.

282 Tate, *The Parish Chest*, p. 12.

283 See e.g., H. Perkin, *The Origins of Modern English Society 1780–1880* (London: Routledge & Kegan Paul, 1969), p. 34; S. Hindle, '"Without the Cry of any Neighbours": a Cumbrian Family and the Poor Law Authorities', ch. 6 in H. Berry and E. Foyster (eds.), *The Family in Early Modern England* (Cambridge University Press, 2007), p. 154.

been noted that 'poor men and women were disproportionately subject to the attention of the authorities (such as church, parish, magistracy, philanthropic, and local and central governments)'.[284] Charity might be contingent on good behaviour (such as attendance at church)[285] and denied to those whose behaviour did not meet the high standards of the donor. Margaret Spencer, for example, refused aid to two 'erring locals' on account of their sexual misconduct;[286] and Hindle similarly found that such misconduct might lead to the forfeiture of payments.[287] While parish relief or charitable donations were not the sole support for the vast majority of the poor, a significant proportion of the poor might find themselves dependent on the parish at some point in their lives.[288] It thus behoved them not to forfeit the good opinion of their neighbours.

The intersection of the poor laws and the law of marriage provided further reasons for the poor to marry. Sometimes the marriage might be brought about at the instigation and expense of parish officials. If a woman was pregnant and the putative father was from another parish, a little expenditure of time and effort to bring about the marriage might result in a considerable saving for the woman's parish in the long term, as responsibility for mother and child would be transferred to the husband's parish.[289]

But the poor laws might also have exercised a more subtle influence on the decision to marry. Under the laws of settlement, a wife took her husband's settlement, as did any children they might have. If misfortune befell the family, they would at least have the right to support from the same parish. By contrast, if the couple were not married the woman would retain her own settlement and any children would be settled where they were

284 A. Levene, T. Nutt, and S. Williams (eds.), *Illegitimacy in Britain, 1700–1920* (Basingstoke: Palgrave Macmillan, 2005), p. 3.

285 It has been noted how endowments 'might stipulate very restrictive codes of conduct on those identified as worthy objects of pity': S. Hindle, *On the Parish? The Micro-Politics of Poor Relief in Rural England, c. 1550–1750* (Oxford University Press, 2004), p. 105.

286 D. T. Andrew, 'Noblesse Oblige: Female Charity in an Age of Sentiment', ch. 14 in J. Brewer and S. Staves (eds.), *Early Modern Conceptions of Property* (London: Routledge, 1995), p. 284.

287 Hindle, *On the Parish?*, p. 387.

288 See P. Slack, *The English Poor Laws, 1531–1782* (Cambridge University Press, 1990), p. 25.

289 See e.g., *R* v. *Edwards* 8 Mod. 320; 88 ER 229, in which parish officials were indicted for conspiracy to marry a female pauper to a pauper from another parish.

born.[290] If the family fell on hard times, each family member would have to look to their parish of settlement for support, and those who did not have a settlement in the place where they were actually resident could be forcibly removed. Given the mobility of the population in the eighteenth century, it was all too likely that the unmarried family would be split up. Snell sums up the advantages of marriage for those who were or might be dependent on the parish:

> one's children would not be shunted off to their respective places of birth under the terms of bastardy settlement; the settlement of man and wife would become as one . . . ; terms of poor relief became more favourable; it was easier to gain aid for children under the poor law; employment and charity were offered more easily, and so on.[291]

In short, therefore, the reasons put forward as to why some couples may have preferred 'consensual marriage' are unconvincing and contradictory, and cannot survive the destruction of the purported evidential basis for such practices.

CONCLUSION

Disentangling the various myths surrounding concepts such as 'informal marriage' and 'common-law marriage' is no easy task. But it is clear that neither concept offers any assistance in understanding the way people set up home in the early eighteenth century. Both are concepts projected back into the eighteenth century by later generations of lawyers and historians, and there is no contemporary evidence for either practice. That a few couples flouted the convention of the time and cohabited outside marriage is clear. That they were not regarded as married by either law or society is equally clear. Indeed, given the penalties that attached to 'suspicious living' and the short-term nature of many such relationships they can at best be described as a *dysfunctional* alternative. The legal expectation that a marriage should be solemnised by a clergyman permeated society: a

290 *Whitechapel* v. *Stepney* (1689) Cart. 433. Under an Act of 1744, however, if a 'wandering' woman was delivered of a child, and then detained by the churchwardens and sent to a justice of peace, the child would take the mother's settlement: An Act to amend and make more effectual the Laws relating to Rogues, Vagabonds, and other idle and disorderly persons, 17 Geo. 2 c. 5, s. 24.

291 Snell, *Annals of the Labouring Poor*, p. 355.

contract *per verba de praesenti* was neither a full nor a functional alternative to a regular marriage.

This being the case, then the implications for the impact of the 1753 Act are profound. If couples did not marry by a simple exchange of consent even prior to 1754, then the impact of the Act would have been lessened, and the need for alternative or evasive practices to have developed after its passage is diminished. Couples from all strata of society had good reason to marry according to the rites of the Church of England, whether they wished to secure property rights or take advantage of the laws of settlement, or simply because they were God-fearing folk who respected the requirements of the Church. Of course, there were some who had objections to the rites of the Church of England: Protestant dissenters, Catholics, and non-Christians. How they married – and how the law regarded marriages conducted according to non-Anglican religious rites – will be considered in the next chapter.

4

THE LITTLE-CONSIDERED MARRIAGE PRACTICES OF NON-ANGLICANS

Since, as discussed in earlier chapters, it has been widely supposed among commentators that the mere exchange of consent constituted a valid marriage before March 1754, little attention has been paid to the status of marriages that were celebrated according to religious rites other than those of the Church of England. It has simply been assumed that dissenters did marry according to their own rites[1] and that such ceremonies were valid, if perhaps clandestine in the eyes of the law,[2] since they would have the same status as a contract *per verba de praesenti*.[3] Yet once it has been established that such a contract was not regarded as a marriage, questions about the status of such ceremonies inevitably arise. Were the marriages of Protestant dissenters treated as no more than contracts, or did the fact that the marriage was celebrated by a minister, albeit a dissenting one, make any difference to the status of such ceremonies? And what about Quaker marriages, which involved no minister, or those of Catholics, who were prevented from practising their faith freely, or those of non-Christians?[4]

1 This is implicit in L. Stone, *Road to Divorce: a History of the Making and Breaking of Marriage in England* (Oxford University Press, 1990), p. 128, who refers to the clergy looking forward 'to forcing the Dissenters back to the Anglican church to obtain legally valid marriages'.

2 See e.g., R. B. Outhwaite, *Clandestine Marriage in England, 1500–1850* (London: Hambledon Press, 1995), pp. 35–7, who includes 'conscientious objections' as a reason for marrying clandestinely.

3 B. L. Manning, *The Protestant Dissenting Deputies* (O. Greenwood (ed.), Cambridge University Press, 1952), p. 5.

4 The scope of this chapter is confined to Judao-Christian religions, since other religious minorities, such as Hindus and Muslims, barely registered in eighteenth-century society and not at all in the case law. There was a small black community in eighteenth-century England but there is evidence that many of them were Christian: see P. Edwards and J. Walvin, *Black Personalities in the Era of the Slave Trade* (London: Macmillan, 1983), pp. 30–1.

While there was no direct legislative provision stating that non-Anglican[5] ceremonies were *not* valid, there are certainly indications that the legislature assumed that this was the case: the penalties imposed on clandestine marriages in the late seventeenth century referred only to marriages celebrated by Anglican ministers;[6] moreover, although the same taxes were levied upon those who had gone through a Quaker, Catholic, or Jewish ceremony of marriage as upon those who had married according to Anglican rites, the legislation expressly distinguished between the two:

> all Quakers, Papists and Jews, or any other Persons who shall cohabit and live together as Man and Wife, shall pay the Duties of Marriage according to their respective Degrees as if they had been married according to the Church of England, to be collected and levied as other Marriages are. The Man so entering into such *pretended Marriage*, shall give Notice thereof ... within five days after, or forfeit 5l. to the King and Informer.[7]

The phrase 'entering into' and the specification of giving notice 'within five days' make it clear that this section was dealing with purported ceremonies of marriage, rather than cohabiting relationships. As if the reference to a 'pretended marriage' was not clear enough, the next section went on to add:

> Provided nothing in this Act shall make good such pretended Marriages, but they shall be in Law as the same force as before.[8]

So it is clear that such marriages were not regarded as 'good' in law, but what force in law did they actually have? And what about the marriages of Protestant dissenters such as Baptists, Presbyterians and Independents? Was it so obvious to contemporaries that such marriages were not valid that no mention need be made of them? Did such groups even celebrate marriage according to their own

[5] The term 'non-Anglican' is used for convenience to denote all ceremonies of marriage conducted according to religious rites other than those laid down in the Book of Common Prayer, although the concept of 'Anglicanism' is itself historically specific: see D. Rosman, *The Evolution of the English Churches, 1500–2000* (Cambridge University Press, 2003), p. 137.

[6] An Act for granting to his Majesty certain rates and duties upon marriages, births and burials, and upon batchelors and widowers, for the term of five years, for carrying on the war against France with vigour 1694, 6 & 7 W. 3 c. 6, s. 52; An Act for the enforcing the laws which restrain marriages without licence or banns, and for the better registering marriages, births and burials 1695, 7 & 8 W. 3 c. 35, s. 2, and see further Chapter 5.

[7] 6 & 7 W. 3 c. 6, s. 202 (emphasis added). [8] *Ibid.* s. 203.

rites? Or was the 1694 Act simply a poorly-drafted piece of legislation that accidentally exempted certain couples from the necessity of paying duties?

If one turns to judicial opinions for assistance, matters are no better. The case law is sparse and scattered over a hundred-year period that witnessed shifting attitudes to dissent.[9] Reported cases are often tantalisingly incomplete.[10] In addition, different issues were decided in different courts:[11] the ecclesiastical courts had exclusive jurisdiction over the question of whether a couple were *validly* married, but in certain contexts (such as the liability of a husband for his wife's debts) the common-law courts could proceed on the basis that a couple had gone through a ceremony of marriage, without enquiring further into the validity of the marriage.[12] As the judge explained in *R* v. *Paty*, the common-law court might be required to consider the existence of a marriage as an incidental matter, 'but their judgment will not bind the Ecclesiastical Court. And therefore, if such a marriage should be adjudged at law to be a good marriage, and yet afterwards the parties should be cited into the Ecclesiastical Court for living in fornication, and excommunicated, and taken upon the *capias excommunicatum*, this court could not discharge them upon a habeas corpus.'[13] This disregard could work both ways: the sentence of the ecclesiastical court was not necessarily binding if it dealt only indirectly with the issue as to whether the parties were married. '[w]here it was incidentally judged

[9] See generally M. R. Watts, *The Dissenters: from the Reformation to the French Revolution* (Oxford: Clarendon Press, 1978).

[10] See e.g., *Hutchinson* v. *Brookebanke* (1693) 3 Lev. 376; 83 ER 738, in which it was argued that after the Toleration Act of 1689, marriages between dissenters in licensed conventicles 'should be good and valid in law; and that no persons should be presented in the Ecclesiastical Court for nonconformity to the Church of England in such marriages; and that the interpretation of all statutes belongs to the common law'. The proceedings in the ecclesiastical court for fornication were subsequently stayed 'and it was agreed a prohibition should go, and that the plaintiff should declare upon the prohibition; so that upon a demurrer the law might be tried'. Unfortunately, it does not appear that the law was ever tested (see further 1 Hag. Con. (App.) 9n; 161 ER 637), and so the summary added in the English Reports ('[m]arriages in conventicles good') is therefore misleading.

[11] See e.g., *Betsworth* v. *Betsworth* (1648) Style 10; 82 ER 490; *Boyle* v. *Boyle* (1687) 3 Mod. 164; 87 ER 106.

[12] See further Chapter 2.

[13] (1705) 2 Ld. Raym. 1105; 92 ER 232, at 1111. A conviction for bigamy in the criminal courts was, however, deemed to be conclusive evidence of the unlawfulness of the second marriage: see e.g., *Boyle* v. *Boyle* (1687) 3 Mod. 164; 87 ER 106.

that the parties were not married, and upon that administration was denied, the court declared their opinion, that it could not be given in evidence in the Courts of Common Law, but where sentence is given in a principal cause it is otherwise'.[14] Thus, if the ecclesiastical court annulled a marriage, or granted a sentence of jactitation of marriage,[15] this was binding on the common-law courts. The result was that a marriage that was recognised for certain limited purposes by the common-law courts might not be regarded as valid by the ecclesiastical courts, since the two were answering different questions.

As Baker has reminded us, we should not look at past cases with the eyes of a modern lawyer, but rather try to view them in context.[16] Within an underdeveloped legal system, the courts attached more significance to the individual point to be resolved than to the articulation of general principles. As I noted in Chapter 1, the concept of cases as binding precedents was still some way off.[17] It is therefore necessary to abandon hope of being able to state the precise status of a non-Anglican ceremony in this period; the question is rather – what remedies would be available to those who had gone through such a ceremony?

Before we begin, it should be recognised that the broad term 'non-Anglican' encompasses a wide range of beliefs and practices, united largely by what they are not.[18] One would not necessarily expect the legal system to treat a Quaker marriage in the same way as one conducted according to Catholic or Jewish rites. It is therefore important to examine each sect or religion separately, to set it in its historical context, to consider its numerical strength, to

[14] *Clues* v. *Bathurst* (1733) Cas. T Hard. 11; 95 ER 7. See also *Blackham's Case* (1709) 1 Salk. 290; 91 ER 258.

[15] See e.g., *Jones* v. *Bow* (1692) Carthew 225; 90 ER 730, at 225–6, holding that as long as the sentence of jactitation was unrepealed, it was conclusive, 'and that the Temporal Courts must give credit to it until 'tis reversed, it being a matter of meer spiritual conusance'.

[16] J.H. Baker, *The Law's Two Bodies: Some Evidential Problems in English Legal History* (Oxford University Press, 2001), p. 57, noting that '[t]he historian must therefore be careful not to read into his sources a legal sophistication which is not there'.

[17] A.H. Manchester, *A Modern Legal History of England and Wales, 1750–1950* (London: Butterworths, 1980), p. 28; M. Lobban, *The Common Law and English Jurisprudence, 1760–1850* (Oxford: Clarendon Press, 1991), p. 82.

[18] See e.g., J. Hoppit, *A Land of Liberty? England 1689–1727* (Oxford: Clarendon Press, 2000), p. 219.

examine whether it developed any distinctive marriage practices and, if so, how such practices were treated by the law. The order in which different groups are considered is roughly chronological, moving from the Reformation and its impact on Catholics (as well as foreign Protestants), to the emergence of non-conformity within (and eventually outside) the Church of England in the seventeenth century, the readmission of Jews in the late seventeenth century, and the evangelical movement of the early eighteenth century. Each section also examines how legal treatment and social practices changed over time, since the approach adopted in one period might well be reversed in another: given the shifts that led to the Reformation, the Civil War and Commonwealth, the Restoration, and the Revolution of 1688, to expect consistency is to be doomed to disappointment.

CATHOLICS

Over the course of the sixteenth century, as England oscillated between Catholicism and Protestantism, that which had been the norm became outlawed.[19] By the end of the century Catholic rites had not only been displaced from the parish church but had become positively dangerous to observe.[20] 'Harbouring' a Catholic priest was an offence in itself.[21] And in the wake of the abortive Gunpowder Plot, [22] Catholics were subjected to new restrictions:

[19] On the effect of such oscillations at parish level, see E. Duffy, *The Voices of Morebath: Reformation and Rebellion in an English Village* (Yale University Press, 2001).

[20] For a review of the penal laws of the sixteenth and seventeenth centuries, see J. A. Williams, 'English Catholicism under Charles II: the Legal Position' (1963) 7 *Recusant History* 123. There was some relaxation of the official stance in the 1630s (see M. Questier, 'Arminianism, Catholicism and Puritanism in England During the 1630s' (2006) 49 *Historical Journal* 53), but the perceived sympathy of the Caroline court towards Catholicism was one of the factors that sparked opposition, and ultimately civil war, and the victorious Parliamentarians had a very different attitude towards Catholics (see e.g., D. L. Smith, 'Oliver Cromwell, the First Protectorate Parliament and Religious Reform' (2000) 19 *Parliamentary History* 38).

[21] See e.g., *Plumpton* v. *Scroope* (1631), in which the bride's father was examined regarding the 'harbouring' of the Catholic priest who had conducted the ceremony 'but said that he did not know him to be a popish priest and did not see him solemnize the marriage'. S. R. Gardiner (ed.), *Reports of Cases in the Courts of Star Chamber and High Commission* (Camden Society, 1886), p. 55.

[22] A. Fraser, *The Gunpowder Plot: Terror and Faith in 1605* (London: Weidenfeld & Nicholson, 1996).

legislation passed in 1606[23] required Catholics to be baptised, married, and buried in the parish church.[24] This spelt out the penalties that would attach to those who failed to marry according to the rites of the Church of England: a husband would lose all rights to his wife's land (and if she had no land would 'forfeit and lose one hundred pounds'), while a wife would not be entitled to dower or jointure.[25] It was therefore the explicit intention of such legislation that a Catholic wedding should not be a full alternative to marriage in the Church of England.[26]

The only detailed study of the status of Catholic marriages that has been published to date focused on cases decided in the early seventeenth century.[27] In these, legal recognition was accorded to such marriages, but all of these were either marriages celebrated by priests who had been ordained during the reign of the Catholic Mary, Elizabeth's predecessor;[28] or ones where the status of the celebrant was left ambiguous,[29] which were decided at a time when there was increasing official sympathy for Catholics. They are therefore not a good guide to the way in which Catholic marriages were treated a hundred years later.

But there are at least some eighteenth-century cases in the common-law courts where a Catholic marriage did have legal consequences – or, rather, in which no attention appears to have been paid to the Catholic nature of the ceremony. In *Hilliard* v. *Phaly*, a dispute concerning entitlement to land, the fact that a couple had cohabited and been reputed to be husband and wife led the jury to hold that they had married before the birth of the child whose title was in question, despite the evidence that the only

23 An Act to prevent and avoid dangers which grow by popish recusants, 3 Jac. 1 c. 5.

24 The terms of the legislation suggest that this was not the practice at the time: 'popish recusants are not usually married, nor their children christened, nor themselves buried according to the law of the Church of England, but the same are done superstitiously by popish persons in secret' (s. 13).

25 Section 13.

26 In practice, the extent to which anti-Catholic legislation was actually enforced has been doubted: see Rosman, *Evolution of the English Churches*, p. 131; J. A. Williams, *Catholic Recusancy in Wiltshire, 1660–1791* (Catholic Record Society, 1968), p. 3.

27 D. H. Aveling, 'The Marriages of Catholic Recusants, 1559–1642' (1963) 14 *Journal of Ecclesiastical History* 68, 78–9.

28 Indeed, had such ordinations not been regarded as valid many parish priests would have required reordination.

29 Aveling, 'The Marriages of Catholic Recusants', 81–2.

ceremony of marriage that had taken place had been conducted by a Catholic priest.[30] However, the Lord Chancellor did express some dissatisfaction with the result, in particular the fact that certain evidence (including the fact that the parties had been prosecuted by the ecclesiastical courts for fornication, and that the 'husband' had paid a sum of money in commutation of penance) had been rejected. One point worthy of note in this case is that the priest in question was part of the retinue of the Portuguese ambassador: such priests were in the country on a regular footing and were not liable to prosecution.[31] This was also the case in *R* v. *Feilding*,[32] in which Robert (otherwise known as 'Handsome' or 'Beau') Feilding was convicted of bigamy, having apparently gone through a Catholic ceremony of marriage with one woman, then 'married' the Duchess of Cleveland (formerly Barbara Palmer, mistress to Charles II). The first ceremony had been conducted by a priest in the envoy of a foreign emperor,[33] although the bride had needed reassurance that the priest was in orders and able to marry them.[34] The report of the judgment makes no mention of the Catholic nature of the first marriage: either it was not relevant, or the high profile of the parties and the flagrant behaviour of the notorious Feilding – marrying two women only months apart – determined the jury in favour of a conviction.

The special status of the priest in these cases would also explain why a different result was achieved in another alleged case of bigamy in 1738. James Lyon's first marriage to Mary Williams had taken place in a private house before an ordinary Roman Catholic priest according to the rites of the Church of Rome.[35] The parties subsequently lived together and Mary 'went for his Wife with every one'. (As one of the witnesses told the court, 'I believe she was his Wife – else she would not have taken the Usage she had from him.')[36] The second 'wife' was allowed to give evidence as to her marriage, which implied that the first marriage was regarded as valid and the second 'wife' therefore no wife at all

[30] (1723) 8 Mod. 180; 88 ER 132.
[31] There is evidence that embassy chapels did celebrate marriages before 1754: see e.g., *The Registers of the Venetian Chapel in London* (London: Catholic Family History Society, 1996). On the position after 1754, see Chapter 9.
[32] (1706) 14 State Trials 1327.
[33] *R* v. *Feilding* (1706) 14 State Trials 1327, at 1341. [34] *Ibid.* at 1335.
[35] *The Proceedings of the Old Bailey*, 6 December 1738, p. 13. [36] *Ibid.* pp. 14–15.

and able to give evidence;[37] this, however, prompted a protest from counsel:

> as all Acts constituting Felonies are to be construed strictly, so a Marriage, strictly and according to the Laws, must be a Marriage according to the Ceremony of the Church of England, and it appearing that there had not been such a Marriage, but one by a Popish Priest, it was submitted, that they had not incontestibly established the first Marriage, nor had they so established it, as to be intituled to produce the second Wife.[38]

Despite this protest, the second 'wife' was admitted and gave evidence that she had married the accused in church, by licence, and that she had brought the prosecution upon learning of the prior marriage from the first wife's brother. Yet James was nonetheless acquitted of bigamy, and it is difficult to see upon what ground this could have been save for the nature of the first, Catholic ceremony.[39] In any case, what is clear is that there was considerable uncertainty as to the legal status of a Catholic marriage in this context, even counsel for the prosecution expressing his doubts as to its sufficiency.

> The Question now is, Concerning a Marriage De Jure and De Facto; Whether a Marriage by a Popish Priest is a Marriage De Jure? She is a Wife De Facto – she has liv'd with him as such, and he has acknowledged her for his Wife; but, I must own, I am not prepared to produce particular Cases to this Purpose.[40]

In the ecclesiastical courts, by contrast, matters were more straightforward. Usefully, a case decided immediately before the Clandestine Marriages Act, in 1752, explains exactly why the ordained status of a Catholic priest[41] did not secure the validity of marriages conducted according to Catholic rites. A priest 'popishly ordained' who converted to the Church of England did not need to be reordained. On that reasoning, a marriage celebrated by such a priest *according to the rites of the Church of England* was

[37] The true wife, by contrast, would not be entitled to give evidence: see e.g., *Broughton* v. *Harpur* (1707) 2 Ld. Raym. 752; 92 ER 2.

[38] *The Proceedings of the Old Bailey*, 6 December 1738, p. 15.

[39] A later commentator suggested that it was because the parties did not understand the Latin service, but it is clear from the evidence that the actual exchange of vows was in English, even if the prayers were in Latin: C. Sprengel Greaves, *Russell on Crimes and Misdemeanors*, 3rd edn (London: Saunders and Benning, 1843), p. 190.

[40] *The Proceedings of the Old Bailey*, 6 December 1738, p. 15.

[41] See e.g., R. Burn, *Ecclesiastical Law* (London, 1763), vol. II, p. 30.

accorded full legal recognition.[42] But a ceremony of marriage conducted by a Catholic priest 'after the Romish ritual' was not: as the judge put it, 'I much doubt whether a marriage in England by a Romish priest after the Romish ritual would be deemed a perfect marriage in this country ... [t]he Roman ritual not being the same with ours, such a ceremony is nothing more than a contract.'[43] And it was very clear that in his view a contract did not constitute a marriage.[44] It was held in this case that the action for restitution of conjugal rights would not be available to those who had married in this way; and there is also evidence that those who married according to Catholic rites were punished by the ecclesiastical courts for fornication.[45]

But how far did such attitudes deter Catholics from celebrating marriages according to their own religious rites? There were certainly contrary pressures from Catholic missioners. One early seventeenth-century treatise condemned even attendance at Protestant weddings, regarding as excommunicated those '"schismatici", who claim to believe all that the Catholic Church teaches and yet who go to the Protestant church'.[46] Priests taught that 'baptism, marriage and burial were ... matters in which there could be no communing with heretics'.[47] Of course, the very vehemence of such protests suggests some Catholics may have been more pragmatic than principled. While there is evidence that many Catholics continued to marry according to their own religious rites,[48] it is clear that some married in the Church of England.[49] After all, the

[42] *Scrimshire* v. *Scrimshire* (1752) 2 Hag. Con. 395; 161 ER 782, at 399.

[43] *Ibid.* at 401–2. [44] *Ibid.* at 401, see further Chapter 2.

[45] See e.g., *Hilliard* v. *Phaly* (1723) 8 Mod. 180; 88 ER 132.

[46] Aveling, 'The Marriages of Catholic Recusants', 71.

[47] J. Bossy, *The English Catholic Community, 1570–1850* (London: Darton, Longman & Todd, 1975), p. 133.

[48] D. J. Steel and E. R. Samuel, *National Index of Parish Registers*, vol. III, *Sources for Roman Catholic and Jewish Genealogy and Family History* (Chichester: Phillimore & Co, 1974), p. 860; Aveling, 'The Marriages of Catholic Recusants'; A. Wilcox, 'Catholics in Parish Registers: Wilcox and Wilcoxon of Maer, Staffordshire' (2003) 8 *Catholic Ancestor* 221 (my thanks to Gerard Wilcox for this reference).

[49] See e.g., V. T. J. Arkell, 'An Enquiry into the Frequency of the Parochial Registration of Catholics in a 17th Century Warwickshire Parish' (1972) 9 *Local Population Studies* 23, 28; M. Wanklyn, 'Catholics in the Village Community: Madeley, Shropshire, 1630–1770', ch. 10 in M. B. Rowlands (ed.), *English Catholics of Parish and Town, 1558–1778* (Catholic Record Society, 1999); Wilcox, 'Catholics in Parish Registers'.

post-Reformation marriage service was not so dissimilar to previous rites,[50] and many churches would have been the site of Catholic worship for centuries.[51] Besides, the importance of safeguarding property rights meant that couples belonging to the gentry or aristocracy had particular reason to go through an Anglican ceremony.[52]

In assessing the significance of Catholic weddings as a functional alternative to marriage in the Church of England it should be borne in mind that by the start of the eighteenth century Catholicism was very much a minority religion. Clusters of Catholics were still to be found in the vicinity of embassy chapels in London, where they could 'meet for worship overtly and regularly',[53] and where manors continued to be held by old Catholic families,[54] but overall numbers were low. Many were isolated: in 1743, when Archbishop Herring sought information on the extent of dissent in Yorkshire, 262 of the 903 parishes required to make a return reported that at least one Catholic family resided in the parish but only 59 suggested that there was a regular congregation.[55] Overall, at the time that the 1753 Act was passed Catholics constituted perhaps only 1 per cent of the population.[56] Even if *all* Catholics had married according to their own rites alone, such weddings would not have constituted a significant number, and if one takes into account

[50] See K. Stevenson, *Nuptial Blessing: a Study of Christian Marriage Rites* (London: SPCK, 1982), pp. 137–41 for an account of the changes that were made by the 1549 and 1552 Prayer Books.

[51] On conformity among the Catholic community more generally, see P. Virgin, *The Church in an Age of Negligence: Ecclesiastical Structure and Problems of Church Reform, 1700–1840* (Cambridge: James Clarke & Co., 1989), p. 17.

[52] See e.g., Steel and Samuel, *Sources for Roman Catholic and Jewish Genealogy and Family History*, p. 860, who suggests that many did so.

[53] G. Rupp, *Religion in England 1688–1791* (Oxford: Clarendon Press, 1986), p. 191.

[54] G. Huelin, 'Some Early Eighteenth Century Roman Catholic Recusants' (1956) 7 *Journal of Ecclesiastical History* 61; see also Bossy, *The English Catholic Community*, p. 175, and C. Haydon, 'The Church in the Kineton Deanery of the Diocese of Worcester, c. 1660-c.1800' in J. Gregory and J. Chamberlain (eds.), *The National Church in Local Perspective: the Church of England and the Regions, 1660–1800* (Woodbridge: Boydell Press, 2003), p. 167.

[55] S. L. Ollard and P. C. Walker (eds.), *Archbishop Herring's Visitation Returns, 1743* (Yorkshire Archaeological Society Record Series vol. 71, 1927).

[56] Steel and Samuel, *Sources for Roman Catholic and Jewish Genealogy and Family History*, p. 832.

the prevalence of inter-marriage[57] and the number who sought solemnisation in the Church of England, the numbers of those who married solely according to Catholic rites would have been even smaller.

REFUGEE PROTESTANTS

Greater latitude had always been shown to the victims of foreign persecution than to domestic dissent. The endorsement of Protestantism at an official level in the sixteenth century attracted Protestants who had been suffering persecution on the Continent, particularly in the wake of the St Bartholomew's Day massacre of 1572.[58] It has been estimated that there were between 10,000 and 15,000 foreign Protestants present in England at the end of the sixteenth century.[59] Far greater numbers (between 80,000 and 100,000) came to England after the revocation of the Edict of Nantes in 1685, but many went on to settle elsewhere.[60] After this, the number of such immigrants plunged 'to no more than 100 in 1695 and to an insignificant trickle after the turn of the century'.[61]

Protestant refugees were specifically exempted from the Act of Uniformity, which meant that they did not need to attend Church of England services and were permitted to establish their own congregations.[62] There is evidence that these congregations also celebrated their own marriages:[63] when registers were yielded up to the Commissioners appointed to examine non-parochial registers in 1838, twenty-four of the thirty-seven Walloon and French churches whose registers had survived produced ones

[57] M. Galgano, 'Out of the Mainstream: Catholic and Quaker Women in the Restoration Northwest', ch. 8 in R. S. Dunn and M. M. Dunn (eds.), *The World of William Penn* (Philadelphia: University of Pennsylvania Press, 1986), p. 120.

[58] See D. Stevens, *UK Asylum Law and Policy: Historical and Contemporary Perspectives* (London: Sweet & Maxwell, 2004), p. 6.

[59] R. Gwynn, *Huguenot Heritage: the History and Contribution of the Huguenots in Britain* (London: Routledge & Kegan Paul, 1985), pp. 29, 33.

[60] Gwynn, *Huguenot Heritage*, p. 35.

[61] D. Desert, 'The Strangers and the Established Church' (2003) 27 *Proceedings of the Huguenot Society of Great Britain and Ireland* 1, 8–9.

[62] Act of Uniformity 1662, 14 Car. 2 c. 4, s. 11. On the treatment of Huguenot churches, see Gwynn, *Huguenot Heritage*.

[63] There is also evidence that some members of the congregation married in Anglican churches: see Gwynn, *Huguenot Heritage*, p. 164.

that included marriages taking place before 1754.[64] Yet the marriages celebrated in these churches were hardly distinguishable from those solemnised in Anglican churches: they were preceded by the calling of banns or the obtaining of a licence,[65] and the credentials of the celebrant would have been recognised by the Anglican authorities.

But even this did not prevent challenges to the status of such marriages. In 1676 the Consistory Court excommunicated a couple for marrying clandestinely in the French church in Canterbury, but '[t]he outcome merely showed that the foreign churches were well-placed to maintain their own ways' as the bishop eventually agreed that they were exempt and so not liable to punishment.[66] It would also appear that this particular marriage was only challenged because the parties were not refugees but second- or perhaps even third-generation immigrants.[67] But in other contexts the status of a marriage celebrated according to such rites was no more certain than that of a Catholic ceremony. Half a century later, in 1724, the status of a marriage celebrated in one of the French churches came under consideration in a bigamy case. There was ample evidence of the two ceremonies, but since the first had been performed 'by a Minister of the French Church of the Presbyterian Persuasion'[68] there was some doubt as to whether the accused could be convicted. The point was reserved for the determination of the judges, and unfortunately there is no information as to the outcome of the case. But again, what is clear is the uncertainty that attached even to marriages of this kind.

Whatever the precise legal status of marriages in a foreign Protestant church, they were clearly a functional alternative for

[64] *Report of the Commissioners Appointed to Inquire into the State, Custody, and Authenticity of Registers or Records of Births or Baptisms, Deaths or Burials, and Marriages in England and Wales, other than the Parochial Registers* (1838), Appendix A. For an account of such a marriage, see C. Jackson (ed.), *The Diary of Abraham de la Pryme* (Publications of the Surtees Society vol. 54, 1869), p. 3, noting the marriage of the diarist's parents 'in the Dutch congregation in the chapple at Santoft'.

[65] See e.g., *Hussare's Case, The Proceedings of the Old Bailey*, 15 April 1724.

[66] R. Gwynn, 'Marital Problems and the Position of Women in the French Church of London in the Later Seventeenth Century' (1995) 26 *Proceedings of the Huguenot Society of Great Britain and Ireland* 214, 215.

[67] Gwynn, *Huguenot Heritage*, p. 164.

[68] At the French church in Spitalfields: *Hussare's Case, The Proceedings of the Old Bailey*, 15 April 1724, p. 4.

those individuals who chose to marry in this way. But such individuals were a diminishing number even before 1754. Half of the twenty-four surviving registers commence in the 1680s or 1690s, reflecting the influx of refugees in that period, but more than one-third of those end over a decade before the 1753 Act came into force. This fall may be due in part to legislation passed in the 1690s in an attempt to regulate marriages;[69] it may also reflect the growing assimilation of refugee families into English society.[70]

PRESBYTERIAN, BAPTIST AND INDEPENDENT

If the reforms of the sixteenth century drove devoted Catholics from the parish church, they also failed to please some of the more radical Protestants. Watts describes the sixteenth-century Church of England as 'neither Protestant nor Catholic, but something in between'.[71] The term 'Separatists' described those 'small groups of extreme Protestants who, impatient of Puritan hopes of reforming the Church of England from within, repudiated the ordinances and disciplines of the established church and met in secret conventicles in the reigns of Elizabeth I and the early Stuarts'.[72] Their view was that marriage was a private matter, and that the consent of the parties would suffice.[73] More numerous, however, were those who tried to work for reform from within: it is important to bear in mind that non-conformism in the early seventeenth century (like evangelism a hundred years later) was a movement *within* the Church of England.[74] In an age when so much attention is paid to the divisiveness of religious differences, it is easy to overlook the way in which people may participate in a communal act of worship while maintaining small but significant differences.[75] The degree of non-conformity in any given parish may have depended on the

69 See Gwynn, *Huguenot Heritage*, p. 162, and for the terms of the legislation see Chapter 5.
70 See Gwynn, *Huguenot Heritage*, p. 163.
71 Watts, *The Dissenters*, p. 15. 72 *Ibid.* p. 1.
73 See e.g., E. J. Carlson, *Marriage and the English Reformation* (Oxford: Blackwell, 1994), p. 48; C. Hill, *The World Turned Upside Down* (London: Temple Smith, 1972; Penguin 1991), p. 311.
74 See e.g., Rosman, *Evolution of the English Churches*, p. 64.
75 See e.g., D. Purkiss, *The English Civil War: a People's History* (London: Harper Perennial, 2007), p. 145; Rosman, *Evolution of the English Churches*, p. 64.

form of conformity that was adopted.[76] Non-conformists may have shared with the Separatists a wish to marry in a form that was less 'popish' than that laid down in the Prayer Book, but while this may have been a factor influencing couples' choice of church,[77] they would have had no reason to marry outside the Church of England.

It is convenient to consider Presbyterians, Baptists, and Independents (otherwise known as Congregationalists) together: partly because these labels were sometimes used interchangeably,[78] or indeed changed according to theological divisions,[79] and partly because in the eighteenth century these three groups co-operated to form the 'Three Denominations'.[80] Presbyterian and Independent ideas on the appropriate form that marriage should take had a significant influence on the law of marriage in the 1640s and 1650s.[81] For this brief period, what had been radical became prescribed,[82] and it was those adherents to the old Church of England who were forced to seek out alternative rites. At the Restoration, however, these initiatives were reversed, and the distinction between conformity and non-conformity was sharpened.[83] Episcopal ordination became compulsory for all Anglican clergymen,[84] those whose ideas did not match those of the new regime were expelled from their livings,[85] and non-conformists were faced with a choice between separation (with the possibility of persecution)[86] and conformity. Yet there was still no hard-and-fast

[76] See e.g., N. J. G. Pounds, *A History of the English Parish* (Cambridge University Press, 2000), p. 264, who notes that '[t]here were Puritans who would have been at home in one parish church but repelled by the services in another which had adopted Laudian practices'.

[77] See e.g., Purkiss, *The English Civil War*, p. 272.

[78] See e.g., Rosman, *Evolution of the English Churches*, p. 55. The distinctions are explored by Rupp, *Religion in England*, chs. 6–8.

[79] See e.g., A. Warne, *Church and Society in Eighteenth Century Devon* (Newton Abbot: David and Charles, 1969), p. 102.

[80] Manning, *The Protestant Dissenting Deputies*, p. 2.

[81] See e.g., Hill, *The World Turned Upside Down*, p. 311.

[82] In the pared-down service provided by the Directory of Worship and the even more attenuated civil marriage required during the Commonwealth: see further Chapter 5.

[83] Rosman, *Evolution of the English Churches*, p. 105.

[84] Those who had been 'ordained by their fellow presbyters' were required 'to seek reordination at the hands of a bishop': Watts, *The Dissenters*, pp. 218–19. See also Rosman, *Evolution of the English Churches*, p. 105.

[85] M. Ashley, *England in the Seventeenth Century, 1603–1714* (London: Penguin, 1952), p. 126; Watts, *The Dissenters*, p. 219.

[86] See Watts, *The Dissenters*, pp. 221–57.

division into 'church' and 'chapel': Whiteman suggests that there 'was much partial conformity on the part of Presbyterians and often Independents'[87] and that attendance at the parish church might fluctuate not only in response to the changing political situation but also more local factors such as 'the popularity or otherwise of the incumbent or his curate as a preacher'.[88] Even when freedom of worship was eventually established under the Toleration Act of 1689 (at least for Protestant dissenters who believed in the Trinity),[89] 'occasional conformity' had its advantages.[90]

One might expect those who practised 'occasional conformity' to gain certain social and legal advantages to be equally pragmatic when it came to the one-off rite of marriage. There is certainly little evidence that Presbyterians, Baptists or Independents regularly conducted their own marriage ceremonies. Of the 505 congregations belonging to the Three Denominations founded prior to 1754, only 8 produced marriage registers relating to that period when requested by the 1838 Commission.[91] There may, of course, have been other records that had not survived: only 123 congregations had *any* surviving records from the period. But even if we take the lower figure of 123, only around 6 per cent of congregations produced marriage registers, and there seems no reason why these registers would be less likely to survive than those of baptisms or burials. Indeed, as we have seen, twenty-four of the thirty-seven Walloon and French churches produced registers of marriage from the period. All this suggests that the low number of surviving registers reflected actual practice within the Three Denominations.[92]

87 A. Whiteman (ed.), *The Compton Census of 1676: a Critical Edition* (London: British Academy, 1986), p. xxxvii.

88 *Ibid.* See also P. Crawford, *Blood, Bodies and Families in Early Modern England* (London: Pearson Education Ltd, 2004), p. 181, noting how a minister ejected in 1662 continued to attend services in the Church of England.

89 See Watts, *The Dissenters*, p. 259.

90 For example, it was a prerequisite for local officials to receive communion in the Church of England: 13 Car. 2 c. 1, s. 9. And, as P. Earle, *The Making of the English Middle Class: Business, Society and Family Life in London, 1660–1730* (London: Methuen, 1989) notes, serving parish offices was 'virtually a precondition of social progress'.

91 *Report of the Commissioners*, Appendix B. A further two of the registers listed as including marriages appear to record only baptisms and burials: Family Records Centre, RG4/2055 (Kingsbury Episcopi) and RG4/3019 (Bridlington Baptist).

92 Others may exist that were not submitted to the Commission, but I have traced only one (relating to Baptist marriages celebrated at Hamsterley) and it records only seven marriages: Society of Genealogists DU/REG/90318/1.

In addition, the eight surviving registers do not suggest that the celebration of marriage in meeting-houses was a regular occurrence ended only by the 1753 Act. Seven end long before 1754 and record only a small number of marriages.[93] The eighth, the register of the Independent chapel in West Street, Dorking, merely records '[p]ersons belonging to the Dissenting Congregation of Dorking marry'd since ye year 1729'.[94] There is no indication that these marriages actually took place in the chapel, and upon investigation it is clear that they did not: of the thirty-one couples who were recorded in the West Street register prior to 25 March 1754, marriages in the Anglican church have been traced for almost 80 per cent.[95] Unfortunately the quality of the register – both in terms of the completeness of the information recorded and the legibility of the handwriting – means that it has not been possible to trace marriages for all of the couples recorded, but there is no reason to suppose that those whose names were incomplete or illegible were any less likely to marry in church.

That *some* marriages were celebrated by dissenters according to their own rites seems clear: the register of the Presbyterian chapel in Flowergate in Whitby states that 'William Hick and Isabel married before a congregation, in the house of Robert Pennock'.[96] But only a minority of dissenters married in this way. Set against the paucity of evidence of non-compliance is ample and positive evidence that the majority of Protestant dissenters married in the Church of England. Caffyn's study of Sussex Baptists, for

[93] Hindley, Wigan, fifteen marriages 1644–77 (Family Record Centre RG4/2115); Stepney Congregational Meeting, Bull Lane, forty marriages 1646–77 (FRC RG4/4414); Stockton-on-Tees Presbyterian chapel, forty-four marriages 1688–1704 (SOG, DU/REG/9031811); Rowell Independent chapel, twenty-six marriages, 1692–1702 (FRC RG4/2476); Scarborough Presbyterian meeting-house, eighteen marriages 1703–20 (FRC RG4/3660); Flowergate, Whitby, Presbyterian chapel, three marriages 1706–19 (Public Record Office RG 4/2020). I have not been able to trace the register of Burlington Zion chapel, but according to the *Report of the Commissioners* it only covers an eight-year period, between 1708 and 1716.

[94] PRO RG 4/3102.

[95] Fourteen couples had married in the Anglican church of St Martin's in Dorking, a further seven elsewhere in Surrey, and at least three in London.

[96] PRO RG 4/2020. See also the certificate of the first Baptist marriage to be celebrated at Melbourne, in 1753, which contains a full account of the ceremony and is signed by no fewer than twenty-two witnesses: T. J. Budge, *Melbourne Baptists: the Story of Two Hundred Years in Melbourne, Derbyshire* (London: Carey Kingsgate Press Ltd, 1951), p. 10.

example, found that at least 70 per cent of his sample could be proved to have married in the Church of England in the late seventeenth and early eighteenth centuries.[97] The percentage of marriages traced for Baptist leaders was even higher, at 79 per cent.[98] While the sample was relatively small, one might have expected couples with this background to be most likely to eschew the Anglican rites.[99] And, as Caffyn points out, these figures must be taken as the minimum, since it is entirely possible that other marriages may not have been traced, given the poor recording of the times and the tendency for couples to marry in parishes to which they did not belong.[100] It is worth bearing in mind that Caffyn was searching without the aid of modern electronic databases: were his study to be revisited it is likely that an even higher proportion would be traced.

Caffyn's findings are confirmed by a number of case studies. The Cardington listing of 1782, discussed in Chapter 3, describes forty-six inhabitants as dissenters. Of these, fourteen had married before the 1753 Act, all of them according to Anglican rites. In Warwickshire, meanwhile, the incumbent of St Nicholas in Kenilworth on occasion noted the birth of children who were not brought to church to be baptised: of the twenty-one fathers listed, fourteen were specifically identified as dissenters, yet still Anglican marriages have been traced for two-thirds of these.[101]

97 J. Caffyn, *Sussex Believers: Baptist Marriage in the 17th and 18th centuries* (Worthing: Churchman Publishing, 1988), p. 101. The three families on which the study was based had a long history of involvement with the Baptist community, and 96 per cent of their members married other Baptists: p. 99.

98 Caffyn, *Sussex Believers*, p. 103.

99 In addition, Baptists are thought to have been *more* likely to solemnise their own marriages than were the other two denominations, partly because of their tradition of inter-marriage: D. J. Steel, *National Index of Parish Registers*, vol. II, *Sources for Nonconformist Genealogy and Family History* (Chichester: Phillimore & Co. Ltd, 1973), p. 551.

100 Caffyn, *Sussex Believers*, p. 101. This possibility undermines Sharpe's conclusion that the fall in the number of marriages celebrated in Colyton Church in the second half of the seventeenth century can be attributed to the prevalence of dissent in the parish (see P. Sharpe, 'Locating the "Missing Marryers" in Colyton, 1660–1750' (1992) 48 *Local Population Studies* 49), since she only searched Colyton's nine neighbouring parishes and the marriage licences. As earlier case studies of Kilsby have shown, it may be necessary to look further afield: see Chapter 3.

101 See H. J. Powell, *A Parson and his Flock: Kenilworth 1690–1740* (Kenilworth, 1981), p. 11; Warwick Record Office DR0101/2 (register of baptisms, marriages and burials 1653–1715); DR0101/2 (register of baptisms, marriages and burials

A larger-scale study of 119 couples[102] whose children's baptisms were recorded in the register[103] of the Independent chapel at Kettering in Northamptonshire between 1744 and 1754 was carried out: marriages in the Anglican church have been traced for at least 69 per cent, and possibly for as many as 87 per cent.[104]

Dissenters who married in this way had the sanction, if not the blessing, of their leaders. The line taken by Baptist leaders, for example, shows that they accepted the necessity of church marriage, if grudgingly: the General Assembly conceded in 1697 that Baptists could be married by an Anglican minister – as long as the minister omitted 'the Ceremonial part thereof respecting Divine Worship'.[105] Those that took a stricter line 'had to pay a heavy price in falling numbers':[106] in the first half of the eighteenth century the Arnesby Particular Baptist Church 'automatically excommunicated those who married unbelievers and those who were married in the parish church, so that by 1751 this once flourishing church was bemoaning that "our number is but few and circumstances low"'.[107]

There were of course grumblings about this state of affairs. One contemporary critic of Anglican ritual demanded to know 'what means the ceremony of the ring in marriage? Why are we forced not only to use it, but to use it in the name of the Father, and of the Son, and of the Holy Ghost?'[108] But such complaints simply illustrate that Baptists did feel compelled to go through an Anglican

1715–64). This relatively low percentage reflects the lack of detail provided: in only four cases is the mother's name supplied and the spelling of the names is highly variable.

102 This excludes eight cases in which the mother of the child was not named and it was therefore impossible to confirm whether or not a marriage had taken place.

103 A. R. Bax, *Northamptonshire Registers*, vol. 1, SOG NH/R39.

104 Inevitably, there are couples whose surname is too common to confirm a potential match, as well as a number for whom the evidence suggests that a mistake may have been made in recording the names.

105 W. T. Whitley, *Minutes of the General Assembly of the General Baptist Churches in England* (London: Baptist Historical Society, 1908), vol. I, p. 50. On other matters a far stricter line was taken: Baptists were in theory forbidden to join in worship with other churches, and marriage with a non-Baptist was deemed highly undesirable (see W. T. Whitley, *A History of British Baptists* (London: Charles Griffin & Co. Ltd, 1923), p. 169).

106 Watts, *The Dissenters*, p. 330. 107 *Ibid.*

108 T. Crosby, *The History of the English Baptists, from the Reformation to the Beginning of the Reign of King George I* (London, 1738–40), vol. IV, p. xvii.

ceremony, and to comply with the service as set out in the Book of Common Prayer.[109]

The evidence is therefore clear, but what is the explanation for this tendency among dissenters to marry in the Anglican church? The obvious and most likely explanation is the uncertainty that existed regarding the status of dissenters' marriages. Once again, what is clear is that the common-law courts were not quite sure how to treat dissenters' marriages but were not willing to grant them the same status as a marriage celebrated by an ordained clergyman.[110] The struggle of the courts to accommodate competing theories is well illustrated by the report of *Wigmore's Case*:

> In the case of a Dissenter, married to a woman by a minister of the congregation, who was not in orders; it is said, that this marriage was not a nullity, because by the law of nature the contract is binding and sufficient; for though the positive law of man ordains that marriages shall be made by a priest, that law only makes this marriage irregular, and not expresly [*sic*] void: but marriages ought to be solemnized according to the rites of the Church of England, to intitle the privileges attending legal marriage, as dower, thirds, &c.[111]

Disentangling the 'ifs' and 'buts', it is clear that a marriage of this kind was not a full alternative to a regular marriage. But it did have some legal consequences. The common-law courts were willing to issue prohibitions to prevent the ecclesiastical courts from treating couples who had married in this way as fornicators,[112] and in one case an Anabaptist who brought an action for criminal conversation succeeded in recovering £500 in damages.[113] By contrast, in

[109] See also R. Lambert, *An Answer to a late pamphlet, entitl'd A Vindication of Marriage, as Solemnized by Presbyterians in the North of Ireland* (Dublin, 1704), p. 11, who commented on the desire of Presbyterians in Northern Ireland not to be married by members of the established church and noted that 'none of their Brethren in England' had raised similar scruples.

[110] Of course, it should be borne in mind that some early dissenting ministers would have been in orders, for example, those ejected from their livings in 1662: see e.g., *Weld* v. *Chamberlaine* (1684) 2 Show KB 301; 89 ER 952, discussed in Chapter 5.

[111] (1707) Holt KB 459; 90 ER 1153, at 459–60.

[112] *Wigmore's Case* 2 Salk. 438; *Hutchinson* v. *Brookebanke* (1693) 3 Lev. 376; 83 ER 738.

[113] *Woolston* v. *Scott* (1753) in F. Buller, *An Introduction to the Law relative to Trials at Nisi Prius* (Dublin, 1768), p. 39: '[i]t has been doubted whether the ceremony must not be performed according to the Rites of the Church; but as this is an action against a wrong doer, and not a claim of Right, it seems sufficient to prove the marriage according to any Form of Religion, as in the case of Anabaptists, Quakers, or Jews'.

addition to the cases in which those who had married in a non-Anglican form were prosecuted for fornication,[114] the ecclesiastical courts held in *Haydon* v. *Gould* that a husband who had married in a Sabbatarian ceremony was not entitled to administration of his wife's estate.[115] And in one respect individual dissenters had *fewer* rights than those who had entered into a contract *per verba de praesenti*: after all, a contract could be enforced if one of the parties proved recalcitrant, but dissenters were not amenable to the same process. As one commentator noted, 'the Dissenters cannot be prosecuted for not solemnizing their Marriages according to the Church of England, being screen'd by the Act of Toleration; whereas those who engage in a Marriage Contract before other Lay-Friends, may be compell'd to solemnize their Marriage at Church'.[116]

Contemporary commentators also expressed doubts regarding the status of dissenters' marriages. One doubted whether a marriage celebrated by a dissenter would be relevant for the purposes of the crime of bigamy: 'I believe no Man will affirm, that a Marriage celebrated by the Dissenters will bring a Man in Danger of the Statute which makes it a Felony to have more Wives than one.'[117] Another took the view that the Marriage Duty Act 1696 had put the matter 'beyond doubt' since it assumed that only those in orders could conduct marriages.[118] Even the body that represented the Three Denominations seems to have taken the same view: when the case of a marriage that had taken place in a meeting-house in Leicestershire in 1752 was raised before the Protestant Dissenting Deputies,[119] the committee refused to offer any assis-

[114] One such case is described by E. Welch, 'The Origins of the New Connexion of General Baptists in Leicestershire' (1995) 65 *Transactions of the Leicestershire Archaeological and Historical Society* 59.

[115] (1711) 1 Salk. 119; 91 ER 113, at 120, and see further Chapter 2.

[116] T. Salmon, *A Critical Essay concerning Marriage* (London, 1724), p. 209. See also *R* v. *Inhabitants of Luffington* (1744) Burr. Sett. Cas. 232 No. 79, at 134, in which it was argued that dissenters were 'virtually dispensed with, by the Toleration Act, from complying with the Common-Prayer Book in this respect'.

[117] Salmon, *Critical Essay*, p. 209.

[118] Anon, *Baron and Feme: a Treatise of Law and Equity concerning Husband and Wives* (London: T. Waller, 1738), p. 6. See also Salmon, *Critical Essay*, p. 207.

[119] The case was raised in 1777, but its validity would have been tested by the law in force at the time of the marriage.

tance to the parties, 'the Dissenters having no right, by law, to perform the marriage ceremony, and the supposed marriage being consequently void, and the children illegitimate'.[120]

So the number of marriages celebrated by Presbyterians, Baptists, and Independents was never large, and there is only one case – and that one, *Woolston* v. *Scott*, decided at a low level[121] – in which the parties to such a marriage were treated any differently from a couple who had simply contracted *per verba de praesenti*. Knowledge that a marriage in a meeting-house would not carry the same rights as a marriage in church was likely to be a significant disincentive to marrying in such a way.[122]

In addition, in assessing the overall significance of such practices, account should be taken of the shrinking numbers of adherents to non-conformity.[123] From an estimated peak of 300,000 at the end of the seventeenth century, their numbers had halved by 1740; moreover, it has further been suggested that by this time 'the fully committed members of Dissenting congregations (as distinct from the penumbra of hearers and sympathisers) scarcely had exceeded 50,000'.[124] Even if *all* Protestant dissenters had married according to their own religious rites, this would have accounted for a very small percentage of marriages; since the overwhelming majority can be shown not to have done so, it was negligible as a social practice.

120 *A Sketch of the History and Proceedings of the Deputies appointed to Protect the Civil Rights of the Protestant Dissenters* (London: Samuel Burton, 1813), p. 45.

121 By Dennison J at Thetford in 1753: Buller, *Introduction to the Law relative to Trials at Nisi Prius*, p. 39.

122 As one commentator noted, the lack of legal rights would enable a man to keep his children and their mother 'in a perpetual Dependence', receiving only what he chose to give them, and 'for these Reasons I think no prudent Parent would chuse to celebrate his Daughter's Nuptials in a dissenting Congregation': Salmon, *Critical Essay*, p. 210.

123 On the pragmatism that might dictate adherence to the Church of England, see e.g., H. Perkin, *The Origins of Modern English Society, 1780–1880* (London: Routledge & Kegan Paul, 1969), pp. 34–5, 72.

124 A. Gilbert, *Religion and Society in Industrial England: Church, Chapel and Social Change, 1740–1914* (London: Longman, 1976), p. 16; see also R. Currie, A. Gilbert, and L. Horsley, *Churches and Churchgoers: Patterns of Church Growth in the British Isles since 1700* (Oxford: Clarendon Press, 1997), p. 23; Watts, *The Dissenters*, Tables I and II.

THE SOCIETY OF FRIENDS

Quakers[125] merit separate discussion, partly because they *were* separate, from both the Church of England and other nonconformists; and, more importantly, because they developed their own distinct marriage practices. The Quaker movement developed against the turbulent backdrop of the Civil War, and even by the standards of the time was regarded as a radical religion.[126] Its key tenet was the existence of an 'inner light' and as a consequence it rejected outward forms of worship.[127] Under the Commonwealth Quakers enjoyed some measure of tolerance, but at the Restoration legislation was specifically directed at their activities.[128] Unlike other dissenters, they did not seek to mitigate their sufferings by 'occasional conformity',[129] and appear to have suffered a higher degree of persecution than other sects.[130] Relief came only with the Toleration Act in 1689, and by this time their numbers had already begun to wane.[131]

It would appear that from the very earliest years of their existence Quakers developed their own marriage practices. Quaker registers contain 203 marriages for the period 1647–59,[132] and, judging from the criticisms within the movement of secret proceedings, there may have been others that were not registered.[133]

125 The term 'Quakers' was a originally a derisory label, coined by a local justice, Gervase Bennett, on the basis that they 'shook and trembled during their meetings': H. Larry Ingle, 'Fox, George (1624–1691)' in *Oxford Dictionary of National Biography* (Oxford University Press, 2004), vol. 20, p. 638.

126 On the radicalism of the early Quakers, see Hill, *The World Turned Upside Down*, ch. 10.

127 J. Stevenson Rowntree, *Quakerism, Past and Present: being an Inquiry into the Causes of its Decline in Great Britain and Ireland* (London: Smith, Elder & Co., 1859), p. 18.

128 See e.g., An Act for preventing the Mischiefs and Dangers that may arise by certaine Persons called Quakers and others refusing to take lawfull Oaths, 1662, 14 Car. 2 c. 1, and see further C.W. Hoyle, *The Quakers and the English Legal System, 1660–1688* (Philadelphia: University of Pennsylvania Press, 1988), p. 16.

129 Hoyle, *The Quakers and the English Legal System*, p. 10; Galgano, 'Out of the Mainstream', p. 126.

130 See e.g., Rupp, *Religion in England*, p. 142.

131 The number of recorded Quaker births and marriages peaked in the decade 1670–9 (at 9,753 and 2,820 respectively) and declined thereafter: see John S. Rowntree, *The Friends' Registers of Births, Deaths and Marriages, 1650–1900* (Leominster, 1902), p. 14.

132 Rowntree, *The Friends' Registers*, p. 14.

133 W.C. Braithwaite, *The Beginnings of Quakerism* (London: Macmillan & Co. Ltd, 1912), p. 146.

As early as 1653 George Fox set out advice to his followers on the procedure they should adopt when entering into a marriage;[134] more importantly, for present purposes, he spelt out the elements of the marriage service that should be dispensed with:

> [the] right joining in marriage is the work of the Lord only, and not the priests or magistrates, for it is God's ordinance and not man's. And therefore Friends cannot consent that they should join them together, for we marry none; it is the Lord's work, and we are but witnesses.[135]

His assertion that church marriage was inappropriate would have appeared less radical at the time it was uttered in 1657, since at this time the law of England and Wales prescribed a civil ceremony for marriage,[136] and the form eventually adopted by the Quakers was not so far removed from that which was current at the time.[137] Other prominent Quakers recommended at least some involvement with the official system: Margaret Fell, for example, insisted that couples should take their certificate of marriage before the justice of the peace after they had exchanged consent before Friends,[138] while in Somerset it was resolved that this would be done 'thus conforming as nearly as possible to the law then in force'.[139] With the abolition of civil marriage at the Restoration, however, such accommodation became impossible.

The Quaker process of marriage, as it crystallised over time,[140] could be a lengthy one. The consent of the meeting was required, whatever the age of those intending to marry. First, the parties announced to the meeting that they intended to marry and established that their parents had consented.[141] Two Friends would then be appointed to make investigations as to whether the parties

134 *A Journal of the Life, Travels, Sufferings, Christian Experiences and Labour of Love of George Fox* (London: Friends' Tract Association, 1891), vol. II, p. 88.

135 Quoted by Hoyle, *The Quakers and the English Legal System*, p. 15.

136 See further Chapter 5.

137 A. Lloyd, *Quaker Social History, 1669–1738* (London: Longmans, Green & Co., 1950), p. 51; see further R. S. Mortimer, 'Marriage Discipline in Early Friends' (1957) 48 *Journal of the Friends' Historical Society* 175.

138 Lloyd, *Quaker Social History*, p. 49.

139 Braithwaite, *The Beginnings of Quakerism*, p. 317.

140 See e.g., Jackson, *The Diary of Abraham de la Pryme*, p. 53.

141 If the parents of either party had died, then the consent of other relatives, guardians, or Friends would be sought: Mortimer, 'Marriage Discipline in Early Friends', 184.

were truly free to marry.[142] They reported back to the next meeting, and if the proposed marriage was approved permission would be given 'for the intention of marriage to be announced at the end of a public meeting for worship'.[143] A certificate recording the publication of the parties' intentions and the lack of any objections to the marriage was then given to the parties, and the marriage itself could then take place. This process in itself took a month, and if there were objections to be investigated, or any doubts about the parties' devotion to Quakerism, it could be longer.

To modern eyes, the system adopted by the Quakers appears extremely careful, and when a Bill for preventing clandestine marriages was before Parliament in 1690 the Quakers submitted copies of the certificate issued to couples who planned to marry, 'to manifest the said people's Christian care and righteous proceedings, not admitting clandestine nor unwarrantable marriages amongst them'.[144] Yet this was not how their marriages were perceived by contemporaries. Accusations that Quakers 'went together like brute beasts' were flung around.[145] As Tual explains:

> The rejection of 'outer manifestations' which belonged to the 'Church of the Apostacy' was not peculiar to Quakerism and had been adopted by many Protestant sects. But what shocked Friends' contemporaries, well-inured to sectarian excesses, was the total discarding of all forms of nuptial ceremonial, the last obstacle it was felt that stood in the way of sexual licence.[146]

But what was the status of such marriages, which were in essence no more than a mere exchange of consent in words of the present tense before witnesses? Once again, the evidence is fragmented and contradictory. A number of commentators have cited a case

[142] See e.g., the record of the marriage of Icabod Bowen and Sarah Wright in Shrewsbury in 1690: it was noted that the former had 'received severall Certificates concerning his clearness from all others' and that she was also known 'to be clear from any other': W. Fletcher (ed.), *Shropshire Parish Registers: Nonconformist and RC Registers* (Shropshire Parish Register Society, 1922), p. 156.

[143] Mortimer, 'Marriage Discipline in Early Friends', 177.

[144] Quoted by Lloyd, *Quaker Social History*, p. 60.

[145] A. Fraser, *The Weaker Vessel* (London: Weidenfeld & Nicolson, 1984), p. 371; Quaker Library, Book of Cases, vol. I, p. 28.

[146] J. Tual, 'Sexual Equality and Conjugal Harmony: the Way to Celestial Bliss – a View of Early Quaker Matrimony' (1988) 55 *Journal of the Friends Historical Society* 161.

heard in 1661 as establishing the validity of Quaker marriages.[147] Certainly, the Quakers' own records confidently headed the entry relating to the attempt of John Ashwell to eject his niece Mary from copyhold land as 'A Case of Marriage amongst the People called Quakers Stated & Maintained Legal'.[148] But there are a number of problems in resting too much weight on this case. First, some caution should be observed in that the only surviving contemporary report of the case is that in the Quakers' own records, the Quakers being no doubt eager to portray their own marriage practices as having been officially vindicated. Secondly, it was decided at a very low level, at the Nottingham Assizes. Thirdly, the marriage in dispute had taken place in 1658, at a time when the rapidly-changing law required marriages to be celebrated before a magistrate but did not invalidate marriages that were not so celebrated.[149] Fourthly, it concerned the question of entitlement to copyhold land: the husband had not been able to do what was necessary to transfer it to his wife before his death, but his infant daughter Mary had subsequently been admitted as tenant of the land. In court, reliance was placed on Sir Edward Coke's statement that a marriage should not be called into question after the death of one of the parties: there is a significant distinction between a marriage not being challenged after death and being afforded recognition during a lifetime. And if the judge did, as the Quakers' report suggest, allude to the marriage of Adam and Eve in Paradise as a reason for upholding the marriage, one inevitably suspects that this was for lack of other more recent precedents.[150]

Furthermore, the above discussion of the marriages of other Protestant dissenters illustrated that cases decided in one particular area of law were not necessarily decisive as to the outcome in other areas. The 1661 case was not regarded by contemporaries as settling the status of a Quaker marriage, as the subsequent litigation

[147] W. Sewel, *The History of the Rise, Increase, and Progress of the Christian People called the Quakers* (London, 1722), p. 292 (although the title hints at Sewel's sympathies); Lloyd, *Quaker Social History*, p. 51; Steel, *Sources for Nonconformist Genealogy and Family History*, p. 665.

[148] Quaker Library, Book of Cases, vol. I, p. 28. See Hoyle, *The Quakers and the English Legal System*, pp. 234–6, for a detailed discussion of the case.

[149] The annulling clause in the original 1653 Act had been removed in 1657: see Chapter 5.

[150] The judge did apparently cite the case of a deathbed marriage, but no details of it are recorded.

noted in the Book of Cases demonstrates. One 1675 case involved Alice Cliffe, who had married William Smith in a Quaker ceremony. After William's death, her entitlement to his assets had been challenged by his brother. Although the dispute resulted in a favourable decision for Alice, the course of litigation did not run smoothly: her counsel, perceiving it would go against her, moved for a special verdict and when it was reargued before the judges three years later, the outcome appears to have turned on the terms of William's will, rather than on the validity of his marriage.[151] Other judgments in favour of the Quakers similarly appear to have been achieved by indirect or roundabout means.[152] As noted in Chapter 3, the common-law courts could in certain contexts take the fact of the marriage into account, together with the cohabitation and reputation of the parties, but in doing so they were explicitly not determining the validity of the marriage.[153] Legal texts would only go so far as to state that '[t]here is a Marriage ... in Reputation, as among Quakers, &c, which is allowed to be sufficient to give Title to a Personal estate'.[154]

151 Book of Cases, vol. I, p. 112.

152 Book of Cases vol. I, pp. 112, 233; R. North, *The Life of the Right Honourable Francis North, Baron of Guilford, Lord Keeper of the Great Seal, under King Charles II and King James II* (London, 1742), p. 68, was critical of Sir Matthew Hale's decision in favour of the Quaker ceremony: 'for if the Circumstances of a Quaker's marriage were stated in Evidence, there was no Colour for a special verdict: for how was a Marriage by a Layman, without the Liturgy, good within the Acts that establish the Liturgy? The Slur, in such Cases, used to be this. In Evidence, a Cohabitation, and owning the Children, as Man and Wife, passeth without entering into the Question of the Right; that properly belongs to another Jurisdiction. But here, though the Right was debated, and could not be determined for the Quakers, yet a special verdict, upon no point, served to baffle the party, that would take Advantage of the Nullity.'

153 See e.g., Book of Cases, vol. I, pp. 216–17; Book of Cases, vol. II, p. 24; Meeting for Sufferings, vol. V, p. 9: 'proving cohabitation at common law is judged enough; tho not in ye Ecclesiastical court'. As emphasised in Chapter 2, statements about the nature of marriage need to be read in context: thus we find at one point an assertion that the Quaker form of marriage 'is a marriage by the common law' but this is immediately qualified by the acknowledgment that the common law will take account of it in 'some' cases and that it is a matter for the jury to determine: Book of Cases, vol. II, p. 2.

154 G. Jacob, *Every Man his Own Lawyer: or, a Summary of the Laws of England in a New and Instructive Method, under the following heads* (London, 1736), p. 299; A. MacDowall Bankton, *An Institute of the Laws of Scotland in Civil Rights, with Observations on the Agreement or Diversity between Them and the Laws of England* (Edinburgh, 1751–3), vol. I, pp. 145–6.

Less favourably, the records of the Meeting for Sufferings recorded numerous challenges to Quaker marriages.[155] And sometimes Quakers themselves appear to have attempted to take advantage of the uncertain status of their unions: Burnet noted that one Quaker, 'sued for some Debts owing by his Wife before he Married her ... pretended, [t]hat it was no Marriage that had past between them, since it was not solemnized according to the Rules of the Church of England'.[156] It is perhaps unsurprising that Sir Matthew Hale rejected this penny-pinching argument (which would have bastardised the man's own children) and held the man liable for his wife's debts; it is equally telling that the fact that he was willing to find in favour of such marriages was seen as requiring comment and explanation by his biographers rather than being a matter of course.[157]

Faced with such challenges, Quakers accordingly sought advice from various sources on the status of their unions. One Thomas Corbett was recorded in 1679 as stating that an exchange of vows in words of the present tense created a good marriage, relying on the fact that such an exchange could invalidate a later marriage. He acknowledged that ministers were enjoined by the Act of Uniformity to use the form there prescribed but argued that there was no statutory provision actually invalidating a marriage not celebrated according to the set form. And he attributed 'the vulgar opinion that marriage cannot be without a priest' to the doctrine of 'popish doctors' that marriage without a minister did not constitute a sacrament.[158] As we have seen in Chapter 2, most of his contemporaries endorsed the 'vulgar opinion'; Corbett's opinion might have had logic on its side, but not the law. Another adviser, Counsellor Conyers, put forward similar arguments to those offered by Corbett, but also suggested, rather tenuously, that since English law recognised marriages solemnised in other countries according to their own usages, it should also recognise

[155] Meeting for Sufferings, vol. I, p. 50; vol. IV, pp. 48–9, 282; vol. V, p. 9.

[156] G. Burnet, *The Life and Death of Sir Matthew Hale* (London, 1696), p. 73. See also Book of Cases, vol. II, p. 222, in which it was advised that 'if the people called Quakers Contest the Payment of the fee for these marriages, they do at the same time admit that their marriages are not good in law'.

[157] See also North, *The Life of the Right Honourable Francis North*, p. 68, who commented on the favour shown by Hale towards dissenters.

[158] Book of Cases, vol. I, p. 65.

Quaker marriages. He pointed out that in certain contexts the marriage was treated by the common-law courts as a question of fact, refraining from mentioning that in other contexts, such as the wife's entitlement to dower, the legality of the marriage *did* have to be proved.[159] But Conyers was forced to admit that 'the matter in Law rests undecided by any Solemn Resolution'.[160] And this state of uncertainty continued: in 1717, Lutwyche acknowledged that Quaker marriages 'have never yet been determined to be Good in Law'.[161]

Indeed, this was the view taken by Parliament. As noted in the introduction, in 1695 Parliament expressly described Quaker marriages as merely 'pretended' marriages, although subject to the same taxes as those celebrated according to the rites of the Church of England. The Quakers took exception to this description, arguing that 'Quakers' marriages being real Marriages, and having obtained a general Reputation as such; now to render them pretended Marriages, may be construed to their great disadvantage in many respects'.[162] But their petition for the Act to be amended was dropped, and, as one commentator noted, the Quakers are 'left, as they were before, to run the Hazard of their Illegal Marriages'.[163]

One such hazard was prosecution by the ecclesiastical courts, whether for fornication or for non-payment of the marriage fees due to the incumbent if a couple married elsewhere.[164] One man presented for 'living incontinently' with a woman pleaded that they had married according to the Quaker form, but the court still proceeded against him 'for that he had not married the said C according to the Canon of the Church of England' and excommunicated him.[165] The legal advice given to the Quakers was that this was a doubtful case, and that the common-law courts might be willing to issue a prohibition in such a case, but it still illustrates the attitude of the ecclesiastical courts. In addition, a suit for

[159] See Chapter 2. [160] Book of Cases, vol. I, p. 233.

[161] Book of Cases, vol. II, p. 222.

[162] Quoted in F. Bugg, *A Retrospective-Glass for the Mis-led Quakers* (London, 1710), p. 497.

[163] Bugg, *A Retrospective-Glass*, p. 498.

[164] See e.g., J. Besse, *A Brief Account of Many of the Prosecutions of the People called Quakers in the Exchequer, Ecclesiastical and Other Courts* (London, 1736), pp. 12, 38, 44, 59, 78, 94–5, 122, 125, 132, 135.

[165] Quaker Library, Book of Cases, vol. II, p. 1.

restitution of conjugal rights brought by a Quaker woman met with the objection that the court did not have jurisdiction as the parties had not married according to the rites of the Church of England.[166] And a Quaker seeking to establish the binding nature of the ceremony had to frame his or her case as one for the enforcement of a contract *per verba de praesenti*, not one for the recognition of a valid marriage.[167]

The continuing doubts about the status of a Quaker marriage meant that some Quakers preferred to marry in the Anglican church.[168] As one commentator noted:

> many persons who worshipped with the Friends, and in the main held their religious principles, shrunk from having their marriages solemnized in a manner which left the legal validity of these unions doubtful, and exposed character and estate to the painful consequences of such doubt.[169]

Steel has further suggested that such doubts may have been one reason for the practice of religious endogamy adopted by the Quakers. The Society would only permit a marriage to go ahead if both parties were convinced Quakers: they 'could not accept the responsibility for the marriage of anyone who was not closely associated with them'.[170] For some, however, it was the strictness of Quaker marriage procedures that drove them to marry in the Church of England,[171] although this course met with disapproval and sometimes disownment from their co-religionists:[172]

166 *Green* v. *Green*, cited in *Andreas* v. *Andreas* (1737) 1 Hag. Con. (App.) 10n; 161 ER 638. According to this note the case was dismissed.

167 See e.g., *Dodgson* v. *Haswell* (1730), PRO DEL/412, and see the note of the case at 1 Hag. Con. (App.) 10n; 161 ER 638.

168 Mortimer, 'Marriage Discipline in Early Friends'; Steel, *Sources for Nonconformist Genealogy and Family History*, p. 666.

169 Rowntree, *Quakerism, Past and Present*, p. 72.

170 Steel, *Sources for Nonconformist Genealogy and Family History*, p. 651.

171 See e.g., R. T. Vann, *The Social Development of English Quakerism, 1655–1755* (Harvard University Press, 1969), p. 187, who notes that 'the offense of "marrying by a priest" – that is, marrying another Quaker, though with a clergyman officiating – was more common than the one of marrying "one of the world"'.

172 See R. Mortimer (ed.), *Minute Book of the Men's Meeting of the Society of Friends in Bristol, 1686–1704* (Bristol Record Society, 1977), pp. 41, 74, 132; and J. V. Wood, *Some Rural Quakers: a History of Quakers and Quakerism at the Corners of the Four Shires of Oxford, Warwick, Worcester and Gloucester* (York: Ebor Press, 1991), p. 64, who notes that marrying out accounted for twenty-one of the thirty-five disownments by the Evesham Monthly Meeting between 1699 and 1812.

> Because thou twice and she once have so notoriously gon contrari to your profession by running confidently against the concent of Friends to be married by the priest, wee thinck it our duty to let you know that your practice therein have shut you out of felowship with us, and by this we publish you disowned.[173]

Despite the legal problems and internal obstacles, there is ample evidence that many Quakers did marry according to their own rites. In sharp contrast to the patchy evidence of a few marriage ceremonies conducted by other Protestant dissenters, the Quaker registers record that 17,823 marriages had taken place according to the procedure of the Society of Friends by 1749.[174] This is all the more striking given the relatively low numbers of Quakers, who constituted only 1 per cent of the population at their peak in 1680.[175] While providing clear evidence of alternative practices among the Quakers, it also sets in context the very small number of marriages according to other rites that have been traced for the period before the 1753 Act.

JEWISH MARRIAGES

For a long period of time the status of Jewish marriages had not taxed the English courts: most Jews were expelled from England in 1290 and the small numbers who remained were unsurprisingly 'a secretive community'.[176] It was not until the 1650s that Jews returned to England in any numbers, and their freedom of worship was not confirmed until the 1680s.[177] Even by the time of the passage of the 1753 Act their numbers remained small, in the region of 8,000.[178]

[173] Mortimer, *Minute Book*, p. 179, 7 April 1701.
[174] Rowntree, *The Friends' Registers*, p. 14.
[175] E.A. Wrigley and R.S. Schofield, *The Population History of England, 1541–1871* (Cambridge University Press, 1981), p. 93.
[176] Stevens, *UK Asylum Law*, p. 14.
[177] H.S.Q. Henriques, *The Jews and the English Law* (London: J. Jacobs, 1908), p. 3; L. Wolf, 'Crypto-Jews under the Commonwealth' (1893–4) 1 *Transactions of the Jewish Historical Society of England* 55.
[178] J. Obelkevich, 'Religion', ch. 6 in F.M.L. Thompson (ed.), *The Cambridge Social History of Britain 1750–1950*, vol. III, *Social Agencies and Institutions* (Cambridge University Press, 1990), and see T.M. Endelman, *The Jews of Georgian England, 1714–1830: Tradition and Change in a Liberal Society* (University of Michigan Press, 1999), p. 172. M. Dorothy George, *London Life in the Eighteenth Century* (London: Penguin 1965; original edn 1925), suggests a lower figure of 5,000.

It has been contended by Henriques that Jewish marriages 'were recognised for some purposes' prior to their expulsion, and that such marriages continued to enjoy legal recognition after their readmission.[179] The evidence for this is, however, somewhat inconclusive. The two thirteenth-century cases cited by Henriques both involved the marriages of Jews who had subsequently converted to Christianity: in one a Jewish wife who had not converted was not entitled to dower upon the death of her now Christian husband; in another the son of a couple who had both converted to Christianity was regarded as the heir to the estate. The later case of *Franks* v. *Martin*[180] concerned the validity of a covenant in a (pre-1754) marriage settlement. From the fact that the House of Lords enforced the covenant one might infer that they regarded the Jewish ceremony of marriage that had taken place as valid, but the question was not directly before the court. Two further pre-1754 cases concerned the jurisdiction of the ecclesiastical courts: in *Mendez da Costa* v. *Da Costa Villa Real*[181] the question was whether two Jews had entered into a binding contract *per verba de praesenti*; while *Andreas* v. *Andreas*[182] involved a suit for restitution of conjugal rights brought by a wife who had married her husband according to the Jewish form. In both an objection was raised on the basis of the religious status of the parties; in both the court decided that it did have jurisdiction; but in neither was the issue of validity actually resolved, since the contract in *Da Costa* v. *Da Costa Villa Real* was held to be conditional only (and therefore unenforceable) and the wife in *Andreas* seems to have abandoned her case. In another case, not cited by Henriques, Domingo de la Sarda, a Jewish merchant, was acquitted of bigamy on the basis that he was not 'within the Statute'[183] but the account of the case is too sparse to determine whether this was because of the nature of his multiple marriages or some other reason.

Yet it does seem that the courts were more willing to recognise a Jewish marriage than a Quaker marriage. In *Andreas* the court distinguished the earlier case of *Green* v. *Green* in which a Quaker

179 H. S. Q. Henriques, 'Jewish Marriages and the English Law' (1908) 20 *Jewish Quarterly Review* 391.
180 (1760) 5 Brown's Parl. Cas. 151; 2 ER 593.
181 (1731) Lambeth Palace Library, E30/4.
182 (1737) I Hag. Con. (App.) 10n; 161 ER 638.
183 *The Proceedings of the Old Bailey*, 8 October 1684, Ref: t16841008-13.

wife's suit for restitution of conjugal rights was dismissed out of hand on the basis that the couple had not married according to the forms of the Church of England. It was suggested that 'as the parties had contracted such a marriage as would bind them according to the Jewish forms, the woman was entitled to a remedy'.[184] It is clear that this did not rest on the classification of the Jewish ceremony as a contract, else the claims in *Green* (and in the later case of *Scrimshire*, discussed above) would also have been admitted. The best explanation is that which appears in later cases: that the matter was regarded as one of Jewish law and would be determined by the application of its principles,[185] just as the validity of a foreign marriage would be determined by the application of foreign law.

MORAVIAN AND METHODIST

The final congregation to yield up a pre-1754 register of marriage to the 1838 Commission was the Moravian church in Bedford. The Moravian church had its origins in medieval Bohemia, but it was not until the eighteenth century that missionaries came to England.[186] This is not the place for a lengthy discussion of Moravian beliefs, but for present purposes a number of points should be made about the nature of the denomination. First, it was Protestant, and was afforded special legal recognition by legislation in 1749 that acknowledged it as 'an antient Protestant Episcopal Church'.[187] Secondly, there was considerable overlap both between Moravians and the evangelical movement and between them and the Anglican church.[188] Even when separate congregations began to be founded, they were envisaged as being a part of, rather than an alternative to, the Church of England. This was reflected in their marriages. In some respects Moravian marriage practices were highly distinctive, since the decision whether – and

[184] *Andreas* v. *Andreas* (1737) 1 Hag. Con. (App.) 10n; 161 ER 636.

[185] See Henriques, 'Jewish Marriages', 409; *Lindo* v. *Belisario* (1795) 1 Hag. Con. 215; 161 ER 530.

[186] E. Welch (ed.), *The Bedford Moravian Church in the Eighteenth Century* (Publications of the Bedfordshire Historical Record Society, vol. 68, 1989), p. 1.

[187] C. Podmore, *The Moravian Church in England, 1728–1760* (Oxford: Clarendon Press, 1998), ch. 8.

[188] Podmore, *The Moravian Church in England*, p. 40.

whom – to marry was one that was made by drawing lots.[189] But in other respects they were entirely conventional: the marriages recorded in the Bedford register took place in the Church of England.

The 1740s also witnessed the emergence of what came to be termed 'Methodism', as part of the evangelical revival within the Church of England.[190] As with the Moravians, early Methodists regarded themselves as part of the Church of England[191] and had no objection to marrying according to the prescribed forms. The rare exception only serves to highlight the general conformity: David Taylor, an evangelistic preacher who oscillated between the Methodists and the Moravians, 'objected to the prayer book marriage and the clergy who administered it. He seems to have simply exchanged vows at home before friends.'[192] He also conducted marriage ceremonies, despite being only a lay preacher.[193] More telling, however, is the fact that his own marriage 'was seen as scandalous by his friends'[194] and damaged Taylor's reputation,[195] and that his fellow Methodists disapproved of his conducting marriage ceremonies.[196]

CONCLUSION

Had it been possible for couples prior to 1754 to marry simply by exchanging consent, one would have expected dissenting groups to adopt this form as an easy means of opting out of the Anglican rites. That they did not is a further indicator that the exchange of consent was not regarded as a marriage. Similarly, if the exchange of consent created a valid marriage, there would have been no occasion

189 See e.g., H. Rimius, *A Candid Narrative of the Rise and Progress of the Herrnhuters, commonly called Moravians*, 2nd edn (London, 1753), p. 94.

190 D. Hempton, *The Religion of the People: Methodism and Popular Religion, c. 1750–1900* (London: Routledge, 1996).

191 See e.g., Warne, *Church and Society*, p. 106; J. Black, *Eighteenth-Century Britain, 1688–1783* (Basingstoke: Palgrave, 2001), p. 136.

192 H. D. Rack, '"But Lord, Let it be Betsy!" Love and Marriage in Early Methodism' (2001) 53 *Proceedings of the Wesley Historical Society* 1, 3–4.

193 S. J. Rogal, *A Biographical Dictionary of 18th Century Methodism* (Lampeter: Edwin Mellen Press, 1999), vol. VIII, p. 26.

194 *Ibid.*

195 H. D. Rack, 'Taylor, David (1715–1783)' in *Oxford Dictionary of National Biography* (Oxford University Press, 2004), vol. 53, p. 876.

196 Rogal, *A Biographical Dictionary*, p. 26.

for the debates as to the validity or consequences of such an exchange. It is clear from the evidence presented in this chapter that the legal system found it difficult to decide exactly how to treat a non-Anglican marriage. That there was no systematic effort to determine the status of such a marriage is consistent with what Perkin has termed 'the English system of partial toleration, or intolerance tempered by inefficiency'.[197] The ecclesiastical courts certainly did not recognise marriages celebrated according to rites other than those of the Church of England, punishing those so marrying for fornication, and refusing to allow them to sustain actions for restitution of conjugal rights or to claim administration of a deceased spouse's estate. The common-law courts, by contrast, were willing to issue prohibitions to the ecclesiastical courts to prevent them prosecuting for fornication couples who had married in this way. But in other areas the powers of the common-law courts were constrained: in relation to dower it was necessary that they seek the view of the bishop as to whether there had been a valid marriage. And the common-law courts could not declare a marriage to be 'valid': a jury might decide that the parties had gone through a ceremony of marriage, but this was not the same as a declaration that the marriage was good for all legal purposes. As one Scottish commentator noted of the law south of the border, the issue as to whether a woman was a particular man's wife could be tried by the jury 'because the lawfulness of the marriage is not in issue, or the point to be tried, but only the fact, whether a marriage was contracted between the parties or was not, or whether the parties lived in a married state'.[198] We can conclude that a non-Anglican marriage was not a full alternative to marriage in the Church of England even before 1754, but that it might, in certain circumstances, have some legal consequences.

By contrast, there is evidence that non-Anglican weddings were viewed as a *functional* alternative to marriage in church, at least for some. But it was an alternative used by a minority of a minority. On the eve of the Clandestine Marriages Act, Protestant dissenters comprised perhaps 6 per cent of the population, Catholics around 1 per cent, and non-Christians a barely visible fraction of a percentage. This places an absolute ceiling of around 7 per cent

[197] Perkin, *Origins of Modern English Society*, p. 73.
[198] MacDowall Bankton, *An Institute of the Laws of Scotland*, p. 146.

on the extent of any alternative practices motivated by religious objections to the Anglican rites. But the true number of non-Anglican weddings was far lower than even that modest figure would suggest. Given the doubts as to the validity and consequences of ceremonies conducted outside the Church of England, and the fact that the distinction between conformity and dissent was a permeable one, it would have been unsurprising if most Protestant dissenters, other than Quakers, had chosen to marry in their parish church. That they did so is attested both by the absence of evidence of non-Anglican ceremonies and by the positive evidence of compliance.[199]

The evidence of practice provides an answer to the question posed in the introduction: Jews, Catholics, and Quakers were singled out for mention in the 1694 legislation on marriage taxes because they were the only groups that regularly – if not inevitably – married according to their own forms;[200] other Protestant dissenters did not need to be named because they did usually comply with the forms of the Church of England. The few that did not can be offset against those Catholics, Quakers, and Jews who married in the Church of England. As a result, a reasonable estimate would be that non-Anglican ceremonies accounted for no more, and possibly less, than 2 per cent of marriages in the first part of the eighteenth century.

So far, the story has been one of compliance, which, of course, raises the question as to why the 1753 Act was needed at all. The answer is to be found in the Act itself – presented as an Act 'for the better preventing of clandestine marriages' – and it is to the phenomenon of clandestine marriages that we shall now turn.

199 W. M. Jacob, *Lay People and Religion in the Early Eighteenth Century* (Cambridge University Press, 1996), p. 72; Steel, *Sources for Nonconformist Genealogy and Family History*, p. 504: 'the majority of Nonconformist marriages and deaths appear in the Church of England registers'.

200 One pamphlet accusing the legislature of partiality to Quakers and Catholics met with a contemptuous response: 'Truly the Papists and Quakers would be much oblig'd to the Author, to make good his Assertion. We allow the *Presbyterian* marriages to be as Valid as either the Papists or Quakers, or any others, who are not Legally Solemnized': Lambert, *An Answer to a late pamphlet*, p. 11.

5

THE UNACKNOWLEDGED REGULARITY OF CLANDESTINE MARRIAGES

As noted in the opening chapter, the term 'clandestine marriage' bore a specific meaning in the period before the 1753 Act, denoting a marriage that was celebrated before an ordained clergyman of the Church of England otherwise than in accordance with the prescriptions of the canon law. As with the informal exchange of vows and non-Anglican ceremonies, it is necessary to pose our two key questions: how far were clandestine marriages a full alternative to a regular marriage, and how far were they a functional alternative? The second and third sections of this chapter address each in turn, examining the legal consequences (good and bad) that flowed from a clandestine marriage, and then considering how prevalent such marriages were in the first part of the eighteenth century.

Yet in this context there is also another important question that needs to be addressed. To view a clandestine marriage simply as an alternative to a regular marriage may be to miss the point. Clandestine marriages varied considerably: at one end of the spectrum there were the more disreputable couplings celebrated within the Rules of the Fleet prison; at the other, there were marriages actually celebrated in church that were clandestine only in that they did not comply with all of the requirements of the canon law. Given this spectrum, simply to state that clandestine marriages constituted a particular percentage of the total number of marriages celebrated is of little assistance in determining the potential impact of the 1753 Act: what we need to know is the form that such clandestinity took. If the majority of clandestine marriages were celebrated outside a church, then the 1753 Act would have required a greater change in public attitudes and practices than if most clandestine marriages were little different from regular marriages. While most accounts of clandestine marriages highlight the extent to which they departed from the form prescribed by the canon law,[1] the final section of this chapter, by contrast, will focus on the elements that clandestine marriages *shared* with regular marriages, and will consider how many technically clandestine marriages actually took place in church.

By way of preliminary, however, some background is required. It is important to bear in mind that the prevalence and nature of clandestine marriages varied over time. In assessing the impact of the 1753 Act it is relevant to ask whether clandestine marriages were a recent craze or an embedded tradition. An overview of the turbulent seventeenth century will illustrate how the meaning and nature of clandestinity changed during that period. It is an obvious point, but worth making, that what is clandestine is defined in relation to what is required by way of conformity; as we shall now see, this was subject to change over the course of the seventeenth century.

CLANDESTINE MARRIAGES IN THE SEVENTEENTH CENTURY

[T]he late times of confusion, criminell divisions, and unhappy warrs[2]

At the start of the seventeenth century what was required for a regular marriage had changed little since the early days of Christianity in England: the canons drawn up in 1604 reiterated that banns were to be called or a licence obtained, and that the marriage was to be celebrated in the church of the parish to which at least one of the parties belonged. It is, of course, possible to find examples of marriages that were not regularly celebrated in every period of history, but it is only in the early decades of the seventeenth century that we regularly find complaints being made about the number of clandestine marriages,[3] and most commentators suggest that it was only after 1660 that such marriages began to

[1] L. Stone, *Road to Divorce: a History of the Making and Breaking of Marriage in England* (Oxford University Press, 1990), ch. 4, especially pp. 116–18; R. B. Outhwaite, *Clandestine Marriage in England, 1500–1850* (London: Hambledon Press, 1995), ch. 2.

[2] J. S. Burn, *The History of the Parish Registers in England*, 2nd edn (London: John Russell Smith, 1862), p. 53.

[3] In 1632 the High Commission noted 'the great mischeifes growinge by clandestine marriages in manie places of this kingdome ... but especiallie ... in the Tower of London': S. R. Gardiner (ed.), *Reports of Cases in the Courts of Star Chamber and High Commission* (Camden Society, 1886), p. 322.

pose a significant problem.[4] In this period clandestine marriages were largely celebrated in church: the problem was perceived to be that some churches were more popular than others.[5] It has generally been assumed that this was because they did not insist on the usual formalities,[6] or were cheaper than their counterparts.[7] But it is worth recalling the religious background of the time. Post-Reformation England was still struggling to determine matters of religious practice, and there were sharp divisions between those who felt that the Reformation had not gone far enough and those who hankered after the traditions of the past.[8] In an era when religious beliefs were passionately held, the choice of a church might be influenced by nuances of religious practice as well as cost or aesthetics.[9]

Nor should the broader political context be overlooked: one would expect disruption at a time of civil strife.[10] This is particularly pertinent in the case of Holy Trinity Minories, which has enjoyed a reputation as a centre for clandestine marriages.[11] The increase dates from the middle of 1644: a mere 15 marriages were celebrated there in the first five months of 1644, but 115 took place

[4] M. Ingram, *Church Courts, Sex and Marriage in England, 1570–1640* (Cambridge University Press, 1987), p. 218; R. A. Houlbrooke, *The English Family 1450–1700* (Harlow: Longman, 1984), p. 86.

[5] See e.g., J. Boulton, 'Clandestine Marriages in London: an Examination of a Neglected Urban Variable' (1993) 20 *Urban History* 191.

[6] See e.g., W. P. W. Phillimore and G. E. Cokayne, *London Parish Registers*, vol. I, *Marriages at St James's Duke's Place from 1668 to 1683* (London: Phillimore's Parish Register Series, vol. XVIII, 1900) who suggest that 'owing to the great number of marriages therein recorded … it may be safely conjectured that they were performed without licence or publication of banns'.

[7] Each church set its own fees, and there were significant variations: see J. Boulton, 'Itching after Private Marryings? Marriage Customs in Seventeenth-Century London' (1991) 16 *London Journal* 15.

[8] D. Rosman, *The Evolution of the English Churches, 1500–2000* (Cambridge University Press, 2003), pp. 73–9.

[9] D. J. Steel, *National Index of Parish Registers*, vol. I, *Sources of Births, Marriages and Deaths before 1837* (London: Society of Genealogists, 1968), p. 59; J. Maltby, *Prayer Book and People in Elizabethan and Early Stuart England* (Cambridge University Press, 1996), p. 232; D. Purkiss, *The English Civil War: a People's History* (London: Harper Perennial, 2007), p. 272.

[10] See e.g., K. Wrightson and D. Levine, *Poverty and Piety in an English Village: Terling 1525–1700* (Oxford: Clarendon Press, 1995), p. 47; and Burn, *The History of the Parish Registers*, p. 57, quoting one vicar who was imprisoned, leaving his parish without any incumbent.

[11] See e.g., Outhwaite, *Clandestine Marriage*, p. 25; J. Gillis, *For Better, For Worse: British Marriages 1600 to the Present* (Oxford University Press, 1985), p. 92.

between June and December.[12] The numbers swelled in subsequent years, from 249 in 1645 to 348 in 1648, after which there is unfortunately a gap in the registers until 1676. Given that the Minories had been taken over by the Parliamentarians in the 1640s,[13] it is possible that this increase reflected popular support (at least within London)[14] for the new, more Puritan form of marriage service that had begun to be used around this time.[15]

More radical change was to come after the Civil War had led to the execution of Charles I and the establishment of the Commonwealth. In 1653 the Barebones Parliament introduced civil marriage:[16] banns could still be called (although provision was also made for the secular alternative of publication in the market-place) but the marriage itself had to take place before a local Justice of the Peace. The recording of the marriage was the role of the Register, who had to be elected by the local ratepayers and approved by the Justice of the Peace. The Act declared forthrightly that after 29 September 1653 no other form of marriage would be valid,[17] but only four years later Parliament backtracked and omitted this clause: the possibility of a civil ceremony remained, but it was accepted that other forms of marriage would also be valid.[18]

12 E. M. Tomlinson, *A History of the Minories, London* (London: Smith, Elder & Co., 1907), p. 232. Tomlinson also suggests that St James' Duke's Place also began to solemnise clandestine marriages at this time: however, there is no evidence of this, and one cannot infer it from its activities in the 1660s, which are considered further below.

13 Tomlinson, *A History of the Minories*, p. 144.

14 On the extent of loyalty to the Book of Common Prayer elsewhere, see Maltby, *Prayer Book and People*.

15 Although Parliament did not pass legislation requiring the use of the new Directory of Public Worship until January 1645, it appears that some churches had begun to use the new service in advance of this: see e.g., Boulton, 'Clandestine Marriages in London', 196.

16 An Act touching Marriages and the registering thereof; and also touching Births and Burials: C. H. Firth and R. S. Rait (eds.), *Acts and Ordinances of the Interregnum, 1642–1660* (London: HMSO, 1911), vol. II, pp. 715–18. For the background to the legislation, see C. Durston, '"Unhallowed Wedlocks": the Regulation of Marriage during the English Revolution' (1988) 31 *Historical Journal* 45.

17 Firth and Rait, *Acts and Ordinances*, vol. II, p. 716.

18 An Act touching several Acts and Ordinances made since the 20th of April 1653, and before the 3rd of September 1654, and other Acts: Firth and Rait, *Acts and Ordinances*, vol. I, p. 1131. For the debates over this particular provision, see J. Towill Rutt (ed.), *Diary of Thomas Burton, Esq.* (New York: Johnson Reprint Corporation, 1974), vol. II, pp. 67–9.

The significance of these changes for present purposes is the response of the public to them. It has been suggested that there was a rush to marry before the Act came into force, although, unfortunately for historians trying to make sense of past practices, increased demand may have meant less regular record-keeping: one parish clerk accounted for the absence of an entry in the church register of a particular marriage by the fact that 'marriages being then very numerous, preceding the [1653 Act], the then clerk had neglected the registry of this marriage'.[19] Further difficulties are posed by the different registration system introduced by the 1653 Act: it was provided that small parishes might unite for this purpose and that one register would serve them all, with the result that it is common to find sudden increases or dramatic falls in the number of marriages being registered in this period.[20] But it is clear that even after the law had changed some couples still chose to marry before an Anglican minister,[21] either instead of the prescribed civil ceremony,[22] or in addition to it.[23] The previously prescribed norm had become the clandestine, but the fact that couples still chose to exchange vows before a minister suggests that there was a deep-rooted commitment to the religious ceremony.[24] As one bride noted in her diary after the underwhelming

19 *The Trial of Mary Moders, alias Stedman, styled the German Princess, at the Old Bailey for Bigamy* (1663) 6 State Trials 274. See also Rosman, *Evolution of the English Churches*, p. 102

20 See D. McLaren, 'The Marriage Act of 1653: Its Influence on the Parish Registers' (1974) 28 *Population Studies* 319, 323–4. Not all commentators have appreciated the reason for such changes: see e.g., L. Bradley, 'Common Law Marriage: a Possible Cause of Under-Registration' (1973) 11 *Local Population Studies* 43.

21 Durston, 'Unhallowed Wedlocks', 49–57.

22 See e.g., *Tarry* v. *Browne* (1661) 1 Sid. 65; 82 ER 972.

23 McLaren, 'The Marriage Act of 1653', 327, argues persuasively that the 1653 Act 'was much more widely and strictly observed than has hitherto been supposed', but this does not preclude the possibility that some couples went through an additional ceremony according to the rites of the Church of England. For examples of this see W.E. Tate, *The Parish Chest* (Chichester: Phillimore & Co. Ltd, 1983; original edn 1946), p. 63; R. Parker, *The Common Stream* (St Albans: Paladin, 1976); K. Wrightson, 'The Nadir of English Illegitimacy in the Seventeenth Century', ch. 6 in P. Laslett, K. Oosterveen, and R. Smith, *Bastardy and its Comparative History* (London: Edward Arnold, 1980), p. 185; A. Plowden, *In A Free Republic: Life in Cromwell's England* (Stroud: Sutton Publishing, 2006), p. 66.

24 P. Crawford, *Women and Religion in England, 1500–1720* (London: Routledge, 1993), ch. 3. See also D. Cressy, *Birth, Marriage and Death: Ritual, Religion and the Life-Cycle in Tudor and Stuart England* (Oxford University Press, 1999), p. 296.

civil ceremony, '[i]f it had not been done more solemnly afterwards by a minister, I should not have believed it lawfully done'.[25]

At the Restoration an Act was passed to confirm the validity of marriages celebrated before Justices of the Peace in the previous two troubled decades.[26] Significantly, the new legislation provided that marriages solemnised in that time should be judged to be as valid as if such marriages 'had been had and solemnized *according to the rites and ceremonies established, or used in the church or kingdom of England*'.[27] Once again, we must recognise that had the exchange of consent by itself been regarded as a marriage, there would have been no need to pass such legislation confirming the validity of marriages that had, if nothing else, involved the exchange of consent in words of the present tense.[28] Indeed, one judge declared the law in operation during the Commonwealth to have been contrary to God's law.[29]

Yet it was not to be expected that stability could be immediately restored after the disruptions of the preceding years.[30] Moreover, the Restoration brought its own tensions. The ejection of many ministers from their livings in 1662 provided a pool of ministers without anything to lose for flouting the canons on the appropriate mode of marriage,[31] and *Weld* v. *Chamberlaine*[32] provides an example of one such minister conducting a wedding service (although there were some doubts as to the status of the marriage).[33]

25 J. Loftis (ed.), *Memoirs of Anne, Lady Halkett and Ann, Lady Fanshawe* (Oxford: Clarendon Press, 1979), p. 85.

26 An Act for confirmation of marriages, 12 Car. 2 c. 33.

27 Section 1 (emphasis added). As one later commentator noted, 'an act of parliament was thought necessary after the grand rebellion, to intitle people who had been married by justices of the peace, to such legal advantages of dower, thirds and the like, as attended marriages duly solemnized according to the rites of the Church of England' (R. Burn, *Ecclesiastical Law* (London, 1763), vol. II, p. 29).

28 Cf. J. Jeaffreson, *Brides and Bridals* (London: Hurst and Blackett, 1872), vol. II, ch. 5, who implausibly attributes the phrasing of the Act to ignorance.

29 *Tarry* v. *Browne* (1661) 1 Sid. 65; 82 ER 972, denying the validity of a dissolution of a marriage that had not complied with the 1653 Act.

30 See e.g., Cressy, *Birth, Marriage and Death*, pp. 181, 333.

31 More than 1,000 ministers left their livings because they would not subscribe to the new Prayer Book, and some retained the loyalty of their parishioners: see e.g., A. Jones, *A Thousand Years of the English Parish* (London: Cassell & Co., 2002), p. 181.

32 (1684) 2 Show. KB 301; 89 ER 952.

33 See further Chapter 2.

In London there may have been a more practical reason for at least some marriages in the wrong parish in this period. In addition to the disruption of political change and the impact of the plague in 1665, the Great Fire of London resulted in the destruction of 87 of the 109 churches in the City of London and damage to a further 3.[34] The rebuilding of the 13,000 destroyed houses began as soon as 1668, and 6,000 had been completed by 1670; the construction of 51 new churches,[35] however, did not begin until 1670 and while most were completed in the 1680s some were not finished until the 1690s.[36] The impact of this is clear in the parish registers. At St Matthew, Friday Street, no marriages were celebrated between April 1666 and December 1672, the incumbent explaining the greater part of this gap with a plaintive note:

> The Parish and Church of St Matthew's Fridaystreet being burnt down Septemb. 3 1666 & the parishioners being scattered & the Church not being rebuilt.[37]

In fact, the numbers marrying in that parish did not recover to their pre-1666 levels until 1687, when the rebuilding of the church was completed. In the meantime, parishioners had to make do with what the register called a 'Tabernacle'. This was a temporary building – a stop-gap measure provided in order for those returning to live in the City to have somewhere to worship.[38] The first of these, at All Hallows the Great, was unflatteringly described as a 'shed'.[39] Baptisms continued to be registered in the parishes whose churches had been destroyed, but marriages, for the most part, were not.[40] These events throw a rather different light on marriage

[34] S. Porter, *The Great Fire of London* (Stroud: Sutton Publishing, 1996).

[35] Those that were not rebuilt were amalgamated with other parishes.

[36] Porter, *The Great Fire*, pp. 138, 143.

[37] A. M. Bruce Bannerman (ed.), *The Register of St Matthew, Friday St, London 1538–1812* (London: Harleian Society, 1933), p. 60.

[38] Porter, *The Great Fire*, pp. 138–9. [39] Porter, *The Great Fire*, p. 139.

[40] A similar pattern could be seen at St Martin Orgar, while at St Clement Eastcheap no marriages were recorded until 1687: A. W. Hughes Clarke (ed.), *The Register of St Clement, Eastcheap and St Martin Orgar*, Part I (London: Harleian Society, 1937). See also A. W. Hughes Clarke (ed.), *The Register of St Michael Bassishaw, London, 1626–1735* (London: Harleian Society, 1943), no marriages recorded 1666–70; Willoughby A. Littledale (ed.), *The Register of St Vedast, Foster Lane, and of St Michael Le Quern, London*, vol. II (London: Harleian Society, 1903), no marriages recorded August 1666–9; A. M. Bruce Bannerman (ed.), *The Register of St Mary Somerset, London 1558–1837*

patterns in London in the late seventeenth century: that many couples chose to be married in a parish to which they did not belong can be interpreted as a desire to be married in a church, rather than in a temporary building.

One apparent oddity is that when these churches began to record marriages once more, many of those marrying were recorded as being from a different parish. One might expect a number of persons in any given year to marry in a parish to which neither belonged, but when *all* the marriages in a particular year involve parties stated to be from a different parish, one's suspicions are inevitably aroused as to what is being recorded. When the parties are described as being from parishes that are not only distant from London, but also from each other (for example, the marriages of 'Gerrald Dannett of Elmbridge co. Worcester & Elizabeth Caldwell of Ridgley co. Stafford' and of 'Thomas Bateman of Gilsborough co. Northampton ... & Sarah Crook of the City of Oxford)[41] it seems more plausible that what we are witnessing is not necessarily couples marrying in a parish to which they do not belong, but the recording of the parties' initial parish(es) of origin or settlement at a time when such issues would have been subject to much disruption.[42] The idea that these individuals eloped to London from their respective counties is untenable: the most plausible explanation is that they were recent immigrants to London who had acquired no permanent settlement there. Caution must therefore be exercised in interpreting apparently 'foreign' marriages as clandestine: the parties may well have been resident in the parish and the marriage consequently perfectly regular.

The fire may have had some impact upon the popularity of marriages at St James' Duke's Place, which stood right on the edge of the affected area. In the first eight months of 1666, 645 marriages

(London: Harleian Society, 1929), no marriages recorded June 1666–71; St Antholin, only seven marriages noted in the register between August 1666 and 1682, some of which had taken place elsewhere.

[41] G. W. G. Leveson Gower (ed.), *A Register of All the Christninges, Burialles & Weddings within the Parish of Saint Peters upon Cornhill* (London: Harleian Society, 1877), p. 61.

[42] Within London this was exacerbated by the fact that those parishes whose churches were not rebuilt were amalgamated with other parishes for ecclesiastical purposes only, and 'retained their own organisations': Porter, *The Great Fire*, p. 114.

were celebrated there, an average of just under 80 per month. The immediate effect of the fire was a small fall in this number, to an average of 76 per month in the final four months of 1666, in all likelihood reflecting the disruption caused by the fire and the fall in the numbers resident in the City of London. But by 1667 numbers were up to an average of 94 per month, and 95 per month were celebrated in the first four months of 1668.[43] Yet even so it is clear that the popularity of St James' Duke's Place and of Holy Trinity Minories in the 1680s and 1690s cannot be attributed to the lack of other venues alone: Boulton has shown that marriages there were cheaper than marriages by licence (the other means of securing privacy) elsewhere in London.[44] While it would be unwise to infer irregular practices from popularity alone, the fact that the incumbent of St James' was suspended for three years in 1687 is a clear indication that the law was being flouted.[45] In *The Way of the World* Congreve portrayed St James' Duke's Place as a place where a marriage could be celebrated without any notice: one couple grew impatient of queuing to be married at St Pancras and so 'drove round to Duke's Place; and there they were riveted in a trice'.[46]

But by the time Congreve's play was performed in 1700 legislation had put an end to this particular abuse of the marriage laws. It was a problem that had attracted critical commentary, and various Bills had been debated in Parliament,[47] although, as one commentator observed, no reform would be necessary if only the canons of the church were properly observed.[48] It is perhaps significant (in terms of illustrating the priorities of the legislators

[43] After this there is unfortunately a gap in the registers until 1679: see W. P. W. Phillimore and G. E. Cokayne, *London Parish Registers*, vol. I, *Marriages at St James's Duke's Place from 1668 to 1683* (London: Phillimore's Parish Register Series vol. XVIII, 1900).

[44] Boulton, 'Clandestine Marriages in London', 206, and 'Itching after Private Marryings?'

[45] T. Benton, *Irregular Marriages in London before 1754*, 2nd edn (Society of Genealogists, 2000), p. 19.

[46] *The Way of the World*, Act 1, Scene 1.

[47] See e.g., the 1689 Bill 'disabling Minors to marry without the consent of their Parents and Guardians, and against their untimely marrying after the Decease of their Fathers, and for preventing all Clandestine marriages for the future' and the 1690 Bill 'for the better preventing clandestine marriages': BL Add 35877/115. A further Bill was debated in 1691: BL Add 35880.

[48] H. Prideaux, *The Case of Clandestine Marriages Stated, wherein are shewn the causes from whence this Corruption ariseth, and the true methods, whereby it might be remedied* (1691; 1744).

of the day)[49] that the first real attempt to tighten up the law occurred in the context of legislation designed to raise revenue, with duties being imposed on licences for and certificates of marriage.[50] However, a succession of statutes had to be passed in the wake of the original legislation in order to ensure its efficacy as the authorities realised precisely what evasive methods were being employed.

First, the legislation passed in 1695 imposed a fine of £100 on any clergyman who performed a marriage ceremony 'at any place pretending to be exempt from the visitation of the bishop of the diocese' without either banns being called or a licence obtained.[51] The penalty for a second offence was suspension for three years.[52] A year later, in 1696, the Preamble to a further piece of legislation noted, with more than a hint of exasperation, that the law was both ineffectual (the penalty, which applied to the person, rather than to each offence, was proving an insufficient disincentive), and was being eluded (by clergymen allowing other ministers to conduct the ceremonies, 'many of which ... have no benefices or settled habitations, and are poor and indigent, and cannot easily be discovered and convicted of the offences aforesaid').[53] The Act therefore provided that £100 would be forfeited by the officiating clergyman for *each* offence,[54] or for allowing another person to conduct such a ceremony in his church.[55] The scope of the offence was also extended, from marriages in places claiming to be exempt

49 See further Chapter 6.

50 An Act for granting to their Majesties several duties upon vellum, parchment, and paper, for four years, towards carrying on the war against France: 5 & 6 Will. & Mar. c. 21, s. 3, which provided that five shillings would be payable '[f]or every skin or piece of vellum or parchment, or sheet or piece of paper, upon which any licence for or certificate of marriage ... shall be ingrossed or written'. The Act came into force on 28 June 1694. On the duties payable, see J. Boulton, 'The Marriage Duty Act and Parochial Registration in London, 1695–1706', ch. 11 in K. Schurer and T. Arkell (eds.), *Surveying the People: the Interpretation and Use of Document Sources for the Study of Population in the Later Seventeenth Century* (Oxford: Leopard's Head Press, 1992).

51 An Act for granting to his Majesty certain rates and duties upon marriages, births and burials, and upon batchelors and widowers, for the term of five years, for carrying on the war against France with vigour: 6 & 7 Will. 3 c. 6, s. 52.

52 *Ibid.*

53 An Act for the enforcing the laws which restrain marriages without licence or banns, and for the better registering marriages, births and burials: 7 & 8 Will. 3 c. 35.

54 Section 2. 55 Section 3.

to marriages that took place anywhere,[56] and it was further provided that 'every man so married without licence or publication of banns ... shall forfeit the sum of ten pounds'.[57]

This legislation had a dramatic effect on the popularity of churches which had previously been noted for the high number of marriages celebrated,[58] suggesting that financial penalties had more persuasive power than ecclesiastical censure. To some extent, it led to more marriages being solemnised in the appropriate parish.[59] But within London it also led to new centres for clandestine marriages emerging. Although clearly not exempt from the legislation, marriages continued to be celebrated in the chapel of the Fleet prison.[60] And a subsequent attempt to stamp out this practice by imposing a fine on any prison keeper who permitted marriages to be performed in a prison[61] resulted in what was to become the most notorious form of clandestine marriage: the celebration of marriages in the Rules of the Fleet.[62]

So the question posed in the introduction to this chapter – whether clandestine marriages were a recent craze or an embedded tradition – has to be answered by reference to the changing nature of clandestinity. As the eighteenth century dawned, there was certainly no tradition of marrying outside a recognised place of worship. Whatever the motivation for those who married otherwise

56 Section 2. 57 Section 4.

58 See Tomlinson, *History of the Minories*, noting the fall in the number of marriages celebrated at the Minories from 1,060 in 1692 to 477 in 1695, 152 in 1700 and an average of only 24 per annum after 1703. See also Benton, *Irregular Marriages*; Boulton, 'Itching after Private Marryings?' and 'Clandestine Marriages in London'.

59 See Boulton, 'The Marriage Duty Act', p. 229; and E. A. Wrigley, 'Clandestine Marriage in Tetbury in the Late Seventeenth Century' (1973) 10 *Local Population Studies* 15, 20, although see below for my challenge to his inference that earlier marriages had taken place outside any church.

60 For an account of 'divers ill practices in the Fleet Prison', see *Journals of the House of Commons*, vol. 15, p. 188.

61 An Act for ... better securing Her Majesties Duties to arise in the Office for the Stamp Duty by Licences for Marriages: (1711) 10 Anne c. 18, s. 192. On the factors influencing this legislation and its implementation see R. L. Brown, 'The Rise and Fall of the Fleet Marriage', ch. 6 in R. B. Outhwaite, *Marriage and Society* (London: Europa Publications Ltd, 1981).

62 The Fleet was a debtors' prison, and its Rules were a defined area outside the actual prison in which those unable to pay their debts were allowed to reside. Its limits were set by statute: 8 & 9 Will. 3 c. 27. See R. L. Brown, *A History of the Fleet Prison: the Anatomy of the Fleet* (Lampeter: Edwin Mellen Press Ltd, 1996).

than according to the strict (although often changing) letter of the law, it is clear that the story of clandestine marriage in the seventeenth century is one of commitment to marrying in church, if not necessarily the church that the canons would have prescribed.[63]

But before attempting to determine how popular marriages outside a church were to become in the eighteenth century we must turn to a further question posed in the introduction: was a clandestine marriage a *full* alternative to a regular marriage?

THE CONSEQUENCES OF A CLANDESTINE MARRIAGE

My dear, don't cry, tho' we were married at the Fleet, I'll marry you again at Church if you desire it.[64]

It was suggested by some early authorities that a marriage celebrated clandestinely did not entitle the parties to the same rights as one celebrated in church,[65] but as early as the sixteenth century it had been confirmed that a wife who had married clandestinely was still entitled to dower.[66] By the eighteenth century it could be confidently stated that: 'if the Marriage be by a Priest of the Church of England, neither the Want of Banns, or License, or the being perform'd at an uncanonical Hour, or in a Closet, by Night or Day, will divest the Parties of any of the Rights, Privileges, or

[63] See e.g., R. Spalding (ed.), *The Diary of Bulstrode Whitlocke, 1605–1675* (Oxford University Press, 1990), pp. 61, 69, 95, 262. His second marriage is particularly worthy of note, since it took place against the opposition of the bride's family. Having got his bride into his coach under the very noses of her family, they 'came away not slowely to Fawley Court ... He caused his gates to shutt, & they went presently into the Chappell, where the Parson of Fawley being ready, they were marryed' (p. 95).

[64] *The trial of Thomas Thomson and Lavinia Whitney, on an Indictment for a Conspiracy, in Procuring one William Gibson, a Sawyer, to Personate Mr Samuel Brooks* (London, 1730), p. 13.

[65] See e.g., H. Bracton, *De Legibus et Consuetudinibus Angliae* (Sir Travers Twiss (ed.), 1879; original thirteenth century), vol. II, p. 51, on the position regarding dower: 'an appointment is not valid, which is made in the bed of death, or in a chamber, or elsewhere, where clandestine unions are made, because if clandestine unions are not valid for the heirs as regard succession, they are not valid for the wives as regards their exaction of the dower'. See also E. J. Carlson, *Marriage and the English Reformation* (Oxford: Blackwell, 1994), p. 29.

[66] See e.g., *A Profitable Booke of Maister Iohn Perkins, Felow of the Inner Temple Treating the Lawes of England* (London, 1559), tit. Dower, fol. 61, noting that the law had changed, and *Wickham* v. *Enfield* (1633) Cro. Car. 351; 79 ER 908.

Advantages of a Marriage solemnized in the Face of the Church'.[67] This is confirmed by the cases in which couples had married clandestinely. If one of the parties refused to live with the other, a suit for restitution of conjugal rights would lie;[68] if one went through a ceremony of marriage with another, he or she would be guilty of bigamy;[69] and on the death of one the survivor was entitled to administration of the estate.[70]

So the parties to a clandestine marriage (which, we should recall, was by definition presided over by an Anglican clergyman) would be entitled to the same legal *rights* as a couple who had married in regular form. But this did not mean that all the *consequences* of a clandestine marriage would be identical to those of a regular marriage: in some cases a court might prevent a person who had married clandestinely from pursuing their legal remedies on the basis that, as Lord Hardwicke noted in *Hill* v. *Turner*, 'it is incumbent on the Court to prevent, as far as they can, persons from profiting themselves by such infamous methods'.[71] In addition, there were two adverse consequences that might flow from a clandestine marriage: first, there were specific evidential difficulties (both legal and practical) in proving that such a marriage had actually taken place, and, secondly, once this was established, there was the risk of being subject to ecclesiastical censure for flouting the requirements of the canon law.

But why did clandestine marriages raise problems of proof? After all, they by definition involved the presence of a clergyman, and many of the informal registers and notebooks of Fleet parsons survive to this day. The difficulties for those attempting to prove that the marriage had taken place related both to the rules as to what evidence would be legally admissible and to the practical

67 T. Salmon, *A Critical Essay concerning Marriage* (London, 1724), p. 210. See also H. Rolle, *Un abridgment des plusiers cases et resolutions del common ley alphabeticalment digest desouth severall titles* (London, 1668), p. 341.

68 *Grant* v. *Grant* (1754) 1 Lee 592; 161 ER 217; *Conran* v. *Lowe* (1754) 1 Lee 630; 161 ER 230.

69 This is evident from the large number of bigamy cases in which the Fleet featured as a venue for one or more of the alleged marriages: see further below.

70 *Taylor* v. *Taylor* (1756) 2 Lee 274; 161 ER 339; *Alfray* v. *Alfray* (1758) 2 Lee 547; 161 ER 435.

71 (1737) West T Hard. 195; 25 ER 892, p. 197. For the facts of the case, see Chapter 6. The jurisdiction of the Court of Chancery was engaged because the marriage had involved a ward of court. His wife was restrained from proceeding in her claim for restitution of conjugal rights and alimony.

problem that those who made their living from conducting clandestine ceremonies might be willing to conceal or disclose evidence according to which side could offer the most money.[72]

In terms of legally admissible evidence, the first problem was that the very circumstances of the marriage might cause the officiating clergyman and any witnesses to be barred from giving evidence.[73] Those present at clandestine marriages could be, and were, excommunicated,[74] and 'such person would not be admitted in the spiritual court to prove such marriage, until he should be legally absolved from the sentence incurred thereby'.[75] Of course, if the witnesses were willing to come before the court, admit the offence, and obtain absolution, they would be able to give evidence, but the very process may have acted as a disincentive to potential witnesses. Even if admissible, little weight would be given to the evidence of a Fleet parson: in one case, evidence as to declarations by one such parson (since deceased) were held inadmissible as evidence since 'even his evidence on oath, if he had been examined, could hardly have had any credit given to it'.[76] In a similar vein, it was noted in *Scrimshire* v. *Scrimshire* that the very fact that the witnesses had been at a clandestine marriage 'in some measure affects their credit'.[77]

In the absence of witnesses (whether excommunicate, deceased, or bribed by the other side), the party seeking to establish the

72 See e.g., the commentary on the Bill that became the 1753 Act in BL Add 35880, fol. 72: 'The only evidence must be that of ye parson or pretended parson who married ye parties. He may be dead; in ye multiplicity of faces he may not remember. He will remember or not as he is paid by either side in ye dispute. If he does remember he is infamous & will not be credited in a court of justice.'

73 See also J. Ashton, *The Fleet: Its River, Prison, and Marriages* (London: T. Fisher Unwin, 1889), who cites a case in which a suit for restitution of conjugal rights failed because the minister had been excommunicated for conducting clandestine marriages and could not be received as a witness.

74 As Lord Hardwicke noted in *Middleton* v. *Croft* (1737) 2 Barn. KB 351; 94 ER 547, p. 352, 'all persons of what sort soever assisting in such clandestine marriage, are within the danger of the penalty'.

75 R. Burn, *Ecclesiastical Law* (London, 1763), p. 24. See also the example, cited in *Middleton* v. *Croft* (1736) Cas. T Hard. 57, at 58, of Sir Edward Coke and those present at his clandestine wedding, *Husbands and Emmerton* v. *Viner and Adams* (1676) 3 Keble 447; 84 ER 815, *Robins* v. *Wolseley* (1754) 1 Lee 616; 84 ER 815, and the discussion in *Grant* v. *Grant* (1754) 1 Lee 592; 161 ER 217.

76 *Plunkett, formerly Sharp* v. *Sharp* (1753) 1 Lee 439; 161 ER 163, at 441.

77 *Scrimshire* v. *Scrimshire* (1752) 2 Hag. Con. 395; 161 ER 782, at 403. See also the report of *Green* v. *Luff* in *The London Magazine* (1732), vol. 1, p. 203: 'notwithstanding a Fleet Parson swore he married them, and a certain woman

marriage might provide as evidence a certificate or entry in a marriage register. The courts were, however, rather suspicious of the registers kept by Fleet parsons, and with ample justification. Fleet parsons were thought to be all too willing to backdate or even forge entries.[78] In *Conran* v. *Lowe*, for example, the court expressed its suspicion that the evidence had been fabricated by the parson 'with a view either of producing it ... or of suppressing it, as it should appear most advantageous to himself'.[79] Small wonder then, if Lord Hardwicke really did tear up one Fleet register that was produced in court, refusing to admit it as evidence.[80] Sir George Lee, presiding over the Prerogative Court in the mid-eighteenth century, was similarly direct in his rejection of the certificate of a Fleet parson: 'it was not evidence, and could not have credit in any Court; and though it was offered only as a circumstance, yet if credit could not be given to it, it could not be received for any purpose'.[81] He acknowledged that he was departing from the practice of his predecessor in taking this strict line but declared that he personally would never admit such evidence unless and until the Delegates stated that it ought to be received.

Those who had genuinely married in the Fleet, albeit clandestinely, would, however, be able to rely on other evidence to support their claim.[82] The claim that a clandestine ceremony had occurred could be supported by evidence that the parties had lived together

deposed she was present; yet, upon the whole Matter, and considering how little Credit is given at Law to Fleet Marriage, it was set aside by the judge, as several have before been'.

[78] See e.g., *Weekly Journal*, 23 February 1717, noting the 'scandalous frauds' contained in the registers kept by John Mottram. The practice regularly appears as a plot-device in contemporary fiction: see e.g., T. Smollett, *Ferdinand Count Fathom*. See also Brown, 'The Rise and Fall of the Fleet Marriage', p. 130; Ashton, *The Fleet*, p. 343. An additional complication was that the parties might give false names: see e.g., *Pool* v. *Sacheverel* (1720) 1 P Wms 676; 24 ER 565, which concerned a man who had married his maidservant in the Fleet under a different name.

[79] (1754) 1 Lee 630; 161 ER 630.

[80] This, at least, was the story that was being told at the end of the eighteenth century. See *Read* v. *Passer* (1794) 1 Esp. 213; 170 ER 332; *Lawrence* v. *Dixon* (1792) Peake 185; 170 ER 123.

[81] *Plunkett, formerly Sharp* v. *Sharp* (1753) 1 Lee 439; 161 ER 163. See also *Conran* v. *Lowe* (1754) 1 Lee 630; 161 ER 230, in which he stated that a Fleet register 'was not evidence' (p. 639).

[82] See e.g., *Beard* v. *Travers* (1749) 1 Ves. Sen. 313; 27 ER 1052, in which it was noted that '[i]n cases relating to clandestine marriages, hearsay evidence and declarations are no defective proof'.

and been reputed to be husband and wife.[83] (Of these two elements, it should be noted that reputation was more important than co-residence: there are cases where a marriage was upheld despite the fact that the parties had never lived together,[84] but none where a claim succeeded without evidence that they had been reputed to be husband and wife.)

But such evidence might be ambiguous, and the clandestine nature of the alleged ceremony an argument against presuming its validity.[85] The case of *Conran* v. *Lowe, otherwise Daniel, calling herself Conran*[86] illustrates this problem – and indeed the other potential problems of proving a Fleet marriage. The case originated in a suit for restitution of conjugal rights brought by Mary Lowe (or Daniel or Conran, depending whose version of events is to be believed). She claimed to have married William Conran in the Fleet in 1741. The parson and the sole other witness to the ceremony were dead. Custody of the parson's register had passed to one Watson, but it contained no detail of the marriage, allegedly because William Conran had given him ten guineas (and a note for forty guineas more to be paid three days after the court had pronounced against the marriage) to tear out the relevant page. When Mary brought her suit in the London Consistory Court, William alleged that she had previously married James Daniel in Ireland, and that he had still been alive at the time of the marriage Mary was now claiming. Although no-one who had been present at this earlier wedding was available to give evidence, there were witnesses who had heard others declare that they had been present at it; there was also evidence that James had come to London to look for his wife and that she had told him that 'it was to no purpose to trouble her; it was better for him to let her live with Conran, and she would

[83] See also *Alfray* v. *Alfray* (1758) 2 Lee 547; 161 ER 435, in which evidence of the parties' courtship was required.

[84] See e.g., *Walton* v. *Rider* (1752) 1 Lee 16; 161 ER 7. In this case the husband, a student at Cambridge, had been courting the wife. When she became pregnant they married in the Fleet, but she and her son (born two months later) lived with her father, and received no financial support from the husband. Similarly, in *Grant* v. *Grant* (1754) 1 Lee 592; 161 ER 217, the cohabitation of the parties was intermittent: the wife continued to reside under her father's roof and her husband boarded there and 'lay with [her] when he pleased'.

[85] See e.g., *Dry* v. *Sutton* (1721), in which evidence of a prior marriage was allowed, 'the second Marriage being clandestine, and no notorious cohabitation to enforce a Presumption': Sir J. Strange, *A Collection of Select Cases relating to Evidence* (London, 1754), p. 79.

[86] (1754) 1 Lee 630; 161 ER 230.

make him remittances of money to Ireland'.[87] As Mary's own witnesses acknowledged, she had 'the character of being a loose woman' and 'owned herself ... to be a common whore'.[88] The court (with some justification, one feels) refused to believe that she was married to Conran.

The problem of proof had another dimension. As we have seen, a couple who set up home together without it being known whether or not they were married might be cited before the ecclesiastical court for 'living and cohabiting scandalously and suspiciously as man and wife without lawful marriage'.[89] Those found guilty of such an offence could be required to do penance. Of course, it was possible for a couple who had married clandestinely to come before the court and inform them of the marriage: the correction books for the Diocese of Carlisle noted this fact on a number of occasions.[90] But confessing a clandestine marriage posed its own problems, since couples could be required to do penance for flouting the canon law in this way.[91] Thus, in 1740 it was noted in the correction book that one couple had been cited two years earlier for cohabiting 'scandalously and suspiciously', and had produced a certificate confirming that they had married clandestinely, but that they had failed to perform the penance enjoined by the court for this offence and were therefore to be excommunicated.[92] Indeed, the authorities sometimes hedged their bets as to which offence had been committed, accusing parties of *either* a clandestine marriage *or* living together without lawful marriage.[93]

The jurisdiction of the ecclesiastical courts to punish couples for marrying clandestinely was challenged in the case of *Middleton* v. *Croft* in 1737,[94] but the challenge was only partially successful.[95]

[87] *Ibid.* at 636. [88] *Ibid.* at 632.
[89] Carlisle Record Office (CRO), DRC/5/7. See further Chapter 3.
[90] CRO, DRC/5/7, Artheret, 1732; Kirkandrews upon Eden, 1735 (a marriage in Scotland); Great Salkeld, 1739; Torpenhow, 1740.
[91] CRO, DRC/5/7, Great Salkeld, 1739; Bampton, 1739; Holm, 1739; St Andrews in Penrith, 1743.
[92] CRO DRC/5/7, Torpenhow, 1740.
[93] CRO, DRC/5/7, Crosby, 1731; Andrews upon Eden, 1739 (fornication or clandestine marriage); Kirkby Stephen, 1743.
[94] (1737) Cas. T Hard. 325; 95 ER 211; Cun. 55; 94 ER 1059; 2 Strange 1057; 93 ER 1030; 2 Barn. KB 351; 94 ER 547.
[95] The narrowness of the point decided has not always been appreciated: see e.g., Stone, *Road to Divorce*, p. 117; P. Langford, *A Polite and Commercial People: England 1727–1783* (Oxford: Clarendon Press, 1998), p. 41.

The case involved a couple who had married before eight o'clock in the morning, in a private house, and without banns or licence, and who were cited into the ecclesiastical court. They sought a prohibition on the basis that the relevant canons did not bind the laity, or, alternatively, that the power of the ecclesiastical courts to punish for marrying clandestinely had been supplanted by legislation imposing financial penalties.[96] The court, presided over by Lord Hardwicke, held that the ancient canon law did bind the laity, although additions made in 1604 did not, and that the power of the ecclesiastical courts to punish a couple for marrying clandestinely had not been abrogated by legislation.[97] The result was that couples could be punished by the ecclesiastical court for flouting requirements that had been confirmed by statute, such as marrying without banns or licence, or outside an Anglican place of worship, but not those set out in the 1604 canons alone, such as marrying between the hours of eight a.m. and twelve noon.[98] It was a decision based both on precedent and on policy grounds: the court noted that the jurisdiction of the ecclesiastical court had received the sanction of the King's Bench,[99] and added 'we think it our duty, not to weaken any lawful method, whereby clandestine marriages may be prevented'.[100]

So far we have been considering the adverse legal consequences that might flow even if a clandestine marriage was valid. It should, however, be noted that those who went through a ceremony of marriage in the Fleet might find that they had no legal status at all. The case of *Taylor* v. *Taylor*[101] illustrates the problem. The question for the court was who was entitled to be granted the administration of the estate of the deceased Thomas Taylor. He had gone through three ceremonies of marriage, two in the Fleet and one before a clergyman in a private house. If the first was valid the second could not be, but the third would be, as the 'wife' to the

[96] As to the details of this legislation, see above.
[97] The history of the ecclesiastical courts' jurisdiction is discussed in Cas. T Hard. 325, at 336.
[98] Cun. 55; 94 ER 1059, at 127.
[99] In *Matingley* v. *Martyn* (1632) Jones, W. 257; 82 ER 134.
[100] (1737) Cas. T Hard. 325; 95 ER 211, at 339. However, a prohibition was granted in relation to the specific charge of marrying outside the hours of eight a.m. to twelve noon. For discussion of the case, see G.R. Bush, 'Dr Codex Silenced: *Middleton* v. *Crofts* Revisited' (2003) 24 *Journal of Legal History* 23.
[101] (1756) 2 Lee 274; 161 ER 339.

first marriage had died before the third was celebrated. But, to make matters even more complicated, there was evidence to suggest that the first 'wife' was already married, in which case the second marriage would be valid but the third would not. After hearing copious and contradictory evidence, Sir George Lee resolved that the second marriage had been valid, since the ceremony was confirmed by 'two express witnesses', and there was tolerable evidence that the first 'wife' was already married to another when she went through a ceremony with Thomas. The risk that one's 'spouse' might already be married was not a problem unique to Fleet marriages, but it was undoubtedly compounded by the speed and anonymity that the Fleet offered.

It is clear, therefore, that while a clandestine marriage offered a full alternative to regular marriage, in that the parties were entitled to the same legal rights as if they had married in church, it was not unproblematic for the parties involved, who might later rue their decision to marry in this way.[102] But how many couples were willing to take such risks?

ESTIMATES OF THE EXTENT OF CLANDESTINE MARRIAGES

Enough has been said already to make it clear that clandestine marriages were both a full and a functional alternative to a regular marriage for many couples.[103] But knowing just how prevalent clandestine marriages were is essential in evaluating the impact of the Clandestine Marriages Act: the more popular they were, the more the Act would have been a break with practice. A global figure for the entirety of England and Wales may, however, be somewhat misleading: urban and rural areas should be considered separately, as should clandestine marriages that took place within a church and those that did not.

[102] No-one could complain that they had not been warned: see e.g., *The Christian's Companion, in the Principles of Religion, and the Concerns of Human Life* (London, 1716), p. 282; J. Barnard, *A Present for an Apprentice: or, a Sure Guide to Gain Both Esteem and Estate* (London, 1740), p. 31.

[103] Although those who married privately in order to keep the marriage secret might not cohabit: see e.g., *Whitaker* v. *Lee alias Whitaker* (1767) PRO DEL 1/588, in which it was alleged that the marriage had taken place in 1737 and was followed by private visits rather than open cohabitation.

London marriages

Eighteenth-century London had a number of places that were famous for the celebration of clandestine marriages. It seems almost compulsory in any account of clandestine marriage to include the tale of the Duke of Hamilton, who wed one of the Gunning sisters at Keith's chapel in Mayfair 'at whirlwind style at midnight ... with a curtain ring'.[104] The chapel in question was actually Alexander Keith's second venue for clandestine marriages: having been appointed incumbent of St George's Chapel, Hyde Park Corner, in the 1730s, Keith celebrated an increasing number of marriages there: 117 in 1741 and 723 in 1742. As a result he was excommunicated; and when he attempted to retaliate by purporting to excommunicate the bishop he was committed to the Fleet prison for contempt.[105] His subsequent venture, a little over a year later, was to set up a rival establishment, directing those who wished to be married to 'Mr Keith's Little Chapel in May-Fair, near Hyde-Park Corner, opposite the Great Chapel, and within Ten Yards of it'.[106] The marriages there were celebrated by parsons operating out of the Fleet prison,[107] who also conducted ceremonies in houses within its Rules, and sometimes further afield.[108] Since the marriages celebrated at the Mayfair chapel, together with many of the marriages celebrated at the Mint, in Newgate, and at the King's Bench prison, appear in what are now collectively termed the Fleet registers,[109] the following discussion

104 E. Mavor, *The Virgin Mistress: a Study in Survival* (London: Chatto & Windus, 1964), p. 62; see also M. Baker, *Wedding Customs and Folklore* (Newton Abbot: David & Charles Publishers Ltd, 1977), p. 47; Burn, *The History of the Parish Registers*, p. 156. The marriage took place on 14 February 1752: *Daily Advertiser*, 15 February 1752.

105 See *Dr Trebec* v. *Keith* (1742) 2 Atk. 498; 26 ER 700; *London Evening Post*, 30 October 1742.

106 *The Morning Advertiser*, 13 May 1748.

107 Keith himself celebrated no more clandestine marriages. It seems that he was less free to leave the Fleet than other prisoners there: he was described as a 'close prisoner' (see e.g., *London Gazetteer*, 2 October 1749) and when his wife died her body was embalmed and kept until he could attend her funeral (see e.g., *Old England*, 20 January 1750; *Penny London Post*, 26 January 1750).

108 See e.g., the notebook kept by one Fleet parson, who recorded celebrating marriages at various taverns, coffee-houses and even a bagnio: PRO RG 7/163.

109 See e.g., G. J. Armytage, *The Register of Baptisms and Marriages at St George's Chapel, May Fair* (London: Harleian Society, 1889); Burn, *The History of the Parish Registers*, pp. 149–50.

will, for convenience, use the terms Fleet parsons and Fleet registers as a shorthand for all such clandestine marriages in London.

The first question has to be, how did the Fleet parsons manage to get away with it? As noted above, the statutory penalties imposed on clandestine marriages had pushed them out of the churches, and then out of prison chapels. But the marriages that took place in alehouses within the Rules of the Fleet were not exempt from the legislation: those celebrating marriages there were exploiting the lack of supervision rather than a legal loophole. As Finn has commented, '[t]he paucity of prison administration, the ready availability of alcohol, and the porous boundaries that divided inmates from the outside world fostered an array of disorderly cultural practices within the unreformed debtors' prison'.[110] Moreover, those who celebrated clandestine marriages generally had much less to lose than their clerical counterparts with comfortable livings: the celebration of a clandestine marriage carried with it the risk of being suspended from one's living for three years,[111] but it has already been noted that this held no threat for clergymen with no livings to lose. Whether the parsons who married couples in the Fleet had actually been imprisoned for debt themselves has been debated,[112] but it is clear that at least some of them had been.[113] Indeed, some of them may have been imprisoned for debt directly as a result of celebrating a clandestine marriage.[114] Those who were in prison for debt had to make money to secure their release by one means or another, and few of their clerical services would have

[110] M. Finn, *The Character of Credit: Personal Debt in English Culture, 1740–1914* (Cambridge University Press, 2003), p. 138.

[111] The canon law prescribed that 'No minister, upon pain of suspension per triennium ipso facto, shall celebrate matrimony between any persons' without a licence or banns being published: canon 62 of the 1604 Canons, see G. Bray (ed.), *The Anglican Canons 1529–1947* (Woodbridge: Boydell Press, 1998). Financial penalties were also imposed by statute, as noted above.

[112] See Brown, 'The Rise and Fall of the Fleet Marriage', p. 120, who suggests that they may have entered the prison on a voluntary basis to gain immunity.

[113] See e.g., *Weekly Journal*, 28 June 1718, noting the imprisonment of John Gaynam in Ludgate for a debt of £500; *London Gazette*, 28 May 1748, in which James Lando gave notice that he intended to take the benefit of recent legislation for the relief of insolvent debtors. See also the report of the committee appointed to consider the issue in 1705, which described the parsons as prisoners: *Journals of the House of Commons*, vol. 15, p. 188.

[114] The legislation had provided that the sums forfeit for marrying contrary to the law were 'to be recovered by action of debt, bill, plaint or information': 6 & 7 Will. 3 c. 7, s. 52. See also 10 Anne c. 19, s. 176, to like effect.

been as lucrative as that of the celebration of matrimony. Such parsons did not escape punishment altogether (John Mottram, for example, was found guilty of solemnising clandestine marriages in 1717,[115] and 'fin'd [£]100 each according to the Statute')[116] but the potential demand made the risk worthwhile.[117]

Once the Fleet became known as a place where clandestine marriages could be celebrated, or a parson procured, it was natural for couples to resort to it when other venues (such as Holy Trinity Minories and St James' Duke's Place) ceased to offer opportunities for clandestine marriage. After all, when embarking on any illicit activity it is always easier to go to a place where one knows one can obtain a particular service than to engage in a potentially futile search elsewhere. To some extent the very size of London ensured that there would always be business for parsons offering clandestine marriages. But London's population was distinctive in other ways as well, in that it had a far higher turnover of residents than other cities. Some were present for a very short period of time: the Fleet lay a stone's throw from the Thames, and sailors formed a significant proportion of the Fleet's clientele in the early eighteenth century.[118] London also attracted a large number of immigrants:[119] Wrigley, for example, has estimated that net immigration into London must have been about 8,000 per year between 1650 and 1750, and 'considerably larger than this' towards the end of that period.[120] Such migrants would primarily have been young and single – and thus eligible to marry – but would not necessarily have had an attachment to any particular parish in London.

115 *Postman*, 16 February 1717. 116 *British Gazetteer*, 23 February 1717

117 Ashton, *The Fleet*, p. 343, notes that Mottram continued to marry couples.

118 Brown, 'The Rise and Fall of the Fleet Marriage', has calculated that sailors accounted for 16.3 per cent of the Fleet's clientele in 1700 and 26.4 per cent in 1710. By 1740 the proportion had fallen to 7.6 per cent, but this should be viewed against a significant increase in overall numbers. See also the engraving 'A Fleet Wedding, between a Brisk Young Sailor, and his Landlady's Daughter at Rederiff', published in 1747, and 'The Sailor's Fleet Wedding Entertainment': Ashton, *The Fleet*, pp. 367–9.

119 One contemporary speculated that it was 'very probable that two thirds of the grown persons at any time in London come from distant parts': G. Burrington, *An Answer to Dr William Brakenridge's Letter concerning the Number of Inhabitants, within the London Bills of Mortality* (London, 1757), p. 37.

120 E. A. Wrigley, 'A Simple Model of London's Importance in Changing English Society and Economy 1650–1750' (1967) 37 *Past and Present* 44, 46.

Certainly the Fleet registers contain a large number of marriages involving parties from outside London. One study noted the records of around 6,500 persons said to be from Hertfordshire marrying in the Fleet,[121] while two couples claiming settlement in the Wiltshire parish of Bradford-on-Avon informed the authorities that they had married in the Fleet.[122] Whether those who gave a parish outside London as their place of residence when they married in the Fleet were recent immigrants or had come to London for the sole purpose of marrying there, is impossible to ascertain in most cases.[123] All too rarely do we find accounts such as that of Mary Cowley, whose story is preserved in settlement examinations for the Buckinghamshire parish of Olney. Born in Olney, Mary was subsequently sent to London with her father, who was settled there. She lived there for some time, and married her first husband in the Fleet. When she came back to Olney for a visit, she met another man: on her return to London she heard that her first husband was dead and married the second man in the Fleet.[124] In this case it is clear that Mary did not travel to London for the sole purpose of marrying in the Fleet. It was otherwise for William Walton and Rachel Rider, who travelled from Ely to London when Rachel became pregnant: they 'came to town and told a relation they were contracted ... [and] were married at the Fleet by Wagstaffe, a priest of the Church of England'.[125] But whether those marrying in the Fleet or Keith's chapel had come to London solely for that purpose[126] or had migrated for economic or other

121 J. Parker, *Fleet Marriages of Hertfordshire People to 1754: an Alphabetical Index of Grooms and Brides* (St Albans: Herts Family and Population History Society, 1999).

122 In one case this was explicit; in the second case the parties claimed to have married in the parish of St Martin Ludgate, but the church register contains no record of their marriage. It is likely that this marriage too took place in the Fleet, since the certificates issued by at least one Fleet parson 'described the place of marriage as either St Bride Fleet Street, St Martin Ludgate or St Sepulchre according to the location of the marriage-house where the wedding was conducted'. Benton, *Irregular Marriages*, p. 32.

123 See also Brown, 'The Rise and Fall of the Fleet Marriage', p. 124.

124 *The People of Olney* (Aylesbury: Eureka Partnership, 2006), p. 17.

125 *Walton* v. *Rider* (1752) 1 Lee 16; 161 ER 7, at 8.

126 That this was the case for many is suggested by the high proportion of couples described as being from the same, distant, parish. Those marrying at Keith's chapel in 1753 included couples from Arrow in Warwickshire, Sherborne in Dorset, and Felbrigg in Norfolk, while on 1 January 1754 James Bone and Jane Summers, both from Northshields in Northumberland, married there: Armytage, *The Register of Baptisms and Marriages at St George's Chapel, May Fair*, pp. 244, 247, 249, 267.

reasons, the implication is that the popularity of Fleet marriages needs to be located in a regional rather than a local perspective.

So, just how many marriages were celebrated by Fleet parsons? As early as 1705 a committee reported that 2,954 marriages had been recorded as taking place at the Fleet between 19 October 1704 and 12 February 1705.[127] The surviving records consist of 545 notebooks and 290 registers and indexes,[128] the former containing the marriages celebrated by individual ministers and the latter recording marriages conducted by various ministers within a certain period of time. To date, the most detailed study of these records is that carried out by Roger Lee Brown.[129] His figures show that the number of marriages recorded initially fell in the wake of the 1711 legislation imposing penalties on gaolers who permitted marriages to be celebrated in prisons,[130] but had risen to a higher level by 1720, and he estimates that in 1740 no fewer than 6,609 marriages were celebrated there. This, however, is an estimate based on an allowance being made for missing registers. Yet the number of marriages recorded does not necessarily correlate to the number of marriages celebrated. As the case of *Conran* v. *Lowe* illustrates, there was good money to be made from revealing or concealing the record of a marriage. The cannier parsons might well keep multiple versions of notebooks and registers, so that one could be produced to confirm or deny allegations of a marriage. The house in which the marriage was celebrated might also have its own register, and there were also clerks who compiled registers from these sources (presumably to charge a fee to those wishing to prove a marriage).[131] As a result, while it is likely that some registers have been lost, the extent of duplication between registers, and between the registers and the parsons' individual notebooks, makes it less likely that all record of any particular marriage has been lost. In addition, there may well be records of some marriages that never took place: some registers are known to be forgeries,[132] and

127 *Journals of the House of Commons*, vol. 15, p. 188.

128 B. Lloyd, *The Fleet Forgeries* (1987, unpublished typescript).

129 'The Rise and Fall of the Fleet Marriage'. 130 See above.

131 M. Herber, *Clandestine Marriages in the Chapel and Rules of the Fleet Prison, 1680–1754* (London: Francis Bootle Publishers, 1998), p. 20.

132 Lloyd, *The Fleet Forgeries*, notes that registers purporting to date from 1674 to 1680 in fact replicate the details in much later registers, save for the name of the officiating parson.

individual records may also result simply from the desire of one of the parties to have it appear that a marriage took place.[133]

A study of the available transcripts confirms the extent of duplication between different sources. Of the first 249 marriages recorded in Herber's (helpfully cross-referenced) transcript of two registers and five notebooks, 62 marriages appear twice, 154 three times, 25 four times, 4 five times and one marriage 6 times out of a possible 7 sources. Only three were recorded only once. This means that 246 marriages accounted for 710 entries in these 7 sources alone. Similarly, an index to the Fleet marriages of Hertfordshire residents[134] enables it to be calculated that approximately 1,100 marriages are represented by 1,522 entries in the registers (266 were mentioned in 2 registers, 44 in 3, 16 in 4, and 5 in all 5), and since this index excluded the parsons' notebooks it is likely that this underestimates the extent of duplication. In each of these cases, cross-referencing further registers and notebooks might well reveal even more duplication.[135] Given such evidence of duplication, it might be more appropriate to reduce any figure based on a count of entries, rather than revising upwards to make allowance for lost registers.[136] Similarly, given that the Fleet registers include details of marriages celebrated in Keith's Mayfair chapel and other locations, it is inappropriate to view these as a separate category to be added to Brown's estimate.[137] A final estimate for the number of marriages celebrated at the Fleet must await the transcription of the existing material, but my suggestion would be that they accounted for less than half of marriages celebrated in London.

This must, of course, be reconciled with evidence from other sources which would seem at first sight to confirm that large numbers

[133] The entries in the registers are often very widely spaced, allowing scope for further entries to be inserted at a later date; in certain places a series of more closely-written entries in a different hand suggests just such a later addition, although other more innocent explanations are possible.

[134] Parker, *Fleet Marriages of Hertfordshire People to 1754*.

[135] See further Lloyd, *The Fleet Forgeries*, p. 7.

[136] Herber, for example, who has transcribed a number of Fleet registers, suggests that the estimated 350,000 entries probably represent 250,000 marriages: M. Herber, *Clandestine Marriages in the Chapel and Rules of the Fleet Prison, 1680–1754* (London: Francis Bootle Publishers, 2001), vol. 3, p. 16.

[137] Cf. Stone, *Road to Divorce*, p. 115, who adds those celebrated at Keith's chapel to Brown's estimate for the Fleet.

of Londoners married in the Fleet. For example, Hitchcock and Black's study of Chelsea settlement examinations between 1733 and 1766 found that half of the 190 marriages where the place of marriage was cited were conducted in the Fleet;[138] Trumbach found similar proportions in the parish of St Margaret's, Westminster,[139] with one-third of those applying for relief between 1714 and 1721 claiming that they had been married in the Fleet, rising to 63 per cent of those claiming relief in the 1740s. But given that the Fleet attracted a disproportionate number of migrants,[140] such figures should not be transposed to London as a whole. It may also be that Fleet marriages appear so often in settlement examinations because the husbands of the women examined had absconded or were already married.[141] As Hitchcock and Black suggest, 'couples married in this way were particularly susceptible to the poverty and insecurity of metropolitan life'.[142] This is reinforced by the number of Fleet marriages that cropped up in the course of bigamy trials. In the 168 trials heard at the Old Bailey between 1715 and 1755, the Fleet was mentioned as the place where at least one of the marriages was celebrated in around half of those reports that give details as to the location of the marriages; this, of course, does not equate to half of the marriages in the sample (there being by definition at least two in every case), and in any case it perhaps indicates simply that the Fleet was a popular venue for marriages that were bigamous.

But even if the Fleet did not account for quite as many marriages as has been thought, it still attracted enough trade for surrounding parishes to complain that few marriages were celebrated in their

138 T. Hitchcock and J. Black, *Chelsea Settlement and Bastardy Examinations, 1733–1766* (London Record Society, 1999), p. xix.

139 R. Trumbach, *Sex and the Gender Revolution*, vol. I, *Heterosexuality and the Third Gender in Enlightenment London* (University of Chicago, 1998), p. 268.

140 A number of settlement examinations available in Hitchcock and Black, *Chelsea Settlement and Bastardy Examinations*, include information as to the parties' place of birth: in this, admittedly small, sample, 69 per cent of marriages that took place in the Fleet involved at least one party from outside London (even when adopting a broad definition of London that would include what were then villages outside the city but which were within an easy day's walk of the Fleet); even more significantly, the proportion of London marriages involving at least one migrant that were celebrated in the Fleet was 83 per cent.

141 See e.g., D. A. Kent, '"Gone for a Soldier": Family Breakdown and the Demography of Desertion in a London Parish, 1750–91' (1990) 45 *Local Population Studies* 27, 39, who notes that Fleet marriages accounted for a high proportion of the broken marriages recorded in settlement examinations.

142 Hitchcock and Black, *Chelsea Settlement and Bastardy Examinations*, p. xix.

churches, and to attribute this to the practice of marrying in the Fleet: according to the churchwardens of Battersea, '[t]he reason why our marriages are so few is because of the evil practice of marrying at the Fleet in a clandestine and scandalous manner'.[143] But the fact that parishioners from Battersea, Hertfordshire, and even Cambridgeshire were choosing to be married in the Fleet does raise a further question: was there nowhere more convenient for them to marry clandestinely?

Clandestine marriages in the provinces

The fact that people travelled to be married at the Fleet is an indication not only of its popularity but also of the lack of facilities for such marriage elsewhere.[144] Indeed, Fleet parsons identified their willingness to travel to other locations when required.[145] When Mary Edes, a ward of court, married the son of a steward, one of those responsible for promoting the match went to London to fetch a Fleet parson to marry the pair of them at Uppark in Sussex.[146]

This is not to say that clandestine marriages did not occur outside London. But it was relatively rare for such marriages to take place outside a church. Individual examples of marriages not celebrated in church can, of course, be found,[147] but when set in context they are a very small minority. The settlement examinations for the parish of Bradford-on-Avon provide only two examples – out of seventy marriages – that took place outside a church: the first, that of John Cripps and Alice Hubert, was celebrated 'at the sign of the Raven in Broad Street, Bath' around

143 W. R. Ward, *Parson and Parish in Eighteenth-Century Surrey: Replies to Bishops' Visitations* (Guildford: Surrey Record Society vol. 34, 1994), p. 6.

144 As Lord Barrington noted in the course of the debates on the 1753 Bill: '[i]n those places they have no Fleet parson nor Keith's chapel to repair to': *Hansard's Parliamentary History*, vol. XV, col. 29. Cf. Stone, *Road to Divorce*, pp. 104–5, whose examples of rural clandestine marriages derive almost exclusively from the seventeenth century.

145 Brown, 'The Rise and Fall of the Fleet Marriage', p. 127; see also S. Richardson, *The History of Sir Charles Grandison* (London, 1753–4), vol. 1, p. 244.

146 *Edes* v. *Brereton* (1738) West T Hard. 347. See also Brown, 'The Rise and Fall of the Fleet Marriage', p. 127.

147 See e.g., *Long* v. *Elways* (1729) Mos. 249; 25 ER 378 (ale-house), and note the examples cited in L. Stone, *Uncertain Unions and Broken Lives: Intimate and Revealing Accounts of Marriage and Divorce in England* (Oxford University Press, 1995), pp. 159, 174, 178, 202.

1730,[148] while the second, that of Samuel and Charity Tucker, took place 'in a private house in Bath'.[149] Given the evidence that the vast majority of the population married in church,[150] the possibility of there being large numbers of untraced clandestine marriages that did not take place in church must be discounted.

One study has, however, advanced a different view and therefore merits closer attention. Wrigley's study of the marriage register of Tetbury in the late seventeenth century led him to infer that a number of the marriages recorded had taken place outside any church.[151] This inference was based on differences in the way in which marriages were recorded in the register in the wake of the 1695 Act: sometimes both the bride and groom were named; sometimes the groom only – and if the latter, he might be described as 'clandestinely married', or just 'married'. Wrigley speculated that '[b]y clandestine marriage [the incumbent] may either have meant a common law marriage contracted by the exchange of vows before witnesses or marriages celebrated by "hedge priests" in private dwellings'.[152] Yet the former interpretation is untenable, given the contemporary meaning of a 'clandestine' marriage, and the latter is an unwarranted assumption in the light of the range of forms that a clandestine marriage might take. Moreover, as we have seen in previous chapters, differences in practice cannot necessarily be inferred from differences in recording.[153]

An examination of Wrigley's sources suggests an alternative possibility. At least one of the fourteen grooms described as having married clandestinely had married in church – only in the wrong church. Henry Gegg was described as being 'of Tetbury' when he married in Cirencester in 1695, as was his bride. The marriage was clearly clandestine, since neither belonged to the parish where it took place, but it involved only a minor infraction of the canon law.[154] It is possible that the other thirteen had also

[148] P. Hembry (ed.), *Calendar of Bradford-on-Avon Settlement Examinations and Removal Orders, 1725–98* (Trowbridge: Wiltshire Record Society, 1990), p. 19.

[149] *Ibid.* p. 28. [150] See Chapter 3.

[151] Wrigley, 'Clandestine Marriage in Tetbury'. [152] *Ibid.* 16.

[153] See the case study of Llansantffraid Glyn Ceiriog, discussed in Chapter 3.

[154] There is a slight time-lag between the date of the marriage and the date it was recorded in the Tetbury register, but a delay in the recording of a marriage celebrated clandestinely in another parish seems more plausible than the swift death of the first wife and clandestine remarriage of the husband in all of these cases: see, for example, the register of Denchworth, Berkshire, in which it was

married in church: possible marriages have been traced in other Gloucestershire parishes for several of the husbands named, but unfortunately none of them are identified in the other registers as being from Tetbury, and without the wife's name it is difficult to be sure that they are the same men as were listed in the Tetbury register. The key point is that there is no evidence that they did *not* marry in church; moreover, given the fact that most clandestine marriages were celebrated in church at this time, it seems inappropriate to assume that these particular marriages were not. This does not affect Wrigley's hypothesis that the high baptism–marriage ratio noted at certain periods may have been due to more couples marrying clandestinely at certain periods, but it is relevant to the explanation of such practices. The question simply becomes one of why certain churches attracted more couples than others, or of why more couples might have chosen to marry away from their parish at different times.

It is clear that many couples did choose to marry in a parish to which neither party belonged. Many parish records reveal at least one marriage involving parties who are recorded as belonging to other parishes,[155] and Snell suggests that 'the very large number of "foreign" marriages conducted in some parishes before 1754 ... was tantamount almost to a local clerical industry in some places'.[156] But the fact that clandestine marriages occurred in other places and at other times does not mean that the facility to celebrate a marriage clandestinely existed at all times in all places. There might be specific reasons for the popularity of a particular parish at any given time.[157] The very popularity of certain places is in itself an indication of the scarcity of other venues.

noted no earlier than July 1697 that the marriage of Joseph Bulcher and Sarah Baker had taken place on 'Lady-day last past but not in this parish': Berkshire Record Office, D/P46/1/3.

155 See e.g., D. Spaeth, *The Church in an Age of Danger: Parsons and Parishioners 1660–1740* (Cambridge University Press, 2000), p. 209, who notes that at least twenty parishes in Wiltshire 'were each the venue of at least one clandestine marriage in the period'.

156 K. D. M. Snell, 'English Rural Societies and Geographical Marital Endogamy, 1700–1837' (2002) 55 *Economic History Review* 262, 274.

157 See e.g., M. F. Snape, *The Church of England in Industrialising Society: the Lancashire Parish of Whalley in the Eighteenth Century* (Woodbridge: Boydell Press, 2003), p. 116, who notes that 'the presence of an obliging curate caused presentments for [clandestine marriage] to rise from time to time'.

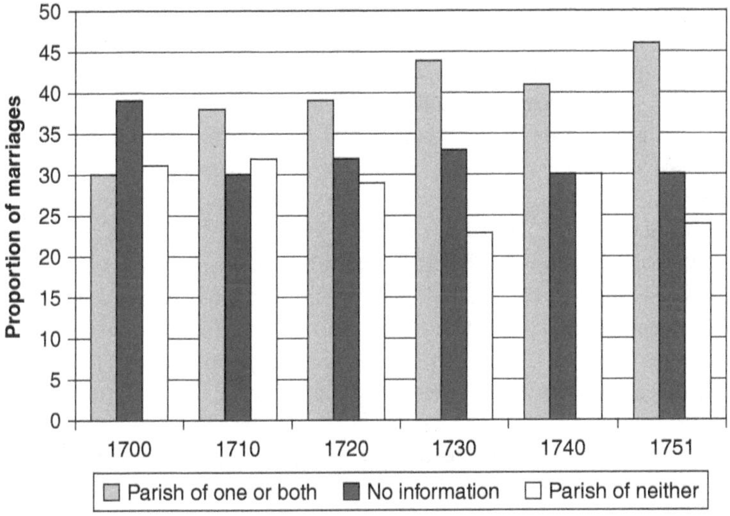

Figure 5.1. Location of marriages

But estimates as to the extent of clandestine marriage in this period have varied considerably because of the different definitions being employed. Some, it would appear, are counting as clandestine only those marriages that did not take place in church;[158] others, by contrast, are including marriages that took place in church but without banns or licence, and in a parish where the parties did not reside.[159] This explains why estimates as to the prevalence of clandestine marriages have varied so widely: if one counts only those that occurred outside a church, then Schofield's estimate that (outside London) a mere 4 per cent of marriages were clandestine in the first quarter of the eighteenth century would fit with the evidence from the Bradford-on-Avon sample, and with

158 See e.g., R. Schofield, 'English Marriage Patterns Revisited' (1985) 10 *Journal of Family History* 2, 14, noting that between 1680 and 1704 '14 per cent of marriages were unregistered and therefore probably clandestine' but that in the decades before and after this was the case for only 4–5 per cent.

159 See e.g., Stone, *Road to Divorce*, p. 115, who offers the 'reasonable guess' that clandestine marriages comprised 15 to 20 per cent of marriages, albeit one based solely on marriages in London; Outhwaite, *Clandestine Marriage*, p. 49, who suggests that around a quarter of marriages were clandestine; and Gillis, *For Better, For Worse*, p. 84, who puts the figure at between one-quarter and one-third.

the few untraced marriages from the Cardington cohort considered in Chapter 3. The practice of marrying in a parish where one was not resident was, however, far more widespread: having carried out a survey of marriages conducted across Northamptonshire at ten-year intervals in the first part of the eighteenth century,[160] it transpired that a significant minority of couples gave a place other than the parish in which they were marrying as their place of residence.[161]

What is equally striking is that the proportion of such marriages seemed to be gradually diminishing over the first part of the eighteenth century, as Figure 5.1 shows, from 31 per cent in 1700 to 24 per cent in 1751; at the same time the proportion of marriages definitely celebrated in the correct parish rose from 30 per cent to 46 per cent.[162]

So it is clear that a sizeable minority of church weddings in the half century before the 1753 Act were technically clandestine in that they were celebrated in a parish to which the parties did not belong. But the impact of the 1753 Act would have depended not merely on the extent of clandestinity, but on the precise form that it took. The final section of this chapter will therefore focus on the attributes of clandestine marriages that were shared with regular marriages.

[160] The study was carried out using the electronic Northamptonshire Marriage Index compiled by A. Clarke and M. Ponting. A search was carried out for every marriage taking place within the years 1700, 1710, 1720, 1730, 1740, and 1751, and each was allocated to one of three categories: parties married in the parish of one or both; parties married in a parish where neither was resident; and 'unknown' where there was no or insufficient evidence about the parties' residence at the time of the marriage. The advantage of carrying out the search electronically was that duplicate entries could be eliminated. Although the methodology was relatively unsophisticated it does at least provide evidence that is not simply derived from secondary sources or single parishes.

[161] In some cases, however, the place identified may in fact have been within the parish itself, but without a knowledge of local terms as used in the eighteenth century this would not necessarily be picked up.

[162] The category of unknowns remained relatively stable, reflecting the fact that whether or not the place of residence was recorded varied between parishes, rather than between individual marriages. There is no reason to believe that this category was comprised of marriages that took place in the wrong parish, and a small test sample found that many of those in this category had in fact been baptised in the parish where they later married. Given the mobility of the population in this period, however, the absence of a baptismal entry in the parish of marriage cannot be taken as evidence that the individual in question was not resident there at the time of the marriage.

THE CONFORMITY OF CLANDESTINE MARRIAGES

Most accounts of clandestine marriages emphasise their irregular aspects: according to Stone, for example, their central characteristic was that they were 'done in secret', 'often in the middle of the night' and were 'usually not recorded in any official parish register'.[163] Such descriptions owe more to romantic fiction[164] than to the prosaic reality of most church-based clandestine marriages. But even the most disreputable of ceremonies shared some features with a regular marriage.

Cost

It is worth making the point that a clandestine marriage was not necessarily a cheap option. If any more proof were needed that couples did not marry by consent alone, it is provided by the evidence of the popularity of clandestine weddings in places such as the Fleet: why would one pay at all if one could achieve the same effect for free and in the privacy of one's own home? Nor were clandestine marriages always cheaper than marriage in church. Boulton's examination of marriage fees found that marriages at both Holy Trinity Minories and the Fleet were more expensive than marriages by banns in some London churches, although less expensive than marriage by licence:[165] '[t]he fees charged for a marriage by banns in St Giles, Cripplegate remained at the exceptionally low level of just 3s 4d between 1636 and 1736'.[166] By contrast, Keith's Mayfair chapel charged one guinea (over six times more) until four p.m., and more thereafter.[167] Nor was marrying in a parish to which one did not belong a cheap option: some parishes charged higher fees to non-parishioners,[168] or stipulated that the incumbent of the parties' home parish was entitled to a fee whether he had married them or not.[169]

163 Stone, *Road to Divorce*, pp. 96–7.
164 See e.g., G. Heyer, *The Reluctant Widow* (London: Arrow Books, 1998; original edn 1946). The backcover proclaims '[b]y midnight she is a bride, by dawn a widow'.
165 Boulton, 'Clandestine Marriages in London', 203–4.
166 *Ibid.* 167 *Penny London Post*, 13 May 1748.
168 See e.g., Boulton, 'Itching after Private Marryings?', 18.
169 Benton, *Irregular Marriages*, p. 43.

The rites of the Church of England

It may be thought somewhat perverse to illustrate the conformity of clandestine marriages by the career of Alexander Keith, who has gone down in history as one of the most famous celebrants of clandestine marriages. But even he made sure that his advertisements announced the presence of 'another regular clergyman' to conduct the service,[170] and Fleet parsons similarly advertised the regularity of their ordination.[171] The fact that the services of a clergyman were sought for even a clandestine marriage indicates once more that the cleric's role 'was accepted as indispensable'.[172] Similarly, even marriages that took place outside the Church of England made use of its forms.[173] Charity Tucker, for example, informed the Bradford-on-Avon justices that when she married her husband in a private house '[t]he form for that purpose (together with the ring) was read over between them, as is written in the Book of Common Prayer according to the Church of England'.[174] John Cripps similarly recalled that the person who performed the ceremony 'read over the ceremony of the Church of England to them'.[175]

'Lawless' churches?

Much has been made of the possibility of marrying in an ecclesiastical 'peculiar', namely a parish that fell outside episcopal jurisdiction.[176] But the term 'peculiar' does not necessarily denote any irregularity: it is simply an area that 'does not fit into the general

[170] *The Morning Advertiser*, 13 May 1748. According to Armytage, *The Register of Baptisms and Marriages at St George's Chapel, May Fair*, p. ix, these were the Rev. Peter Symson, Francis Denevau, the Rev. John Grierson (whom we shall meet again in Chapter 7) and Mr Walker. Keith's emphasis on the credentials of those who performed the ceremony was particularly important in the light of his own excommunicate status.

[171] Brown, 'The Rise and Fall of the Fleet Marriage', p. 127.

[172] Spaeth, *The Church in an Age of Danger*, p. 195. See also John Tomlinson's account of a wedding conducted while the bride, locked in her room by her father, was leaning out of the window: *Six North Country Diaries* (Durham: Publications of the Surtees Society vol. 118, 1910), p. 150.

[173] See e.g., *Whitaker* v. *Lee alias Whitaker* (1767) PRO DEL 1/588. See also Stone, *Uncertain Unions*, pp. 121, 140, 159, 174.

[174] Hembry, *Calendar of Bradford-on-Avon Settlement Examinations*, p. 28.

[175] *Ibid.* p. 19.

[176] See e.g., Outhwaite, *Clandestine Marriage*, pp. 24–6; J. C. Cox, *The Parish Registers of England* (London: Methuen & Co., 1910), p. 93.

scheme of jurisdiction within the Church ... its jurisdiction is "peculiar" to itself'.[177] The nature of the supervision exercised over peculiars depended on the nature of the peculiar, whether episcopal, extra-diocesan, or extra-provincial.[178] Spaeth has commented of the peculiars within his study that many such parishes were 'not lawless at all, for each not only had its own court and visitations, presided over by the prebend himself or by his surrogate, but also was subject to the dean's court'.[179] Others might not fit into this structure but had their own court; indeed, 'peculiar' courts outnumbered the ordinary ecclesiastical courts.[180] Of course, some peculiars may have exploited their status by flouting the law, but in highlighting the regularity of much clandestinity it is the fact that these marriages still took place in a church that is more important.

The use of licences and banns

One particular advantage of a peculiar might be the possibility of obtaining a licence there.[181] The popularity of certain parishes has been accounted for by the fact that the incumbent had (or claimed) the power to grant licences.[182] Others attracted a high proportion of outsiders because they were conveniently located close to the registry where licences were granted. In Oxford, for example, St Mary Magdalen was a popular venue for marriage as the Bishop of Oxford's registry was located at the back of the church: 'nearly all the couples married there came from outside the parish'.[183] Similarly, in early eighteenth-century London it 'became the

177 P. Barber, 'What is a Peculiar?' (1993–95) 3 *Ecclesiastical Law Journal* 299.

178 *Ibid.* 179 Spaeth, *The Church in an Age of Danger*, p. 207.

180 See R. B. Outhwaite, *The Rise and Fall of the English Ecclesiastical Courts, 1500–1860* (Cambridge University Press, 2006), ch. 1, on the prevalence of such courts.

181 Outhwaite, *Clandestine Marriage*, p. 31, suggests that 'licensed clandestinity' was 'the most widespread breach of the ecclesiastical marriage laws'. See also his *Rise and Fall*, p. 56.

182 The power to grant licences could quite legitimately be delegated from bishop to vicar-general and from vicar-general to surrogates: see the discussion by C. C. A. Pearce, 'The Roles of the Vicar-General and Surrogate in the Granting of Marriage Licences' (1990–2) 2 *Ecclesiastical Law Journal* 28; see also R. B. Outhwaite, 'Sweetapple of Fledborough and Clandestine Marriage in Eighteenth Century Nottinghamshire' (1990) 94 *Transactions of the Thoroton Society of Nottinghamshire* 35.

183 C. Harris, 'Marriages in Oxford before 1754' (1982) 2 *Oxfordshire Family Historian* 278.

practice for marriages [by licence] to take place in the churches close to Doctors' Commons, the main beneficiaries from this trade being the churches of St Benet Paul's Wharf, St Mary Magdalen Old Fish St and St Gregory by St Paul'.[184] Accounts of clandestine marriages have tended to stress the abuses of the licence system;[185] for example, the fact that the person granting the licence did not have the authority to do so, or the practice of issuing licences with blanks that could be filled in at a later date, rather than with the place that the marriage was to be celebrated being specified,[186] or the flouting of the canonical requirement that the marriage should take place in the parties' parish of residence.[187] Such abuses undoubtedly existed, but the fact that couples actually obtained licences before marrying is perhaps a more striking consideration.

Similarly, some clandestine marriages were preceded by banns. Although the canon law stipulated that the banns should be called in the parish or parishes where the parties were resident, and that the marriage should be celebrated there, some clergymen were willing to marry a couple from another parish on the strength of a certificate that the banns had been published by the minister of the parish where they were resident.[188] The ecclesiastical court disapproved of this practice, and the clergymen in question were subjected to correction.[189] It was suggested, however, that it would be acceptable if the incumbent of the parish where the banns had been published gave explicit permission for the marriage to be celebrated in another parish.[190] It may be, therefore, that many

[184] Benton, *Irregular Marriages*, p. 39.

[185] See e.g., Stone, *Road to Divorce*, pp. 102–3; Outhwaite, *Clandestine Marriage*, pp. 31–5.

[186] See e.g., *Mr Herbert's Case* (1731) 3 P Wms. 116; 24 ER 992, in which an Oxford undergraduate 'was drawn in to marry a common servant maid'.

[187] See e.g., the complaint to this effect by Prideaux, *The Case of Clandestine Marriages Stated*, p. 4.

[188] M. G. Smith, 'An Interpretation of *Argar v. Holdsworth*' (1998–2000) 4 *Ecclesiastical Law Journal* 34, notes that the practice can be seen in parish registers.

[189] C. Wheatly, *A rational illustration of the Book of Common Prayer of the Church of England* (London, 1722) p. 390.

[190] J. Johnson, *The Clergyman's Vade Mecum; or, an Account of the Antient and Present Church of England* (London, 1706), p. 159, noted that 'indeed this was forbid by our Ancient Canons, as well as by our present 62 Canon: But then the Licence of the Curate, whose Parishioners they were, was sufficient by the Constit. of Archbishop Stratford. L. 5. T. 1. c. Humana; and so it should in

of the marriages that appear to be celebrated in the wrong parish were there by the permission of their own incumbent.

The reasons for the choice of church

Nor did marriage in a different parish necessarily mean marriage before a different minister. The fact that many incumbents were pluralists,[191] holding more than one living, meant that the marriage of parishioners from one parish might well take place in the parish where the incumbent lived. Harris, for example, noted that towards the end of the seventeenth century 'it became the custom for college fellows (who were often the incumbents of nearby college livings) to marry their country parishioners in their Oxford college chapels'.[192] Similarly, research by Benton found that there was a series of weddings of parishioners of West Ham at St Alphage London Wall: 'both parishes were in the care of the same clergyman, Hugh Wyat'.[193] Clerical non-residency – another pressing problem for the Church of England in the eighteenth century[194] – was perhaps another factor encouraging some couples to resort to other parishes when they married. And in some cases clandestine marriages may actually have been motivated by religious factors: it has been suggested that in Exeter the popularity of the cathedral showed that 'it was the custom for all and sundry to come to the mother church for so important an office'.[195]

reason be now; but then the Curate must do more than certifie the Publication of Banns, he must expressly, under his hand, give leave to be married in another Church, and to the Curate of that other Church to marry them.'

191 On the extent of pluralism, see A. Warne, *Church and Society in Eighteenth Century Devon* (Newton Abbot: David and Charles, 1969), ch. 3; J. Hoppit, *A Land of Liberty? England 1689–1727* (Oxford: Clarendon Press, 2000), p. 212; W. Gibson, '"A Happy Fertile Soil which Bringeth Forth Abundantly": the Diocese of Winchester, 1689–1800', ch. 5 in J. Gregory and J. Chamberlain (eds.), *The National Church in Local Perspective: the Church of England and the Regions, 1660–1800* (Woodbridge: Boydell Press, 2003).

192 Harris, 'Marriages in Oxford before 1754', 282.

193 Benton, *Irregular Marriages*, p. 44.

194 P. Virgin, *The Church in an Age of Negligence: Ecclesiastical Structure and Problems of Church Reform, 1700–1840* (Cambridge: James Clarke & Co., 1989), p. 193; Snape, *The Church of England in Industrialising Society*, ch. 5; Warne, *Church and Society*, ch. 3.

195 W. U. Reynell-Upton and H. Tapley Soper (eds.), *The Registers of Baptisms, Marriages and Burials of the City of Exeter* (Exeter: Devon and Cornwall Record Society, 1910), p. viii. See also Lambeth Palace Library, Fulham papers,

Studies of clandestine marriage have tended to focus on those parishes that functioned as a centre for such marriages. It is, of course, more romantic to imagine parishes that celebrated clandestine marriages as precursors of Gretna Green, and to embellish one's account with a few eloping heiresses.[196] But although this may tell us something about those couples who chose to marry clandestinely, it tells us nothing about the majority who did not. In order to redress the balance, I decided to look at the marriage patterns of all couples from a particular parish who married in the first half of the eighteenth century, in order to ascertain how many married in their own parish and to try to learn what the motivations might be of those who did not.

Two hundred marriages involving one or more Kilsby residents were traced for the period between 1706 (when the Kilsby records begin) and 25 March 1754.[197] These were divided equally between marriages where both husband and wife were from Kilsby and marriages where only one party was. The patterns of marriages among these two groups were very different. If both parties were from Kilsby, they were far more likely to marry in Kilsby itself: sixty-four did so, compared to only seventeen of those couples where only one party was from Kilsby. Nor was this due to the fact that the latter group were marrying in the parish of the other party: twenty of them married in the wife's parish, and seven in the husband's parish, leaving fifty-six who married in a parish to which neither belonged. Overall, out of these 200 couples, 92 (or 46 per cent) married in a parish to which neither belonged.

Terrick 6, fol. 39, noting the practice of those from Harwich marrying at Dovercourt before 1754, it being 'the Mother Church when they could take the liberty'.

196 Outhwaite has noted how successive accounts of the activities of William Sweetapple, the Rector of Fledborough, grew more and more elaborate, and admitted to adopting a similar style himself in his previous work; in setting the record straight, he showed how all but a handful of couples marrying there in the period under consideration came from within a twenty-mile radius of the parish, that the mean age of those marrying was no different from that of their counterparts who married in their own parish, and that most were of middling rank: Outhwaite, 'Sweetapple of Fledborough'.

197 Three sets of couples were included in the sample: those who married in Kilsby itself, those who had a child baptised there and whose marriage had been traced as part of a separate study, and those listed in the Northamptonshire Marriage Index who stated that they were from Kilsby. The conveniently round numbers were quite fortuitous.

This would suggest a very high level of clandestinity in this particular cohort. But on closer inspection matters prove to be more complicated. While parental opposition, bridal pregnancy, or the desire for privacy may have been a factor in some clandestine marriages,[198] there is no direct evidence that they were the motivations for the couples in this sample. There is certainly no evidence that under-age brides or grooms were more likely to marry clandestinely.[199] Only one of the seventeen Kilsby brides who married a Kilsby man in another parish but had their children baptised in Kilsby was obviously pregnant on her wedding day; this was the case for three of the forty Kilsby brides who married a Kilsby man in Kilsby, and another appears to have had a child by her husband before the marriage. In fact, one could turn the suggestion that a clandestine marriage was intended to hide a pregnancy on its head and argue that if a woman was clearly pregnant it was all the more important that the marriage should be public and local.

One noteworthy feature is that those couples who married outside Kilsby were far less likely to have their children baptised in Kilsby. No children are recorded for seventy-seven of the ninety-two couples who married elsewhere. Indeed, some couples disappear from the Kilsby records altogether, suggesting that they had set up home in a new parish. And others may have had only a tenuous connection to Kilsby to start with: in a number of cases a bride or groom who states that she or he is from Kilsby is the only person of that name in the Kilsby records. It would be understandable if a person who was only temporarily resident in Kilsby (perhaps for work) preferred to marry in a parish where he or she had family or other connections, now unreconstitutable.[200]

198 See e.g., Outhwaite, *Clandestine Marriage*, pp. 60–2.

199 Cf. Stone, *Uncertain Unions*, p. 155, who claims that the 'clandestine marriage system was mainly used by young couples seeking to arrange to marry without the knowledge or consent of their relatives and friends'; see also *Road to Divorce*, p. 98.

200 It is difficult enough to discern the motivations of those whose lives are well documented. Samuel Johnson, for example, married Elizabeth Porter at Derby in 1735 – 'not the most obvious place for the marriage', as one biographer comments: H. Hitchings, *Dr Johnson's Dictionary: the Extraordinary Story of the Book that Defined the World* (London: John Murray, 2005), p. 25. Even diarists do not always provide such information: see e.g., S. Markham (ed.), *John Loveday of Caversham, 1711–1789: the Life and Tours of an Eighteenth-Century Onlooker* (Wilton: Michael Russell, 1984), p. 357.

We can, however, examine the parties' choice of parish. The twenty-two couples who married in Lilbourne, five miles from Kilsby, would at first sight appear to be taking advantage of a local centre for marriages: throughout the first half of the eighteenth century, most marriages celebrated in Lilbourne involved outsiders. But nine of these twenty-two marriages coincided with a period in which (judging from the baptism records) Kilsby appears not to have had a permanent incumbent: four marriages took place between March 1724 and May 1726 when no baptisms at all were recorded; while the other five were celebrated between 1726 and 1730, when the baptism register bears the signatures of two different curates and a vicar. Five marriages took place in Brockhall, another local centre for marriages,[201] in the same period. Without a permanent incumbent, couples may have been forced to travel to marry.

More puzzling was the popularity of Long Buckby, around seven miles to the south-east: twenty marriages involving Kilsby residents took place there between 1731 and 1743. In two cases the marriage was perfectly regular, since it involved a spouse from Long Buckby, but in twelve cases both parties were from Kilsby, and six Kilsby residents were marrying spouses from a third parish. The choice of this parish, which was not otherwise a particularly popular destination for marriages, seemed inexplicable, until it was discovered that the vicar of Long Buckby, the Reverend William Taylor, was also officiating at Kilsby. William Taylor solemnised a handful of marriages in Kilsby in this period, but most took place in the parish where he was resident. Such marriages can only be regarded as 'clandestine' in the most technical sense: what turns out to be more striking than scandalous tales of elopements in high society is the conformity of much apparent clandestinity.[202]

[201] Six hundred marriages were celebrated there between 1707 and 1753, at a time when Brockhall had a mere twelve houses: see J. M. Smith (ed.), *The Registers of the Church of St Peter and St Paul, Brockhall, Northamptonshire* (Northamptonshire Record Office, 2001).

[202] This was confirmed by a further study of the 229 apparently clandestine marriages that took place across Northamptonshire in 1745. In the vast majority of cases the parties appeared to have had a family link with the parish where they married or were marrying in a neighbouring parish (sometimes because their own parish had no church). Such marriages could hardly be said to be secret from family and friends. Moreover, in some cases the place of residence specified turned out to be located within the parish of marriage: these marriages were therefore perfectly regular.

CONCLUSION

A clandestine marriage might carry all of the same legal rights as a regular marriage, but it exposed the parties to certain penalties, and those that took place outside a church might well be difficult to prove. In London there was a critical mass of both persons and parsons to sustain a trade in clandestine marriage, but in the provinces such opportunities were far more limited and such clandestine marriages as did take place were usually conducted in church, after banns or licence.

But how far were marriages of this kind seen as a *public* problem, and why did several decades elapse between the legislation described above and the passage of the Clandestine Marriages Act in 1753? It is to these questions that we shall turn in the next chapter.

6

THE EVENTUAL PASSAGE AND ACTUAL TERMS OF THE 1753 ACT

So far, it has been shown that contracts *per verba de praesenti* were neither a full nor a functional alternative to regular marriage; that most non-Anglicans married in the Church of England rather than according to their own religious rites; and that although clandestine marriages were common, most differed little from regular marriages. Given this evidence of regularity, the reader may well wonder why legislation was needed at all. But of course *some* types of clandestine marriage were highly problematic. The previous chapter focused on the problems posed by clandestine marriages for the parties themselves – in terms of proof and potential punishment – but there was a further dimension that was more likely to interest the propertied men who made up Parliament, namely the possibility of their minor children marrying without their consent or knowledge. This, and other problematic aspects of clandestine marriages, is considered in the first part of this chapter.

The fact that clandestine marriages were problematic may indicate why reform was necessary but does not explain the timing of the reform. After all, clandestine marriages were hardly a novel problem in 1753. Nor was the Bill introduced in that year the first to try to address the problem. The second section examines the various theories that have been advanced to explain the passage of the 1753 Act, and puts forward a rather simpler explanation that takes account of other contemporary reforms.

This brings us to the Act itself, which, in broad terms, made certain formalities essential to the validity of a marriage. In order to undertake a proper evaluation of the effect of the Act, it is necessary to be clear about what formalities were mandatory, in the sense that any failure to comply would render the marriage void, and which were merely directory, and so had no effect on the marriage's validity. It is also important to appreciate which provisions were novel, and which built on existing rules and practices. The third part of the chapter is therefore devoted to a close reading of the legislation, set in the context of the existing canonical requirements for a marriage.

In evaluating the requirements of the Act it is, of course, necessary to go beyond the terms of the legislation. The significance of a piece of legislation does not lie merely in its terms, but in the way it is interpreted by the courts. The harshest law may be modified in practice by the way in which it is interpreted, while apparently permissive provisions may be given unexpected force. Contemporary judicial comments are of use in illustrating the way in which a piece of legislation was perceived, while changing conditions may require judges to apply the terms of a piece of legislation to circumstances unforeseen at the time that it was passed. So it was with the 1753 Act, and certain requirements of the Act only became apparent over time, as the result of judicial interpretation. The final part of the chapter accordingly examines the judicial decisions that dealt with the question of how the provisions of the Act should be interpreted.

THE SEEDY SIDE OF CLANDESTINITY

There have been so many mischievous Consequences attending these Fleet Practices, that it is hoped the Legislature, in order to prevent such scandalous Attempts for the future, will take the same into Consideration.[1]

The case of *Hill* v. *Turner* epitomises exactly why Fleet marriages were regarded with disfavour by the ruling elite.[2] A seventeen-year-old lad who was entitled to substantial property was taken to an ale-house in the vicinity of the Fleet, intoxicated,[3] and married to a woman 'in mean circumstances and of bad character'.[4] She then sued him in the ecclesiastical court for restitution of conjugal rights and demanded alimony. Since her reluctant husband was a ward of court, the assistance of the Court of Chancery was sought. It held that the validity of the marriage could not be impugned, but

[1] *London Evening Post*, 19 January 1751.

[2] (1737) West T Hard. 195; 25 ER 892; 1 Atk. 516; 26 ER 326.

[3] The Fleet was one of the places where gin could still be purchased after its sale was banned by the 1736 Gin Act: J. Warner, *Craze: Gin and Debauchery in an Age of Reason* (London: Profile Books Ltd, 2003), p. 46.

[4] 1 Atk. 515; 26 ER 326, at 515.

that it did have the power to restrain the wife from proceeding further in the ecclesiastical courts, and to issue a prohibition to prevent the husband from being excommunicated. Lord Hardwicke, presiding over the court as Lord Chancellor, noted the 'misfortune [of] ... the want of a sufficient law to restrain such clandestine marriages'.[5] Of course, *mésalliances* of this kind were not representative of Fleet marriages, which catered for a broad cross-section of London society.[6] Nor did many members of the aristocracy marry outside their caste.[7] But, as today, the reality was perhaps less important than the perception: as Ogborn has noted, the Fleet was understood in terms of the 'disreputable transgressions, disruptions and deceptions it made possible'.[8]

Certainly the stories that appeared about the Fleet emphasised the seedier aspects of weddings celebrated there. The *Weekly Journal* described the 'scandalous frauds' perpetrated by John Mottram.[9] Fleet parsons were invariably depicted in a bad light: when Daniel Wigmore was convicted 'of selling Spirituous Liquors contrary to Law' it was noted that he was also 'one of the Parsons noted for marrying People within the Rules of the Fleet'.[10] The author of *The Morning Walk*, published in 1751, pulled no punches:

> Where lead my wand'ring footsteps now? the Fleet
> Presents her tatter'd sons in luxury's cause;
> Here venerable crape and scarlet cheeks
> With nose of purple hue, high eminent
> And squinting leering looks, now strike the eye.
> B__sh__p of Hell once in the precincts call'd,
> Renown'd for making thoughtless Contracts: here
> He reign'd in bloated reeling majesty
> And passed in sottishness and smoke his time –
> Rever'd by GIN's adorers, and the tribe
> Who pass in brawls, lewd jests, and drink, their days,
> Sons of low, groveling riot and debauch.[11]

5 *Ibid.* at 515. See also *More* v. *More* (1741) 2 Atk. 157; 26 ER 499.

6 R.L. Brown, 'The Rise and Fall of the Fleet Marriage', ch. 6 in R.B. Outhwaite, *Marriage and Society* (London: Europa Publications Ltd, 1981), Table III.

7 D. Thomas, 'The Social Origins of Marriage Partners of the British Peerage in the Eighteenth and Nineteenth Centuries' (1972) 26 *Population Studies* 99.

8 M. Ogborn, '"This Most Lawless Space": the Geography of the Fleet and the Making of Lord Hardwicke's Marriage Act of 1753' (1999) 37 *New Formations* 11.

9 *Weekly Journal*, 23 February 1717. 10 *Daily Post*, 26 May 1738.

11 W.H. Draper, *The Morning Walk, or, City Encompassed* (London, 1751), p. 42.

One commentator described the Fleet as 'the common place for joining all Rogues and Whores together'.[12] Others depicted those marrying at the Fleet as drunk,[13] devious,[14] or debauched,[15] and a Fleet marriage as a mechanism for fraud[16] or even forced marriage.[17] The mercenary motives of those so marrying were stressed: there were reported to be men who married women to fleece them of their possessions,[18] and women who married in order to throw liability for their debts upon a man who was either legally or physically unavailable to pay them,[19] or upon an innocent third party, unaware that another person had borrowed his name when marrying for this purpose.[20]

Other underhand practices were also highlighted: in 1741 the *London Evening Post* reported that the churchwardens of one City parish had bribed 'a miserable blind Youth, known by the name of Ambrose Taily, who plays on the Violin in Moorfields'[21] to marry one of their parishioners at the Fleet and so transfer her settlement – and the cost of maintaining her – to his parish. For this they were, according to the report, willing to pay Ambrose forty shillings and 'the Expence of a Fleet Marriage', which one parish

12 A. Smith, *A Compleat History of the Lives and Robberies of the Most Notorious Highwaymen, Footpads, Shop-lifes, and Cheats, of both Sexes*, 5th edn (London, 1719), vol. II, p. 218. See also *Select Trials for Murders, Robberies, Rapes, Sodomy, Coining etc at the Sessions-House in the Old-Bailey* (London, 1734–5), p. 406.

13 See e.g., *Hansard's Parliamentary History*, vol. XV, col. 47. 14 *Ibid.* col. 43.

15 See e.g., the reported marriage of a young apprentice and a woman double his age 'said to be a woman of the town': *Memoirs of the Society of Grub Street* (London, 1737), p. 100.

16 *British Gazetteer*, 23 February 1717.

17 T. Lucas, *Authentick Memoirs relating to the Lives and Adventures of the Most Eminent Gamesters and Sharpers*, 3rd edn (London, 1744).

18 See e.g., the case of Hugh alias John Coleman, alias John Davis, alias Hugh Roberts, prosecuted for bigamy at the Old Bailey: *The Proceedings of the Old Bailey*, 27 February 1718, p. 5.

19 See e.g., *The History of the Lives and Actions of Jonathan Wild ... Joseph Blake ... and John Sheppard*, 3rd edn (London, 1730), p. 78, where it was reported that the man in question was about to be transported. The practice was not unique to Fleet marriages as the memoirs of the courtesan Con Phillips made clear: she alleged that in 1723, in order to foil her creditors, she had gone through a ceremony of marriage with a married man who assumed a different name (see *An Apology for the Conduct of Mrs T.C. Phillips* (London, 1750), p. 85).

20 *The Trial of Thomas Thomson and Lavinia Whitney, on an Indictment for a Conspiracy, in Procuring one William Gibson, a Sawyer, to Personate Mr Samuel Brooks* (London, 1730).

21 *London Evening Post*, 9 July 1741.

official attended to ensure that the ceremony had been performed. The practice of throwing the expense on another parish was condemned, as was 'their unjustifiable abetting and encouraging an Irregularity so much and so justly complain'd of, these Fleet Matches'.[22]

As one contemporary pamphleteer demanded rhetorically, '[w]hat then *were* the legislature to do?'[23] Abolish the existing regulations of marriage altogether? Stand by and see them flouted? Or provide a more effective means of enforcing them?[24]

> [I]f political prudence would not admit a Repeal in the whole, or in Part, of the old Law ... nor the credit of Government consist with Connivance at the standing Practice of violating that Law, nothing remained for Parliament, but to invent Means of rendering effectual those Precautions of their Ancestors, so scandalously fallen into Contempt.[25]

THE PASSAGE OF THE ACT

> As we are now at Peace with our Neighbours, we cannot make a better Use of our present Situation, than by considering the internal state of the nation, and rectifying those Disorders, which have arisen, or encreased, whilst the Necessity of Affairs carried our Thoughts abroad.[26]

The explanations offered by academic commentators for the passage of the 1753 Act have been many and various. At a macro level, it has been linked to changing views as to the legal capacity of minors,[27] the rise of affective individualism[28] and the insidious creep of middle-class notions of respectable behaviour,[29] the self-interested actions of an aristocratic elite concerned to protect their

[22] *Ibid.*

[23] *A Letter to the Public: Containing the substance of what hath been offered in the late Debates upon the subject of the Act of Parliament for the better preventing of Clandestine Marriages* (London: Charles Marsh, 1753), p. 8.

[24] See H. Gally, *Some Considerations on Clandestine Marriages* (London, 1750), p. 28 on the inefficacy of the existing sanctions.

[25] *Letter to the Public*, p. 8. [26] Gally, *Some Considerations*, p. 3.

[27] See H. Brewer, *By Birth or Consent: Children, Law, and the Anglo-American Revolution in Authority* (Chapel Hill: University of North Carolina Press, 2005), pp. 314–24.

[28] L. Stone, *The Family, Sex and Marriage in England 1500–1800* (Harmondsworth: Penguin, 1979).

[29] C. Lasch, 'The Suppression of Clandestine Marriage in England: the Marriage Act of 1753' (1974) 26 *Salmagundi* 90, 104.

children from fortune-hunters,[30] or, alternatively, to the demands of political economy and the desire to maximise the productive part of the population.[31] At the micro level, historians have analysed the case that appeared to be the catalyst for the Bill,[32] and discussed the role of its most famous backer, Lord Hardwicke,[33] sometimes in very unfavourable terms.[34]

Any fundamental change in the law inevitably prompts reflection on the causes of such change and encourages commentators to locate it within other observed trends and grand narratives. But once it has been shown that the legislation was *not* the imposition on past practice that has been assumed, much less needs to be explained as to why it was passed. Legislators were not riding rough-shod over customary practices, but simply addressing the specific problem of clandestine marriages. So much is clear from the face of the Act itself, which declared in its Preamble that it was a response to that very issue – 'great Mischiefs and Inconveniences have arisen from Clandestine Marriages'[35] – and noted darkly that 'many Persons do solemnize Matrimony in Prisons and other Places without Publication of Banns'.[36]

Of course, the fact that the legislation aimed to eliminate the practice of marrying in the Fleet is not necessarily incompatible with the various explanations that have been offered by other commentators: such marriages were regarded as problematic precisely because they were seen as a danger to heedless teenagers who might find themselves saddled with an inappropriate spouse for

30 K. O'Donovan, *Sexual Divisions in Law* (London: Weidenfeld & Nicholson, 1985), p. 44; W. Mansell, B. Meteyard, and A. Thomson, *A Critical Introduction to Law*, 2nd edn (London: Cavendish, 1999), p. 92; A. Diduck and F. Kaganas, *Family Law, Gender and the State: Text, Cases and Materials*, 2nd edn (Oxford: Hart Publishing, 2005), p. 60.

31 E. Tavor Bannet, 'The Marriage Act of 1753: "A Most Cruel Law for the Fair Sex"' (1997) 30 *Eighteenth Century Studies* 233, 235–6.

32 See L. Leneman, 'The Scottish Case that Led to Hardwicke's Marriage Act' (1999) 17 *Law and History Review* 16.

33 L. Stone, *Road to Divorce: a History of the Making and Breaking of Marriage in England* (Oxford University Press, 1990), pp. 20, 122–3.

34 See e.g. S. Parker, *Informal Marriage, Cohabitation and the Law, 1754–1989* (Basingstoke: Macmillan, 1990), p. 38: '[i]f Lord Hardwicke had a likeable side to his character it has been firmly hidden from history'. Contrast the positive contemporary appraisal of Hardwicke in 'Character of the Late Earl of Hardwicke' (1764) *Annual Register* 279.

35 Section 1. 36 Section 8.

life,[37] as well as to the personal interests of the elite,[38] the public interest in prudential marriages,[39] legal certainty,[40] and moral probity.[41] But the fact that one can find support for all of these propositions in the parliamentary debates does highlight the difficulty of attributing the passage of a piece of legislation to any one trend: different legislators may have had different reasons for approving reform; indeed, any one individual might well have been influenced by a number of different factors. Thus, if one takes any speech in Parliament (for example, the speech of Ryder, the Attorney-General, who set out the provisions of the Bill for the House of Commons) it is possible to find in it a number of different themes. His statement that clandestine marriages were 'an evil by which many of our best families have often suffered'[42] may be seen as endorsing the power of the elite to control the marriages of their offspring; his description of the idea that a marriage once solemnised by a man in holy orders could not be annulled as 'superstitious'[43] invites parallels with other secularising trends of the Enlightenment;[44] his emphasis on the need for adequate proof reflects the lawyer's desire for certainty;[45] and his analogies between marriage and other legal transactions entered into by minors[46] reflects the shifts that were occurring in this context.[47] Given this melange of influences – and since we can only guess at the views of the majority who did not speak in the debates[48] – any explanation that posits a single cause should be regarded as flawed.

And there is a further problem with the explanations that have been advanced by other commentators. Looking at Fleet marriages and the problems that they posed, not just for patrician parents bent on control but also for the parties themselves, the most

[37] MPs harped on the risk of the heir marrying 'a common strumpet' or an heiress 'an infamous sharper': see *Hansard's Parliamentary History*, vol. XV, cols. 3, 41–2.
[38] *Ibid.* cols. 3–4, 41. [39] *Ibid.* cols. 46–7, 63, 76–7. [40] *Ibid.* cols. 7, 65–6.
[41] The idea that clandestine marriages encouraged polygamy was a particular theme: *ibid.* cols. 7 and 30.
[42] *Ibid.* col. 3. [43] *Ibid.* col. 6.
[44] See e.g., R. Porter, *Enlightenment: Britain and the Creation of the Modern World* (London: Penguin, 2000), ch. 9.
[45] *Hansard's Parliamentary History*, vol. XV, col. 7. [46] *Ibid.*
[47] See generally Brewer, *By Birth or Consent.*
[48] The Bill passed the House of Commons by 125 votes to 56, but only 10 speeches are recorded in *Hansard's Parliamentary History*.

puzzling issue is not why the law was reformed, but why it took so long. Any explanation for the passage of the 1753 Act must be able to identify not only why it was passed, but also why it was passed at that particular point in time.

But grand narratives do not lend themselves to such specific details. For example, the trend identified by Brewer, whereby minors gradually lost their capacity to enter into legal transactions,[49] occurred over such a lengthy period that it is of little assistance in explaining why legislation was passed at this particular time; moreover she underestimates the extent to which parents could exercise control over the marriages of minors even prior to the 1753 Act.[50]

Similarly, the argument that there was a move towards affective individualism over the course of the eighteenth century (which has in itself been contested)[51] is far too general to be of much assistance. Indeed, scholars advancing that argument have struggled to accommodate the 1753 Act within it. Stone, for example, suggests that although parental powers had been strengthened by the 1753 Act, parents were by that time influenced by affective individualism and did not exercise those powers to their full extent,[52] but this, of course, raises the question as to why the Act was passed at all if affective individualism had already pervaded the mindset of the elite who dominated Parliament. Trumbach has attempted to provide an answer that reconciles the passage of the 1753 Act with his contention that the strict settlement[53] reduced parental power and that the eighteenth century did indeed witness a rise in affective individualism.[54] He argues that previous attempts to control

[49] Brewer, *By Birth or Consent*.

[50] See further R. Probert, 'Control over Marriage in England and Wales, 1753–1823: the Clandestine Marriages Act of 1753 in Context' (2009) 27 *Law and History Review* 413.

[51] See e.g., H. Berry and E. Foyster (eds.), *The Family in Early Modern England* (Cambridge University Press, 2007), p. 17, who suggest that Stone was 'emphatically wrong' in his theory that the English family had passed through progressive stages.

[52] Stone, *Road to Divorce*, p. 58.

[53] For definition and discussion see J.H. Baker, *An Introduction to English Legal History*, 4th edn (London: Butterworths, 2002), pp. 293–6.

[54] R. Trumbach, *The Rise of the Egalitarian Family: Aristocratic Kinship and Domestic Relations in Eighteenth-Century England* (New York: Academic Press, 1978).

clandestine marriages had been rejected by the House of Commons 'primarily because younger sons were jealous of their right to run off with an heiress and by this means repair the disabilities that primogeniture inflicted on them'.[55] The adoption of the strict settlement, however, freed children from the threat of disinheritance; the position of younger sons improved; it was no longer necessary to marry for money and became distasteful to do so. By such arguments he arrives at the somewhat counter-intuitive conclusion that 'it was because romantic love had become so acceptable that the act was finally passed'.[56] Yet it is difficult to see how a commitment to marrying for affection rather than money would translate into support for a measure that increased parental control over marriage. And Lemmings has convincingly contested this interpretation of the Act, contending that the life-histories of the opponents of the Bill 'suggest that far from being driven by the ideology of love and affection as the proper foundations for marriage, they were actually fortune-hunters, who wanted only to keep the marriage market open for fellow spirits'.[57]

The adoption of the strict settlement has, however, been seen as providing a further and more practical reason for the passage of the Act, and one that was more closely linked to the interests of elite parents. According to Harth, legislation was needed because of the financial demands generated by the strict settlement.[58] The basic assumption is that under the strict settlement there was no discretion as to the amount each child was to receive,[59] and that families had therefore to ensure that money coming into the family (through marriages to heiresses) balanced money paid out in

[55] *Ibid.* p. 71. [56] *Ibid.* p. 108.

[57] D. Lemmings, 'Marriage and the Law in the Eighteenth Century: Hardwicke's Marriage Act of 1753' (1996) 39 *Historical Journal* 339, 356. See also J. Cannon, *Aristocratic Century* (Cambridge University Press, 1984), p. 75, who describes the opposition as 'personal, factious and synthetic'.

[58] See E. Harth, 'The Virtue of Love: Lord Hardwicke's Marriage Act' (1988) 9 *Cultural Critique* 123.

[59] It should be noted that the extent of flexibility under a strict settlement has been debated: see E. Spring, 'The Strict Settlement: its Role in Family History' (1988) 41 *Economic History Review* 454; S. Staves, 'Resentment or Resignation? Dividing the Spoils among Daughters and Younger Sons', ch. 10 in J. Brewer and S. Staves (eds.), *Early Modern Conceptions of Property* (London: Routledge, 1995), pp. 201–2, but cf. L. Bonfield, 'Marriage, Property and the "Affective Family"' (1983) 1 *Law and History Review* 297 and his 'Strict Settlement and the Family: a Differing View' (1988) 41 *Economic History Review* 461, 464.

portions. And Bonfield's suggestion that the cumulative burden of debt occasioned by the payment of portions 'would not have been pressing until mid-century'[60] does seem to fit very neatly with the timing of the legislation. But would the 1753 Act really have assisted debt-pressed patrician parents to ensure that their sons made suitable matches with brides whose portions could be used to provide for other family members? At the very most it gave them a right of veto until their child reached the age of twenty-one, and even this was not absolute. Since aristocratic sons tended to marry at a considerably later age[61] – and would have had the means to take advantage of the loopholes in the Act[62] – it is difficult to see how the Act would have addressed this particular problem.

Moreover, had the financial demands of the strict settlement been the main motivation for the Act, many of the terms of the 1753 Act would have been otiose. It is instructive to consider the terms of an earlier, unsuccessful Bill, promoted by Viscount Thomas Gage in 1736. This noted the problem that 'many Persons under age, who are intitled to considerable Fortunes, are frequently married without the Consent of their Parents and Guardians, to the great Prejudice and Ruin of many Families';[63] among the solutions proposed was the equally class-specific suggestion that agreements to marry would not be regarded as contracts of marriage if either party to the marriage, or their parents, owned property above a certain value. Had the 1753 Act been in these terms, the accusation that the ruling elite were acting only in their own interests might have had some force; in the event, however, the 1736 Bill failed to become law.

The fact that the 1753 Act did regulate the poor as well as the rich has led one commentator to suggest a still grander design behind the Act – nothing less than the production of a suitable population to advance Britain's impending industrial revolution. Bannet describes the Act as 'one of the first fruits of the new

60 L. Bonfield, *Marriage Settlements, 1601–1740: the Adoption of the Strict Settlement* (Cambridge University Press, 1983), pp. 115, 117.

61 See e.g., T.H. Hollingsworth, 'Marriage' (1964) 18 *Population Studies: Supplement* 8, 14, Table 4.

62 See further below, and Chapter 7.

63 A Bill for the more Effectual preventing of clandestine marriages, 27 February 1736.

discipline of political economy' that 'represented the best contemporary thinking about how to manage population in order to increase Britain's wealth'.[64] This argument is not entirely convincing, since the thinkers she cites were mainly political economists writing some time after the passage of the 1753 Act.[65] Moreover, the House of Commons seemed to be more concerned with the question of whether the proposed new regulations would enable the aristocracy to monopolise heiresses, wealth, and, as a result, power,[66] than with the production of a suitable labour force.[67]

Nor should one be overly cynical about the motivations of those individuals who pressed for reform. While Lord Bath,[68] who introduced the Bill that became the Clandestine Marriages Act, had on previous occasions instigated general legislation with an eye to his own advantage,[69] on this occasion he must be acquitted of any self-interested motive.[70] In 1753 his only son was already aged twenty-two, and so beyond the reach of the new statutory controls

[64] Bannet, 'The Marriage Act of 1753', 235.

[65] James Steuart's *An Inquiry into the Principles of Political Economy* was published in 1767, and Adam Ferguson's *Institutes of Moral Philosophy* in 1768, while Adam Smith's *An Inquiry into the Nature and Causes of the Wealth of Nations* was not published until 1776. I am grateful to John Snape for assistance on this point.

[66] See e.g., *Hansard's Parliamentary History*, vol. XV, col. 14 ('if this Bill passes, our quality and rich families will daily accumulate riches by marrying only one another'); col. 38 ('which in a few years must greatly influence the property and influence of the other House of Parliament, to the manifest danger of our present happy constitution'); cols. 68–9 ('for a factious majority of the other House having by means of their elective power, got a majority in this, will soon force the crown to put the whole military power of the kingdom into their hands'). For counter-arguments see cols. 45–6.

[67] Although Lord Barrington suggested that 'the good of society' and 'the propagation of the species' were 'the two great ends we should have in view when we are making any laws relating to marriage' (*Hansard's Parliamentary History*, vol. XV, col. 29) it is clear from the context that it was the moral good of the country, rather than its economic needs, to which he was referring. The Earl of Hillsborough was similarly making a broader point about the need to ensure that parents could support children when he stated that 'the prosperity and happiness of a country does not depend upon having a great number of children born, but upon having always a great number well brought up, and inured from their infancy to labour and industry' (*Hansard's Parliamentary History*, vol. XV, col. 63).

[68] William Pulteney, 1684–1764, created Earl of Bath in 1742.

[69] S. Handley, M. J. Rowe, and W. H. McBryde, 'Pulteney, William, Earl of Bath (1684–1764)' in *Oxford Dictionary of National Biography* (Oxford University Press, 2004).

[70] Cf. R. B. Outhwaite, *Clandestine Marriage in England, 1500–1850* (London: Hambledon Press, 1995), p. 93.

on the marriages of minors proposed in the Bill.[71] And even Lord Hardwicke does not appear to have been an inflexible advocate of controlling the marriages of minors. Such power could be exercised, he allowed, but not arbitrarily: in a number of cases he held that once consent had been given, it could not be withdrawn. This, he opined, would be 'a delusion on the young folks, and it is not to be imagined, after they had fixed their affection by such encouragement, they will be very easily induced to alter it'.[72] And in another case where a lady was only entitled to a sum of money if she married with the consent of her trustees, he expressed the view that the restriction imposed by the condition was harsh, and since there could be no objection to the person or estate of the suitor, and the lady 'had a strong inclination for the match', consent should have been given.[73] It would be going too far to represent Hardwicke as a champion of romantic love – he was clearly influenced by the suitability of the contested matches – but it seems that his ire was reserved for *mésalliances* and the improper marriages of wards, which specifically flouted the authority of the Court of Chancery.[74]

But what of the case that is alleged to have led Lord Bath to introduce the Bill in the first place?[75] If the problem with the macro-level explanations considered above is their failure to explain the timing of the reform, the problem with ascribing the introduction of the Act to the Scottish case of *Cochran* v. *Campbell* is that it is difficult to perceive exactly what it was about that particular case that might have motivated reform. The court was called on to decide who was the true widow of John Campbell: Magdalen, who claimed to have married him in 1724,[76] or Jean, who had married him in 1725 and lived with him for twenty years

[71] And apparently beyond parental control, according to Horace Walpole, who in May 1753 gossiped that Lord Bath had lost 'his only son, who is run away from thirty thousand pounds a year': W.S. Lewis (ed.), *Horace Walpole's Correspondence* (Oxford University Press, 1983), vol. IX, p. 147.

[72] *Lord Strange* v. *Smith* (1755) Amb. 263; 27 ER 175, at 264. See also *Merry* v. *Ryves* (1757) 1 Eden 1; 28 ER 584, at 6.

[73] *Daley* v. *Desbouverie* (1738) 2 Atk. 261; 26 ER 561.

[74] See e.g., *Hill* v. *Turner* (1737) West T Hard. 195; 25 ER 892; *More* v. *More* (1741) 2 Atk. 157; 26 ER 499.

[75] See Stone, *Road to Divorce*, p. 122.

[76] *The Case of Mrs. Magdalen Campbell, Widow, Impartially Stated* (London, 1751), p. 2.

until his death.[77] It is true that the case therefore revealed one of the problems with the law, namely the potential for a challenge to a marriage that had existed for many years, but this was hardly revelatory. Moreover, the case could also be seen as illustrating the willingness of the courts to fend off such challenges: the House of Lords, upholding the decision of the lower courts, held that Magdalen had not proved her claim. And had *Cochran* v. *Campbell* been the sole motivating factor, it is rather odd that the Bill did not extend to Scotland, where the relevant events had occurred. At the most it could be said that this case provided the opportunity for the House of Lords to act to deal with a long-standing problem.

So we are still left with the question as to why Parliament had not acted before. One possible answer might be that clandestine marriages grew in popularity over the first half of the eighteenth century, and that Parliament only acted when the number of such marriages in London had reached epidemic proportions. If one examines the estimates of clandestine marriages produced by Roger Lee Brown, this has a veneer of plausibility. Yet one must bear in mind that eighteenth-century legislators would not have had the benefit of such information: the registers and notebooks in which Fleet parsons inscribed marriages were not conveniently located in one place and open to public inspection but secreted in ale-houses and private pockets.[78] And complaints that Fleet marriages were on the increase were hardly new: in *Middleton* v. *Croft*, for example, Lord Hardwicke had noted that 'as we are all sensible, the evil of clandestine marriages is a growing one'.[79]

But perhaps we need to pose the question in a different way. After all, to ask why Parliament took so long to respond to a particular problem implicitly assumes that the legislators of the day were quick to respond to social problems. But clandestine marriages were not the only problem affecting London in the early eighteenth century. This was the violent London of Hogarth's 'Gin Lane', in which

[77] Both marriages were apparently irregular: see Leneman, 'The Scottish Case', 163.

[78] Robert Nugent claimed that he had been told 'that at Keith's chapel there have been 6,000 married in a year': *Hansard's Parliamentary History*, vol. XV, col. 19, but the extant registers do not bear this out: see G.J. Armytage, *The Register of Baptisms and Marriages at St George's Chapel, May Fair* (London: Harleian Society, 1889).

[79] (1737) 2 Str. 1057; 93 ER 1030, at 1062.

Fielding's newly-appointed Bow Street Runners had as yet made little progress. So the answer as to why Parliament did not reform the law of marriage until the middle of the century may simply be that it reformed very little else. Even those who have challenged the popular image of eighteenth-century legislators as uninterested in law reform have only been able to point to three relatively brief flurries of activity.[80] And it was during one of these that the 1753 Act was passed, along with yet more legislation attempting to address the consumption of gin,[81] and the long overdue reorganisation of the calendar.[82]

And perhaps one can hardly blame Parliament for not acting sooner. One writer has suggested that '[f]or early eighteenth-century legislators, domestic issues came a poor third to foreign policy and the serious business of raising revenue'.[83] It was unsurprising that foreign policy should have dominated Parliament's attention for much of the early eighteenth century: the Treaty of Aix-la-Chapelle in 1748 signalled a brief respite from war, but that this was far from the norm is clear from Langford's comment that the Pelham ministry responsible for this achievement was 'the only ministry which negotiated a peace and survived it for more than a few months between the Revolution of 1688 and the comparable success of Lord Liverpool's ministry in 1815'.[84]

The fact that Parliament now had time to turn to domestic matters does not, of course, explain why this particular Bill on clandestine marriages should pass into law. The pivotal role played by Lord Hardwicke has been emphasised by a number of commentators,[85] as well as his political influence at this particular time,[86]

[80] W. Priest, 'Law Reform in Eighteenth Century England', ch. 7 in P. Birks (ed.), *The Life of the Law* (London: Hambledon Press, 1991).

[81] P. Dillon, *The Much-lamented Death of Madam Geneva: the Eighteenth-Century Gin Craze* (London: Review, 2002), ch. 15.

[82] See F. O'Gorman, *The Long Eighteenth Century: British Political and Social History 1688–1832* (London: Hodder Headline, 2004; original edn 1997), p. 91, who concludes that '[f]ew, if any, eighteenth-century administrations can boast a record of reform to match that of Henry Pelham'.

[83] Dillon, *The Much-lamented Death of Madam Geneva*, p. 70. See further P. Langford, *A Polite and Commercial People: England 1727–1783* (Oxford University Press, 1998), p. 28, on Walpole's prioritising of issues pertaining to taxation.

[84] Langford, *A Polite and Commercial People*, p. 209.

[85] Stone, *Road to Divorce*, pp. 122–3.

[86] See, in particular, Outhwaite, *Clandestine Marriage*, p. 95. Given that Hardwicke had been part of the ruling Whig triumvirate (along with Pelham and Newcastle) since 1744, it is clear that his political clout alone cannot explain the timing of the Bill.

but the passage of the Bill should not be attributed solely to political pressure and successful cajolery. Ultimately, the reason why the Bill introduced in 1753 passed when others had failed was that it was quite simply a better Bill. In contrast to earlier Bills, the terms of the 1753 Act were broad-ranging in their application rather than addressing narrow sectional interests.[87] And it dealt with the regulation of marriage as a whole, rather than simply the single issue of preventing clandestine marriages. But the scope of the Act can only be fully appreciated by a careful examination of its terms, to which we shall now turn.

THE TERMS OF THE ACT

> [T]here is no ceremony or solemnity required by this Bill, but what is absolutely necessary for ascertaining the marriage and rendering it public, which every marriage ought to be.[88]

As noted in the introduction, it is essential to understand exactly what the Act required of the nuptial pair, since there is a tendency among commentators to exaggerate the demands of the Act,[89] and to imply that the bureaucratic elements of the marriage were now of primary importance.[90] Such portrayals strengthen the perception that the Act constituted a profound change in the law. In fact, as we shall see, there was general continuity between the canon law and the new statutory requirements. It is also important to view the Act

87 See also Outhwaite, *Clandestine Marriage*, p. 94.

88 *Hansard's Parliamentary History*, vol. XV, col. 11.

89 See e.g., Baker, *Introduction to English Legal History*, pp. 482–3, who states that 'the publication of banns or purchase of a licence ... the presence of at least two witnesses and the recording of the marriage in a public register, *all became essential requirements for validity*' (emphasis added); Brown, 'The Rise and Fall of the Fleet Marriage', p. 135; Stone, *Road to Divorce*, pp. 123–5.

90 See e.g., L. O'Connell, '"Matrimonial Ceremonies Displayed": Popular Ethnography and Enlightened Imperialism' (2002) *Eighteenth Century Life* 98, 99, who asserts that the marriage rite 'came more and more to represent a practical reiteration of governmental regulations that bound citizens to the nation-state', and her 'Marriage Acts: Stages in the Transformation of Modern Nuptial Culture' (1999) *Journal of Feminist Cultural Studies* 68, in which she claims that the effect of the Act was 'to reduce and rigidify matrimony's social meanings'. See also C. Flint, *Family Fictions: Narrative and Domestic Relations in Britain, 1688–1798* (Stanford University Press, 1998), p. 54, who suggests that the Act 'appears to mark a change in conception as well from regarding matrimony (and therefore family) as a private spiritual sacrament to a public event inseparable from secular political activities'.

as a whole, in order to appreciate the way in which it adopted a more holistic approach to the regulation of marriage than had been evident in earlier attempts at legislation.

Contracts to be unenforceable

The Act declared that no suit might be brought in any ecclesiastical court to compel celebration *in facie ecclesiae* of a contract *per verba de praesenti* or *per verba de futuro* that was entered into on or after 25 March 1754.[91] It is significant that it did not declare future contracts to be *void*: had a contract *per verba de praesenti* indeed been regarded as the equivalent of a marriage before this date, the Act would have been of little effect, since upon that view solemnisation would not be necessary to the validity of the union, nor would it affect the rights flowing from it. But, as Chapter 2 has demonstrated, a contract *per verba de praesenti* was not the same as a marriage, and the only real right that it conferred on the parties was the right to compel celebration. The very terms of the 1753 Act itself are the final confirmation (should any be needed) of this.

Of course, the fact that a contract could no longer be enforced did in itself constitute a break with the past. Yet the effect of this was mitigated by the fact that it had in any case become difficult to enforce a contract.[92] And, of course, the moral force of a promise to marry remained: couples who vowed to take each other as husband and wife after 24 March 1754 could still regard themselves as married 'in the sight of God', just as the jilted party to an unenforceable private contract might have appealed to the other's conscience before that date.[93] Most couples, before and after the Act, would have married in church without the need to invoke the legal enforceability of any contract. For those few who were impervious to the prompting of conscience or other forms of community pressure, after March 1754 there was still the threat of an action

[91] Section 13. The original Bill also declared that a marriage that had been lawfully solemnised could not be invalidated by a precontract, but it was subsequently decided that such a clause was otiose if such a contract could not be enforced: BL Add 35880, fol. 72.

[92] See Chapter 2.

[93] We might recall the Rev. Goole and his dark threat of eternal punishment, referred to in Chapter 2.

in the common-law courts for breach of promise,[94] which had been developed by the courts some years earlier to deal with those who reneged on promises to marry.[95] To draw again on the analogy with the purchase of a house, all the 1753 Act did was abolish specific performance as a means of enforcing a contract: the remedy of damages remained.

Preliminaries to the marriage

The Act required that every marriage be preceded either by the calling of banns or by the parties' obtaining a licence. As has been made clear, such formalities were far from novel: banns had been required since at least the twelfth century and licences had been introduced in the sixteenth.[96] And in requiring that the banns should be called in the parish where the parties dwelt,[97] the Act was only echoing the (admittedly not always observed) prescriptions of the canon law.[98]

In some respects, however, the Act did tighten up the existing preliminaries. The rubric in the Book of Common Prayer had stipulated that banns were to be published 'in the Church three several Sundays or Holy-days, in the time of Divine Service'.[99] The Act was more restrictive, providing that banns could only be

94 As developed in cases such as *Holder* v. *Dickeson* (1673) 1 Freem. 96; 89 ER 70; *Harrison* v. *Cage* (1698) 1 Ld. Raym. 387; 91 ER 387; *Hutton* v. *Mansell* (1705) 6 Mod. 172; 87 ER 928; *Cork* v. *Butler* (1717) 1 Strange 34; 93 ER 367; *Atkins* v. *Far* (1738) West T Hard. 589; 25 ER 1100. On the subsequent development of the action for breach of promise, see G. Frost, *Promises Broken: Courtship, Class and Gender in Victorian England* (Charlottesville: University of Virginia Press, 1995).

95 Prior to 1754 it applied only to contracts *per verba de futuro*: see e.g., *Collins* v. *Jessot* (1705) 6 Mod. 155; 87 ER 913. After 1754, the tense used was immaterial.

96 Previously it had been possible to obtain a dispensation: see Outhwaite, *Clandestine Marriage*, pp. 5–6.

97 Section 1. Residency was a factual question, and did not depend on one's place of birth or legal settlement. Under the Act, as under the canon law, if the parties lived in separate parishes, the banns were to be published in both. As not all parishes had their own church or chapel where banns could be published, special provision was made for such extra-parochial places, with couples resident in such places being required to solemnise the marriage in a neighbouring parish: see ss. 1, 2 and 5.

98 See further E.J. Carlson, *Marriage and the English Reformation* (Oxford: Blackwell, 1994), p. 133.

99 Church of England, *The Book of Common Prayer* (London, 1662), 'The Form of Solemnization of Matrimony'. As had been pointed out during the debates on the Bill, this meant that at certain times (such as Christmas, Easter, and Whitsuntide)

called on Sundays.[100] Since it retained the requirement that the banns be called three times, this meant a wait of at least sixteen days (assuming solemnisation on the following Monday) and ideally longer, since the minister was under no obligation to publish the banns unless he had seven days' notice.[101] A slightly longer period of residence was required in the case of a licence, which would only be granted to solemnise the marriage in the place of worship of the parish or chapelry where at least one of the persons had resided for four weeks.[102] Once the licence had been granted the marriage could take place immediately,[103] so the overall period of residence was intended to be roughly the same in both cases.

The more fundamental change introduced by the Act was that compliance with such preliminaries (either the calling of banns or the obtaining of a licence) would henceforth be essential to the validity of a marriage. On this point the legislation was unambiguous:

> all Marriages solemnized ... without Publication of Banns, or Licence of Marriage from a Person or Persons having Authority to grant the same first had and obtained shall be null and void to all Intents and Purposes whatsoever.[104]

a marriage by banns could take place within as little as four days: *Hansard's Parliamentary History*, vol. XV, col. 70. Opponents of the bill argued that couples would not marry if they had to wait for longer (see e.g., cols. 39, 57, 70), ignoring the fact that for most of the year holy days were not so conveniently clustered.

100 Section 1.

101 See s. 2, which stipulated that the minister should be notified in writing of the names and abodes of the parties.

102 Section 4.

103 This possibility meant that a marriage could still be celebrated speedily. One Sussex churchwarden, Thomas Turner, recorded that on 23 October 1757 Anne Stevenson forbade the banns of marriage between Richard Parker and Mary Vinal. Anne had had a child by Richard three years earlier and claimed that he had promised to marry her. The following day Mary told the churchwardens that she was with child by Richard. Two days later, Thomas Turner took out a warrant to apprehend Richard, acted as Richard's bondsman in the obtaining of a licence, attended his marriage to Mary, took the parties before the Justice of the Peace so that Richard could swear that he belonged to a different parish, and delivered them to that parish – all between 2 a.m. and 9 p.m. on the same day: D. Vaisey (ed.), *The Diary of Thomas Turner, 1754–1765* (Oxford University Press, 1984). Cf. D. Jarrett, *England in the Age of Hogarth* (New Haven: Yale University Press, 1986), p. 120, who suggests that the process would take 'several months'.

104 Section 8.

The force of the new provisions was, however, seriously undermined by an amendment usually attributed[105] to Henry Fox,[106] which provided that once a marriage had been celebrated, it could not be invalidated on the ground that the parties had not in truth resided in the place where the banns were published or the marriage solemnised.[107] The result was that the detailed provisions of the earlier sections were directory rather than mandatory. As long as banns were called *somewhere*, or a licence obtained, the requirements of the Act would be satisfied. Although the Act forbad the granting of a licence to solemnise a marriage in a parish to which the parties did not belong,[108] it introduced no new sanctions for surrogates who did so.[109] While a marriage was void if celebrated without a licence 'from a Person or Persons having Authority to grant the same',[110] there was no stipulation that the licence itself had to be properly obtained.[111] Thus, whether the marriage was preceded by banns or by licence it would be perfectly valid even if it was celebrated in a parish where the parties were unknown, just as it had been before 1754.[112]

Parental control

The same points can be made in relation to the Act's requirement of parental consent: it was not an innovation, nor was it absolute.[113]

105 Since Murray, the Solicitor-General, instanced this clause as one that had been added in the House of Lords, this seems unlikely: *Hansard's Parliamentary History*, vol. XV, col. 75.

106 Fox's loudly-voiced opposition to the Bill may have been due in part to his own clandestine marriage to the daughter of the Duke of Richmond: S. Tillyard, *Aristocrats* (London: Chatto & Windus Ltd, 1994), pp. 88–9.

107 Section 10. For contemporary discussion of the clause see BL Add 35880 fol. 72.

108 Section 4.

109 Although they had to give security of £100 for the proper performance of their office: s. 7.

110 Section 9.

111 And note the decision in *Argar* v. *Holdsworth* (1758) 2 Lee 515; 161 ER 424, which held that a licence was a legal authority for the marriage to proceed and that a clergyman could be prosecuted for breach of clerical duty if he refused to proceed, unless he had reason to believe that it was fraudulently obtained.

112 See e.g., *Robinson* v. *Grant* (1811) 18 Ves. Jun. 290; 34 ER 327. The significance of this as a means of evading the Act is considered in more detail in Chapter 7. On occasion the choice of an alternative parish might be dictated by necessity, as in *R* v. *Hind* (1813) Russ. & Ry. 253; 168 ER 788, where the church in the parties' parish was being repaired, forcing them to marry in the neighbouring parish.

113 For a more detailed discussion of the previous requirements, see Probert, 'Control over Marriage in England and Wales'.

Even before 1754, parental consent to the marriages of minor children had been required by the canon law.[114] Those who wished to marry by licence had been required to swear that they were of age or had parental consent,[115] and were required to give security in support of such statements.[116] The canons further directed that two witnesses should swear that parental consent had been obtained.[117] Similarly, those whose banns were called in the parish church might have found them forbidden by an irate parent. Indeed, the canon law had directed that advance consent should be given to the marriage of a minor marrying by banns.[118] What changed in 1754 was not the requirement of parental consent, but the penalty for failing to obtain it. Under the canon law, the fact that a marriage had been celebrated in the face of parental opposition did not affect its validity. Under the Act, by contrast, this might render the marriage void.

The possibility that a marriage might be rendered void on the basis that parental consent had not been given necessitated more precise rules as to whose consent was necessary. The Act accordingly laid down a strict hierarchy. Heading the list was the minor's father: if he consented, the dissent of the mother was irrelevant, as was her approval if he dissented. A father's control could also extend beyond the grave, as he could appoint a guardian whose consent would be required. Only if there was no such guardian was

[114] Canon 100 of the 1604 code had prescribed that 'No children, under the age of one and twenty years compleat, shall contract themselves, or marry, without the consent of their Parents, or of their Guardians and Governours, if their Parents be deceased.'

[115] Canon 102 required the parties to swear 'that they have obtained thereunto the express Consent of their Parents (if they be living) or otherwise of their Guardians or Governours'.

[116] Canon 101 stipulated that licences should be granted 'unto such persons only as be of good state and quality, and that upon good Caution and Security taken'.

[117] Canon 103 prescribed that '[f]or the avoiding of all fraud and collusion in the obtaining of such Licences and Dispensations: We further constitute and appoint, that before any Licence ... be had or granted, it shall appear to the Judge by the Oaths of two sufficient Witnesses, one of them to be known either to the Judge himself, or to some other person of good reputation then present, and known likewise to the said Judge, that the express consent of the Parents or Parent, if one be dead, or Guardians, or Guardian of the Parties, is thereunto had and obtained.'

[118] Canon 62 prescribed that in the case of a marriage by banns, the minister was not to marry the couple 'before the Parents or Governours of the Parties to be married, being under the age of twenty and one years, shall either personally, or by sufficient testimony, signify to him their consents given to the said marriage'.

the mother entitled to give consent,[119] and if she remarried she lost even this right. If she had remarried or was dead, the consent of a guardian appointed by the Court of Chancery was required.[120] The increased significance of parental consent also necessitated some exceptions being devised. It was recognised that the requisite consent might not be forthcoming for various reasons,[121] for example, if a guardian or mother was '*non compos mentis*, or ... in Parts beyond the Seas, or ... induced unreasonably, and by undue Motives to abuse the Trust reposed in him, her, or them, by refusing or withholding his, her, or their Consent to a proper Marriage'.[122] In such cases the parties could apply to the Lord Chancellor, who could decree that consent should be deemed if the marriage was thought 'proper'.[123] Significantly, this provision did not apply where a father was refusing consent, reflecting the fact that the law reposed confidence in the paterfamilias to exercise his duties responsibly, and saw mothers as merely agents carrying out the trust bequeathed to them rather than as acting in their own right. An unreasonable mother could be overridden. It was not acknowledged that a father could be unreasonable – or, for that matter, insane or absent.[124] In such cases the unfortunate young lovers would simply have to wait until they attained their majority, or marry by banns, safe in the knowledge that the father, the only person who could forbid them in law, was unable to do so.

So the Act introduced a stricter and more structured requirement of parental consent than had existed under the canon law. Yet it was less prescriptive as to how such consent should be signified than the canon law had been, not requiring witnesses to swear that

[119] This was itself a consolidation of existing practice: see *Shaftsbury* v. *Shaftsbury* (1725) Gilb. Rep. 172; 25 ER 121, at 177, where it was noted that 'the Mother can't marry her Child without the consent of the Testamentary Guardian. For the Father who had the Power over his child by law, has placed it under the Power of the Testamentary Guardian. Therefore it is taken out of the Power of the Mother.'

[120] See e.g., *In the matter of Martha Lavinia Woolscombe, an Infant* (1816) 1 Madd. 213; 56 ER 79; *Ex parte Becher* (1783) 1 Bro. C.C. 1296; 28 ER 1296 in which a seventeen-year-old girl whose father was dead and whose mother resided in the East Indies asked the court to appoint a guardian. The court approved of her proposed marriage and her uncle was appointed guardian.

[121] For discussion see BL Add 35877, fol. 119.

[122] Section 12. [123] *Ibid.*

[124] And see the interpretation of the similarly-worded provision in the Marriage Act 1823: *In the matter of the 4 G. 4 c. 76* (1838) 3 My. & Cr.471; 40 ER 1008.

parental consent had been obtained.[125] And, contrary to the claims of most commentators,[126] not every under-age marriage without parental consent would be void. There was an important distinction between marriages by banns and those by licence. Marriages by licence where either or both of the parties was under the age of twenty-one years were void unless the minor had the consent of the appropriate person, or was a widow or widower.[127] By contrast, the marriage of a minor by banns was valid unless the person whose consent was required had publicly voiced his or her *dissent* when the banns were published. If this occurred the publication of the banns would be void and the marriage could not take place.[128] But if no objection were made, the marriage could go ahead and could not later be impugned on the basis of lack of parental consent.

When combined with section 10, this left a serious loophole in the Act. The fact that a marriage could not be invalidated on the basis that the parties did not reside in the parish where the banns had been published meant that under-age couples could escape parental notice by marrying in a more distant parish, unknown to their parents. There would be no chance for the parent or guardian to express dissent in such a case. As a result, a marriage by banns would be legal even if celebrated without parental consent and in a place where the parties were not known.[129]

125 It was also less prescriptive that the original version of the Bill, which would have required consent to a minor's marriage by licence to be signified in writing and attested by two credible witnesses: BL Add 35880, fol. 7, clause 3, fol. 51, clause 1. This was dropped from the final version.

126 See e.g., Stone, *Road to Divorce*, pp. 58 and 124; Trumbach, *The Rise of the Egalitarian Family*, p. 107; K. O'Donovan, *Sexual Divisions in Law* (London: Weidenfeld & Nicholson, 1985), p. 44; R. Porter, *English Society in the Eighteenth Century*, 2nd edn (Harmondsworth: Penguin, 1990), pp. 28–9; A. Macfarlane, *Marriage and Love in England: Modes of Reproduction 1300–1840* (Oxford: Basil Blackwell Ltd, 1986), p. 127; J. Gillis, *For Better, For Worse: British Marriages 1600 to the Present Day* (Oxford University Press, 1985), p. 88; G. Treital, 'Jane Austen and the Law' (1984) 100 *Law Quarterly Review* 549; O'Connell, 'Matrimonial Ceremonies Displayed', 86; Diduck and Kaganas, *Family Law*, p. 60.

127 Section 11. Those remarrying had also been exempted from the requirement of parental consent under the canon law: see canon 104.

128 Section 3.

129 The extent of such evasive practices is considered in the next chapter, how the courts dealt with them in Chapter 8.

This might be viewed as simply a matter of oversight, or poor drafting,[130] were it not for a letter written by Lord Hardwicke himself. The Bill drawn up by the Scottish judges in 1754 to abolish clandestine and irregular marriages in Scotland appeared to make the consent of parents or 'curators' necessary to the marriages of minors in all cases. At least, this was how it was interpreted by Hardwicke, and he clearly did not approve: '[a]s this Clause extends to persons of all degrees, even the lowest, in that part of the United Kingdom, it may possibly deserve a reconsideration whether that Clause ought not to be in some measure limited'.[131] In England, it was generally the poorer classes who married by banns, and who therefore would have been best placed to take advantage of the fact that parental consent was not actually necessary to such marriages under the 1753 Act. Hardwicke's letter suggests that he was fully aware of this and was content that the new controls should mainly affect those of higher status, who tended to marry by licence.[132]

The Ceremony

The Act stipulated that the marriage itself should take place 'in one of the Parish Churches or Chapels where such Banns have been published',[133] while a licence would only authorise the celebration of the marriage in the church or chapel of a parish where at least one of the parties resided; marriages not so solemnised would be void.[134] It has been suggested that insofar as couples had had a choice as to where to celebrate their marriage prior to 1754, this choice was extinguished by the 1753 Act.[135] But of course, given

[130] See e.g., Parker, *Informal Marriage*, p. 29.

[131] See B. Dempsey, 'The Marriage (Scotland) Bill 1755: Lord Hardwicke's Attempt to Abolish Clandestine and Irregular Marriage in Scotland' (2009) *Stair Society Miscellany* (forthcoming).

[132] Of course, it was not impossible for minors of higher status to marry by banns specifically to avoid the necessity of parental consent to marriages by licence, and examples of this are to be found in Chapter 7.

[133] Section 1. The 'chapels' referred to were, of course, Anglican rather than dissenting chapels: and see further below.

[134] Section 8: 'all Marriages solemnized ... in any other Place than a Church or such Publick Chapel ... shall be null and void to all Intents and Purposes whatsoever'.

[135] See e.g., M. G. Smith, 'An Interpretation of *Argar v. Holdsworth*' (1998–2000) 4 *Ecclesiastical Law Journal* 34.

the terms of section 10, such provisions were merely directory as regards the residence of the parties.

The content of the ceremony continued to be governed by the Book of Common Prayer and the canon law.[136] The Act itself made no stipulation that any particular words be included as part of the ceremony. The fact that an Anglican minister would usually declare 'I now pronounce you man and wife' did not mean that a marriage would be invalid if he omitted these words.[137]

Registration

Three lengthy sections were devoted to the issue of registration, and the level of detail to which the Act descended[138] suggests concern about the ease with which falsified entries could be inserted in registers, and the risk of registers that were not carefully kept being lost.[139] Again, the recording of marriages in the parish register was hardly a novelty, as legislation had ordered that parish registers be kept as early as 1538, but the Act altered the form and time of registration. The canon law had stipulated that christenings, weddings, and burials be recorded on a weekly basis by the minister every Sunday, after morning or evening prayer, in the presence of the churchwardens.[140] Such a requirement, even when

136 For the evolution of the liturgy, see K. Stevenson, *Nuptial Blessing: a Study of Christian Marriage Rites* (London: SPCK, 1982).

137 See e.g., *Hemmings* v. *Smith* (1784) 4 Dougl. 33; 99 ER 753. Cf. O'Connell, 'Matrimonial Ceremonies Displayed', 86–7, who has claimed that 'the essence of marriage was no longer exclusively situated in the utterance of the consensual vow . . . but now had to be supplemented by an Anglican minister's declaration: "I now pronounce you man and wife"'.

138 See e.g., s. 14, which directed the churchwardens to 'provide proper Books of Vellum, or good and durable Paper, in which all Marriages and Banns of Marriage respectively, there published or solemnized, shall be registered, and every Page thereof shall be marked at the Top . . . and every Leaf or Page so numbered, shall be ruled with Lines at proper and equal Distances from each other . . . and all Books provided as aforesaid shall be deemed to belong to every such Parish or Chapel respectively, and shall be carefully kept and preserved for publick Use'. This is only a sample of the sixteen lines of small print in the Act, but suffices to give a flavour of the legislature's concerns.

139 The idea of improving the registration of marriages met with the support even of those who otherwise opposed the Bill (see e.g., *Hansard's Parliamentary History*, vol. XV, col. 55), and had been the topic of a separate Bill that session: see *Hansard's Parliamentary History*, vol. XV, col. 75.

140 Canon 70. For discussion of this requirement see R. Wall, 'English Population Statistics before 1800' (2004) 9 *History of the Family* 81, 83–5.

properly observed, was all too conducive to errors and omissions, as anyone who has waded through pre-1754 marriage registers will appreciate.[141] Under the 1753 Act, by contrast, 'in order to preserve the Evidence of Marriages, and to make the Proof thereof more certain and easy', it was directed that the registration of the marriage should take place 'immediately after the Celebration of every Marriage', and should be signed by the minister, the parties themselves, and two attesting witnesses.[142]

The law had long tried to prevent tampering with the evidence and punished those who falsified entries in the parish register.[143] The 1604 canons warned sternly that 'if the Minister or Churchwardens shall be negligent in performance of any thing herein contained, it shall be lawful for the Bishop or his Chancellor to convent them, and proceed against every of them as Contemners of this our Constitution'.[144] In reinforcing the penalties imposed on those who made false entries or destroyed part of the register, the 1753 Act replaced such general warnings with specific threats. For once the overused adjective 'Draconian' may be justified: under the Act, 'every person so offending, and being thereof lawfully convicted, shall be deemed and adjudged to be guilty of felony, and shall suffer death as a felon, without benefit of clergy'.[145] At a time when England was moving from an oral to a written culture, the sanctity of the written word had to be upheld:[146] in the late

[141] See e.g., D. Ashurst, 'St Mary's Church, Worsbrough, South Yorkshire: a Review of the Accuracy of a Parish Register' (1995) 55 *Local Population Studies* 46, 52, who notes that events were generally entered on a yearly basis in that parish, and see generally D.J. Steel, *National Index of Parish Registers*, vol. I, *Sources of Births, Marriages and Deaths before 1837* (London: Society of Genealogists), ch. 2.

[142] Section 15. The legislation was also more prescriptive about the detail to be recorded, directing that it should be recorded whether the marriage was celebrated by banns or licence (and, if the latter, whether either party was under-age).

[143] See canon 70. Those who did not comply might find themselves before the correction court: see e.g., Carlisle Record Office, DRC/5/7 Scalesby, 1731.

[144] Canon 70. However, the penalty for such negligence was hardly harsh: '[i]n all the three Injunctions of Henry VIII, Edw. VI and Queen Elizabeth, the penalty on the person in fault, was, 3s. 4d. one half to the Poors-box, the other half to the Repairs of the Church': E. Gibson, *Codex juris ecclesiastici Anglicani* (London, 1713), p. 229.

[145] Section 16. Draco's code set out a number of offences for which the penalty was death: see R. Trask, *Mind the Gaffe* (London: Penguin, 2001), p. 104.

[146] A. Fox, 'Custom, Memory and the Authority of Writing', ch. 3 in P. Griffiths, A. Fox, and S. Hindle (eds.), *The Experience of Authority in Early Modern England* (Basingstoke: Macmillan Press, 1996).

eighteenth century being convicted for forgery was more likely to lead to execution than any other felony apart from murder.[147]

Yet since (just as before 1754) the parties were married once they had exchanged their vows before the presiding clergyman, anything done, or not done, afterwards could not affect the validity of the marriage. Thus, it is simply wrong to claim, as some commentators have done, that 'registration of a ceremony was considered more important than the marriage ceremony itself',[148] or that the record of a marriage 'became as crucial a part of the ceremony as the words spoken by the bride and groom'.[149] A failure to register the marriage did *not* invalidate it.[150] The provisions of the Act, while detailed, were directory rather than mandatory, and the penalty for 'falsely making, altering, forging or counterfeiting' entries was borne by the person responsible. The legislators were keen to ensure that proper proof of marriages would be easily available, but it would have been unreasonable to expect possibly illiterate brides and grooms[151] to bear the responsibility for failures in the registration process. Similarly, the absence of a (or any) witness to the ceremony did not render the marriage void. The Act did not direct that the marriage be celebrated in the presence of witnesses, only that they should attest the registration of the marriage – and as already explained, deficiencies in registration did not render the marriage void.

Penalties

The Act tried to ensure compliance with its terms by stipulating a harsh penalty (transportation to America for fourteen years) for any person who solemnised a marriage in defiance of the provisions

147 C. Emsley, *Crime and Society in England, 1750–1900*, 3rd edn (Harlow: Pearson Education Ltd, 2005), Table 10.2.

148 M. Collins, 'Centlivre v. Hardwicke: Susannah Centlivre's Plays and the Marriage Act of 1753' (1999) 33 *Comparative Drama* 179, 193.

149 Ogborn, 'This Most Lawless Space', 31.

150 Cf. Stone, *Road to Divorce*, p. 124; Baker, *Introduction to English Legal History*, pp. 482–3. For explicit confirmation that registration was not necessary, see *St Devereux* v. *Much Dewchurch* (1762) Burr. Sett. Cas. 506; No. 162, at 507, *Read* v. *Passer* (1794) 1 Esp. 213; 170 ER 332, at 214, and *R* v. *Allison* (1806) Russ. & Ry. 109; 168 ER 709 (a case of bigamy).

151 On contemporary illiteracy levels, see J. Black, *Eighteenth-Century Britain, 1688–1783* (Basingstoke: Palgrave, 2001), p. 96.

of the Act.[152] The offence was only committed if he did so 'knowingly and wilfully' and, once again, not every departure from the terms of the Act incurred the penalty. It was only if the marriage was solemnised 'in any Place other than a Church or Public Chapel, where Banns have been usually published', or if the marriage was celebrated without the necessary preliminaries having been observed, that the celebrant might be subject to prosecution.[153] This meant that if a clergyman conducted the marriage of a minor after the publication of banns without knowledge of parental opposition, no crime had been committed. Indeed, the Act actually modified the rigours of the canon law in providing that a clergyman would not be punishable even by ecclesiastical censure for solemnising a marriage by banns without the requisite consents unless he had had notice 'of the Dissent of such Parents or Guardians'.[154]

Exemptions

The provisions outlined above were not of universal application. Exemption from publicity could effectively be purchased by means of a special licence, while the territorial application of the legislation was limited to England and Wales. And three groups were automatically exempted from the provisions of the Act: Quakers, Jews, and members of the Royal Family. These exemptions will be considered in turn.

Members of the elite who desired privacy could still ensure it by means of a special licence, which allowed a marriage to go ahead at any time or place. There were, however, a number of restrictions on obtaining such a licence, which meant that it was by no means an easy option. First, it could only be obtained from the Archbishop of Canterbury. Secondly, it was expensive. Thirdly, further restrictions on the granting of such licences were quickly added by the Archbishop of Canterbury himself: in 1759 he spelt out that such licences might only be granted to 'Peers, and Peeresses in

152 Section 8.

153 Section 9 further prescribed that any prosecution had to be commenced within three years of the offence.

154 Section 3. This was in sharp contrast to the direction in the 1604 canons that a minister should not solemnise a marriage of a minor unless he had positive knowledge of parental consent: see canon 62, above.

their own right of Great Britain and Ireland, to their sons and daughters, to Dowager Peeresses, to Privy Councillors, to Judges of his Majesty's Courts in Westminster Hall, to Baronets and Knights and to members of the House of Commons'.[155] Even personages of this rank had no automatic right to a special licence, which remained a privilege in the gift of the Archbishop.[156] Those who did not fall within these narrowly-defined groups would not be granted a licence 'unless they allege very strong and weighty reasons for such Indulgence arising from the particular circumstances of their case'.[157] It was, therefore, an exemption of very limited scope.[158] Nor did it offer aristocratic youngsters a means of evading the requirements of the 1753 Act: the rules laid down by the Archbishop required diligent checks to be made as to the parties' status and age, and if there was a risk that either party might be under the age of twenty-one, officials were directed to 'insist on the fullest evidence that the intended marriage is approved by the Person or Persons whose consent the said Act ... requires'.[159]

Of even more limited significance was the provision that the Act would 'not extend to the Marriages of any of the Royal Family'.[160] It seems likely that this exemption was intended to protect royal personages from the possible embarrassment of having their marriages declared null and void in court.[161] Another motivation may have been to preserve the privacy of royal weddings: in sharp contrast to the public nature of modern royal weddings,

[155] Lambeth Palace Library (LPL), Moore 5, fol. 273.

[156] See e.g., LPL, Moore 5, fols. 272, 276. [157] LPL, Moore 5, fol. 273.

[158] The social cachet carried by such licences explains the reaction of the snobbish Mrs Bennet upon learning of her daughter's intended marriage to Mr Darcy: 'You must and shall be married by a special licence!' (J. Austen, *Pride and Prejudice* (London: Penguin Popular Classics, 1994; original edn 1813), p. 292). Whether this would have been possible is a moot point: the restrictions laid down in 1759 were still in force (T. Poynter, *A Concise View of the Doctrine and Practice of the Ecclesiastical Courts in Doctors' Commons* (London, 1824), p. 51), and Mr Darcy, despite his £10,000 per year, does not seem to meet the criteria. Perhaps Jane Austen was simply seizing another opportunity to satirise Mrs Bennet's shaky grasp of legal matters.

[159] LPL, Moore 5, fol. 273. [160] Section 17.

[161] The exemption was replicated in all subsequent legislation, including the 1836 Marriage Act which introduced civil marriage: see S. Cretney, 'Royal Marriages: the Law in a Nutshell' (2005) *Family Law* 317; R. Probert, 'Royal Privileges and Human Rights: the Wedding of the Prince of Wales' (2005) *Child and Family Law Quarterly* 363; S. Cretney, 'Royal Marriages: Some Legal and Constitutional Issues' (2008) 124 *Law Quarterly Review* 218.

eighteenth-century royal marriages were 'held at St. James's Palace, and usually at night with little emphasis on ceremonial'.[162] Moreover, to strengthen the powers of parents might risk creating a clash of authority. Within the Royal Family, the consent of the sovereign was more important than the consent of a parent, and those who married without such consent were liable to punishment.[163]

The exemption of Quakers and Jews was of wider application, although, as Chapter 4 has shown, these were very much minority religions. The puzzle as to why these two, of all non-Anglican denominations or religions, were exempted, has been resolved by considering previous practice: Quakers and Jews were the only non-Anglicans in the jurisdiction (except for Catholics) who regularly celebrated marriages according to their own religious rites, and conferring special privileges on Catholics was unthinkable in the light of the numerous legal disabilities they suffered and the persistent anti-Catholicism of Georgian England.[164]

Another factor was that the Quakers actually asked to be exempted from the legislation, whereas those representing England's Catholic community did not. The organisation of the Quakers was such that they regularly made representations to Parliament if there was a risk that legislation might prejudice their position.[165]

[162] R. Mullen, 'The Last Marriage of a Prince of Wales, 1863' (1981) 31 *History Today* 10, 12. The reigning monarch at the time the Act was passed, George II, had himself married in Hanover before ascending to the throne, but his children Frederick and Anne married at the Chapel Royal, St James' Palace. Of his remaining children, Mary and Louisa both married by proxy and the rest died unmarried: A. Weir, *Britain's Royal Families: the Complete Genealogy* (London: Pimlico, 1996).

[163] See C. d'O. Farran, 'The Royal Marriages Act, 1772' (1951) 14 *Modern Law Review* 53, 54. The sovereign's control over marriages within the Royal Family was subsequently strengthened by the Royal Marriages Act 1772, passed in the wake of two secret and unsuitable marriages within the family circle. See further Cretney, 'Royal Marriages'.

[164] 'So insignificant a minority, thankful as it was for the barest toleration, could not hope to make its voice heard to effect': E. Burton, *The Life and Times of Bishop Challoner* (London: Longmans, Green & Co., 1909), vol. I, pp. 328–9. On attitudes to Catholics in the eighteenth century, see C. Haydon, 'Parliament and Popery in England, 1700–1780' (2000) 19 *Parliamentary History* 49.

[165] See generally C.W. Hoyle, *The Quakers and the English Legal System, 1660–1688* (Philadelphia: University of Pennsylvania Press, 1988), and note the representations made by the Quakers when there was an earlier attempt to legislate against clandestine marriages: Quaker Library, Yearly Meetings, vol. V, pp. 356–7.

In this case they were quick off the mark: at the start of March 1753, it was noted that '[m]ention being made of A Bill brought in or likely to be brought into Parliament respecting clandestine marriages, the Friends following are desired to make Enquiry, and take the necessary care therein, lest any thing be inserted to the Prejudice of Friends'.[166] Over the following weeks the course of the Bill was tracked, and suggestions as to the appropriate wording of an exemption were made.[167] The willingness of Parliament to accede to the request of the Quakers to be exempted from the legislation may have been encouraged by the close control exercised by Quakers over their marriages: there was no risk that members of the wider community might be able to evade the provisions of the 1753 Act by pretending to be Quaker and so marrying according to their rites. The same was true of Jews. It should also be noted that the Act did not declare that marriages conducted according to Quaker or Jewish rites would be valid. Instead, it simply stated that the Act did not extend to such marriages.[168] Just as the Act consolidated many aspects of the existing law, so it could be said to have captured the ambiguous status of Quaker and Jewish marriages.[169]

By far the most significant exemption, however, was the provision that the Act only applied to England and Wales.[170] The marriage law of Scotland had long differed from that of its southern neighbours, and the terms of the Act of Union precluded legislation relating to religion.[171] Since the validity of a marriage was tested by the law of the country where it had been celebrated,[172]

166 Quaker Library, Meetings for Sufferings, vol. XXV, p. 234.

167 *Ibid.* pp. 241–2, 244, 248, 252, 261. The final version adopted by Parliament was very similar to that proposed by the Quakers: see *ibid.* p. 245.

168 It was grafted on to a provision that the Act should not extend to Scotland.

169 See further Chapter 9.

170 Section 18: 'nothing in this Act shall extend to that Part of Great Britain called Scotland ... nor to any Marriages solemnized beyond the Seas'.

171 As noted in *Middleton* v. *Janverin* (1802) 2 Hag. Con. 437; 161 ER 797.

172 See e.g., *Scrimshire* v. *Scrimshire* (1752) 2 Hag. Con. 395; 161 ER 782. By contrast, it was assumed that it would not be possible to bring an action to compel celebration of a contract made elsewhere, reflecting the difference between the recognition of a marriage validly celebrated overseas in accordance with the laws of that country, and a contract to marry entered into abroad: see the arguments of counsel in *Robinson* v. *Bland* (1760–1) 1 Black. W 234; 96 ER 129, at 241.

this raised the possibility that the Act might be evaded by elopements out of the jurisdiction.[173]

Viewed in context, therefore, the terms of the 1753 Act were far from being a radical break with the past; moreover, once its loopholes are exposed, it is obvious that there were ways of evading its prescriptions. And it could, after all, have been much stricter: one earlier Bill had attempted to make the seduction of a minor by a servant an imprisonable offence;[174] and in an earlier draft the death penalty had been prescribed for those ministers who solemnised marriages other than according to the legal requirements.[175] From these perspectives the Act, as passed, seems positively lenient. But how was it interpreted by the courts?

THE INTERPRETATION OF THE ACT

It is impossible to provide by express words, in any law, for all the minute accidents that may afterwards happen in practice. When such accidents happen, it is always deemed sufficient if the general intent and meaning of the statute be pursued.[176]

The operation of any piece of legislation is bound to throw up questions and problems that were not anticipated at the time of its drafting, and the 1753 Act was no exception. The Act had, for example, omitted to deal with the question of jurisdiction: did the fact that marriage was now regulated by statute preclude the ecclesiastical courts from exercising jurisdiction? Two early decisions on the Act illustrated the expanded powers of the common-law courts: first, they were no longer required to refer the issue of validity to the ecclesiastical courts for determination;[177] secondly, they had the exclusive right to determine whether a felony had been committed by a clergyman flouting the provisions of the Act, and

[173] See further Chapter 7. [174] See Outhwaite, *Clandestine Marriage*, pp. 69–70.

[175] BL Add 35880, fol. 12, cl. 8.

[176] *Hansard's Parliamentary History*, vol. XV, col. 79 (William Murray, then Solicitor-General, who as Lord Mansfield was later to put this principle into practice in interpreting the Act).

[177] *R* v. *Inhabitants of Preston near Faversham* (1759) Burr. Sett. Cas. No. 154. See also *Ilderton* v. *Ilderton* (1793) 2 H. Bl. 145; 126 ER 476. However, in dower cases the appropriate course remained for the bishop to certify whether the parties were married or not: see e.g., *Robins* v. *Crutchley* (1760) 2 Wils. 118; 95 ER 718.

the church authorities consequently lost the power to censure ministers guilty of such an offence.[178]

Questions also arose regarding the position of illegitimate minors: did the provisions of the Act apply to them in the same way as it did to legitimate children? The Act itself was silent on this point. In the first case to consider the issue, *R* v. *The Inhabitants of Edmonton*,[179] it was assumed that no difference was intended. Willes J stressed that the Act should have a liberal construction, and pointed out that the Act did not state that it applied only to 'lawful' children. The decision of the court was perhaps influenced by the fact that this was not a case in which the parties had intended to flout the law: the father of the illegitimate minor had consented to her marriage. Thus, as Buller J pointed out, 'it was unnecessary to decide whether a putative father were within the act or not; for taking it either way, the marriage was good: if the consent of the putative father were necessary, it had been obtained, if it were not necessary, then the marriage was good without'.[180] The issue was revisited in another settlement case, *R* v. *The Inhabitants of Hodnett*.[181] In this case both of the parties to the marriage were illegitimate minors, no-one had consented to their marriage, and the groom had obtained a licence by swearing that both were of age. Unsurprisingly, the court had no reservations in declaring the marriage to be void: as Lord Mansfield pointed out, 'here there is no consent by any one; consequently, in my opinion, it is void by the marriage act'.[182] As in *Edmonton*, however, the decision was based on the assumption that illegitimate minors should be treated no differently from those who were legitimate: the Act applied to all, and, as Lord Mansfield said, there was 'no reason to except illegitimate children, for they are within the mischiefs intended to be remedied by the act'.[183]

One possibility was left unexplored in these two cases, namely, that the consent of the illegitimate minor's parents was not sufficient and that the consent of a guardian appointed by the Court of

[178] See *Campbell, Clerk* v. *Aldridge* (1757) 2 Wils. KB 79; 95 ER 697. The ecclesiastical courts did, however, retain jurisdiction over those more minor breaches of canon law that did not amount to a felony: *Wynn* v. *Davies* (1835) 1 Curt. 69; 163 ER 24.

[179] (1784) Caldecott 435.

[180] Cited in *R* v. *The Inhabitants of Hodnett* (1786) 1 TR 96; 99 ER 993, at 97.

[181] (1786) 1 TR 96; 99 ER 993. [182] *Ibid.* at 100. [183] *Ibid.*

Chancery was required instead. It was not until the end of the century that Sir William Scott affirmed this to be the case,[184] holding the marriage of an illegitimate minor to be void despite the fact that her mother had consented to the match. Policy and pragmatism were mixed in his judgment. As a matter of policy, he argued that the privilege of giving consent should not be given to 'those who bear the title of parents not as a title of honour and privilege, but of discredit and disability'.[185] One might have imagined that holding the consent of a whole class of parents to be insufficient would undo many marriages, but Sir William denied that this would occur, instead asserting that it had been the practice of the Court of Chancery to appoint guardians for illegitimate children since the Act and that such marriages would be invalidated if it were to be decided at such a late stage that parental consent was necessary.[186] Despite such confident assertions, Scott later made attempts to modify the rule, describing it as 'this strict principle of law, the growth of later times', and suggesting that the law on this point was not settled.[187] In the light of such uncertainty, illegitimate minors had three options: apply to the court for such a guardian to be appointed; wait until the age of twenty-one to marry, or – most simply – marry by banns. Since unmarried parents were now deemed to be disqualified from consenting to their child's marriage by licence, they were equally disqualified from forbidding the banns.[188] Most illegitimate children (hardly a large category in any case)[189] would have married by banns, while those born to parents of higher social standing would have had the wherewithal to apply for a guardian to be appointed.

[184] In *Horner* v. *Liddiard* (1799) 1 Hag. Con. 337; 161 ER 573.

[185] *Ibid.* 357.

[186] There had been a number of cases in which the Court of Chancery accepted the guardians named in the putative father's will, even though such a person technically had no authority to appoint a guardian: *Peckham* v. *Peckham* (1788) 2 Cox 46; 30 ER 22; *Ward* v. *St Paul* (1789) 2 Bro. CC 583; 29 ER 320. Scott's assumption that a guardian would be appointed for an illegitimate minor should be viewed in context: he was, of course, discussing marriages by licence, which were generally used only by the more monied sections of society.

[187] *Fielder* v. *Smith* (1816) 2 Hag. Con. 193; 161 ER 712, at 194.

[188] A point noted in *Priestly* v. *Hughes* (1809) 11 East 1; 103 ER 903.

[189] Even by the end of the century, the illegitimacy rate was only 6 per cent: see P. Laslett, *Family Life and Illicit Love in Earlier Generations* (Cambridge University Press, 1977), ch. 3.

What might appear at first sight to be a harsh interpretation of the law had very little impact in practice.

The suggestion in *R* v. *The Inhabitants of Edmonton* that the Act should be liberally construed may come as a surprise to those who assume, as many commentators have done,[190] that the Act was strictly interpreted. But it was a policy that was echoed in other eighteenth-century cases. One question that arose for consideration by the courts was how compliance or non-compliance should be proved. Again, this was a point that had not been elaborated in the Act. The approach of the courts was that *non*-compliance had to be proved: in the absence of evidence to the contrary, it would be presumed that the banns had been properly called or a licence obtained;[191] that parental consent had been given; and that the clergyman conducting the ceremony was lawfully ordained.[192] It was further held that a marriage could be proved even if the register was missing or had not been signed by the parties.[193] As noted in Chapter 3, cohabitation and reputation of marriage could be taken into account by the common-law courts when determining certain issues, and the courts appear to have been even more willing to accept such evidence after 1754,[194] perhaps because the Act had made it more likely that the marriage would have taken place within the parties' own parish church and with the required publicity.

The Act was liberally construed in other contexts, too. It was one thing to presume that a marriage had been properly celebrated in the absence of evidence to the contrary, but one might think it was quite another to overlook obvious deficiencies in the

[190] See e.g., W.P. Eversley, *The Law of the Domestic Relations* (London: Stevens & Haynes, 1885), p. 26; G.E. Howard, *A History of Matrimonial Institutions* (University of Chicago Press, 1904; New York Humanities Press, 1964), pp. 463–4; O.M. Stone, *Family Law* (London: Macmillan Press, 1977), p. 30; R.L. Brown, 'The Rise and Fall of Fleet Marriages', ch. 6 in R.B. Outhwaite, *Marriage and Society* (London: Europa Publications Ltd, 1981), p. 135; A.H. Manchester, *A Modern Legal History of England and Wales 1750–1950* (London: Butterworths, 1980), p. 365; and S. Parker, *Informal Marriage, Cohabitation and the Law, 1750–1989* (Basingstoke: Macmillan Press, 1990), p. 61.

[191] *St Devereux* v. *Much Dewchurch* (1762) 1 Wl. Bl. 367; 96 ER 205, at 367–8.

[192] *R* v. *The Inhabitants of Haslingfield* (1814) 2 M & S 558; 105 ER 489, at 490.

[193] *St Devereux* v. *Much Dewchurch* (1762) 1 Wl. Bl. 367; 96 ER 205.

[194] See e.g., *St Devereux* v. *Much Dewchurch* (1762) 1 Wl. Bl. 367; 96 ER 205, at 367–8. The only contexts in which such evidence did not suffice were prosecutions for bigamy and suits for criminal conversation: see *Morris* v. *Miller; Birt* v. *Barlow* (1779) 1 Doug. KB 171; 99 ER 113; *Hemmings* v. *Smith* (1784) 4 Dougl. 33; 99 ER 753.

celebration of the marriage. Yet there are a number of cases in which the courts did just that, on the basis that the form set out in the Act did not have to be followed precisely. In *Standen* v. *Standen*,[195] for example, Lord Kenyon directed the jury that it was not necessary to comply with all of the requirements set out in the Act of Parliament, since 'the form prescribed by the Act is merely directory and need not be strictly followed. If the substance is followed it is sufficient.'[196] The jury accordingly found for the plaintiff – whose legitimacy hinged on the validity of his parents' marriage – despite the facts that the marriage had taken place in the chapel of the Savoy in 1755[197] and that the father had subsequently claimed that the banns had not been adequately published.

An even more robustly liberal attitude was displayed in *Wilkinson* v. *Payne*,[198] in which the court progressed from ignoring evidence that might invalidate a marriage to presuming that a second, valid ceremony had taken place. Two key policy factors underpinned this fiction. The first was the justice of the case. The defendant had promised his future son-in-law £180 upon marriage. The ceremony had taken place, and the couple were treated as husband and wife by the family, but the wife then died and her father, the defendant, tried to avoid paying his son-in-law the money by arguing that the marriage had been invalid. There were good grounds for this argument, as the parties had been married by licence during the minority of the orphaned husband, and no guardian had been appointed to consent to the marriage. The person whom his dying mother had asked to act as his guardian had approved of the match, but since a mother had no power to appoint a guardian, and a mere verbal request would not have been sufficient to create a valid appointment in any case, such approval was irrelevant to the legal validity, although it was crucial to the merits of the case. This leads on to the second policy consideration: as Lord Kenyon pointed out, the parties had not intended to elude the 1753 Act: 'all their friends were fully informed of and concurred in the former marriage'.[199] The jury found in favour of the plaintiff, and the judges refused to grant a

[195] (1791) Peake 45; 170 ER 73. [196] *Ibid.* 48.

[197] In 1755 a number of marriages were solemnised in the Savoy chapel contrary to the requirements of the Act, the minister claiming (unsuccessfully as it turned out) to be exempt from the Act: see further Chapter 7.

[198] (1791) 4 Term Rep. 468; 100 ER 1123. [199] *Ibid.* 469.

new trial, both agreeing that this result was consistent with justice and equity.[200]

A similarly purposive interpretation of the Act was adopted in *Stallwood* v. *Tredger.*[201] In this case the church was being repaired at the time of the parties' marriage in 1792. It was thus deemed an extra-parochial place for the purposes of the Act, and the banns were called in the neighbouring parish, as the 1753 Act stipulated. However, the marriage was then solemnised on the site of the home church, contravening the provision that 'the Marriage shall be solemnised in one of the Parish Churches or Chapels where such Banns have been published, and in no other Place whatsoever'.[202] This provision could hardly be clearer. Yet the Court of Arches upheld the marriage, and the decision was affirmed by the High Court of Delegates. Sir John Nicholl stated trenchantly that 'nothing but the most imperious demands of judicial interpretation could induce me to hold this marriage invalid'.[203] He pointed out that this was not the type of marriage that the Act was designed to prevent: both of the parties were of age, there was no attempt at concealment, and the marriage had subsisted for twenty years before its validity was questioned. Moreover, the minister had done all that he could to comply with the spirit and letter of the law, even making an entry in the register to explain the circumstances.

Yet sometimes the spirit of the law mandated a stricter approach to the letter. This was apparent in the case of *Early* v. *Stevens*, in which it was held that the true names of the parties had to be published in the banns.[204] A further issue arose as to *where* banns could be published. The Act had stipulated that banns should be called in 'the Parish Church, or in some publick Chapel, in which publick Chapel Banns of matrimony *have been*

[200] They did, however, differ on the reasoning by which it could be supported as a matter of law. Buller J suggested that the fact of the marriage would be sufficient in this particular case: the £180 was payable when a ceremony of marriage took place, and the nullity of the marriage would not affect the plaintiff's entitlement. Lord Kenyon preferred the more artificial route of presuming that a second valid marriage had taken place after the plaintiff had attained the age of twenty-one, although as this birthday had occurred when the 'wife' was on her death-bed this interpretation rather strains credulity.

[201] (1815) 2 Phill. Ecc. 287; 161 ER 1147. [202] Section 1.

[203] (1815) 2 Phill. Ecc. 287; 161 ER 1147, at 290.

[204] *Early* v. *Stevens* (1785), cited in *Pouget* v. *Tomkins* (1812) 2 Hag. Con. 142; 161 ER 695.

usually published'.[205] The aim of this section was clearly to ensure that the Act could not be evaded through the use of private chapels outside the jurisdiction of the Church of England. *R* v. *Northfield* raised the question of whether it by implication excluded the celebration of marriages in *newly-built* churches or chapels: the marriage of the woman whose settlement was in question had taken place in a church that had been erected in 1765. Lord Mansfield, rather reluctantly, held that the Act clearly meant structures existing when the Act was passed.[206] The effect of this was most unfortunate, since it meant that marriages by banns in churches or chapels built after 1754 could not be valid.[207] The decision required a succession of Acts of Parliament to ratify such marriages retrospectively.[208]

At first sight, this decision appears harsh and out of line with those that adopted a more purposive interpretation of the legislation. After all, an alternative interpretation of the Act had been argued for by counsel, namely that 'usually published' should refer to when the marriage took place, not when the Act was passed. Against this was the argument of opposing counsel that Lincoln's Inn chapel was no longer used for the celebration of marriages, as banns had not been published there prior to the Act, and that it would be absurd if a new chapel were to be treated more favourably. The latter argument had force, and the decision was consistent with a purposive interpretation of the Act. If the marriage had been upheld on the basis that banns had 'usually' been published in the church in question, then the authority to publish banns would depend simply on the practice of publishing them. Such an interpretation would have opened up the possibility for any private chapel to publish banns and claim the right to celebrate marriages and it is unsurprising that Mansfield moved swiftly to prevent this.[209]

205 Section 1 (emphasis added).

206 *R* v. *Northfield* (1781) 2 Dougl. 658; 99 ER 418.

207 And see *Taunton* v. *Wyborn* (1809) 2 Camp. 297; 170 ER 1161 on the evidence required to raise a presumption that banns had been published in an existing church or chapel prior to 1754.

208 Such Acts were passed in 1781, 1804, 1825, and 1830. The fact that Parliament acted so quickly in response to the decision in *R* v. *Northfield* to address this obvious deficiency in the drafting of the Act (the Bill was introduced on 28 May and had passed all its stages in the Commons by 7 June) does rather suggest a lack of any widespread perception that other aspects of the Act might be in need of reform. On later reform initiatives, see Chapter 8 below.

209 This may have been why the initial Bill did not deal with newly-built churches, although the issue was raised at the time: see BL Add 35877 fol. 119, clause 4.

Reading such cases, the indictment that the Act was harshly interpreted would appear to be unsustainable. The reason why other commentators have come to such a different conclusion is because they have focused on a later set of cases, largely decided in the second decade of the nineteenth century, that dealt with the application of the Act to a specific problem, that of couples who deliberately flouted the spirit of the Act, evading parental disapproval by having the banns called in a parish to which neither belonged. But in contextualising the 1753 Act it is important both to separate out those cases that dealt with the interpretation of new rules from those that dealt with the application of well-established rules to specific facts, and to set each body of case law in its historical context. The analysis of these cases is therefore a task for another chapter.

CONCLUSION

To a generation used to a wide choice of wedding venues the options available under the Clandestine Marriages Act may seem limited indeed, and its approach unduly prescriptive. Yet the Act should not be viewed from the perspective of a twenty-first-century bride or groom, but from that of their eighteenth-century counterparts, for whom marriage in church was the norm. All that the Act did, in essence, was to reinforce the requirements of the canon law by invalidating those marriages that failed to comply with its key provisions: as Lord Mansfield pointed out in *R* v. *The Inhabitants of Hodnett*, the Act 'only made that less practicable which was before illegal'.[210]

It is significant that Mansfield said 'less practicable' and not 'impracticable'. For, as this chapter has shown, loopholes did exist under the new statutory scheme. Neglect of the residential requirements did not render a marriage void, and neither did the failure of a minor to obtain parental consent to a marriage by banns. The extent to which these loopholes were exploited in practice – and the ways in which the judiciary subsequently sought to plug them – form the subject of the next two chapters.

[210] (1786) 1 TR 96; 99 ER 993.

7

THE UNAPPRECIATED SUCCESS OF THE 1753 ACT

It has been contended by many scholars that the Act was a failure, and that a significant proportion of couples continued to marry according to their own rites – religious or regional – or simply lived together outside marriage.[1] One commentator has gone so far as to suggest that cohabitation actually increased in the wake of the Act: 'as the law became stricter, the resort to common-law [*sic*][2] rites became more frequent'.[3] Others have suggested that while the 1753 Act was intended to replace custom with law, in practice its operation saw the triumph of custom over law.[4] But we must carefully consider the evidential basis for such claims.

[1] See e.g., J. Gillis, *For Better, For Worse: British Marriages 1600 to the Present* (Oxford University Press, 1985); K. O'Donovan, *Sexual Divisions in Law* (London: Weidenfeld & Nicholson, 1985), p. 49; L. Davidoff, 'The Family in Britain', ch. 2 in F. M. L. Thompson (ed.), *The Cambridge Social History of Britain 1750–1950* (Cambridge University Press, 1990), vol. II, p. 90; O. Hufton, *The Prospect before Her: a History of Women in Western Europe*, vol. I, *1500–1800* (London: HarperCollins, 1995), p. 135; W. Mansell, B. Meteyard, and A. Thomson, *A Critical Introduction to Law*, 2nd edn (London: Cavendish, 1999), p. 92; S. Parker, *Informal Marriage, Cohabitation and the Law, 1754–1989* (Basingstoke: Macmillan, 1990); C. Gibson, *Dissolving Wedlock* (London: Routledge, 1994), p. 49; A. Diduck and F. Kaganas, *Family Law, Gender and the State: Text, Cases and Materials*, 2nd edn (Oxford: Hart Publishing, 2005), p. 61; T. Evans, *'Unfortunate Objects': Lone Mothers in Eighteenth-Century London* (Basingstoke: Palgrave Macmillan, 2005), p. 48; A. Barlow, S. Duncan, G. James, and A. Park, *Cohabitation, Marriage and the Law: Social Change and Legal Reform in the 21st Century* (Oxford: Hart, 2005), p. 51. L. Stone, *Road to Divorce: a History of the Making and Breaking of Marriage in England* (Oxford University Press, 1990), p. 129, suggests that some 'relapsed into concubinage' but is more tentative about the scale of non-compliance.

[2] See further Chapter 3 on the anachronistic nature of this term.

[3] J. Gillis, 'Married but not Churched: Plebeian Sexual Relations and Marital Nonconformity in Eighteenth Century Britain' in R. Maccubbin (ed.), *'Tis Nature's Fault: Unauthorized Sexuality during the Enlightenment* (Cambridge University Press, 1987), p. 37.

[4] D. Hay and N. Rogers, *Eighteenth-Century English Society: Shuttles and Swords* (Oxford University Press, 1997), p. 37.

The work of Griffiths, Fox, and Hindle provides a useful starting-point for thinking about attitudes to, and compliance with, the 1753 Act. In considering the broader issue of experiences of authority in the early modern period, they note that the spectrum of interpretative positions included 'conformity, resignation, passivity, creativity, mockery and opposition'.[5] This encapsulates how individuals may comply with rules willingly, reluctantly, indifferently, or indeed not at all. The vast majority of the population – today as in the past – generally accepts new laws with neither wild enthusiasm nor execration. Even those who actively oppose new laws may recognise that they have no choice but to comply with them once they have been enacted.

This chapter, then, examines five different ways in which the populace might have reacted to the 1753 Act. The opening section looks at the immediate reaction to the Act: whether there was any overt opposition at the time of its passage or any rush to marry before its provisions came into force. The following two sections consider whether there is any evidence that couples 'opted out' by refusing to engage in any way with the legislative requirements, and whether many couples simply avoided the Act by eloping to another jurisdiction. There is a danger that these tales of elopements, with their romantic associations, will leave a stronger impression than the necessarily less exciting account of conformity, and so, at the risk of giving away the ending, I will state here that the fourth section shows clearly that the vast majority of the population complied with the requirements of the Act. Yet the story of compliance is not a straightforward one, and the fifth section demonstrates that at least some couples complied with the letter but not the spirit of the law.

It should also be noted by way of preliminary that, just as previous chapters focused on the period immediately *before* the Clandestine Marriages Act, so this chapter will focus on the period immediately *after* 1754. Too often nineteenth-century practices have been cited as evidence of the popular reaction to the Act.[6] Yet it is crucial to remember that in the 1750s England stood on the

[5] P. Griffiths, A. Fox, and S. Hindle (eds.), *The Experience of Authority in Early Modern England* (Basingstoke: Macmillan Press, 1996), p. 6.

[6] See e.g., B. Meteyard, 'Illegitimacy in Eighteenth-Century England: a Reply' (1981) 11 *Journal of Interdisciplinary History* 507, citing the writings of Henry Mayhew (from the 1850s) and L.A. Tilly, J. Scott, and M. Cohen, 'Women's Work and

cusp of profound economic and social changes.[7] By the start of the nineteenth century the dislocating effects of agricultural and industrial change were already being experienced in many parts of the country;[8] by the time Mayhew was writing in the 1850s the population had almost trebled,[9] and parts of London had become, in the view of mid-Victorian investigators, an alien place inhabited by strange people.[10] Quite simply, the fact that couples were cohabiting in the nineteenth century does not mean that they were doing so in the eighteenth,[11] nor does it imply that the 1753 Act was the cause.

One section of the population that is not considered in this chapter comprises those persons who may have had *religious* objections to a marriage in the Church of England. The sheer diversity of dissent in eighteenth-century England and Wales means that the topic requires separate treatment, while changes in the nature of dissent over the course of the late eighteenth and early nineteenth centuries provide the backdrop to the legislation enacted in 1836. This made radical changes to the law of marriage and is the natural end-point of an analysis of the 1753 Act. All these issues will therefore be considered in a later chapter.

OPPOSITION

Pamphleteers and MPs easily work themselves up to think the cause in hand of the last moment.[12]

European Fertility Patterns' (1976) 6 *Journal of Interdisciplinary History* 447, whose sources mostly relate to developments in Europe but who also rely on Mayhew; see also Parker, *Informal Marriage*, p. 67, citing Mayhew and Booth (from the 1890s).

7 See e.g., M. J. Daunton, *Progress and Poverty: an Economic and Social History of Britain 1700–1850* (Oxford University Press, 1995); K. D. M. Snell, *Annals of the Labouring Poor: Social Change in Agrarian England, 1660–1900* (Cambridge University Press, 1985).

8 See e.g., D. Levine, *Family Formation in an Age of Nascent Capitalism* (London: Academic Press, 1977).

9 M. Anderson, 'The Social Implications of Demographic Change', ch. 1 in Thompson, *The Cambridge Social History of Britain 1750–1950*, vol. II.

10 See e.g., J. Walkovitch, *City of Dreadful Delight: Narratives of Sexual Danger in Late-Victorian London* (London: Virago Press, 1992), pp. 18–19.

11 See e.g., R. Trumbach, *Sex and the Gender Revolution*, vol. I, *Heterosexuality and the Third Gender in Enlightenment London* (University of Chicago Press, 1998), p. 261, who examined the poor-law examinations for Shoreditch from the last four decades of the eighteenth century and noted that '[t]here was not yet present in eighteenth-century Shoreditch the practice attributed to the weavers in the 1830s of not "having lawful married wives" but keeping instead "women whom they call tacks"'.

12 *A Letter to the Public: Containing the substance of what hath been offered in the late Debates upon the subject of the Act of Parliament for the better preventing of Clandestine Marriages* (London, 1753), p. 14.

While the Act certainly gave rise to heated debates in Parliament, a flurry of pamphlets,[13] and a rather bad novel,[14] there are no indications that it was widely resented among the populace as a whole.[15] There is a tradition that Henry Fox was acclaimed and carried through the streets of London because of his opposition to the Act,[16] but I have been unable to trace any contemporary report confirming this.[17] Even if it were true, Fox's own biographer (and descendant) acknowledges that 'these signs of popular approval soon died away'.[18]

Similarly, Parker's dramatic statement that '[t]he immediate effect of Lord Hardwicke's Act appears to have been a riot in Oxfordshire'[19] is rather misleading. There certainly appears to have been friction in Oxfordshire in 1754,[20] in the context of one of the most bitterly contested elections of the eighteenth century, but it owed more to the rabble-rousing of the Tory gentlemen there on a range of issues than to any groundswell of opinion against the 1753 Act in particular. According to Jarrett, they 'trotted out every possible slogan in order

[13] See e.g., A. Keith, *Observations on the Act for Preventing Clandestine Marriages* (London, 1753); H. Stebbing, *A Dissertation on the Power of States to Deny Civil Protection to the Marriages of Minors made Without the Consent of their Parents or Guardians* (London, 1754) and *An Enquiry into the Force and Operation of the Annulling Clauses in a late Act for the Better Preventing of Clandestine Marriages, with respect to Conscience* (London, 1754). For discussion of this literature see R. B. Outhwaite, *Clandestine Marriage in England, 1500–1850* (London: Hambledon Press, 1995), ch. 5.

[14] J. Shebbeare, *The Marriage Act: a Novel Containing a Series of Interesting Adventures* (London, 1754).

[15] Cf. B. Rizzo, '"The Bite" – Kitty Smart to Henry Fox' (1986) 37 *Review of English Studies* 215.

[16] See e.g., Stone, *Road to Divorce*, p. 123; D. Lemmings, 'Marriage and the Law in the Eighteenth Century: Hardwicke's Marriage Act of 1753' (1996) 39 *Historical Journal* 339, 340; Outhwaite, *Clandestine Marriage*, p. 97.

[17] The only eighteenth-century source I have traced was written several decades later: G. A. Bellamy, *An Apology for the Life of George Anne Bellamy* (London, 1786), vol. III, p. 47, noted that 'Mr Fox's popularity was at this time arrived at such a height, from the opposition he made to the Marriage Act, that his chariot was carried upon the shoulders of the crowd for several days together, from the Parliament House to Conduit-Street.' It is a good mile from Parliament to Conduit Street: either the crowd was both enthusiastic and strong or there is an element of exaggeration in this account.

[18] Earl of Ilchester, *Henry Fox, First Lord Holland, His Family and Relations* (London: John Murray, 1920), p. 196.

[19] Parker, *Informal Marriage*, p. 61.

[20] See e.g., J. Stevenson, *Popular Disturbances in England, 1700–1832*, 2nd edn (London: Longman, 1992), p. 34, who does not mention the 1753 Act as a factor.

to smear the Whigs and their government'.[21] Since Jarrett, Parker's source for his claim, is discussing Hogarth's depiction of the election, the inference that there was a riot on this particular issue seems to rest solely on the fact that Hogarth included an oblique reference to the 1753 Act in one of his paintings.[22]

It might be argued that the lack of other protests was because the majority of the population was generally too cowed by patrician power to make their views known. But the response to other pieces of legislation does not suggest that this was the case. One might contrast the reaction to the contemporaneous Jewish Naturalisation Act, also passed in 1753. A vicious press campaign followed, public protests were made, and the Act was repealed. As Langford comments, '[i]f Pelhamite government was an oligarchy, it was evidently one which was remarkably sensitive to the opinions of those whom it governed'.[23] The repeal of the Jewish Naturalisation Act evidently made Hardwicke somewhat nervous lest the same fate be meted out to the Clandestine Marriage Act: thinking that the passage of a similar measure in relation to Scotland might provide opportunity for further criticism, he besought those responsible for drafting the Scottish Bill to delay sending it.[24]

Nor can the failure to protest against the Act be attributed to ignorance of its terms. It was hardly a hidden reform, since incumbents were required to read it in full from the pulpit.[25] There is

[21] D. Jarrett, *England in the Age of Hogarth* (New Haven: Yale University Press, 1986), p. 25.

[22] The slogan 'marry and multiply in spite of the devil and the court' appears, as does 'give us our eleven days'. The latter is discussed by R. Poole, '"Give Us Our Eleven Days!": Calendar Reform in Eighteenth-Century England' (1995) 149 *Past and Present* 95, 104, who concludes that the supposed riots over the calendar change that accompanied the 1754 election 'can be asserted with confidence [to be] a myth'.

[23] P. Langford, *A Polite and Commercial People: England 1727–1783* (Oxford University Press, 1998), p. 225. A similar point is made by E. P. Thompson, 'Patrician Society, Plebeian Culture' (1974) 7 *Journal of Social History* 382: 'the tetchy sensibilities of a libertarian crowd defined, in the largest sense, the limits of what was politically possible'.

[24] B. Dempsey, 'The Marriage (Scotland) Bill 1755: Lord Hardwicke's Attempt to Abolish Clandestine and Irregular Marriage in Scotland' (2009) *Stair Society Miscellany* (forthcoming).

[25] Section 19. This was not an uncommon practice: the incumbent of the parish was under a duty to read the Canons of 1604 and certain Acts of Parliament from the pulpit each year: see J. Shaw, *Parish Law*, 7th edn (London, 1750), p. 62. In an era when absence from church might still incur penalties, this practice was a useful way of informing the populace of new developments.

evidence that this did happen: historians have often quoted a report in the *Gentleman's Magazine* that the congregation in Kingston began to leave when the minister started reading the Act,[26] suggesting this was an example of the populace's dislike of the new legislation.[27] Yet when the story was reported in November 1753 the congregation would have already heard the new provisions read out at least twice, since the Act directed that it was to be published every month from September to December of that year: familiarity, rather than resistance, may have been the explanation for the mass exodus.

Of course the Act had its critics, many of whom were violent in their language if not in their actions. Alexander Keith, who had himself benefited from the phenomenon of clandestine marriages and whose championship of 'rash and inconsiderate marriages' was clearly self-interested,[28] suggested that enforced waiting periods would mean that 'there would not be one in twenty, nay, I might say, one in fifty who would marry'.[29] The results, he suggested, would be fornication, concubinage, and (not entirely consistently) depopulation. Another writer predicted dire consequences, including the destruction of the nation.[30] Opposition of this kind was characterised more by heat than by light: like their modern journalistic counterparts, eighteenth-century commentators did not always have a sound knowledge of the law preceding the reforms. As Smollett dryly noted in his account of the Act, opponents 'foresaw a great number of evils in the train of this bill, which have not yet been realized'.[31]

It is true that some couples took advantage of the delay between the passage of the Act and its implementation to marry clandestinely before 25 March 1754. Horace Walpole wrote to George Montagu on 17 July 1753 that 'Lady Anne Powlett's daughter is eloped with a country clergyman; the Duchess of Argyll harangues against the marriage bill's not taking place immediately and is

[26] *Gentleman's Magazine* (1753) 23 588.

[27] See e.g., Outhwaite, *Clandestine Marriage*, p. 124. [28] See Chapter 4.

[29] Keith, *Observations on the Act*, p. 19.

[30] *Essays on several subjects, viz. 1. on the late Act to Prevent Clandestine Marriages* (London, 1769).

[31] T. Smollett, *Continuation of the Complete History of England* (London, 1762–5), vol. I, p. 148.

persuaded that all the girls will go off before next Lady Day.'[32] There was apparently a last rush to marry in the Fleet and at Keith's chapel: sixty-one marriages were celebrated at the latter on 24 March 1754.[33] Elsewhere, however, reactions were more muted. Across Northamptonshire, for example, the numbers marrying in the first three months of 1754 were higher than was usual for this time of year, but the forty-four couples married in March included six who married on the day that the Act actually came into force.[34]

'OPTING OUT'

As noted above, it has been argued that a substantial proportion of the population resorted to 'self-marriage' in the wake of the 1753 Act. The claim that informal unions continued after the 1753 Act is based on the assumption that they existed before – an assumption that Chapter 3 has already shown to be false. There have, however, been a number of specific claims about post-1754 practices; mostly, although not exclusively, from modern historians rather than contemporaries. This section considers three separate sets of arguments: first, the specific claim that around 20 per cent of couples cohabited outside marriage after the 1753 Act; secondly, the link that has been made between the 1753 Act and the rise of illegitimacy in the second part of the eighteenth century; and thirdly, the suggestion that cohabitation was common in certain geographical areas or among certain occupational groups.

The reputed popularity of 'self-marriage'

The main proponent of the claim that 'self-marriage' was popular in the second half of the eighteenth century is Gillis, who talks of 'massive non-compliance'[35] and suggests that:

> it would not be exaggeration to suggest that as much as a fifth of the population may, at one time or another in their lives, lived in an illicit

[32] W. Lewis (ed.), *Horace Walpole's Correspondence* (Oxford University Press, 1983), vol. IX, p. 154.

[33] G. J. Armytage, *The Register of Baptisms and Marriages at St George's Chapel, May Fair* (London: Harleian Society, 1889).

[34] Calculations based on A. Clarke and M. Ponting, *The Northamptonshire Marriage Index, 1700–1837* (2004).

[35] Gillis, 'Married but not Churched', p. 34.

relationship, most no doubt as a prelude to legal marriage, but some also as a substitute for it.[36]

The idea that a significant number of couples were cohabiting in the late eighteenth century has been widely accepted and repeated by historians,[37] sociologists,[38] demographers,[39] and lawyers,[40] usually without the significant qualifications with which Gillis surrounds his claim. There is a tendency for any statistic to take on a momentum of its own, especially when there are so few for the period. In addition, there is considerable sympathy for the idea that customary rituals survived in this sphere at a time when the common law was riding rough-shod over other long-established customs.[41] But even if one takes Gillis' claim at face value, it should be noted, before we go any further, that the suggested figure of one-fifth hardly suggests that such practices were the norm either before *or* after the 1753 Act.

More significantly, Gillis' own sources do not support this figure. His estimate of one-fifth is based on four statistics: in ascending order, they are Frith's statement that '10 per cent of marriages in Gloucestershire cannot be located in the official record';[42] Newman's suggestion that 15 per cent of unions in the Kentish parish of Ash-next-Sandwich might be attributable to non-marital

36 Gillis, *For Better, For Worse*, p. 219.

37 See e.g., Hay and Rogers, *Eighteenth-Century English Society*, p. 49. Leah Leneman argues that the Scottish experience was similar: *Alienated Affections: the Scottish Experience of Divorce and Separation, 1684–1830* (Edinburgh University Press, 1998), p. 330. Trumbach, by contrast, cites Gillis' argument with approval but notes that his own study of London produced rather different results: *Sex and the Gender Revolution*, p. 267.

38 S. McRae (ed.), *Changing Britain: Families and Households in the 1990s* (Oxford University Press, 1999), p. 3; Gibson, *Dissolving Wedlock*, p. 49.

39 See e.g., M. Murphy, 'The Evolution of Cohabitation in Britain, 1960–95' (2000) *Population Studies* 43; K. Kiernan, 'Unmarried Cohabitation and Parenthood in Britain and Europe' (2004) 26 *Law and Policy* 33.

40 K. O'Donovan, *Sexual Divisions in Law* (London: Weidenfeld & Nicholson, 1985), p. 49; Parker, *Informal Marriage*, p. 66; W. R. Cornish and G. N. de Clark, *Law and Society in England, 1750–1950* (London: Sweet & Maxwell, 1989), p. 362: 'up and down the country, and particularly in its less conspicuous corners, there were people who resorted to folk ceremonies – exchange of rings, broom-jumping and the like – to notarise their arrangements'.

41 Hay and Rogers, *Eighteenth-Century English Society*, p. 50, and see generally ch. 7; C. Hill, *Liberty Against the Law: Some Seventeenth Century Controversies* (London: Penguin, 1996), p. 205; Mansell *et al.*, *Critical Introduction*, p. 84.

42 See B. Frith (ed.), *Marriage Allegations in the Diocese of Gloucester, 1681–1700*, (Bristol and Gloucestershire Archaeological Society Records, 1954), vol. II.

unions;[43] Gandy's findings of an illegitimacy rate of 30 per cent in Culcheth, Lancashire;[44] and the suggestion of Gwenith Gwynn that in the late eighteenth century numerous couples in the parish of Llansantffraid Glyn Ceiriog married by jumping over a broomstick.[45] Together, these pieces of evidence might seem to build a compelling case for country-wide non-compliance. The last, however, has already been shown to be based on a complete misunderstanding,[46] and on further examination all of the other sources can also be shown to be irrelevant to his claim or of dubious authority.

Let us start with the data supplied by Frith and Newman. They are based on absences from the parish registers, but the fact that a marriage has not been traced in a given parish, or even a given county, does not mean that it did not take place elsewhere.[47] In any case, Frith's estimate relates to the late seventeenth century and cannot be taken as evidence for the prevalence of informal unions over half a century later, especially when we know that some parishes suffered from defective registration in the late seventeenth century but saw an increase in recorded marriages in the eighteenth.[48] Similarly, Newman's calculations relate to the early nineteenth century, a lifetime *after* the Act was passed, and are hardly conclusive proof of popular reactions to it. More fundamentally, the reasoning underpinning her speculation that 'a proportion of up to 15 per cent for non-church unions might be reasonable at this time'[49] is flawed. It is based solely on the fact that, of those bringing their children to be baptised in the parish of Ash-next-Sandwich between 1814 and 1837, no marriage has been traced for 20 per cent.

43 A. Newman, 'An Evaluation of Bastardy Recordings in an East Kent Parish' in P. Laslett, K. Oosterveen, and R. M. Smith (eds.), *Bastardy and its Comparative History* (Cambridge, 1980).

44 G. N. Gandy, 'Illegitimacy in a Handloom Weaving Community: Fertility Patterns in Culcheth, Lancashire, 1781–1860' (unpublished DPhil. dissertation, University of Oxford, 1978).

45 G. Gwynn (W. Rhys Jones), 'Besom Wedding in the Ceiriog Valley' (1928) 39 *Folk-lore* 149.

46 See Chapter 3.

47 See further Chapters 1 and 3 on the multifarious reasons why a marriage might not be traced.

48 See Chapter 4. E. A. Wrigley, 'Clandestine Marriage in Tetbury in the Late Seventeenth Century' (1973) 10 *Local Population Studies* 15, 20; P. Sharpe, 'Locating the "Missing Marryers" in Colyton, 1660–1750' (1992) 48 *Local Population Studies* 49.

49 Newman, 'An Evaluation of Bastardy Recordings', p. 151.

The reduction to 15 per cent is intended to take account of marriages that took place further away and have not been traced, but this does not seem to make sufficient allowance for the fact that information about marriages outside the parish was only available for the years after 1813, and then only for marriages taking place within the county. A comparison with the Northamptonshire parish of Kilsby in the same period found that 8 per cent of parents baptising children there had married in another parish before 1813, and a further 12 per cent had married outside the county: these two obvious factors alone would exactly account for the 20 per cent of marriages not traced by Newman. While this is a very rough-and-ready comparison, which might not reflect differences between parishes situated in different parts of the country[50] and with very different social experiences, it is at least preferable to plucking a figure out of thin air.

Next, the link made by Gillis between supposed 'common-law unions' and Gandy's finding of a high illegitimacy rate in Culcheth is in fact directly contradicted by Gandy's own research. Two quotations will suffice to make the point:

> in Culcheth ... their mothers, even if they had more than one child, appear not to have been cohabiting with a man.[51]

> The existence of consensual unions does not, to my knowledge, contribute directly to the illegitimate births with which the parish registers are studded.[52]

In fact, Gandy attributes a mere 4 per cent of births to 'consensual unions' for the period 1801–50, and less than 1 per cent for the years between 1781 and 1800.[53] Moreover, the true levels of cohabiting unions may be still lower, since the children of these unions were not baptised as illegitimate.[54] This could indicate that the incumbent was willing to baptise children of consensual unions as

[50] It should be noted that Ash is to be found just a short distance inland from several of Kent's busy coastal towns, thus enabling relatively easy access by water to more distant parishes.

[51] Gandy, 'Illegitimacy in a Handloom Weaving Community', p. 21.

[52] *Ibid.* p. 170.

[53] *Ibid.* Table 14. Cf. the version in Hay and Rogers, *Eighteenth-Century English Society*, p. 49, who state that '[a]mong the handloom weavers of Culcheth ... women entered into common-law unions as often as they were married in church'.

[54] Gandy, 'Illegitimacy in a Handloom Weaving Community', p. 170.

legitimate,[55] but a more likely explanation is that the couples in question had in fact married elsewhere – as Gandy notes, there is no evidence that this was not the case,[56] and we have seen from other studies how couples do not always marry in the most obvious parish. The fact that there was very little to distinguish the behaviour of such couples from those known to have married in church, and no evidence that they had to have been living together for a significant period of time before their children were baptised as legitimate,[57] is also more consistent with the latter explanation. Another genuine possibility is that some of the missing couples actually went through a civil ceremony after this became a possibility in 1837, since Gandy's study is based only on the church records. This alone would explain the higher percentage attributed to consensual unions in the later period.

It is clear, therefore, that the idea that one-fifth of the population cohabited outside marriage has no evidential foundation whatsoever.

The claimed link with the rise in illegitimacy

A second argument that needs to be explored is that the rise in illegitimacy in the second half of the eighteenth century was linked to the passage of the 1753 Act. This time the demographic evidence is clear: there was a sustained rise in the number of children born outside marriage in the second half of the eighteenth century.[58] A number of commentators have attributed this rise at least in part to the 1753 Act, the suggestion being that relationships that would previously have been considered to be marriages had to be classified as concubinage in the wake of the 1753 Act.[59] This, of course, assumes that the children of informal unions (i.e., ones in which the parties had exchanged consent or simply lived together) would have been

[55] As Gandy hypothesises: *ibid.* p. 392.

[56] *Ibid.* p. 380, acknowledging that only 'some' registers for surrounding parishes were checked.

[57] *Ibid.* ch. 5.

[58] P. Laslett, *Family Life and Illicit Love in Earlier Generations* (Cambridge University Press, 1977), Table 3.1.

[59] See in particular B. Meteyard, 'Illegitimacy and Marriage in Eighteenth-Century England' (1980) 10 *Journal of Interdisciplinary History* 479; J. Schellekens, 'Courtship, the Clandestine Marriage Act, and Illegitimate Fertility in England' (1995) 25 *Journal of Interdisciplinary History* 433.

regarded as legitimate *prior* to the 1753 Act. But it has already been shown that such children would not have been regarded as legitimate,[60] and that there is little evidence that such unions occurred.[61]

A further problem is that the pattern of illegitimate births does not suggest that the parents were living in a stable non-marital relationship. Studies of illegitimate children have shown that the parents of such children were rarely cohabiting. Gandy's research, discussed above, repudiated the idea that mothers of illegitimate children were cohabiting with the fathers. An examination of the baptism register of Llansantffraid Glyn Ceiriog reinforces this impression. Of the thirty-four entries in which the child was described as illegitimate, seven gave the father's name only, eleven the mother's, and three neither. In only fourteen cases were both parents recorded. No subsequent marriages have been traced for any of the couples who produced illegitimate children. Nor were they necessarily cohabiting: in nine cases the register states that they were from different parishes. There are few repeaters: parents of base children tended to appear only once in the baptism register, suggesting that bearing an illegitimate child was a one-off event rather than an element of a stable union. A rare exception is Mary Roberts: when recording the birth of Sarah Roberts (Parry) in 1799, David Jones wrote indignantly that 'the said Sarah is ye fifth base child to ye said wicked debauched animal Mary Roberts'.[62] But Mary was certainly not living in a stable non-marital union: the five children all had different fathers, including one John Williams from Elsmere, who was presumably just passing through the parish.

The same is true of the Kilsby records. Ten children were designated as 'base' during the twenty years after the 1753 Act came into force, born to nine combinations of parents.[63] Ann French was

[60] See Chapter 2. Moreover, if contracts *per verba de praesenti* had constituted valid marriages, then any children born to the parents after the 1753 Act would equally have been regarded as legitimate: the law tests the validity of a marriage according to the law in force at the time it was celebrated.

[61] See Chapter 3.

[62] Denbighshire Record Office, PD75/1/1, 18 January 1799; Clywd Family History Society, *Llansantffraid Glyn Ceiriog Parish Registers 1754–1814* (CFHS, 1992), p. 14.

[63] It should be noted that calculating illegitimacy according to the number of *parents* involved gives a rather different picture from simply calculating the proportion of baptised infants designated as base. If the latter calculation is made, Kilsby had in this period an illegitimacy rate of 4 per cent. But just under 10 per cent of the couples in the study brought an illegitimate child to be baptised.

the only 'repeater' in this sample, with two base children by two different men (which is hardly suggestive of a stable relationship with either); another couple, John Hollis and Mary Hirons, had two children baptised at the same time. By contrast, the other ninety-one sets of parents baptising children in this period produced an average of 4.3 children each.[64] Nor were these illegitimate births necessarily a prelude to marriage: at least two of the fathers and one of the mothers went on to marry a different partner (evidence that the first relationship had not been considered a 'marriage' in any meaningful sense) and no subsequent marriage has been traced for any of the others.

The mothers of illegitimate children were far more likely to be dependent on the parish, or living with their own parents, than to be cohabiting with the father of their child. The presence of a workhouse in the parish of St Olave in York accounts for the remarkably high number of illegitimate births recorded in its baptism register. Between 1770 and 1785 seventy-two mothers (accounting for 26 per cent of the total cohort) had an illegitimate child baptised there. One was recorded as being at her mother's house at the time of the baptism; most of the others, however, were resident in the workhouse.[65] The evidence does not suggest that illegitimate children were the product of stable relationships.

Of course, the 1753 Act may have had an effect on the illegitimacy rates by reducing the protection available to women who trusted men to make good on their promises of marriage. If the Act was responsible for the rise in illegitimacy in this sense, one would expect there to be a sharp increase in the immediate aftermath of the Act,[66] probably followed by a slow decline as a new generation grew up accustomed to its requirements. In fact, the increase in births outside marriage had begun before 1754,[67] and

64 In addition to the 255 children born to these parents during the period under review, the couples in question had a further 136 children born outside this period.

65 This was the case for forty-nine of the mothers, or 67 per cent of this group. In the remaining cases the mother's residence was unstated.

66 Although the Act was unlikely to catch anyone out, since it only prohibited the bringing of an action to compel solemnisation of a contract entered into after 25 March 1754. Those who could establish that such a contract had been made prior to 1754 could still bring an action to enforce it; those who could not were in no worse position than they would have been had the Act not been passed.

67 See e.g., R. K. McClure, *Coram's Children: the London Foundling Hospital in the Eighteenth Century* (Yale University Press, 1981).

grew steadily over the course of the century.[68] As Laslett has noted, the 1753 Act had 'no sudden effect on the number of illegitimates'.[69] Of course, some of the women who gave birth outside marriage in the later part of the eighteenth century may have been seduced upon a promise of marriage and then abandoned – as many had been before the Act. But this was certainly not the case for all.[70] Besides, the number of legitimate births (and proportion of prenuptial pregnancies)[71] also increased, suggesting that the causes of the rise in illegitimacy were more complex than a simple shifting of categories.[72] Other countries that witnessed a similar increase had not made changes to their marriage laws.[73] Thus, the only possible conclusion is that the 1753 Act had little impact on the increase in illegitimacy in the later part of the eighteenth century.

The suspected irregularity of certain groups

The third set of claims regarding the popularity of 'self-marriage' in the wake of the 1753 Act relates to practices in specific locations or among particular occupational groups. These are based largely on complaints by contemporaries about the irregular lifestyles of

68 See e.g., A. Levene, T. Nutt, and S. Williams (eds.), *Illegitimacy in Britain, 1700–1920* (Basingstoke: Palgrave Macmillan, 2005), ch. 1. A. Newman, 'An Evaluation of Bastardy Recordings in an East Kent Parish', ch. 1 in P. Laslett, K. Oosterveen, and R. Smith (eds.), *Bastardy and its Comparative History* (London: Edward Arnold, 1980), p. 148, does suggest that the numbers 'jump' after 1754, but a total of six bastards in the period 1751–60 is not out of line with previous decades. The rise over the subsequent decades is clear – twenty illegitimacies in the 1760s and fifty-six in the period 1811–20 – but the link to the 1753 Act is not.

69 Laslett, *Family Life and Illicit Love*, p. 132. See also L. Stone, 'Illegitimacy in Eighteenth-Century England – Again' (1981) 11 *Journal of Interdisciplinary History* 507; R. Adair, *Courtship, Illegitimacy and Marriage in Early Modern England* (Manchester University Press, 1996), p. 9.

70 Evans, *'Unfortunate Objects'*, p. 116, examined petitions to the Foundling Hospital and found that only 18 per cent of mothers mentioned that a promise of marriage had preceded the sexual relationship that resulted in her pregnancy.

71 Levene *et al.*, *Illegitimacy in Britain*, p. 6.

72 J. Black, *Eighteenth-Century Britain, 1688–1783* (Basingstoke: Palgrave 2001), p. 16, argues that the rise reflected 'increased freedom of labour and living arrangements'.

73 The Europe-wide increase in illegitimacy in the late eighteenth century was noted by P. Laslett, 'Introduction: Comparing Illegitimacy over Time and between Cultures' in P. Laslett, K. Oosterveen, and R. Smith (eds.), *Bastardy and its Comparative History* (London: Edward Arnold, 1980).

certain sections of the community.[74] As with any historical source, it is important to consider both the knowledge and motivation of those responsible for these claims. It would be rather ironic if fulminations intended to discredit a particular section of the community were taken as literally true by a later generation and used to celebrate that group as ahead of their time.

The danger of an over-literal reliance on contemporary complaints is illustrated by the deficiencies of one early estimate of the extent of cohabitation provided by Patrick Colquhoun, a stipendiary magistrate based in London at the end of the eighteenth century. He suggested that there were 50,000 prostitutes in London alone, 25,000 of whom 'live partly by Prostitution, *including the multitudes of low females, who cohabit with labourers and others without matrimony*' (my emphasis).[75] A number of points need to be made about this source, and the reliance that has been placed on it. First, Colquhoun was not claiming, as one commentator has suggested, that there were '25,000 common-law wives'[76] in London at this time: the unspecified 'multitudes' of cohabiting women are a sub-set of the 25,000 said to be living partly by prostitution. Secondly, it should be obvious that these figures are suspiciously round and very large. The population of London was under one million at the time, which would mean that one in every ten females, whether adults or children, was living partly or wholly by prostitution. Thirdly, Colquhoun's methods have not gone uncriticised. As Schwarz has noted:

> Colquhoun's attitude to the statistics of London's population combined an occasional scrupulous count ... with another set of figures that were almost biblical in the sweep of their range ... [H]is renown in the field of social statistics when his work was first published might be thought to have come from the willingness of his alarmed readers to believe any figure he gave them, provided it was large.[77]

[74] Such complaints were a standard feature of the debate as to the effect of industrialisation: see e.g., H. Perkin, *Origins of Modern English Society 1780–1880* (London: Routledge & Kegan Paul, 1969), pp. 149–60.

[75] P. Colquhoun, *A Treatise on the Police of the Metropolis: containing a detail of the various crimes and misdemeanors by which public and private property and security are, at present, injured and endangered and suggesting remedies for their prevention*, 6th edn (London: J. Mawman, 1800), p. 340.

[76] A. Clark, 'Whores and Gossips: Sexual Reputation in London 1779–1825' in A. Angerman *et al.* (eds.), *Current Issues in Women's History* (London: Routledge, 1989), p. 232.

[77] L. Schwarz, 'English Servants and their Employers during the Eighteenth and Nineteenth Centuries' (1999) 52 *Economic History Review* 236, 238. See also

In this particular case there was no such scrupulous count: Colquhoun merely asked the reader to consider the numbers that might resort to prostitutes, and infer the potential number of prostitutes from this. He acknowledged that his claims would 'at first view ... seem to excite doubts, and require investigation' but claimed that in view of 'the profligate state of Society in vulgar life, the intelligent mind will soon be reconciled to the statement'.[78] So Colquhoun's figures were, by his own admission, only a guess, to be taken on outraged trust rather than supported by evidence. And he was not even attempting to produce a census of cohabitants but to convince readers that prostitution was a growing evil – and for this purpose, as he himself remarked airily, a few thousand either way was hardly relevant.[79] For the purposes of gauging responses to the 1753 Act, Colquhoun's alarmist[80] guess is equally irrelevant.

The importance of taking account of the purpose for which a particular source was produced is also apparent when considering claims that specific groups were particularly prone to cohabitation. Miners crop up frequently in accounts of alternative marriage practices: in Wales, Wednesbury, and Kingswood.[81] There are two possible responses to such claims. The first is to emphasise the distinct nature of mining communities and to argue that miners were untypical in their moral and marital behaviour. Malcolmson, for example, has argued that colliery villages tended to be inward-looking, with their own distinctive culture, 'commonly regarded by genteel observers as a strange, uncouth and rather frightening breed of men'.[82] This leads onto the second response, which is to ask who was reporting the practices of the miners. Were they

B. Wilson, *Decency and Disorder: the Age of Cant, 1789–1837* (London: Faber & Faber Ltd, 2007), p. 103. And 'even Colquhoun's admirers admitted that he was pompous and prone to "hyperbolic notions"': R. Paley, 'Colquhoun, Patrick (1745–1820)' in *Oxford Dictionary of National Biography* (Oxford University Press, 2004).

78 Colquhoun, *A Treatise on the Police of the Metropolis*, p. 340.

79 *Ibid.* p. 341.

80 E. P. Thompson, *The Making of the English Working Class* (Harmondsworth: Penguin, 1968), pp. 61–2, notes that these 'impressionistic estimates' were produced 'in the atmosphere of panic in the aftermath of the French Revolution', a context which was 'not ... conducive to accurate social observation'.

81 Gillis, *For Better, For Worse*, pp. 190–2.

82 Robert W. Malcolmson, *Life and Labour in England, 1700–1780* (London: Hutchinson, 1981), p. 54.

merely perceived to be different? Wood has commented on the way in which miners 'were presented in elite descriptions as a culturally degenerate and socially subversive isolated mass, cut off from normal society'.[83] But he points out that those describing them had had little contact with them and attributes such views to class hostility towards a group who were perceived to be unruly industrial workers. Similarly, Levine and Wrightson noted a pervasive stereotype depicting denizens of the colliery districts as 'a race apart' that by the mid-nineteenth century 'had achieved the status of unquestioned historical fact'.[84] The fact that claims about sexual non-conformity were regularly used to discredit certain groups should make us cautious about the truth of such assertions, and indeed about the social acceptability of cohabitation.[85]

An examination of one small cohort of colliery workers suggests that their marriage practices were no different from those of the general population. The cohort consists of the ninety-two men who died in an accident at the Felling Colliery near Newcastle in the early nineteenth century, whose names were listed in a pamphlet published by the local vicar.[86] Only thirty-one of them were married, but this low figure is explicable by the young age of those who died: fifty-eight of them were under the age of twenty-five, the youngest being only eight years old. Only two of those under the age of twenty-five were married, which means that twenty-nine of the thirty-three over that age (or 88 per cent) *were* married. Nor was the writer of the pamphlet simply sparing the feelings of the survivors by glossing over the marital status of the deceased men: marriages in church have been traced for all of those in the cohort where this was a realistic exercise.[87]

The stereotyping of certain groups as a 'race apart' should also warn us to exercise caution in relying on the accounts of local

[83] A. Wood, 'Custom, Identity and Resistance: English Free Miners and their Law, c. 1500–1800', ch. 8 in P. Griffiths, A. Fox, and S. Hindle (eds.), *The Experience of Authority in Early Modern England* (Basingstoke: Macmillan Press, 1996), p. 254.

[84] D. Levine and K. Wrightson, *The Making of an Industrial Society: Whickham 1560–1765* (Oxford: Clarendon Press, 1991), p. 276.

[85] See further Chapter 9 on religious sects accused of sexual non-conformity.

[86] Rev. J. Hodgson, *The Funeral Sermon of the Felling Colliery Sufferers* (Newcastle, 1813).

[87] Given the absence of information about the wives (save in one case) one can only be certain of a match where the man's name is relatively unusual.

customs penned by travellers. Again, we should ask: what was their source of information and who was the intended audience? The account of 'little weddings' in Wales provided by the Rev. Evans may appear at first sight to provide evidence of alternative marriage practices,[88] but one might wonder just how much a clergyman intent on carrying out botanical researches actually knew about the marital practices of the inhabitants of the districts through which he was travelling. It is almost certain that Evans drew his account from the writings of Lewis Morris published in the *Gentleman's Magazine* a few years earlier. His version of the 'little wedding' is certainly similar to that given by Morris: both refer to it as a trial,[89] with the possibility of the women being dismissed or left;[90] both note that the practice did not affect the woman's reputation;[91] and both identify Cardiganshire and its borders as having distinct marriage practices.[92] In addition, Evans' version of the 'great' wedding is practically identical to that of Morris, even down to the cheese.[93]

The difficulties in interpreting Morris' account have already been discussed in Chapter 3; for present purposes the issue is whether he is suggesting that these were practices that had survived the Act or not. Given that he seems to have been writing at the time when the 1753 Act had only just been passed, this is difficult to ascertain: at one point he predicted that 'the marriage-act will have no effect upon it';[94] but at another he suggested that 'the late act of parliament is looked upon only as a cruel and wicked restraint upon the liberties of the mine country',[95] which might suggest that it was resented and flouted but might equally indicate that it was resented precisely because it had to be observed. Certainly it provides no evidence that any dubious practices continued. If, as seems likely,

88 Rev. J. Evans, *A Tour through Parts of North Wales in the Year 1798, and at other times, Principally undertaken with a view to Botanical Researches in that Alpine Country* (London: J. White, 1800), pp. 359–60.

89 *Ibid.* p. 359; 'Morrisian Miscellany' (1791) 61 *Gentleman's Magazine* 13.

90 Evans, *A Tour*, p. 359; L. Morris, 'Cardigan Weddings' (1792) 62 *Gentleman's Magazine* 325.

91 *Ibid.*

92 Evans, *A Tour*, p. 359; 'Cardigan Weddings' (1791) 61 *Gentleman's Magazine* 1103. In this context, however, Morris appears to be referring to the bidding wedding described in Chapter 3.

93 See Chapter 3.

94 'Morrisian Miscellany' (1791) 61 *Gentleman's Magazine* 13.

95 'Cardigan Weddings' (1792) 62 *Gentleman's Magazine* 325.

Morris' writings were the sources for the Rev. Evans' claims, then the latter's statement that, at the time he was writing, such practices were 'chiefly now confined to the borders of Cardiganshire' can be attributed to his belief that Morris' account was a contemporary one, there being nothing in the *Gentleman's Magazine* to indicate that Morris had in fact died in 1765.

In short, accounts based on hearsay rather than actual observation should not be relied upon without independent verification. While there may be a kernel of truth, as with many myths of people living in remote places, one cannot rule out the possibility that accounts were exaggerated or even invented to make a better story and pander to the new taste for folklore.[96]

AVOIDANCE

The focus now switches to those who avoided the Act or its effects by marrying in a jurisdiction to which it did not extend. There were some early attempts to find loopholes within the Act that would allow ministers to celebrate marriages within England and Wales in locations to which the legislation did not apply. The Rev. Wilkinson, minister of the Savoy, clearly thought that he had discovered one, as his son explained:

> [M]y father began the dreadful experiment of exerting his supposed rights as minister of the Savoy ... [H]e judged he had a right to grant licences as usual; and that it was a privilege annexed to the Savoy, as being extra-parochial.[97]

In 1754 and 1755 numerous marriages were celebrated at the Savoy chapel, located between the Strand and the Thames. Some of these marriages were preceded by banns, and some by licences granted by the Bishop of London or Archbishop of Canterbury, but most depended on a licence granted by Wilkinson himself. Wilkinson was confident enough to advertise the attractions of the chapel, although after an attempt was made to arrest him another clergyman, the Rev. John Grierson, conducted the actual ceremonies.[98] But the authorities were swift to clamp down on this practice. Grierson only solemnised marriages between 20 May and 4 July 1755; and in December 1755 he

[96] See e.g., E. Mavor, *The Ladies of Llangollen* (London: Penguin, 1973), p. 40 on the newly-fashionable Welsh tour.

[97] T. Wilkinson, *Memoirs of his own Life* (York, 1790), vol. I, p. 74.

[98] *Ibid.* p. 77.

stood trial at the Old Bailey on the basis that he 'did unlawfully, knowingly, wilfully and feloniously solemnize marriage' without banns or licence at the Savoy chapel;[99] was found guilty, and was sentenced to transportation for fourteen years. The same sentence was subsequently meted out to Wilkinson.[100] Such examples of the rigour of the law (rendered all the more dreadful by Wilkinson's death on board ship)[101] are likely to have been influential in deterring other ministers from following suit.[102]

Of course, Wilkinson's initiative also reveals the extent of the public demand for such a loophole. At Grierson's trial the clerk of the chapel, one Philips, estimated that 1,400 couples had been married there since the Act came into force.[103] While this is clearly a substantial number, it still suggests that fewer couples were taking advantage of this apparent loophole than had married in the Fleet at its height. Philips also suggested that many – perhaps as many as 900 – 'came distress'd from out of the country, big with child'.[104] For obvious reasons this is less easy to verify, but any image of desperate, heavily pregnant women toiling long miles to be married at the Savoy is dispelled by the evidence from the register of the parties' parishes of residence, which (when available) indicates that most had travelled relatively short distances: in mid-eighteenth-century London, 'the country' was far closer than it is today.[105]

99 *The Proceedings of the Old Bailey*, 4 December 1755, p. 47.

100 *The Proceedings of the Old Bailey*, 14 July 1756.

101 Admittedly this was due to the gout, rather than the conditions on board ship: Wilkinson, *Memoirs*, p. 91.

102 They certainly influenced Richard Mason, who had himself been employed to celebrate marriages at the Savoy but who ceased to do so as soon as Grierson had been found guilty. This was a factor relied upon at his trial as evidence that he had not 'knowingly and wilfully' flouted the Act, and he was acquitted: *The Proceedings of the Old Bailey*, 26 October 1757. His was the last such case to be heard at the Old Bailey. The diarist Thomas Turner did note the presence of two clergymen in Horsham gaol 'for marrying contrary to the Marriage Act', but not the outcome of their cases: D. Vaisey (ed.), *The Diary of Thomas Turner, 1754–1765* (Oxford University Press, 1984), p. 130.

103 This was denied by Wilkinson but has been verified by checking the original registers of the Savoy: 1,406 marriages were solemnised there between the coming into force of the Act and Grierson's trial.

104 *The Proceedings of the Old Bailey*, 4 December 1755, p. 52.

105 Care should, however, be taken in interpreting the evidence as to residence: Philips claimed that one couple had come from Dunbar in Scotland, but it is obvious that they had not made the journey to the Savoy solely for the purpose of marriage. Quite apart from the distance involved, Scotland allowed couples to marry with far less formality.

Those who had the inclination and the resources could avoid the requirements of the Act by marrying outside the jurisdiction. In one of the earliest cases to be heard after the 1753 Act, *Butler* v. *Freeman*,[106] the parties had run away together to marry in Antwerp. Lord Hardwicke, presiding over the Court of Chancery, was clearly furious that the Act he had long fought for had not had the effect of preventing all clandestine marriages.[107] Others eloped to the Channel Islands.[108] In 1760, the *Gentleman's Magazine* noted the elopement of an heiress to Guernsey and commented that 'there are always vessels at Southampton to smuggle contraband goods into the land of matrimony'.[109] Such elopements did have certain disadvantages. In addition to the cost, as Jeaffreson has noted, no bride 'was ever known to reflect with satisfaction on her experiences in a slow sailing boat on the rough waters off Alderney and the Casketts'.[110]

Scotland offered an easier alternative, particularly for those living close to the border. Yet there are no signs of a mass exodus from English parishes close to the Scottish border.[111] Couples in Northumberland and Cumberland continued to marry in their own parish churches,[112] and one even finds some Scottish brides and grooms marrying on the English side of the Border.[113] Moreover, for those living further south money was generally necessary for such an elopement, although in 1816 Edward Gibbon Wakefield spent three

[106] (1756) Amb. 301; 27 ER 204.

[107] This was reflected in his willingness to hold that the Court of Chancery had jurisdiction to punish the bride and those who had brought about the marriage on the basis that the husband was a ward of court. Perhaps fittingly, it was to the Fleet prison that they were committed.

[108] See e.g., C. Smith, *The Old Manor House* (Broadview Press Ltd, Ontario 2002; original edn 1794), pp. 339, 428, 484.

[109] (1760) 30 *Gentleman's Magazine* 30–1.

[110] J. Jeaffreson, *Brides and Bridals* (London: Hurst and Blackett, 1872), vol. II, p. 204.

[111] Cf. Parker, *Informal Marriage*, p. 63.

[112] Examining the parochial registers for the period 1734–73 established that there was a steady rise in marriages at Lanercost (T. W. Willis (ed.), *The Register of the Parish of Lanercost, Cumberland* (Beverley, 1912)), and no obvious effect at Alnham (Rev. W. Nall, *The Registers of Alnham in the County of Northumberland* (Sunderland: Durham and Northumberland Parish Register Society, 1907)). The numbers marrying at Norham in the second half of the period did appear to fall (*Northumberland Registers*, vol. 11, SOG NU/REG/123980), but since a number of the marriages that did take place there involved a bride or groom from Scotland, it seems unlikely that Scottish elopements were the primary cause for the decline.

[113] See e.g., Norham, *Northumberland Registers*, vol. 11, SOG NU/REG/123980.

weeks trudging from Tunbridge Wells to Scotland with the seventeen-year-old heiress who became his first wife.[114] But those with more money could travel by horse or even carriage, and improvements to the road network in the 1750s and 1760s meant that they could do so with increasing speed.[115] Smollett's last novel, *The Expedition of Humphry Clinker*, published in 1771, depicted an elopement to Edinburgh (diverted en route, with a different groom, to Coldstream, 'where there was a parson who dealt in this branch of commerce').[116] And the hitherto obscure village of Graitney, just over the Scottish border, began to prove a popular destination for eloping couples,[117] to such an extent that 'Gretna Green' is today known for little else.[118]

Such elopements posed new issues for the courts. What, for example, was the legal status of the resulting marriages? The courts had begun to develop the principle that the formal validity of a marriage should be tested according to the place where it had been celebrated, the *lex loci*.[119] But should the same rule apply if the parties had intended to evade English law?[120] Some thought not,

114 A. Ashby and A. Jones, *The Shrigley Abduction: a Tale of Anguish, Deceit and Violation of the Domestic Hearth* (Stroud: Sutton Publishing, 2005), pp. 41–2.

115 Langford, *A Polite and Commercial People*, p. 397, notes that 'journey times between major centres were slashed more dramatically during this period than at any time before the railway age'.

116 T. Smollett, *The Expedition of Humphry Clinker* (Ware: Wordsworth Classics, 1995; original edn 1771), p. 199. See also M. Dresser (ed.), *The Diary of Sarah Fox née Champion, Bristol 1745–1802* (Bristol Record Society, 2003), p. 14, noting the elopement of her brother from Bristol to Edinburgh in 1764.

117 There appear to have been few references to Gretna as a place of clandestine marriage prior to the 1770s, but by 1776 it was assumed that people knew what 'Gretna' signified (see e.g., C. Melmoth, *The Pupil of Pleasure* (London, 1776), p. 28). This is also the first year in which Gretna appears in D. Paterson's *A New & Accurate Description of all the Direct and the Principal Cross Roads in Great Britain* (London, 1776), first published in 1771 and again in 1774. It is likely that Gretna did not become a popular place to marry until improvements to the local toll-roads made it easier to reach.

118 Elopements to Gretna featured in a number of novels of the period: see e.g., F. Burney, *Camilla, a Picture of Youth* (Oxford University Press, 1972; original edn 1792), p. 806; S. Ferrier, *Marriage* (Oxford University Press, 2001; original edn 1818), p. 5.

119 See e.g., *Scrimshire* v. *Scrimshire* (1752) 2 Hag. Con. 395; 161 ER 782. For a contemporary discussion of the requirements of Scottish law, see R. Burn, *The Justice of the Peace, and Parish Officer* (London, 1766), pp. 330–2.

120 This question was raised but not tested in the first case to come before the courts: the husband's father did initiate a suit (*Butler* v. *Dolben* (1756) 2 Lee 312; 161 ER 352), but as the couple went through a further, valid ceremony of marriage after the husband came of age the case never came to trial.

others thought that it did.[121] Bills introduced in 1764, 1765, and 1772 sought to remove doubts regarding the validity of Scottish marriages, but, being incorporated with proposals for wholesale reform, all failed to become law.[122] The 1769 decision of the High Court of Delegates in *Compton* v. *Bearcroft* – refusing to annul a runaway marriage celebrated in Scotland – was thought to have settled the matter, but there were still potential challenges and questions.[123]

Moreover, clandestine marriages in Scotland, and indeed elsewhere, were not necessarily any easier to prove than Fleet marriages had been. 'Indeed, a plaintiff would have the greatest difficulty in proving a marriage of that sort' commented one judge.[124] Although it was the practice to give a certificate to the newly-weds, such certificates were not always admitted as evidence of the marriage.[125] And, just as modern couples (most famously Mick Jagger and Jerry Hall) jetting off to exotic locations to marry may fail to observe the local formalities, so, on occasion, did their eighteenth-century counterparts. The Guernsey marriage of an heiress and an apprentice in *Bathurst* v. *Murray* was accordingly held to be void, although the Court of Chancery accepted the match and ordered them to go through a valid ceremony.[126] Other couples chose to go through

[121] The objections to the validity of such a marriage were overruled by Sir Thomas Clarke in *Brook* v. *Oliver* in 1759, and by Lord Northington in *Bedford* v. *Varney* in 1762: see L. Shelford, *A Practical Treatise of the Law of Marriage and Divorce and Registration* (London: S. Sweet, 1841), ch. 2. See also *Phillips* v. *Hunter* (1795) 2 H. Bl. 403; 126 ER 618, at 412.

[122] See Outhwaite, *Clandestine Marriage*, pp. 112–16.

[123] In *Harford* v. *Morris* (1776) 2 Hag. Con. 423; 161 ER 792, for example, it was questioned whether the *lex loci* would be applicable if the parties were not actually resident in the country where they had married: 'I conceive the law to be clear that it is not the transient residence, by coming one morning and going away the next day, which constitutes a residence to which the *lex loci* can be applied; so as to give a jurisdiction to the law' (p. 431). See also *Ilderton* v. *Ilderton* (1793) 2 H. Bl. 145; 126 ER 476, in which the process to be followed when determining a wife's entitlement to dower was discussed.

[124] *Bain* v. *Mason* (1824) 1 Car. & P 202; 171 ER 1162.

[125] *Bain* v. *Mason* (action for criminal conversation); *Nokes* v. *Millward* (1824) 2 Add. 386; 162 ER 336 (nullity on basis of prior marriage); *Graham's Case* (1837) 2 Lewin 96; 168 ER 1091 (bigamy). In *Montague* v. *Montague* (1824) 2 Add. 373; 161 ER 331 it was held that the certificate was inadmissible qua certificate, but could be allowed as a declaration by the parties under their own hands that they were husband and wife.

[126] (1802) 8 Ves. Jun. 74; 32 ER 279.

a second ceremony in England to ensure the validity of their marriage.[127]

Yet the popularity of elopements overseas and north of the border should be kept in perspective. While such adventures formed a staple plot device in the fiction of the time, in reality it was a very small proportion of the population who resorted to such means. As the next section will show, the reaction of the overwhelming majority of the population to the 1753 Act was not evasion or avoidance but simply obedience.

OBEDIENCE

> [T]o have such dictates of reason and scripture established by the authority of parliament, must certainly increase our obligation to a conscientious compliance.[128]

One could infer compliance with the Act from the fact that evidence of non-compliance is lacking, but, of course, absence of evidence is not evidence of absence. Fortunately, my thesis that the vast majority of the population complied with the requirements of the 1753 Act does not rest on individual and equivocal sources, but is based on the black-and-white evidence of the parish registers.

The first immediate sign of compliance is the difference between the old records of marriage – interspersed with baptisms and burials in no particular order – and the new, neatly kept registers that were acquired as required by the legislation and which recorded information in a standard form.[129] Compliance with this aspect of the 1753 Act was almost universal:[130] as one contemporary noted,

127 See e.g., *Ex parte Hall* (1812) 1 V & B 112; 35 ER 44; *Population according to the Census of 1821* (1822), vol. 15, p. xxiv.

128 *Antenuptial Fornication Considered, in a letter to a young gentleman* (London, 1766), p. 55.

129 Printers, spotting a new market, supplied special books that satisfied the new legislation's exacting specifications: e.g., *A Register Book for the Registering of all Banns and Marriages Published or Solemnized in the Parish Church of the Parish of [name] Provided by the Churchwardens of the Said Parish, in pursuance of the Statute of the Twenty-Seventh Year of his present Majesty King George the Second, Intituled, An Act for the Better Preventing of Clandestine Marriages, which Act commenced from the Twenty-Fifth Day of March in the Year of Our Lord Seventeen Hundred and Fifty-Four.*

130 In Hampshire, for example, the bishop's visitations of 1765 asked the incumbents whether they had separate register books for marriages, as required by the 1753 Act. Of the 183 parishes visited, only four replied in the negative, of which only one had actually celebrated marriages. Others anxiously boasted that their

'a regular form for the enrolment of marriage has been universally adopted and approved'.[131] Record-keeping improved considerably:[132] it has been noted that the 1753 Act 'had an immediate impact in reducing the proportion of months with defective marriage registration',[133] down to 0.6 per cent between 1754 and 1812. Incumbents were clearly keen to comply with the Act.

But was this true of their parishioners? Contemporary returns for a number of parishes in London found a significant recovery in the number of marriages recorded.[134] As the Rector of St Andrew Holborn noted in his letter to the Archbishop of Canterbury, '[t]his is not owing to the increase of buildings in this Parish, as that has bin Inconsiderable, but most probably due to the opperations of the Marriage Act'.[135] Such parishes had, of course, previously lost marriages to the Fleet.[136] The returns from Colchester and St Albans were rather more equivocal, with some parishes seeing an increase and some a fall.[137] But this simply reflected the inevitable consequence that any parish which had been a 'net importer' of couples for the purpose of clandestine marriages experienced a fall in the number of marriages,[138] while any parish that had been a 'net

register books were 'provided and duly kept', while the parish of Farlington specified that its register was 'printed and ruled ... pursuant to the said Act of Parliament': W.R. Ward (ed.), *Parson and Parish in Eighteenth-Century Hampshire: Replies to Bishops' Visitations* (Winchester: Hampshire County Council, 1995), pp. 175, 185.

131 J. Lucas, *An Impartial Inquiry into the Present State of Parochial Registers; Charitable Funds; Taxation and Parish Rates* (Leeds, 1791), p. 14.

132 D. J. Steel, *National Index of Parish Registers*, vol. I, *Sources of Births, Marriages and Deaths before 1837* (London: Society of Genealogists, 1968), p. 34.

133 E. A. Wrigley and R. S. Schofield, *The Population History of England 1541–1871: a Reconstruction* (Cambridge University Press, 1989), p. 30. Deciding that the register was defective was 'based on statistical grounds alone and reflects a wide variety of circumstances: missing registers, torn out pages, illegible entries, absent or apathetic incumbents, or parishioners who were indifferent or hostile to the religious celebration of vital events' (pp. 23–4).

134 Lambeth Palace Library, Fulham Papers, Terrick 6. 135 *Ibid.* fol. 54.

136 As noted in the reply from the clerk of St Botolph Aldersgate: *ibid.* fol. 67.

137 *Ibid.* fols. 6–8.

138 See e.g., W. U. Reynell-Upton and H. Tapley Soper (eds.), *The Registers of Baptisms, Marriages and Burials of the City of Exeter* (Exeter: Devon and Cornwall Record Society, 1910). The Act put an end to the practice of attending the cathedral for marriage: the number of marriages there fell from twenty-nine in 1752 and twenty-one in 1753 to a single marriage in 1755. See also W. A. Fearon and J. F. Williams, *The Parish Registers and Parochial Documents in the Archdeaconry of Winchester* (Winchester: Warren & Son, 1909), p. 9.

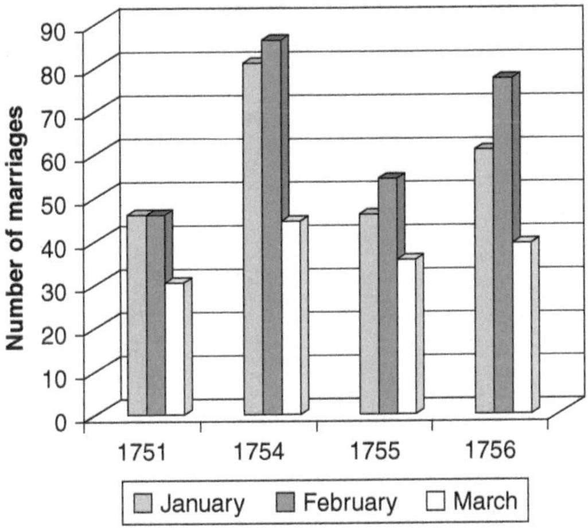

Figure 7.1. January–March marriages

exporter' saw an increase. If one looks at the numbers marrying across a large number of parishes, however, these gains and losses evened out and the overall numbers marrying showed no dramatic change, as Figure 7.1 shows. Across Northamptonshire, 771 marriages were celebrated in the 12 months immediately preceding the Act, and 682 in the succeeding 12 months. The higher number in the year preceding the Act can be accounted for by the fact that, as noted above, more couples had married in the first three months of 1754 than was usual. After this, the numbers marrying steadied, with 814 marriages being celebrated in 1755 and 819 in 1756. The stability in the overall number marrying reflected the fact that in the provinces clandestine marriages before 1754 had, by and large, taken place in church: after 1754 marriages were simply being redirected to the parties' own parish church, as Figure 7.2 shows.

Further evidence of conformity is provided by a number of different test groups in different communities. In Kilsby, an examination of the baptism register between 25 March 1754 and 24 March 1774 (the first twenty years of the Clandestine Marriages Act's operation) yielded a list of 265 children.[139] By omitting

[139] See further R. Probert and L. D'Arcy Brown, 'The Impact of the Clandestine Marriages Act: Three Case-Studies in Conformity' (2008) 23 *Continuity and Change* 309.

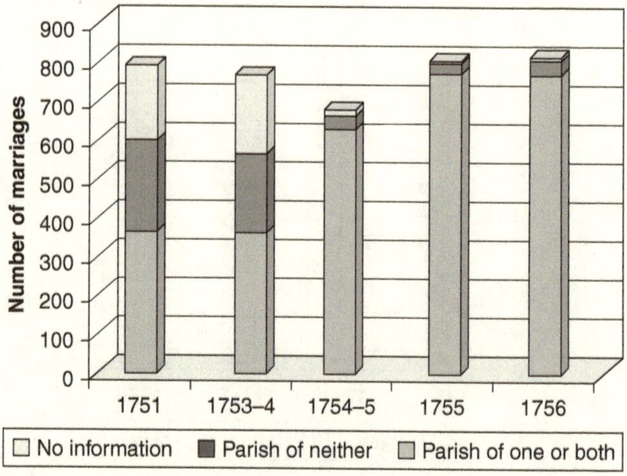

Figure 7.2. Location of marriages

Joseph Russell (baptised in 1755 without either parent being noted in the register) a test group of (quite fortuitously) 100 combinations of parents was drawn up. The nine who produced base children have already been considered above; of the remaining ninety-one combinations, a marriage has been traced for all but five, and of these, three appear only once in the registers and appear not to have been resident in the parish.[140] If one omits those couples who produced illegitimate children (who do not seem to have been cohabiting) then 95 per cent of marriages have been traced for this cohort.[141] Of course, many of those bringing children to be baptised in the twenty years immediately after the Act had married before 1754. So a further test group was therefore drawn up of those who brought their children to be baptised in Kilsby between 25 March 1774 and 24 March 1794.[142] The effect of the Act in redirecting couples to marry in their own parish church is clear in the higher percentage marrying in Kilsby

[140] The three couples (Thomas and Mary Hammons, Robard and Judy Ivesson, and John and Elizabeth Holles) all had a son baptised in Kilsby in 1771 or 1772 but none of the men appear on the 1771 Militia List, which recorded all males between the ages of eighteen and forty-five.

[141] See further Table 7.1.

[142] One couple in this cohort had married before 1754, reflecting the fact that child-bearing was spread over a long period of time for many women in this period.

Table 7.1 *Proportion and location of marriages traced*

	Parish studied	Adjacent parishes	Same county	Different county	Number and % traced
Kilsby, 1754–74	44	11	22	9	86
– all births	(44%)	(11%)	(22%)	(9%)	(86%)
– excluding illegitimate births	(48%)	(12%)	(24%)	(10%)	(95%)
Kilsby, 1774–94	123	21	20	15	179
– all births	(63%)	(11%)	(10%)	(8%)	(92%)
– excluding illegitimate births	(67%)	(11%)	(11%)	(8%)	(97%)
Colyton, Devon, 1765–77	118	22	22	6	168
– all births	(58%)	(11%)	(11%)	(3%)	(83%)
– excluding illegitimate births	(65%)	(12%)	(12%)	(3%)	(92%)
St Olave, York, 1779–85	47	66	45	8	166
– excluding illegitimate births	(23%)	(33%)	(22%)	(4%)	(83%)
Bradford-on-Avon settlement	100	36	13	24	173
examinations post-1754	(51%)	(18%)	(7%)	(12%)	(88%)
Cardington 1782 listing	86	26	46	8	166
post-1754 marriages	(50%)	(15%)	(27%)	(5%)	(97%)

itself.[143] Overall, 92 per cent of marriages have been traced for the 194 combinations of parents in this cohort, and once illegitimate children are excluded[144] this rises to 97 per cent.

Similar results have been achieved for parishes in other parts of the country. In the Devon parish of Colyton, marriages have been traced for at least 83 per cent of the 204 mothers whose children were baptised there between 1765 and 1777, a figure that rises to 92 per cent

143 The location of the marriages traced is set out in Table 7.1.

144 Again, there was nothing to suggest that the parents of the child were cohabiting in any of these cases.

once illegitimate children are excluded.[145] At St Olave in York the high number of illegitimate children baptised there on account of its poorhouse requires us to exclude such cases from the start: once this has been done, 83 per cent of marriages have been traced for those whose children were baptised between 1770 and 1785.[146] The lower percentage traced in this particular case reflects the fact that York's urban population was drawn from a wider catchment area, as the evidence about the parents' original parish of birth showed; it also reflects the fact that there is as yet no index for Yorkshire as a whole.

Of those examined as to their settlement in Bradford-on-Avon, marriages have been traced for 88 per cent of the 196 who claimed or are known to have married after the Act came into force.[147] One acknowledged irregular marriage took place *after* the 1753 Act: Hester Bishop and John Vennell had agreed to marry, and the banns were called in Bradford church. However, John's mother forbade the banns, so the couple went through a ceremony of marriage in a chapel in Bath. That this did not comply with the legal requirements is indicated by the fact that the unfortunate Hester was removed from the parish to her last place of settlement. This aside, there is no evidence in the Bradford records of any attempts to flout the 1753 Act. The failure to trace the few missing marriages can be attributed to a lack of information or the absence of an extant record.[148] It is significant that 8 per cent of marriages remained untraced even when information as to the place of marriage was supplied by the examinant: even after the Act some allowance must still be made for missing or deficient registers.[149]

[145] This period was chosen because of the extra information provided in the register in this period, including the wife's maiden name and her father's parish. There are some errors in the register, however, and since nine of the fifteen couples for whom no marriage has been traced had only one child baptised in Colyton, it is possible that mistakes as to their names have gone undetected.

[146] Again, this specific period was chosen because of the extra information available in the register for this period.

[147] See further Probert and D'Arcy Brown, 'The Impact of the Clandestine Marriages Act'.

[148] For example, for the six soldiers examined in 1771 who were accompanied by wives for whom only first names were recorded and who came from distant parts of the country: see P. Hembry (ed.), *Calendar of Bradford-on-Avon Settlement Examinations and Removal Orders, 1725–98* (Trowbridge: Wiltshire Record Society, 1990).

[149] In seven cases the simple problem is that the register for the relevant period has not survived, whether 'lost or stolen or strayed'. In five cases one must presume

The evidence of compliance is stronger still for the Cardington cohort, as one would expect given its location, the information available, and the fact that it comprised those actually resident in the parish.[150] Of the 171 combinations in the cohort,[151] marriages have been traced for all but five, a demonstrable compliance rate of over 97 per cent. But it would be entirely reasonable to assume that compliance approached 100 per cent. Only one couple were definitely unmarried: 'John Nesbitt Esqr' is described as occupying a gentleman's house together with 'Children by Sarah Lancaster his Mistress'.[152] In the remaining four cases the failure to trace a marriage can be attributed to a lack of information: the anonymous helpmeets of John Wyche and Luke Heywood are merely listed as 'wife' and no ages are provided for any of the parties or their children. Similar problems arise in tracing the first marriage of Thamas (*sic*) Frankerling, while Edward Gulever came from another county and his eldest child was not baptised in Cardington.

Overall, these six cohorts, comprising over 1,000 combinations of couples, show that the vast majority of couples can be proven to have married in church after 1753. The fact that it was not possible to trace 100 per cent should not be attributed to a failure to comply with the Act. Only two couples in this sample are known to have been cohabiting or to have married otherwise than in accordance with the Act. Those for whom marriages are missing are almost invariably those for whom the personal information is incomplete or from parishes for which the registers are missing, or who, as discussed in Chapter 3, had only a limited connection with the parish being studied; indeed, I have deliberately included cohorts for which a lower proportion was traced in order to highlight the reasons that might lead to such a result. The fact that a higher proportion of marriages have been traced for those marrying after 1754 should not, however, be taken as an indication that couples were less likely to marry formally before that date: as the survey of

defective recording: three of the couples for whom no marriage has been traced claimed to have married in Bradford itself, and two in not-too-distant churches in Bath and Bristol.

150 See further Chapter 3, and Probert and D'Arcy Brown, 'The Impact of the Clandestine Marriages Act'.

151 This is comprised of 125 couples living in the same household; 20 individuals who had been married before and repartnered, and 25 widow(er)s.

152 The published version of the list does not have this information, which appears in a second copy.

Northamptonshire shows, the number of marriages did not rise significantly in the wake of the Act. The increase in the proportion traced after 1754 should instead be attributed to the higher percentage marrying in the appropriate parish church, as set out in Figure 7.1, and to the improvements in recording that now enable positive links to be made where the marriage took place in a different parish.

Table 7.1 sets out exactly where those in the different cohorts married, whether in their own parish, an adjacent parish, another parish in the same county, or a different county. It also calculates the proportion traced to each location both as a percentage of each cohort and as a percentage of the cohort excluding those whose children were baptised as illegitimate and who do not appear to be living as a couple.[153] (Thus, John Nesbitt Esq and Sarah Lancaster are included in both calculations for the Cardington cohort, since they were known to be sharing a home, but those women who had just one illegitimate child, or more than one by different fathers, are not.)

Of course, even the fact that the parties had gone through a ceremony of marriage in church does not necessarily mean that they were validly married, since they might have failed to comply with one of the mandatory requirements of the 1753 Act. But a number of factors justify the inference that widespread invalidity was unlikely. First, all of the parties would usually have good reason to ensure that the necessary formalities were observed: for the parties themselves, there would be little point in going through a ceremony that was not valid, while a minister solemnising a marriage in defiance of the requirements relating to banns or licence would be guilty of a felony and vulnerable to transportation for fourteen years.[154] Of course, mistakes might happen, but an unsuspected mistake was effectively irrelevant.[155] And a mistake that was discovered in time could be rectified, as the following account illustrates:

> the first Publication of the banns between Thos. Small and Jenny Benham were made (thro' a mistaken conformity to the Rubrick in the Common Prayer Book) on Easter-day, Easter Monday, and Easter Tuesday, and the

[153] Percentages are rounded to the nearest whole number, with the result that the two different calculations may produce the same percentage where the numbers are small.

[154] Section 8. [155] See further Chapter 8.

first marriage was accordingly solemnized. But, upon perusing the Marriage Act of the 26th of George the 2nd, which orders the Banns to be published on Three Sundays, it was thought proper to publish the Banns afresh on the 1st and 2nd Sundays after Easter, and a Marriage between the above mentioned Parties was again solemnized after such fresh Publications.[156]

Similarly, when William Brown married Sarah Sargent in Bradford-on-Avon, the banns were by mistake called in the name of Sarah *Sartain*. The register recorded that the banns were republished in the correct name and the marriage resolemnised.[157] Even if the mistake was not rectified and was subsequently relied on in a challenge to the validity of the marriage, minor and genuine mistakes could often be overlooked. The courts generally adopted a purposive approach to the interpretation of the Act: there are very few cases of accidental non-compliance that resulted in a marriage being held to be invalid.[158]

COMPLIANCE 'ON TERMS'

When the month is expired and the Law fulfilled, Live and be happy.[159]

The reader might be forgiven for thinking that the evidence of obedience to the Act is too good to be true. Had all the motivations for clandestine marriages disappeared, or were they insufficiently strong to risk the penalty of invalidity? Of course, even before 1754, the majority of the population had married regularly in church. But both before and after the Act, there was a minority for whom marriage in the local parish church was unattractive, whether because of religious differences, a desire for privacy, or the wish to escape parental control. Before 1754 the clandestine marriage offered an alternative that brought with it the same legal status and rights as a regular marriage; although, as we have seen, outside London it is likely that most clandestine marriages themselves took place in church. After 1754 the only real alternative that offered the

156 Quoted by Fearon and Williams, *The Parish Registers and Parochial Documents in the Archdeaconry of Winchester*, p. 27.

157 *Wiltshire Marriages: Bradford-on-Avon 1566–77, 1779–1799*, Society of Genealogists, WL/R 113.

158 See Chapters 6 and 8.

159 J. Uglow, *The Lunar Men: the Friends who Made the Future, 1730–1810* (London: Faber and Faber Ltd, 2002), p. 63.

same legal status and rights, given the doubts about the validity of a marriage celebrated in another jurisdiction, was to marry within the Act, but on the parties' own terms.

Those whose wish, for whatever reason, was simply for a quiet marriage could still achieve this under the 1753 Act.[160] The option of a special licence, which would allow a marriage to be celebrated at any time and in any place, was still available for a few.[161] Marrying by common licence, especially soon after eight a.m.,[162] would avoid publicity. Erasmus Darwin adopted this approach when he married his first wife Mary in 1757, 'as the Voice of Fame makes such quick Dispatch with any News in so small a Place as Lichfield'.[163] The Act required that two witnesses be present at the registration, but this was no more than had been required to prove the marriage under the old law and in any case was merely directory.

Those who feared local objections to their marriage might go a step further and marry in a parish to which neither belonged. The improvements in road transport that facilitated a flight to the Border were also of assistance to those travelling shorter distances.[164] If they had time, they might be able to establish a residence that satisfied the requirements of the Act.[165] In 1760, for example, Matthew Boulton married his deceased wife's sister in London 'where no one who knew them was around to oppose the banns'.[166]

160 See e.g., A. Foreman, *Georgiana: Duchess of Devonshire* (London: HarperCollins, 1999), p. 20.

161 Outhwaite, *Clandestine Marriage*, p. 130, notes that the number granted 'soared' immediately after the 1753 Act. This might seem to indicate a desire among the elite to avoid its provisions, although as the average was still only thirty-six per year it was not particularly significant as an evasive practice. Stricter rules were introduced in 1759, as set out in Chapter 6, and the numbers fell back again.

162 See e.g., Fanny Burney, *Cecilia* (Oxford: World Classics, 1999; original edn 1782).

163 Uglow, *The Lunar Men*, p. 42.

164 See Langford, *A Polite and Commercial People*, pp. 397–405, on the links between different centres of population.

165 One contemporary suggested that marriages at Holy Cross in Shrewsbury were 'generally between strangers who occasionally reside here so long as to make a place of abode according to the act of parliament made in 1754': *Philosophical Transactions of the Royal Society of London* (1782), pp. 56–7. See also R. Bigland, *Observations on Marriages, Baptisms, and Burials, as Preserved in Parochial Registers* (London, 1764), p. 56.

166 Uglow, *The Lunar Men*, p. 63. At this stage marriage with one's deceased wife's sister was forbidden by canon law, but not by the common law.

He later advised his friend Edgeworth, who was in a similar predicament: 'say nothing of your intentions but go quickly and snugly to Scotland or some obscure corner in London ... and there take lodgings to make yourself a parishioner. When the month is expired and the Law fulfilled, Live and be happy.'[167] There is an intriguing combination here of precise compliance with the terms of the law and a willingness to flout its spirit.[168] In some cases, the parish officials appear to have connived at marriages that breached the spirit, if not the letter, of the Act. In *Priestly* v. *Lamb*, for example, the husband alleged that the clerk had told him that if he did not live in the parish he must take a lodging there. The Lord Chancellor refused to believe this and noted that 'in any case it must have been an evasive residence, no longer than a week'[169] – evasive of the spirit of the Act, but not of the letter, and the marriage was upheld.

In addition, the parties might simply lie about their residence. After all, the 1753 Act contained no clause that would invalidate a marriage simply on the basis that the parties had not fulfilled the residential requirements. A marriage could even be had without an actual elopement in towns and cities where there were numerous parishes, and where the news of the marriage would not so easily filter back to those who might oppose it.[170] An Episcopal Visitation of 1788 found that a number of Surrey parishioners were marrying in London: in Mitcham, for example, the churchwardens reported that '[i]t is the custom of the common people of this and neighbouring parishes to go to Lambeth church to be married'.[171] The popularity of Lambeth is confirmed by an examination of Mitcham's settlement examinations: around 10 per cent of those examined as to their settlement claimed that they had married in

167 *Ibid.* p. 63.

168 Edgeworth took the advice and married Mary, his deceased wife's sister, in London after the local bishop had forbidden any clergymen in the diocese to marry them.

169 (1801) 6 Ves. Jun. 421; 31 ER 1124.

170 See e.g., *Harford* v. *Morris* (1776) 2 Hag. Con. 423; 161 ER 792, at 429, where the judge commented that 'if instead of going abroad the parties had been married in any great parish of this town or country ... [n]o law says that it shall be void'.

171 W. R. Ward, *Parson and Parish in Eighteenth-Century Surrey: Replies to Bishops' Visitations* (Guildford: Surrey Record Society, 1994), vol. 34, p. 122. It was similarly noted for the parish of Great Bookham that '[m]any persons, my parishioners, get married in London or its neighbourhood' (p. 92).

Lambeth.[172] And it may be explained by the policy adopted by its parish officials: as one outraged judge reported, '[b]y the affidavit of the clerk of the parish of Lambeth it is disclosed, that they conceive in that parish, that they do their duty to the public, and to the individuals ... whom they are to marry, never making any inquiry as to the residence of the parties'.[173] The judge did not share this view as to the legitimacy of this practice, opining that the parish officials were guilty of an offence in deliberately failing to make enquiries, and expressing the hope that such cases would not reoccur. The evidence suggests that he was disappointed in this hope: the census of 1821 found low marriage rates in Middlesex and Hertfordshire and noted that 'the custom of surreptitiously marrying in the Metropolis increase[d] the number of marriages therein, at the expense of the adjacent counties'.[174]

Some clergymen were clearly more assiduous than others in checking the credentials of parties wishing to be married. William Holland, the incumbent of Monkton Farley in Somerset, recorded in his diary how one of his parishioners 'spoke to me about marrying a couple tomorrow, his sister and another. I told him that it could not be unless 21 days resident'[175] – although the refusal, and the fact that this detail was deemed worthy of comment, might be accounted for by his dislike of the individual in question. Others clearly did not make adequate inquiries. In *Nicholson* v. *Squire* an actor eloped with a young ward of court and married by banns in a parish to which neither belonged.[176] Lord Eldon LC reluctantly upheld the validity of the marriage but stressed that the clergyman was much to blame for not making enquiries as to the residence of the parties. He pointed out that under the 1753 Act clergymen were not obliged to publish banns unless they had been given seven days' notice, and that enquiries into residence could be made during this time – he 'has only to repair to the house, in which they are

172 B. Berryman (ed.), *Mitcham Settlement Examinations* (Guildford: Surrey Record Society, 1973).

173 *Priestly* v. *Lamb* (1801) 6 Ves. Jun. 421; 31 ER 1124, at 422–3.

174 *Population according to the Census of 1821* (1822), PP vol. 15, p. xxv. It was noted in *The Case of Queens' College, Cambridge* (1828) Jac. 1; 37 ER 750, that '[t]here are churches in the metropolis, where more than 20 couples are sometimes married at one and the same time'.

175 J. Ayres, *Paupers and Pig Killers: the Diary of William Holland – a Somerset Parson, 1799–1818* (Stroud: Sutton Publishing, 2003), p. 175.

176 (1809) 16 Ves. Jun. 259; 33 ER 983.

represented to have lived, and to inform himself whether the statement is true'.[177]

Nor did the residential requirements for marriage by licence ensure that the incumbent was acquainted with both of the parties, since the law only required that one party be resident in the parish where the marriage was to take place.[178] Once a licence had been obtained it was regarded as authority for the marriage to proceed, and there was no rule equivalent to that in the context of banns that would sanction delay. In *Argar* v. *Holdsworth*,[179] a vicar who refused to marry a couple was cited into the ecclesiastical court, which held that he should have performed the marriage unless he had reasons to believe that the licence had been fraudulently obtained and was only delaying in order to make proper enquiries. Given the risk of admonition or suspension for not performing a marriage, clergymen might well have taken the view that their best course was to stifle any suspicions and simply conduct the marriage.

It was even possible for minors to evade the requirement of parental consent. As Chapter 6 pointed out, although consent was necessary for a marriage by licence to be valid, a marriage by banns was valid as long as there had been no public *dissent*. The legislation also provided that a clergyman would not be punished for celebrating a marriage by banns between minors who did not have parental consent unless he actually had notice of the parents' dissent, with the result that ministers would not have been inhibited from marrying under-age couples by the fear of criminal penalties. Minors could therefore validly marry without parental consent if the banns were called and their parents did not object, even if the banns were called in a parish where the parties were unknown and their parents had no knowledge of the intended marriage.

In many cases this would have been easily achieved, if, for example, the parties had left home at an early age and established

177 See also *Warter* v. *Yorke* (1815) 19 Ves. 451; 34 ER 584, another marriage involving a ward of court, in which the judge commented on the mischief that might be caused by clergymen marrying persons of whom they knew nothing.

178 See e.g., M. Beardsley and N. Bennett, *'Grateful to Providence': the Diary and Accounts of Matthew Flinders*, vol. I, *1775–1784* (Lincoln Record Society vol. 95, 2007), p. 148: the groom arrived in the bride's parish with the licence the night before the intended marriage and 'waited on Mr Vesey (the Clergyman) that evening to inform him'.

179 (1758) 2 Lee 515; 161 ER 424.

a residence elsewhere. Of course, the likelihood of this varied according to both class and gender.[180] Among the lower orders, children tended to move out at a fairly young age to work as servants or apprentices,[181] rather than living at home until they married.[182] This depended to a great extent on the employment opportunities available.[183] As Wall has noted, 'the varying requirements of service, parental ability to make use of the labour of sons and daughters, and greater male earning power generally make it difficult to predict whether sons would, or could, be retained in preference to daughters'.[184] Of course, exit from the parental home did not guarantee that a child would be living sufficiently far away for news of his or her intended marriage not to filter back, but some children moved considerable distances. In one Bedfordshire sample, for example, 23 per cent had moved to the anonymity of London.[185] For such individuals parental control was effectively rendered nugatory.

For those higher up the social scale, opportunities to live away from home were more extensive for males embarking on careers. Daughters tended to marry from home.[186] For them, an elopement – or at least a temporary absence from home – would be necessary to

180 See further R. Probert, 'Control over Marriage in England and Wales, 1753–1823: the Clandestine Marriages Act of 1753 in Context' (2009) 27 *Law and History Review* 413.

181 R. Malcolmson, *Life and Labour in England 1700–1780* (London: Hutchinson, 1981), ch. 3.

182 Snell, *Annals of the Labouring Poor*, Table 7.2, estimates that the mean age of leaving home was 14.6 for male agricultural workers and 17 for female agricultural workers in the period 1700–1760. This fell to 13.9 and 16.2 respectively in the two succeeding decades, before rising again to 14.9 and 16.6 at the end of the eighteenth century

183 R. Schofield, 'Age-Specific Mobility in an Eighteenth Century Rural English Parish' (1970) *Annales de Démographie Historique* 261, noted that in one Bedfordshire parish in 1782, only 22 per cent of boys aged between fifteen and nineteen remained at home, although 71 per cent of girls of this age were still living with their parents, probably because of the availability of employment in lace-making in that particular locality.

184 R. Wall, 'Leaving Home and the Process of Household Formation in Preindustrial England' (1987) 2 *Continuity and Change* 77, 79.

185 Schofield, 'Age-Specific Mobility'. See also Malcolmson, *Life and Labour*, ch. 3 on the mobility of those in their teens, and P. Horn, *Flunkeys and Scullions: Life Below Stairs in Georgian England* (Stroud: Sutton Publishing, 2004), ch. 3.

186 See M. Hunt, *The Middling Sort: Commerce, Gender and the Family in England, 1680–1780* (Berkeley: University of California Press, 1996); A. Vickery, *The Gentleman's Daughter* (New Haven: Yale University Press, 1998).

avoid parental control.[187] Yet even those who lived at home might pay extended visits to friends and relations, giving them the opportunity to thwart their parents' wishes. The novels of Jane Austen provide a number of fictional examples: Lydia's visit to Brighton facilitates her elopement with Wickham, and Jane Fairfax becomes secretly engaged to Frank Churchill while living with friends.[188] Real-life examples appear in the case law: in *Wheeler* v. *Warner*, for example, Mrs Warner had objected to her daughter visiting Wheeler's family, observing 'that she was aware of the attachment that existed between Mr Wheeler and her daughter; and that, if she was permitted to go to Birmingham, a marriage would be the consequence; but the testator said that he had promised his daughter she should go, and that he would not disappoint her'.[189] The mother was ultimately proved right when the couple married without telling either set of parents. Thus, at all levels of society there might be the possibility of marrying while away from home,[190] but such possibilities were obviously far more extensive for those who had already established an independent residence away from their parents.

Thus, the desire for privacy or the wish to escape parental control – factors that had prompted clandestine marriages prior to 1754 – could still be accommodated under the new system. Indeed, some saw these means of avoiding the Act as a necessary safety-valve. One judge commented that 'the act makes particular exceptions, without which the purpose of the marriage act, though an exceeding good act, might have been questioned before this time, if there had not been so many ways to avoid the restraint put on the marriage of minors'.[191]

Yet the reality of marrying in a parish to which the parties did not belong should not be exaggerated. There is evidence that the residential requirements of the 1753 Act were observed to a greater extent than the equivalent prescriptions of the canon law had been. A survey of 18,442 marriages from 69 parishes in 8 counties has

[187] See e.g., *Dobbyn* v. *Corneck* (1813) 2 Phill. 102; 161 ER 1090; *Meddowcroft* v. *Gregory* (1816) 2 Hag. Con. 207; 161 ER 717; *Sullivan* v. *Sullivan* (1818) 2 Hag. Con. 238; 161 ER 728; *Green* v. *Dalton* (1822) 1 Add. 289; 162 ER 101.

[188] J. Austen, *Pride and Prejudice* (London, 1813) and *Emma* (London, 1816).

[189] (1823) 1 Sim. & St. 304; 57 ER 123, at 308.

[190] See also A. Blacker Kerr (ed.), *The Diary of a Young Lady of Fashion in the Year 1764–1765* (London: Thornton Butterworth Ltd, 1926), pp. 100–1.

[191] *Harford* v. *Morris* (1776) 2 Hag. 423; 161 ER 792, at 429, per Sir George Hay.

been carried out by Snell, who found that all counties showed a dramatic reduction in the number of 'foreign' marriages – those clandestine marriages where both parties came from outside the parish.[192] He concluded that 'Hardwicke's Act ... shows itself to have been highly effective over all counties'.[193] The pattern of marriages after the 1753 Act came into force suggests that most couples were not merely pretending to comply with the law and misstating their parish of origin.[194] As we have seen, in each of the parishes studied the percentage of marriages celebrated in that parish rose in the wake of the Act.[195] In Colyton, 65 per cent of parents named in the baptism register had married in that parish; in addition, the fact that the baptism register often gives details as to the parents' original parish of residence[196] enables it to be ascertained that a further 17 per cent married in a parish where at least one of them was resident. Of course, the extent of mobility in this period makes it unsafe to conclude that an individual was *not* resident in a parish simply because he or she was not baptised there;[197] equally, of course, evidence of baptism in a particular parish is not conclusive evidence of residence there later in life. A further analysis of the cohort who married in Kilsby between 1774 and 1794 was therefore carried out. This specific cohort was chosen not merely because all couples bar one married after the 1753 Act came into force, but also because of the additional information available about those resident in Kilsby in this period, in the form of militia listings[198]

[192] K. D. M. Snell, 'English Rural Societies and Geographical Marital Endogamy, 1700–1837' (2002) 55 *Economic History Review* 262.

[193] *Ibid*. 274.

[194] As they could do without invalidating the marriage: see Chapter 6.

[195] See Table 7.1. Nor does the fact that the parties married in a parish different to that where their child was baptised necessarily indicate that they did not belong there: the baptism, rather than the marriage, might have taken place in a different parish. See e.g., Lucas, *An Impartial Inquiry*, p. 20.

[196] Specifically, it identifies the husband's parish, and the parish of the wife's father.

[197] See e.g., M. Long and B. Maltby, 'Personal Mobility in Three West Riding Parishes, 1777–1812' (1980) 24 *Local Population Studies* 13; R. Tinley and D. Mills, 'Population Turnover in an Eighteenth-Century Lincolnshire Parish in Comparative Context' (1994) 52 *Local Population Studies* 30; A. J. Pain and M. T. Smith, 'Do Marriage Horizons Accurately Measure Migration? A Test Case from Stanhope Parish, County Durham' (1984) 33 *Local Population Studies* 44.

[198] Northamptonshire Record Office, Kilsby Militia List 1771, 1774, 1777. For an explanation of the criteria for inclusion on such lists, see V. A. Hatley (ed.), *Northamptonshire Militia Lists 1777* (Kettering: Northamptonshire Record Society, 1973), p. ix.

and a list of those who owned land drawn up for the purposes of enclosure.[199] In most cases the men who appeared in the Kilsby marriage register as residents of Kilsby had either been baptised there, or appeared on the militia list as an adult; in the remaining few cases it was clear from the coincidence of names that there were other members of their family present in the parish.

And in Llansantffraid Glyn Ceiriog, the fact that a high number of couples married in Llangollen,[200] but had their children baptised in Llansantffraid, is in fact evidence of conformity. The much larger parish of Llangollen extends south from the town of Llangollen, across the mountains of the lower Ceiriog valley, and tucks neatly into the curve of the river Ceiriog as it flows through Llansantffraid village itself. For those living on the south bank of the Ceiriog valley, it was far easier to carry their new-born babies a mile or so to Llansantffraid parish to be baptised in its church than to struggle over the steep, exposed mountains to their parish church of Llangollen. That they made this journey to get married is in fact a testimony to their willingness to comply with the requirements of the 1753 Act.

CONCLUSION

In conclusion, then, there is virtually no evidence that couples failed to comply with the requirements of the 1753 Act. Some did attempt to avoid the Act altogether by marrying in another jurisdiction, but doubts about the validity of such evasive measures (and the fact that marriages on the Continent required just as many formalities as English marriages) limited the scope of such measures. The parish case studies suggest that the vast majority of the population complied with the Act. Yet, as the final section has demonstrated, there were ways in which a couple could enter into a marriage according to the terms of the Act and yet evade parental control or achieve the privacy they desired. How far the courts were willing to find flaws in marriages that flouted the spirit of the 1753 Act will appear in the next chapter.

199 I am grateful to Gren Hatton for providing me with this information.

200 Thirty-seven of the fifty-seven whose marriages have been traced to another parish: see Chapter 3 and see further R. Probert, 'Chinese Whispers and Welsh Weddings' (2005) 20 *Continuity and Change* 211.

8

THE UNEXPLORED JUDICIAL INTERPRETATION OF THE 1753 ACT

The prevalent view among modern commentators is that the Act was interpreted extremely harshly. Stone, for example, has claimed that 'the slightest mistake, however accidental or trivial'[1] might invalidate a marriage, even if this was simply a matter of misstating the age of the parties or omitting their middle name, and similar views have been advanced by other commentators.[2] Yet such a synthesis of the case law is misleading: it is true that there were cases in which marriages were annulled on the basis that one party's middle name had been omitted from the banns, and that there were cases in which marriages were annulled because of an (accidental) failure to comply with the law, but there are no reported cases in which a marriage was annulled because of an *accidental* omission of one party's middle name. Some commentators have based their indictment of the entire Act on one single case[3] – and when one finds the same case being cited by a number of commentators one does begin to wonder whether there are any other examples. Moreover, reporting the bare facts of a case may not indicate why that particular marriage was annulled: any decision, shorn of its context, may appear harsh or inexplicable.

[1] L. Stone, *Road to Divorce: a History of the Making and Breaking of Marriage in England* (Oxford University Press, 1990), p. 132.

[2] See e.g., W. P. Eversley, *The Law of the Domestic Relations* (London: Stevens & Haynes, 1885), p. 26; G. E. Howard, *A History of Matrimonial Institutions* (New York: Humanities Press, 1964; original edn 1904), pp. 463–4; O. M. Stone, *Family Law* (Macmillan Press, 1977), p. 30; R. L. Brown, 'The Rise and Fall of Fleet Marriages', ch. 6 in R. B. Outhwaite, *Marriage and Society* (London: Europa Publications Ltd, 1981), p. 135; A. H. Manchester, *A Modern Legal History of England and Wales 1750–1950* (London: Butterworths, 1980), p. 365; and S. Parker, *Informal Marriage, Cohabitation and the Law, 1750–1989* (Basingstoke: Macmillan Press, 1990), p. 61.

[3] Manchester, *A Modern Legal History*, p. 365; Parker, *Informal Marriage*, p. 61.

In order to understand exactly when and why a marriage might be annulled on the basis of the parties' failure to comply with the required formalities, we need to pay close attention not only to the reasoning of the case, but also its context. One factor that is of particular importance is the identity of the person who was seeking to annul the marriage. Under the Act there were two groups of persons who might challenge the validity of a marriage. On the one hand there were irate parents whose minor children had married without their consent (whether by banns or licence) and who sought to have the marriage annulled. On the other, there were individuals who claimed that their own marriage was void because of their own failure to comply with the law. As we shall see, the courts treated these two groups very differently.

The argument advanced in this chapter is not that the judicial interpretation of the Act was always liberal, nor that it was particularly harsh, but that it was sensitive to the purposes for which the legislation had been enacted.[4] This meant that in certain contexts (for example, where a claim was brought by a parent) a strict interpretation of the legislation was appropriate. Conversely, where the challenge to the marriage was brought by one of the parties, perhaps after many years of matrimony, the courts would try to uphold the marriage and ignore any defects as far as possible.

To show this, a detailed study of the reported[5] case law[6] is necessary. Marriages by banns are considered separately from marriages

[4] For an earlier version of these arguments, see R. Probert, 'The Judicial Interpretation of Lord Hardwicke's Act 1753' (2002) 23 *Journal of Legal History* 129.

[5] Unreported cases are of less assistance in evaluating the judicial interpretation of the Act, since it is not usually possible to ascertain why a particular marriage was annulled or upheld. Fortunately, however, the reported cases are not in this period confined to those that broke new ground and there is a sample of around fifty cases for analysis, together with those referred to in the judgments.

[6] The reported case law is largely drawn from nullity suits in the London Consistory Court and the Court of Arches. Whether the approach of these courts was replicated in other ecclesiastical courts is impossible to ascertain in the absence of reported case law from such other courts. But the London courts were the most important, both because of the appellate jurisdiction exercised by the Court of Arches over all the ecclesiastical courts in the Province of Canterbury and because of the volume of cases heard there. In addition, a number of the cases discussed in this chapter were decided in the common-law courts, for example in cases concerning the settlement of the parties, but since the approach adopted was substantially the same these cases are not differentiated from the others.

by licence, since different requirements applied to each.[7] It will be noted that the cases cited date for the most part from the early decades of the nineteenth century, and the third part of the chapter will offer some explanations as to why this should be the case. This leads us into the story of how the increased number of cases led to proposals for reform being advanced – although, as will be shown, it was easier to criticise the operation of the Act than to find a workable alternative.

MARRIAGES BY BANNS

It is the doctrine of all courts that every thing is to be presumed in favour of a matrimonial union which has produced children, and united parties by a long cohabitation.[8]

On the face of the Act, a marriage would be valid if banns had been called three times in the church where the parties married, and would only be void if this preliminary was omitted altogether or had been opposed by the person whose consent was required.[9] This seemed to leave little scope for ambiguity or argument. But before long it was realised that the whole purpose of publishing the banns – that of bringing the intended marriage to the notice of the community and those who might wish to object[10] – would be undermined if the names of the parties were misstated.[11] The Court of Arches therefore held that if the true names were not used, there was simply no publication of banns.[12] This in itself

[7] See further Chapter 6 for the legal requirements.

[8] *Diddear* v. *Faucit* (1821) 3 Phill. Ecc. 580; 161 ER 1421, at 581.

[9] See e.g., *Robinson* v. *Grant* (1811) 18 Ves. Jun. 290; 34 ER 327 (marriage to ward of court; banns not published in wife's parish but marriage upheld under s. 10 of the 1753 Act).

[10] See e.g., *Frankland* v. *Nicholson* (1805) 3 M & S 259n; 105 ER 607: 'marriage is a contract by which the relation of the parties to the public is materially altered ... nothing can be more clear than that the publication should notify what it is fit the world, for public purposes, should know, that such persons are going to enter into that state and condition of life'.

[11] This may seem an obvious point, but since banns had not been essential to the validity of a marriage prior to 1754 it would not have mattered what names had been used (see e.g., *Pool* v. *Sacheverel* (1720) 1 P Wms. 676; 24 ER 565, which involved a Fleet marriage under an assumed name), and so the point had never had to be resolved.

[12] *Early* v. *Stevens* (1785), cited in *Pouget* v. *Tomkins* (1812) 2 Hag. Con. 142; 161 ER 695. A similarly strict approach was taken in other legal contexts: see e.g., *Jones* v. *Macquillian* (1793) 5 TR 195; 101 ER 110 (misnomer in declaration – reversal of defendant's first two names – successfully pleaded in abatement).

was hardly a harsh interpretation of the Act, but one consistent with the purposive approach generally taken by all courts in construing its provisions.[13] But how strictly did subsequent courts interpret this requirement? Did the full names of the bride and groom have to be set out? Did spelling mistakes matter? And what was the 'true name' of an individual anyway?

Before addressing such questions, we should first examine the case most often cited as 'proof' that the Act was harshly interpreted, *Pouget* v. *Tomkins*.[14] At first sight, the case does indeed support such an interpretation. The groom, William Peter Pouget, was described as 'William Pouget' in the banns, the marriage was challenged, and the court held that the banns had not been properly called, with the result that the marriage was held to be void. But if we examine the context of the case this apparently absurd decision becomes explicable.

In fact, *Pouget* v. *Tomkins* epitomises the type of marriage that the 1753 Act was designed to prevent. Sixteen-year-old William Pouget, who was usually known as Peter, and who was tellingly described as a 'boy' throughout the report, formed a relationship with his grandmother's maid. The report does not mention her age, but Sir William Scott assumed that she was older than her purported husband. Clearly, she was seen as a designing, lower-class woman, inveigling a young gentleman into marriage.[15] Unsurprisingly, Peter did not have the consent of his family to this disadvantageous union. The couple had sought to have the banns called in a more distant parish, but this had been refused on the basis that they were not resident there. They eventually settled for a church closer to home, but had the banns called in the name of William, rather than Peter. The incumbent did not insist on seven days' notice, or check the background of the parties, and married them. The couple managed to keep the wedding a secret for a few months, but eventually the Pouget family was informed of the marriage, and the father took steps to annul it on the ground of undue publication of banns.

In these circumstances, the omission of the name 'Peter' was held to be sufficient to invalidate the marriage, the judge noting

13 See further Chapter 6. 14 (1812) 2 Hag. Con. 142; 161 ER 695.

15 Maidservants who enjoyed liaisons with their masters' sons were seen as 'artful, libidinous young women corrupting naïve, untutored boys': P. Langford, *A Polite and Commercial People: England 1727–1783* (Oxford: Clarendon Press, 1998), p. 119.

that the name of William Pouget 'would not have described him to most persons so as to notify him'.[16] It was explicitly stated that, where no fraud was intended, the omission of one of the baptismal names would not invalidate the marriage, but that this was not such a case. Sir William Scott made it clear that the strict interpretation of the Act in this case was to further the purposes for which the legislation was passed:

> Where ... there is a fraud intended, and where the omission is not casual, but intentional, and made a principal part of the machinery of the fraud, I should hold that the Court would be bound to enforce the most literal interpretation *for the purpose of supporting the true spirit of the act*.[17]

So the decision in *Pouget* was avowedly a harshly literal interpretation of the law – but only for the purpose of promoting the spirit of the Act. But *Pouget* also illustrates the fact that a person wishing to challenge a marriage had to overcome two obstacles: first, he must show that the banns were not called in the true names of the parties, and, secondly, he must show that any omission or alteration of the names was fraudulent. And there is an interesting body of case law on both of these elements.

Proving that the true names of the parties were not used

Pouget illustrates that the 'true name' of a person was not necessarily the name in which he or she had been baptised. The approach taken by the courts was a pragmatic one. Since the purpose of the requirement was to ensure public knowledge of the intended wedding, the names in which the banns were to be published were the names that were most likely to attract the attention of those who knew the parties.[18] This would usually be the baptismal name, but it could be supplanted by a name acquired by reputation.[19] As Lord Ellenborough CJ explained:

16 (1812) 2 Hag. Con. 142; 161 ER 695, at 145.

17 *Ibid.* at 143–4 (emphasis added).

18 *Frankland* v. *Nicholson* (1805) 3 M & S 259n; 105 ER 607; *Wakefield* v. *Mackay* (1807) SC 1 Hag. Con. 394; 161 ER 937n; see also *Cope* v. *Burt* (1809) 1 Hag. Con. 434; 161 ER 608, at 438.

19 *Mayhew* v. *Mayhew* (1812) 3 M & S 266n; 105 ER 611; *R* v. *Inhabitants of Billinghurst* (1814) 3 M & S 250; 105 ER 603; *Wilson* v. *Brockley* (1810) 1 Phill. Ecc. 132; 161 ER 937.

It would lead to perilous consequences if in every case an inquiry were to be instituted, at the hazard of endangering the marriage of a woman, who had every reason to think she was acquiring a legitimate husband, whether the name by which the husband was notified in the banns was strictly his baptismal name, or whether at the period of his baptism he may not have received some other name.[20]

Indeed, the fact that a certain name was used for the purpose of the marriage might itself convince the court that it was the 'true' name. In one case the bride had had five surnames before she married and was passing under the name of Thorpe at the time she was married.[21] The banns were then called in the name of Jackson, her mother's maiden name. The court held that this was her true name:

taking all the evidence together, that it was the name of her mother, that it was the name impressed upon her at her birth, *that she has used that name in the most solemn acts of her life civil and religious* ... the court could not be warranted to say ... that Jackson is so clearly demonstrated to be the untrue name of this person ... as to destroy the validity of the marriage.[22]

Since marrying in a particular name would constitute using it 'in the most solemn acts' of that person's life, this made it even more difficult to show that a false name had been used. Similar generosity was shown to another under-age bride who used her mother's maiden name as a middle name.[23] The court noted that it was not surprising that she had not used it before, as she would be unlikely to use it on ordinary occasions and, as a minor, would not have executed any formal documents. It was assumed that she had used the name because she had thought that she was entitled to do so, rather than from any motives of concealment, and so the marriage was upheld.

It is significant that these were both cases where the brides thought that they were entitled to the names they used, and where they had no reason to conceal their identity. A less favourable approach was adopted if the court thought that the individual in question had something to hide. Ann Nicholson was described in the banns by the assumed name of Ross, and could provide no evidence that she had acquired this name by reputation.[24] There

20 *R* v. *Inhabitants of Billingshurst* (1814) 3 M & S 250; 105 ER 603, at 257.
21 *Wakefield* v. *Mackay* (1807) SC 1 Hag. Con. 394; 161 ER 937n.
22 *Ibid.* at 939 (emphasis added).
23 *Sullivan* v. *Sullivan (falsely called Oldacre)* (1818) 2 Hag. Con. 238; 161 ER 728.
24 *Frankland* v. *Nicolson* (1805) 3 M & S 259n; 105 ER 607.

are hints in the case that Ann may have used the name to conceal her reputation: it was noted that if she had been described by her proper name 'there might have been persons acquainted with her conduct, which might have influenced, and fairly influenced, the party himself'.[25] The assumed name was seen as a fraud on the groom as to her condition and situation, as well as a fraud on the officiating minister and the public. Alas, the report does not give any further details as to Ann's condition, simply declaring the marriage void.

Thus, the 'true name' was the name by which one was usually known, but could even be a name used only at the time of the marriage, as long as it was not assumed for the sole purpose of bringing about the marriage. And a further hurdle faced a person who wished to challenge the marriage – how could it be *proved* that the false name had been read out in church? The Act required the minister to certify in writing that the banns had been published, but even such written evidence did not necessarily satisfy the court. In one case the entry in the register stated that the banns had been published in the name of Fanon, but Follon had signed his true name below.[26] The court held that it would not presume that the banns had been improperly published, preferring to assume that the minister had made a mistake in entering the names in the register rather than in publishing them. And when the converse case occurred (as in *Heffer* v. *Heffer*, where the register described Anna Colley as Ann *Sophia* Colley) the court again preferred to assume that it was the minister who had made a mistake in issuing the certificate, rather than inferring that the wrong name had been used in calling the banns.[27] Since the court was willing to give the parties the benefit of the doubt in this way, the party trying to prove that the banns were published in the wrong name had to provide convincing evidence.

[25] *Ibid.* at 260.

[26] *Coppe* v. *Follon* (1794) 1 Phill. Ecc. 145n; 161 ER 943. Note too the comments of the poet-parson George Crabbe: 'How fair these Names, how much unlike they look/To all the blurr'd Subscriptions in my Book/ . . . Much have I tried to guide the Fist along/But still the Blunderers plac'd their Blottings wrong': 'The Parish Register' in N. Dalrymple-Champneys and A. Pollard (eds.), *George Crabbe: the Complete Poetical Works* (Oxford: Clarendon Press, 1988), vol. I, pp. 244–5.

[27] *Heffer* v. *Heffer* (1812) 3 M & S 265n; 105 ER 611. *Pouget* v. *Tomkins* was explicitly distinguished as a case of 'clear fraud against the rights of the father' (p. 266).

Proving that the wrong name had been used fraudulently

Once it had been proved that a mistake had been made, it then had to be shown that it was fraudulent. In those cases where the name used was completely at variance with the true name the bare evidence of publication was sufficient, such publication being regarded as fraudulent in itself. As Sir William Scott explained,[28] there could be no true publication where the names used were totally different from the real names of the parties:

> nor could one have supposed that such names could have been used but for the purposes of gross fraud, if the case of *Mather* v. *Ney*[29] had not occurred, in which the woman from a mere idle and romantic frolic insisted on having her banns put up in the name of Wright, to which she had no sort of pretension. Such a publication, whether fraudulently intended or not, operates as a fraud and is therefore held to invalidate a marriage.[30]

The same principles applied where the discrepancy in names was thought to 'disguise the name and confound the identity, nearly as much as a total variation would do'.[31] The suggestion that no fraudulent intent was necessary should be read in the light of this construction rather than taken as evidence that marriages would be invalidated even where the mistake was accidental.[32]

It is difficult to think of innocent reasons for choosing to marry in a completely false name, and few grooms matched James Farquharson for duplicity. He was courting two women and married one by the name of the other so that the marriage could be concealed from their respective parents.[33] The marriage was held to be void upon the wife's suit for nullity. The reaction of the jilted woman whose name had been published in the banns is not

[28] *Sullivan* v. *Sullivan (falsely called Oldacre)* (1818) 2 Hag. Con. 238; 161 ER 728.

[29] (1807) 3 M & S 265n; 105 ER 610.

[30] *Sullivan* v. *Sullivan*, at 254. See also *Wilson* v. *Brockley* (1810) 1 Phill. Ecc. 132; 161 ER 937.

[31] *Sullivan* v. *Sullivan*, at 255.

[32] See e.g., *Wakefield* v. *Mackay* (1807) SC 1 Hag. Con. 394; 161 ER 937n, in which Sir William Scott noted that the court had annulled marriages where a false name had been inserted, even though no fraud had been intended. He did not cite any cases to support this, although he may have been thinking of *Mather* v. *Ney*, decided in the same year.

[33] *Stayte, otherwise Farquharson* v. *Farquharson* (1826) 3 Add. 282; 162 ER 483.

recorded. Another deliberate case of fraud involved the bigamous Thomas Henry: in this case the fact that he had changed his name to Charles was less critical than the fact that he was already married.[34]

By contrast, where the variation of the name was less significant, the court would allow an explanation of the discrepancy to be put forward, recognising that such variations might occur 'not only from fraud, but from negligence, accident, error from unsettled orthography or other causes consistent with honesty of purpose'.[35] Such allowances were important at a time when literacy was far from universal, and pronunciation far from homogeneous. If the explanation implied that the variation had been made for fraudulent purposes, 'that fraud will decide any doubt concerning the sufficiency of the name to disguise the party'.[36] However, if a credible explanation of an innocent mistake was offered 'the Court will decide for the explanation and against the sufficiency of the variation to operate as a disguise where no such effect was intended'.[37] Thus in *Dobbyn* v. *Corneck*[38] a robust approach was taken to the allegations that the husband had been married under the name Dobbyns, and that an additional Christian name had been added to the wife's name. It was thought impossible that any person present could have been misled by these discrepancies.[39] This is all a far cry from the general assumption among later commentators that a trivial and accidental mistake could invalidate a marriage.

This raises the question as to the circumstances in which the court would hold that the parties *had* been fraudulent. One relevant factor was whether the parties had had the consent of their parents. While only parental dissent that had been voiced during the calling of the banns would invalidate the marriage, the fact that a parent or guardian was seeking to annul a marriage might raise the inference that a variation in the names of the parties had been intended to conceal the marriage and frustrate the purposes of the Act. In

[34] *Wyatt* v. *Henry* (1817) 2 Hag. Con. 215; 161 ER 720. [35] *Ibid.* at 255.

[36] *Ibid.* See e.g., *Fellowes* v. *Stewart* (1815) 2 Phill. Ecc. 257; 161 ER 1136.

[37] *Ibid.* at 256. [38] (1813) 2 Phill. Ecc. 102; 161 ER 1090.

[39] By contrast, the son of the Earl of Harrington was clearly trying to conceal his marriage when he caused the banns to be called in his third name of Edward, by which he was never known, and disguised himself as a labourer: *Stanhope* v. *Baldwin* (1822) 1 Add. 93; 162 ER 33.

Meddowcroft v. *Gregory*,[40] for example, a suit brought by the father of the husband, then a minor, the banns had been read in the name of Widowcroft, rather than Meddowcroft. The husband's argument that it was unlikely that this had deceived anyone, as his relations would have been unlikely to attend the distant church in which the marriage had been celebrated, did not find favour with the court. The concealment of the marriage in this way was 'the very effect which it is the object and the policy of the Act to prevent'.[41] The marriage was held to be void.[42] By contrast, in *Mayhew* v. *Mayhew*, where the bride had achieved her majority, the court held that there was no-one on whom fraud could operate and upheld the marriage.[43]

A strict approach to the letter of the law in such cases is perfectly consistent with a generally more purposive interpretation of the Act. But these strict decisions should be contrasted with that in *Sullivan* v. *Sullivan*,[44] which also involved the addition of a middle name, a marriage in a parish to which neither belonged, and a suit for nullity brought by the father of the groom. The court thought that the variation did not confound the identity of the bride and pointed out that if the parties had had a fraudulent intention they would have concealed the bridegroom's name, rather than the bride's, as it was his father who disapproved of the match, while the bride's parents actually attended the wedding.[45] The marriage was upheld.

The willingness of the courts to find that small but deliberate differences might invalidate the marriage where the father of one of the parties was responsible for bringing the suit for nullity contrasted sharply with their approach where the marriage was

[40] (1816) 2 Hag. Con. 207; 161 ER 717. [41] *Ibid.* at 213.

[42] The fraudulent intention of the parties in *Green, falsely called Dalton* v. *Dalton* (1822) 1 Add. 289; 162 ER 101 was less obvious, but the court may have been swayed by the lack of parental consent and the fact that the parties had been married in a parish to which neither belonged. See also *R* v. *Longley* (1794) 1 Phill. Ecc. 148n; 161 ER 943.

[43] (1812) 3 M & S 266n; 105 ER 611. The case can be distinguished from that of Ann Nicholson in *Frankland* v. *Nicolson*, discussed above, on the basis that here the husband was apparently aware of all the facts.

[44] (1818) 2 Hag. Con. 238; 161 ER 728.

[45] See also *Tree* v. *Quin* (1812) 3 M & S 266n; 105 ER 611, a case brought by the bride's father on the basis of undue publication of banns (in this case the insertion of a middle name). The court admitted the libel but delayed a decision until evidence of fraud had been adduced. In the event, no further proceedings were taken.

challenged by one of the parties themselves, especially if the marriage had subsisted for a considerable time. One contemporary noted the more relaxed approach of the court 'in cases wherein, (from a continued cohabitation, from there being no disparity in the ages or conditions of the parties, and from the presumptive consent of parents) all circumstances of fraud and clandestinity have been negatived'.[46] *Diddear* v. *Faucit*[47] was one such long-standing union. In this case one of the wife's Christian names had been omitted and there was uncertainty as to the true surname of the husband, an actor. The difference between 'Saville' (the name used) and 'Faucit' (the name by which he was apparently known) might be thought to be sufficiently clear to confound the identity of the groom but the court held that it was not satisfied that he was universally known by the latter name. The lack of parental approval at the time of the marriage may have made these variations tactical, but the parents had ultimately been reconciled to the marriage and had received him into the family. Sixteen years later, when the wife instituted a suit to annul the marriage, Sir William Scott stated that the length of the relationship meant that everything would be presumed in favour of it that could not be explicitly proved against it. The marriage was upheld.[48] Even where the marriage was relatively short – in *Dobbyn* v. *Corneck*,[49] less than two years elapsed between the wedding and the husband's suit for nullity – the courts were reluctant to let one of the parties plead its invalidity.

In addition to parental views and the identity of the person seeking to annul the marriage, a third factor that might affect the decision of the court was the suitability of the match. If there was no disparity between the parties in terms of age or condition, the court did not encourage the suit.[50] By contrast, differences in class and age clearly attracted the disapproval of the

[46] T. Poynter, *A Concise View of the Doctrine and Practice of the Ecclesiastical Courts in Doctors' Commons, relative to the subject of Marriage and Divorce*, 2nd edn (London: J. & W. T. Clarke, 1824), p. 32.

[47] (1821) 3 Phill. Ecc. 580; 161 ER 1421.

[48] See also *Heffer* v. *Heffer* (1812) 3 M & S 265n; 105 ER 611, at 266, in which Sir William Scott held that 'the court would be very unwilling to question the validity of the marriage after the long cohabitation of the parties'.

[49] (1813) 2 Phill. Ecc. 102; 161 ER 1090.

[50] See e.g., *Dobbyn* v. *Corneck* (1813) 2 Phill. Ecc. 102; 161 ER 1090.

court.[51] It was generally thought desirable that a wife should be younger than her husband: in *Sullivan* v. *Sullivan* the fact that a wife was two years older than her husband was noted but described as 'no very revolting disproportion',[52] especially since the husband was mature for his age. Sir William Scott went on to speculate that a disparity of rank and condition might prevent 'that correspondence and harmony of mind, without which the comfort of a married life cannot exist' but suggested that marriage would level such differences and the wife was 'of an age susceptible of better impressions'.[53]

The emphasis on suitability required that the parties should have had an opportunity to acquaint themselves with each other. Accordingly, an associated factor was whether the use of the false name may have misled one of the parties about the other.[54] In one case it was assumed the extra names had been inserted to prevent the bride from finding out that the groom was not, as he had pretended, the heir of the Earl of Moray but rather the son of a man who kept a vintner's cellar.[55] The disappointed bride succeeded in her attempt to annul the marriage.[56]

In short, the ecclesiastical courts were trying to achieve two different aims: on the one hand, to plug the loophole in the Act that allowed minor couples to marry by banns in a parish to which they did not belong and so evade parental notice; on the other, to

[51] See e.g., *Pouget* v. *Tomkins* (1812) 2 Hag. Con. 142; 161 ER 695; *Meddowcroft* v. *Gregory* (1816) 2 Hag. Con. 207; 161 ER 717 (attempted marriage of a minor to a thirty-year-old widow). The sequel to the latter case shows that the balance of power in the relationship was not as it might at first appear: the 'wife' was apparently persuaded not to contest the case upon being offered the (somewhat contradictory) inducements of a continuing pension from her first husband and Meddowcroft's promise that he would marry her again if the marriage were to be declared void. The latter promise was not fulfilled, and their son's claim to an interest in his father's estate failed: *Meddowcroft* v. *Huguenin* (1842) 3 Curt. 403; 163 ER 771.

[52] (1818) 2 Hag. Con. 238; 161 ER 728, at 244. [53] *Ibid.* at 246.

[54] See e.g., the settlement case of *R* v. *The Inhabitants of Burton-upon-Trent* (1815) 3 M & S 537; 105 ER 712, in which the husband's name had been assumed sixteen weeks before the wedding to conceal his desertion from the army. The marriage was upheld as there had been no intention to impose on the wife. Contrast *Frankland* v. *Nicolson* (1805) 3 M & S 259n.

[55] *Fellowes* v. *Stewart* (1815) 2 Phill. Ecc. 257; 161 ER 1136.

[56] An analogy may be drawn with contemporary cases on breach of promise, which recognised material misrepresentations as a defence: *Wharton* v. *Lewis* (1824) 1 C & P 529; 171 ER 1303.

ensure that the parties themselves could not rely on minor defects to escape from a no-longer-desired marriage. The approach developed by the courts could not invalidate marriages where the banns had been called in the true names of the parties, however fraudulent their intention in choosing to marry in a distant parish, but it did at least enable the more egregious evasions of the law to be punished with annulment. The courts were more successful in their second aim: although judges showed sympathy to those who had entered into a marriage on account of the other party using a false name,[57] there were no other successful petitions for annulment instigated by the parties themselves.[58]

MARRIAGES BY LICENCE

> [I]t is necessary to prove the negative of consent, together with the other circumstances relied on, in the strongest terms.[59]

The rules relating to marriages by licence were rather different. The court had no discretion to uphold a marriage by licence where it was proved that, first, one of the parties was under-age at the time that it was celebrated and, secondly, that parental consent had not been given.[60] Such a marriage was void however close the minor had been to the age of twenty-one and however long the marriage had subsisted in fact.[61] However, both age and lack of consent had to be proved, and the strictness of the proof required obviously affected the likelihood that the marriage would be held to be valid. Moreover, consent was not defined in the Act, and thus some latitude was allowed to the court in determining this issue.

[57] See e.g., *Frankland* v. *Nicolson* (1805) 3 M & S 259n; 105 ER 607; *Fellowes* v. *Stewart* (1815) 2 Phill. Ecc. 257; 161 ER 1136.

[58] Nor did assuming a false name for a second marriage protect an individual from a conviction for bigamy: see *R* v. *Allison* (1806) Russ. & Ry. 109; 168 ER 709.

[59] *Days, falsely called Jarvis* v. *Jarvis* (1814) 2 Hagg. CR 172, 161 ER 705, at 173.

[60] It should, however, be noted that, in contrast to marriages by banns, the fact that the true names were not used did not affect the validity of a marriage by licence: see e.g., *Cope* v. *Burt* (1809) 1 Hag. Con. 434; 161 ER 608; *Ewing, falsely called Wheatley* v. *Wheatley* (1814) 2 Hag. Con. 175; 161 ER 706; *Cockburn* v. *Garnault* (1792) 1 Hag. Con. 435n; 161 ER 608.

[61] See e.g., *Jones, falsely called Robinson* v. *Robinson* (1815) 2 Phill. Ecc. 285; 161 ER 1146 (sixteen-year marriage); *Johnston* v. *Parker, falsely called Johnston* (1819) 3 Phill. Ecc. 39; 161 ER 1251 (twenty-two-year marriage and seven children).

Proving that one party was not of age

The first issue was whether both parties were of age – i.e., twenty-one or over – when they married. The court tended to lean in favour of finding that the parties were of age when they married if this was at all possible on the evidence before it. There had to be very clear evidence that the parties were not of age at the time of the marriage. Thus, in one case it was held that the wife had not succeeded in proving her minority (which was in any case no more than a matter of seventeen days) as there were contradictory declarations as to the time of her birth.[62] In another, the court found several reasons for not relying on the evidence from the family bible that the wife was four months under-age at the time of the wedding.[63] Her father had been away at sea at the time of her birth and had copied the date of birth from another bible that had subsequently been lost. The court noted a later mistake that had been erased and corrected, holding that this showed 'how little reliance is to be placed on a transcript made by ignorant persons of this kind'[64] and opined that many people, especially among the lower class, mistake the year in which they or their children were born. This approach meant that where the parties were only slightly under-age at the time of the marriage, it was possible that the available evidence might be dismissed as ambiguous and the marriage upheld.[65]

Proving that the wrong person had given consent

Should it be decided that either of the parties to the marriage had not been of age at the time of the wedding, the second issue to be determined was whether parental consent had been given. One of the problems that faced minors who wished to marry by licence was the question of who should give consent. The court had no discretion to alter the strict hierarchy of persons who were able to give

[62] *Hodgkinson* v. *Wilkie* (1795) 1 Hag. Con. 262; 161 ER 946.

[63] *Agg* v. *Davies* (1816) 2 Phill. Ecc. 341; 161 ER 1164. [64] *Ibid*. at 347.

[65] See also the discussion in *Osborn* v. *Goldham* (1808) 1 Phill. Ecc. 298n; 161 ER 990. Of course, there were also cases where the parties marrying were so far from attaining the age of twenty-one, or where clear evidence of age was available, that this approach was not possible: see e.g., *Droney, falsely called Archer* v. *Archer* (1815) 2 Phill. Ecc. 327; 161 ER 1159 (evidence of family); *Johnston* v. *Parker, falsely called Johnston* (1819) 3 Phill. Ecc. 39; 161 ER 1251 (birth certificate).

consent[66] and as a consequence a number of marriages were invalidated simply because the wrong person had done so. For example, the Act had stipulated that testamentary guardians should be 'lawfully appointed',[67] and the invalidity of a will would mean that the consent of the guardians appointed by that will was null – and therefore so was the marriage.[68] Consent given by the mother during the lifetime of the father was of no effect, which led to a seemingly harsh decision in *Hayes* v. *Watts*.[69] In this case the father had emigrated to America before the marriage, and was presumed dead. The mother gave her consent to the marriage. The father then returned to England, alive and well. His daughter's marriage was annulled after it had lasted for eighteen years – but before condemning the provisions of the Act it should be noted that she herself brought the action to annul it.

More complicated still was the situation in *Robinson* v. *Dickenson*.[70] The bride, still under-age, was the reputed illegitimate daughter of a gentleman, and the marriage accordingly took place with the consent of guardians appointed by the Court of Chancery. It was later discovered that her mother had been married (to a different man) at the time of the birth. Since the law presumed that the husband was the father of any child born within the marriage, it was assumed that this was the person whose consent to the marriage was technically required, and that the marriage was therefore void. In this case the story had a happy ending: the parties went through a second, valid ceremony, and the case only came to court because of a question about the validity of the marriage settlement.

While the court could not alter the statute, its approach to findings of fact could be designed to avoid harsh results. In *Osborn* v. *Goldham*[71] the wife brought an action to annul her marriage of twelve years' standing on the basis that her mother, having remarried, was not competent to consent. The court was not keen to agree. Sir William Wynne noted that it was 'not the intent of the Act to annul a marriage of this kind'[72] and managed to uphold it on the basis that the mother's remarriage was not valid and that she was thus eligible to consent (what the mother thought

66 See further Chapter 6. 67 Section 11.
68 *Reddall* v. *Leddiard* (1820) 3 Phill. Ecc. 256; 161 ER 1318.
69 *Hayes, falsely called Watts* v. *Watts* (1819) 3 Phill. Ecc. 43; 161 ER 1252.
70 (1828) 3 Russ. 399; 38 ER 625. 71 (1808) 1 Phill. Ecc. 298n; 161 ER 990.
72 *Ibid.* at 298n.

of this is not recorded!). In the absence of a father, a testamentary guardian was entitled to give consent to the marriage of a legitimate minor, and clear evidence that such a person had not been appointed would be required before the court would hold the marriage to be void.[73]

As noted in Chapter 6, by the end of the eighteenth century it had been decided that the parents of an illegitimate minor could not consent to their child's marriage. But despite one or two hard cases, it is unlikely that this rule invalidated many marriages. Given the popularity of marriages by banns, especially among the poorer classes, only a few illegitimate minors would have been affected. Moreover, the court was reluctant to decide that a child was in fact illegitimate: in *Fielder* v. *Smith*, for example, Sir William Scott assumed that the wife was legitimate on the basis that it would need the 'strongest attainable evidence' to show that the wife's parents were living in unlawful cohabitation.[74] Despite the evidence of two witnesses that the father's former wife was still alive and the lack of any register relating to the marriage between the father and the mother, it was concluded that the parents had been married, and that a valid consent had therefore been given to the wife's marriage. This is perhaps difficult to square with the court's somewhat cavalier approach to the marriage of the mother in *Osborn* v. *Goldham*, but the two cases can be reconciled on the basis that the evidence was construed in the way most favourable to the validity of the marriage under challenge.

Proving that consent had not been given

The question of what constituted consent was rather more malleable than that of the age of the parties or the decision as to who was entitled to give that consent.[75] Since the onus of proof was on the party who wished to show that the marriage was void, it was necessary to prove that the necessary person had not actually given

[73] See e.g., *Days* v. *Jarvis* (1814) 2 Hagg. CR 172; 161 ER 705, in which Sir William Scott ordered that a due search be made for the father's will to ensure that no guardian had been appointed. See also *Clarke, falsely called Hankin* v. *Hankin* (1814) 2 Phill. Ecc. 331; 161 ER 1160n.

[74] (1816) 2 Hag. Con. 193; 161 ER 712, at 195.

[75] Had the initial draft of the Bill been passed, such flexibility would not have existed: see Chapter 6.

consent to the marriage in order to invalidate it. Sir William Scott emphasised that 'it is necessary to prove the negative of consent, together with the other circumstances relied on, in the strongest terms'.[76] This task was rendered all the more difficult by the generous concept of consent, which did not have to be expressly stated. Nor did consent have to be given to a marriage at a particular place or time: general approval of the match would suffice.[77] The court was even willing to infer consent from conduct:

> Where the courtship has been known and not prohibited, and *a fortiori*, where it has been countenanced and encouraged, the law must and ought to presume that the party was consentient, and had given that sort of consent which the law requires. Such conduct is equivalent to saying 'Get your marriage solemnized whenever you please, I have no objection, I consent'.[78]

In that case Henry Smith was seeking an annulment after four years of marriage on the basis that his wife had been under-age and her father had not consented. However, there was evidence that there had been a twelve-month courtship, during which period he had visited Afra Huson at her father's house. Henry himself had obtained the licence swearing that Afra, then only seventeen, was of age, his intention being to avoid the calling of banns so that he could conceal the marriage from his friends until he was established in business. The father had since died, but his widow gave evidence that he would not have allowed Smith to visit if he had not thought that his intentions were honourable, and that he had wanted Smith to marry his daughter. Afra's sister also gave evidence that her father had said that he would not oppose his daughters' inclinations in point of a husband. It is possible that this was simply a matter of the family closing ranks against Henry and fabricating evidence, but the court declared that where the person whose consent would have been necessary had since died, it would be willing to presume that the deceased had given consent. After all, it was up to the person impugning the marriage to show lack of consent, not for those defending it to show that consent

[76] *Days, falsely called Jarvis* v. *Jarvis* (1814) 2 Hagg. CR 172; 161 ER 705. See also *Cresswell* v. *Cosins, by her guardian, falsely calling herself Cresswell* (1815) 2 Phill. Ecc. 281; 161 ER 1145.

[77] *Selby* v. *Selby* (1771) and *Stoney* v. *Terry* (1771), cited in *Smith* v. *Huson, falsely called Smith* (1811) 1 Phill. Ecc. 287; 161 ER 987. See also *Hodgkinson* v. *Wilkie* (1795) 1 Hag. Con. 262; 161 ER 546 (match initially had mother's approbation).

[78] *Smith* v. *Huson, falsely called Smith* (1811) 1 Phill. Ecc. 287; 161 ER 987, at 299.

had been given. As with the cases on banns, the fact that there was no disparity in the social status of the parties (she was the daughter of a plumber, he the shopman to a grocer) was noted by the court and may have influenced its decision to uphold their marriage.

Conduct indicating consent could even include disapproval short of active prohibition: in one case, where the father of the bride had expressly disapproved of the wedding, the court pointed out that he had not ordered the connection to be broken off. It also noted that his objection had been based on the disapproval of the groom's father and speculated that he may have told his prospective son-in-law that he would not object if the latter could get the consent of his friends. The case was ultimately decided on the basis that the wife was of age, but illustrates the extent to which the courts were willing to presume that consent had been given.[79]

Moreover, despite the clear wording of the Act, it was held that it was not even necessary that consent should precede the wedding. *Post facto* acquiescence would be sufficient. Thus, in *Osborn* v. *Goldham* the mother expressed surprise but not disapproval when she learned of her daughter's marriage, and her acquiescence in that marriage was inferred from the fact that she went to live with the couple.[80] Once again, the approach of the courts was consistent with a purposive approach to the 1753 Act, which ensured that the types of marriages that the legislature had been so keen to prevent would be void, while at the same time marriages that were accepted by the families would not be rendered vulnerable by too strict an insistence on the formal requirements. As one contemporary commentator noted, 'so strictly was this proof of non-consent insisted on, that the Courts have almost gone the length of requiring proof of an actual dissent, presuming (in virtue of the general presumption in favour of marriage) that due consent had been had, until the contrary was shown'.[81] Thus, a marriage would only be void for lack of parental consent where it could be proved by clear and convincing evidence that the parents had ordered the connection to be broken off, or where they had no knowledge of the intended marriage until it had taken place and then did not acquiesce in it. This greatly reduced the likelihood that a nullity suit would

[79] *Agg* v. *Davies, falsely calling herself Agg* (1816) 2 Phill. Ecc. 341; 161 ER 1164.
[80] (1808) 1 Phill. Ecc. 298n; 161 ER 990. [81] Poynter, *A Concise View*, p. 65.

succeed, although, inevitably, there were some cases in which the evidence was so clear-cut that the marriage had to be annulled.[82]

It must be remembered, however, that there was one context in which the invalidity of a marriage was a positive advantage, namely where an individual would otherwise risk a criminal prosecution for bigamy. In contrast to the ecclesiastical court's approach of finding marriages valid if at all possible, the criminal courts held marriages to be *void* if at all possible where this would ensure the defendant being acquitted of the crime of bigamy. Once the defendant had shown that he or she was under-age at the time of the wedding, that the marriage was by licence, and there was no record of parental consent, the burden of proof shifted to the prosecutor to show that the licence had been duly obtained.[83] In *R* v. *James*,[84] for example, it was decided that the absence of any statement in the register that the under-age groom's father had consented, together with the fact that his parents were not known ever to have visited England, was *prima facie* evidence that the marriage was had without consent; although, of course, while the absence of the groom's parents may have made a secret marriage easier, it did not necessarily denote the absence of consent. Their absence from the country would also have made it difficult for the prosecutor to show the 'subsequent countenance' of the match that might afford grounds for presuming that consent had been given.[85] James' first marriage was therefore held to be void and he was acquitted.

Overall, then, the approach of the courts was consistent with the Act's aim of preventing clandestine marriages. Marriages that had clearly been celebrated in defiance of the provisions of the Act, or which represented the type of marriages that the Act was trying to prevent, were more likely to be invalidated than those where the mistake appeared to have been accidental and the parties were well-matched in terms of age and social station. The desire to channel marriages into a standard form was tempered by a more purposive approach. As one contemporary noted, '[t]he principles applied by

[82] See e.g., *Turner* v. *Felton* (1812) 2 Phill. Ecc. 92; 161 ER 1088; *Days* v. *Jarvis* (1814) 2 Hagg. CR 172; 161 ER 705; *Clarke, falsely called Hankin* v. *Hankin* (1814) 2 Phill Ecc 331; 161 ER 1160n.

[83] *R* v. *Thomas Morton* (1789) Russ. & Ry. 17; 168 ER 661n.

[84] (1802) Russ. & Ry. 17; 168 ER 660.

[85] *R* v. *Charles Butler* (1803) Russ. & Ry. 61; 168 ER 683.

the ecclesiastical courts ... seem to have proceeded rather upon views of natural equity than upon a strict interpretation of the statute'.[86]

But even the most purposive judicial interpretation could neither ensure that every marriage that flouted the spirit of the Act was annulled, nor prevent individuals from exploiting the legislation to free themselves from their own marriages. For that, more fundamental reform was needed.

REDUCING THE SCOPE FOR CHALLENGES

Had the effects of the 1753 Act been as drastic as has sometimes been claimed, it is rather surprising that it was not until the nineteenth century that any serious attempts were made to change the law. There had, of course, been earlier attempts to repeal the Act, but the arguments for reform were characterised more by rhetoric than by the identification of specific problems.[87] Those who had argued for reform in the 1760s, 1770s, and 1780s had not suggested that minors were evading the controls laid down by the Act by marrying by banns, or that the terms of the legislation were being exploited by individuals as a means of self-divorce.[88]

If the volume of litigation is anything to go by, both problems – evasion of the law by minors, and attempts by those who later regretted their choice to undo marriages – increased in the early decades of the nineteenth century.[89] While the discussion of

86 E. Jacob, 'Addenda No. 1' to R. S. Donnison Roper, *A Treatise on the Law of Property Arising from the Relation between Husband and Wife*, 2nd edn (London: Butterworth & Son, 1826).

87 See Chapter 6.

88 On these earlier attempts at reform, see R. B. Outhwaite, *Clandestine Marriage in England, 1500–1850* (London: Hambledon Press, 1995), pp. 112–16. Charles James Fox introduced Bills to repeal the Act in both 1772 and 1781, but his commitment to this cause apparently did not extent to reading the Act before pressing for its repeal and his biographer suggests that he found the racing at Newmarket so engrossing that he missed part of the debate on his own Bill: see S. Ayling, *Fox: the Life of Charles James Fox* (London: John Murray, 1991), p. 36.

89 However, the claim made by both Stone, *Road to Divorce*, p. 132, and Outhwaite, *Clandestine Marriage*, p. 154, that sixty marriages were annulled by the London Consistory Court and the Court of Arches between 1810 and 1822 is somewhat misleading. It is based on a misunderstanding of Dr Phillimore's statement to Parliament in 1822 that since 1810 'at least forty cases of nullity of marriage on account of lack of consent have been decided in the Consistory Court of London and at least twenty in the Arches Court' (*Hansard*, 2nd Series, vol. 6, col. 1342, 27 March 1822). Two points should be made: first, the fact that a case was decided does not mean that the marriage was annulled, and, secondly, since the Court of

the case law is inevitably skewed by the availability of reported cases,[90] the other records of the Court of Arches and the London Consistory Court confirm that there was far less litigation on this point in the eighteenth century.[91] In the Court of Arches, for example, before 1800 only six suits for nullity had alleged that a minor had married by licence without parental consent, while eight such cases were brought between 1800 and 1810 and seventeen between 1811 and 1820.[92]

A number of trends may have contributed to the increased number of cases of nullity at the start of the nineteenth century. There is evidence to suggest that there was an eagerness to comply with the 1753 Act in the early decades of its operation, which had slackened by the 1780s.[93] Clergymen may have been more zealous in checking the details of the banns or licence in the immediate wake of the Act, with the result that there were fewer marriages that could later be avoided because the incorrect name or age had been given. In addition, urbanisation and population growth made it more likely that some ministers would have no real knowledge of their parishioners (and therefore would be unable to spot any

Arches was the appellate court for the London Consistory Court, many of the twenty cases heard there would have been appeals from the forty decided in the lower court (as Stone himself noted in a different context, the London Consistory Court supplied between one-quarter and one-half of the cases going to the Arches). Phillimore's point that other ecclesiastical courts across the country would also have been dealing with such cases is a valid one, but at this time most cases were heard in London.

90 There are a few reported cases from the 1750s, but apart from these decisions the ecclesiastical courts were not fully reported until the 1790s. The information that is available does suggest, however, that a similarly purposive interpretation operated in the earlier cases: see e.g., *Selby* v. *Selby* (1771) and *Stoney* v. *Terry* (1771), discussed in *Smith* v. *Huson, falsely called Smith* (1811) 1 Phill. Ecc. 287; 161 ER 987.

91 For the London Consistory Court, see *Royal Commission to inquire into the Practice and Jurisdiction of the Ecclesiastical Courts in England and Wales* (1831–2), Appendix C, Part II, p. 379. See also Stone, *Road to Divorce*, Table 1.8.

92 J. Houston, *Index of Cases in the Records of the Court of Arches at Lambeth Palace Library 1660–1913* (London: British Record Society, 1972). Of these six, the earliest dates from 1774: *Price* v. *Stone* (1774) Lambeth Palace Library (LPL) Aa 69/2; *Davies* v. *Battishill* (1777) LPL Aa 72/6; *Perkins* v. *Perkins* (1778) LPL Aa 73/13; *Smyth* v. *Wright* (1781) LPL Aa 76/4; *Dobree* v. *Bushnell* (1784) LPL B18/78; *Cockburn, falsely called Garnault* v. *Garnault* (1793) LPL Aa 87/14.

93 See W. Edwards, 'National Marriage Data: a Re-Aggregation of John Rickman's Marriage Returns' (1976) 17 *Local Population Studies* 25. This eagerness to comply is inferred from the degree of inaccuracy in the parish registers during this period: in the 1750s and 1760s, the degree of inaccuracy is only 5 per cent, but it rises to over 10 per cent in the 1780s.

errors or omissions). And, as identified in the previous chapter, changing social conditions made it easier to travel to, and marry in, a parish where one was not known.

Demographic trends may also have contributed to the increase in the number of cases.[94] Increasing longevity and earlier marriage meant that in the second half of the eighteenth century the majority of parents survived to see the marriages of their children.[95] It has been estimated that only 12 per cent of children born in 1741 would have lost both parents by the age of twenty-five,[96] while the age at first marriage fell throughout the course of the eighteenth century, from an average of 27.6 for men and 26.9 for women in the first quarter to 26.1 and 24.7 in the final quarter.[97] But this varied according to class. Within the peerage, men were likely to marry later, and women earlier: Hollingsworth, for example, calculated the median age at first marriage of those who actually married to be around thirty years for aristocratic men, and just under twenty-three years for the cohort of aristocratic women born 1725–74.[98] The likelihood of parental death would also have varied according to the class of the parties: longevity was greater amongst the upper classes.[99] Moreover, the likelihood that a dying father would appoint

[94] See R. Probert, 'Control over Marriage in England and Wales, 1753–1823: the Clandestine Marriages Act of 1753 in Context' (2009) 27 *Law and History Review* 413.

[95] L. Stone and J. C. Fawtier Stone, *An Open Elite? England 1540–1880* (Oxford: Clarendon Press, 1984), Fig. 3.10; D. Levine, '"For their Own Reasons?" Individual Marriage Decisions and Family Life' (1982) 7 *Journal of Family History* 255, 258.

[96] It is estimated that 36 per cent would have lost their father and 34 per cent their mother: see M. Anderson, 'The Social Implications of Demographic Change', ch. 1 in F. M. L. Thompson (ed.), *The Cambridge Social History of Britain 1750–1950*, vol. II, *People and their Environment* (Cambridge University Press, 1990), Table 1.5.

[97] E. A. Wrigley, 'Marriage, Fertility and Population Growth in Eighteenth-Century England', ch. 7 in Outhwaite, *Marriage and Society*, Table III. For regional variations see D. Levine, *Family Formation in an Age of Nascent Capitalism* (London: Academic Press, 1977), Tables 5.1 and 6.6.

[98] T. H. Hollingsworth, 'Marriage' (1964) *Population Studies: Supplement 18* 8, 25, Table 17. I have chosen to cite the figures for those who did marry, rather than those for the aristocracy as a whole, because the proportion never marrying was significantly higher within the aristocracy than in the general population: contrast Hollingsworth, Table 11, and E. A. Wrigley and R. S. Schofield, *The Population History of England 1541–1871: a Reconstruction* (Cambridge University Press, 1989), Table 7.28. N. Rogers, 'Money, Marriage, Mobility: the Big Bourgeoisie of Hanoverian London' (1999) 24 *Journal of Family History* 19 similarly found that late marriage was common within his sample of London businessmen.

[99] T. H. Hollingsworth, 'Mortality' (1964) *Population Studies: Supplement 18* 52.

a guardian whose consent was required would also have varied according to the class of the parties. A final factor was that more couples were choosing to marry by licence;[100] again, of course, this was more likely among those of higher status.[101] These factors combined would increase the number of cases that would potentially be vulnerable to challenge in the absence of parental consent.

It is also possible that the desire to take advantage of such defects increased. At a time when divorce was only available by means of a private Act of Parliament, a suit for nullity offered the only judicial means by which the parties to a marriage could be freed to (re)marry, and it is unsurprising that some couples sought to take advantage of this. From this perspective, the rise in the number of suits after 1810 could simply indicate a general increase in the number of individuals wishing to leave unsatisfactory marriages:[102] it is significant that the increase in the number of nullity suits instigated by the parties themselves coincided with an increase in the number of suits for separation.[103]

The inference that the increase in the case law was the product of external changes, rather than any inherent defects of the Act, is supported by the fact that it was only in the early nineteenth century that serious attempts were made to change the law. It is clear from the Bills that were introduced into Parliament in the early decades of the nineteenth century that both the laxity of marriages by banns and the potential invalidity of marriages of minors by licence where the appropriate consent had not been given were being perceived as a problem. A Bill introduced in March 1812 initially dealt only with the issues of authorising the publication of banns in consecrated places of worship and consent to the marriage

[100] There was a sharp rise in the number of licences granted after 1795: *Vicar-General Marriage Licences Surname Index* (London: Society of Genealogists, 1996).

[101] V. Elliott, 'Marriage Licences and the Local Historian' (1973) 10 *Local Historian* 282, 288.

[102] According to Dr Phillimore, one opportunistic husband instituted proceedings after reading about other successful cases in the newspapers: *Hansard*, vol. 40, col. 1466, 24 April 1819.

[103] Forty such suits were brought before the Court of Arches in 1800–10, and seventy in the following decade: Stone, *Road to Divorce*, Table 1.3, and see also p. 40. See generally V. Murray, *High Society in the Regency Period, 1788–1830* (Penguin, 1998), ch. 7 on the prevalence of and attitudes towards adultery in this period.

of an illegitimate minor,[104] but a subsequent version put forward in May of that year recited the 'evils' arising when marriages by licence without lawful consent were held to be void and proposed that such marriages could be confirmed by the cohabitation of the parties or the lack of any challenge to the marriage within a specified period.[105] Five years later, a further Bill set out to tighten up the law relating to banns,[106] while an 1818 Bill would have validated under-age marriages by licence that were not challenged by the parties' parents but invalidated marriages where the banns had been called in a parish to which the parties did not belong.[107] From then on the Bills considered by Parliament set out to deal with both problems.[108]

But it was easier to criticise the 1753 Act than to find a workable alternative. A number of Bills tried to impose mandatory residence requirements for marriages by banns and to uphold marriages by licence where the parties had lived together for a specified period. The difficulties of reform can be illustrated by the fact that no fewer than three pieces of legislation were passed between 1822 and 1823, with the result that for a few years the courts had to apply three different statutes, depending on precisely when the marriage had been celebrated.

The first successful attempt at reform, in 1822, focused on marriages by licence.[109] It applied retrospectively to validate marriages of minors by licence where parental consent had not been given but where the parties had continued to live together until death or the passage of the new Act. This meant that couples could no longer use nullity as a substitute for divorce. By contrast, past marriages by banns were unaffected. For future marriages, stricter

[104] A Bill to amend Act for better preventing of Clandestine Marriages (1812), House of Commons Sessional Papers, vol. I, p. 477.

[105] A Bill to amend Act for better preventing of Clandestine Marriages (1812), House of Commons Sessional Papers, vol. I, p. 481.

[106] Bill for further Regulation of Marriages to be solemnized after Publication of Banns of Matrimony (1817), House of Commons Sessional Papers, vol. II, p. 197.

[107] Bill to amend Act for better Preventing of Clandestine Marriages (1818), House of Commons Sessional Papers, vol. II, p. 95.

[108] Bill to amend Act for better Preventing of Clandestine Marriages (1819), House of Commons Sessional Papers, vol. I, p. A.349; Bill to amend Act for better Preventing of Clandestine Marriages (1820), House of Commons Sessional Papers, vol. I, p. 81.

[109] An Act to amend certain provisions of the [Act] for the better preventing of clandestine marriages, 3 Geo. 4 c. 75.

procedures were to be observed. To obtain a licence, both parties, rather than just one, were to swear that they believed there were no impediments to the marriage and that both were of age, or, if not, that parental consent had been obtained. They were also required to provide an extract from the register of baptism as proof of their age.[110] Parental consent had to be signified in writing, signed in the presence of two witnesses and describing the nature of their authority to consent to the marriage.[111] Obtaining a licence falsely was to be a felony, for which the punishment was potentially transportation for life and the forfeiture of any benefits derived from the marriage.[112] However, in a drastic reversal of the principle of the 1753 Act, it was provided that failure to comply with these processes, or the new, more stringent processes for banns,[113] would not render the marriage void.[114]

But the operation of the 1822 Act was short-lived. As Dr Phillimore ruefully noted in presenting a Bill for its repeal only a few months later, many of the oaths required of the parties had been found to be 'unnecessary and vexatious'.[115] Thus, most of its provisions were repealed in March 1823 and the principles of the 1753 Act restored for subsequent marriages.[116] The retrospective provisions of the 1822 Act continued to apply, with the result that marriages prior to 22 July 1822 were governed by the 1753 Act but could be saved by the retrospective provisions of the 1822 Act.[117] Marriages celebrated between 22 July 1822 and 26 March 1823 were

[110] Section 8. [111] Section 9. [112] Section 10.

[113] Before the banns were read, each party was required to deliver to the minister an affidavit stating their name, age, and residence (s. 16).

[114] Sections 15 (licences) and 19 (banns).

[115] It is interesting to note that the *repeal* of the 1753 Act and its replacement by the stricter 1822 Act sent more couples to marry over the border in Scotland than had previously been the case: at Annan, for example, more irregular marriages involving at least one partner from England were celebrated in 1822 and 1823 than in the previous twenty years combined: see A. Brack, 'English Marriages at Annan, Dumfrieshire, 1797–1854', Society of Genealogists, SC.G/50305.

[116] An Act to repeal certain Provisions of the Act ... intituled An Act to amend certain provisions of the [Act] for the better preventing of clandestine marriages, 4 Geo. 4 c. 17.

[117] *King* v. *Sansom, otherwise King* (1826) 3 Add. 277; 162 ER 481; *Duins* v. *Donovan* (1830) 3 Hagg. Ecc. 299; 162 ER 1165; *Poole* v. *Poole* (1831) 2 C & J 66; 149 ER 28. In *R* v. *The Inhabitants of St John Delpike* (1831) 2 B & D 226; 109 ER 1128 it was held that a marriage which would have been void under the 1753 Act but had been validated by virtue of the 1822 Act because of the parties' cohabitation should continue to be treated as valid, even though the wife had subsequently gone through a ceremony with another man.

governed by the 1822 Act, while marriages after that date were governed by the 1753 Act. The old law thus became the new law – at least for a while. The repealing Act was only a holding measure, its final clause stating that it might be amended that same session.

A few months later the Marriage Act of 1823, the third piece of legislation on this topic in two years, finally established what was to form the basis of Church of England ceremonies until the present day.[118] It retained the basic structure of the 1753 Act in requiring that a marriage be preceded by banns or a licence and celebrated in the church of the parties' parish of residence. A few minor procedural changes were made, reflecting the litigation to which the 1753 Act had given rise. The position of illegitimate minors, for example, was addressed, not by allowing their parents to consent to their marriage, but by recognising that there was no person able to consent.[119] It was specifically provided that churches built since 1754 would be able to host marriages, subject to authorisation by the bishop of the diocese, which obviated the need for *ex post facto* statutory approval.[120] But the key innovation of the 1823 Act was the provision that a marriage would only be void if the parties 'knowingly and wilfully' failed to comply with certain provisions.[121] The purpose of this was to invalidate only those marriages that involved a deliberate flouting of the rules. Moreover, not all requirements of the Act were subject to this provision. If the couple 'knowingly and wilfully' married without either a licence or the due publication of banns, outside an authorised church, or by a person who was not in holy orders, the marriage would be void.[122] If they knowingly married outside the prescribed hours of

118 An Act for amending the Laws respecting the Solemnization of Marriages in England, 4 Geo. 4 c. 76.

119 Section 14: 'if there shall be no such Person or Persons having Authority to give such Consent, then upon Oath made to that Effect by the Party requiring such Licence, it shall be lawful to grant such Licence notwithstanding the Want of any such Consent'. It was perhaps realised that there was little to be feared, and much to be gained, from allowing (almost exclusively lower-class) illegitimate minors to marry.

120 Section 3. 121 Section 22.

122 *Ibid.*: 'if any Persons shall knowingly and wilfully intermarry in any other Place than a Church, or such Public Chapel wherein Banns may be lawfully published, unless by Special Licence as aforesaid, or shall knowingly and wilfully intermarry without due Publication of Banns, or Licence from a Person or Persons having Authority to grant the same, ... or shall knowingly and wilfully consent to or acquiesce in the Solemnization of such Marriage by any Person not being in Holy orders, the Marriages of Such Persons shall be null and void to all Intents and Purposes whatsoever'.

eight a.m. to midday, the marriage would still be valid, although the celebrant would be guilty of a felony and liable to transportation for fourteen years.[123]

But how much difference did this make in practice? It was clear that under the Marriage Act 1823 an accidental failure to comply with the provisions of the Act would never have the effect of rendering the marriage void. Yet, as we have seen, under the 1753 Act the courts had been keen to avoiding annulling marriages for trivial and accidental reasons. One contemporary commentator, a proctor in Doctors' Commons, noted that it was 'difficult to anticipate any material variation', at least in the principles applied to marriages by banns, as a result of the 1823 Act.[124] This was borne out by the first cases in which it was necessary to consider the new provisions relating to banns, in which the facts were remarkably similar to those in *Pouget* v. *Tomkins*. In *Wiltshire* v. *Prince*,[125] for example, the under-age husband, who was usually known as 'Henry John', married his parents' thirty-year-old cook – it is hardly necessary to add without their consent – and was described as 'John' in the banns. The court held that there was sufficient evidence that both parties knew of the false publication of banns and avoided the marriage. Similarly, in *Tongue* v. *Allen*, a schoolboy entered into a marriage with a thirty-five-year-old widow who acted as the school housekeeper.[126] The banns were published in his first name, rather than in his middle name by which he was more usually known, 'and that this was done for the purpose of concealment and in fraud of the father's rights, there can be no doubt'.[127] It was assumed that both parties knew of the undue publication, and the marriage was held to be void, the court noting that this was 'precisely the case against which the legislature must have intended to provide'.[128] The fact that these cases were now based on statute rather than on the case law of the ecclesiastical courts should not obscure the underlying continuity in practice.[129]

[123] Section 21.

[124] Poynter, *A Concise View*, p. 43; see similarly L. Shelford, *A Practical Treatise of the Law of Marriage and Divorce and Registration* (London: S. Sweet, 1841), p. 240.

[125] (1830) 3 Hagg. Ecc. 332; 162 ER 1176. [126] (1835) 1 Curt. 38; 163 ER 13.

[127] *Ibid.* at 41. [128] *Ibid.* at 49.

[129] See further *Brealy, falsely called Reed* v. *Reed* (1841) 2 Curt. 834; 163 ER 601; *Tooth* v. *Barrow* (1854) 1 Sp. Ecc. & Add. 371; 164 ER 214.

The provisions relating to banns in the 1823 Act can be seen as a codification of what was happening in practice rather than a change in policy, and provided a more subtle way of achieving what the 1753 Act had set out to do.

The change effected by the 1823 legislation in respect of marriages by licence, however, was more dramatic. Lack of parental consent ceased altogether to be a ground for annulling a marriage by licence.[130] Not everyone was enthusiastic about the change. The same contemporary commentator observed that 'it remains for time to determine which is the greater evil – the unqualified Nullity so justly complained of, with reference to a certain class of cases under the late Marriage Act – or the positive validity, as indiscriminately conferred on marriages of the same class, by the present [Act]'.[131] But it is clear that the motivation for this reform was to close off the avenue of exploiting the law of nullity as a substitute for divorce, rather than to undermine parental control over marriage, since a new provision was introduced to provide aggrieved parents with some remedy if their children flouted their authority: the Act stipulated that a person who obtained a licence by false oaths would not be entitled to any property as a result of the marriage,[132] thereby removing the incentive for fortune-hunters to inveigle minors into secret marriages. There was, in fact, a precedent for this: if a ward of court married without the consent of the Court of Chancery, the court had the power to order a settlement of

[130] Only the absence of a licence would invalidate the marriage, and only then if the parties 'knowingly and wilfully' married without a licence: Marriage Act 1823, s. 21.

[131] Poynter, *A Concise View*, p. 1.

[132] Section 23. The provision is lengthy, so its essential points will be summarised. It applied only to the marriages of minors (widows and widowers excepted) if one party had brought about the marriage by knowingly, wilfully, and falsely 'swearing as to any Matter or Matters to which such Party is hereinbefore required personally to swear' (which included the age of the parties, parental consent, their residence, and the lack of any impediments: section 14). The minor's aggrieved parent had three months after the discovery of the marriage to inform the Attorney-General, who would then bring a suit in the Court of Chancery or the Court of Exchequer. Both courts had the power to order that the property that would have accrued for the benefit of the offending party should be settled for the benefit of the innocent party and any children of the marriage (or, if both parties were equally guilty of flouting the law, for the benefit of the children). The provision also applied to marriages by banns, although in such cases only one party, by definition, would have flouted the law, else the marriage would not be valid. See further Probert, 'Control over Marriage'.

the ward's property.[133] Extending a similar power to all cases where the marriage was by licence enhanced the deterrent effect: forfeiture of property would no longer depend on the happenstance of the minor party being a ward of court.[134] The provisions of the 1823 Act may have been different to those of the 1753 Act in certain crucial respects, but they were not necessarily more generous to young lovers chafing under parental fiats.[135]

CONCLUSION

The myth that the 1753 Act had been harsh, and that the 1823 Act had introduced new principles,[136] was quick to emerge. Dr Lushington, who became judge of the London Consistory Court in 1828, was of the opinion that there were 'striking differences' between the 1823 Act and the 1753 Act, since the latter had been intended to enforce formalities 'with the utmost vigour'.[137] As a result, it was actually after 1823 that we find the harshest decisions of the courts in the few cases that still had to be decided by reference to the 1753 Act.[138] In a number of these cases it was decided that the banns had not been duly published, even though the bride had some claim to the name used.[139] Perhaps it was more difficult to take a flexible approach applying an Act that had been reformed on the basis of its apparent harshness.

133 See e.g. *Priestly* v. *Lamb* (1801) 6 Ves. Jun. 421; 31 ER 1124; *Salles* v. *Savignon* (1801) 6 Ves. Jun. 572; 31 ER 1201; *Bathurst* v. *Murray* (1802) 8 Ves Jun 74; 32 ER 279; *Warter* v. *Yorke* (1815) 19 Ves. 451; 34 ER 584; and see generally Probert, 'Control over Marriage'.

134 See Probert, 'Control over Marriage', on the circumstances in which the Chancery Court had jurisdiction.

135 Note too the increased willingness of the courts to uphold conditions in restraint of marriage whereby those who married without the stipulated consents would forfeit the property to which they would otherwise have been entitled: see Probert, 'Control over Marriage'.

136 See e.g., Howard, *A History of Matrimonial Institutions*, p. 464: 'new and juster rules were substituted'.

137 *Dormer* v. *Williams* (1838) 1 Curt. 870; 163 ER 301.

138 By the combined effect of 3 Geo. 4 c. 75, 4 Geo. 4 c. 17 and 4 Geo. 4 c. 76, the 1753 Act continued to apply to marriages celebrated by banns before 1 September 1822, and to all marriages between 26 March 1823 and 1 October 1823.

139 *R* v. *The Inhabitants of Tibshelf* (1830) 1 B & Ad. 190; 109 ER 758 (grandfather's surname, as used in baptism); *Allen* v. *Wood* (1834) 1 Bing. (NC) 8; 131 ER 1020 (maiden name).

The 1823 Act did not, however, address all the complaints that were being voiced about the marriage law of the time. England had changed considerably in the seventy years that had elapsed since the passage of the 1753 Act, and in the early decades of the nineteenth century a new demand for reform was being put forward by those who did not subscribe to the tenets of the Church of England. How and when that demand was articulated is the subject of the next chapter.

9

THE OVERLOOKED RESPONSE OF NON-ANGLICANS

As discussed in Chapter 4, non-Anglicans were very much in the minority at the time the 1753 Act was passed, and the Church of England 'controlled something approaching a monopoly of English religious practice'.[1] Yet this period of unrivalled popularity was to be brief, as new sects sprang up in the second half of the century, and older ones attracted new adherents. Since it has been widely assumed that non-Anglicans could marry according to their own rites before 1754, the impact of the 1753 Act on such groups is often presented in stark terms. According to Gibson, for example, the Act 'forced Catholics and Dissenters to flout either the law or their consciences'.[2] Most commentators take the view that, faced with such a choice, couples preferred to comply with the law and that the requirements of the legislation were observed by all denominations, with Protestant dissenters and Catholics alike submitting to the Anglican rite.[3]

Yet there have been remarkably few studies devoted specifically to this topic, and one must be as sceptical of views that agree with one's own as of those that do not, unless and until those views are supported by clear evidence. Certainly evidence is lacking in the arguments of the few who have put forward the alternative

[1] A. D. Gilbert, *Religion and Society in Industrial England: Church, Chapel and Social Change, 1740–1914* (London: Longman, 1976), p. 27. See also W. M. Jacob, *Lay People and Religion in the Early Eighteenth Century* (Cambridge University Press, 1996), p. 19, and generally D. Spaeth, *The Church in an Age of Danger: Parsons and Parishioners 1660–1740* (Cambridge University Press, 2000).

[2] C. Gibson, *Dissolving Wedlock* (London: Routledge, 1994), p. 42.

[3] See e.g., D. J. Steel, *National Index of Parish Registers*, vol. II, *Sources for Nonconformist Genealogy and Family History* (Chichester: Phillimore & Co. Ltd, 1973), p. 552; P. E. H. Hair, 'Bridal Pregnancy in Rural England in Earlier Centuries' (1966) 20 *Population Studies* 233, 241; J. Gillis, *For Better, For Worse: British Marriages 1600 to the Present Day* (Oxford University Press, 1985).

view: O'Donovan, for example, states simply that Catholics and Dissenters 'did not conform';[4] Parker notes the existence of 3,451 dissenting chapels and speculates – his own word – that 'a large proportion of these conducted their own marriage services',[5] while Olive Stone has suggested that up to one-third of all marriages were non-Anglican and so void but provides no authority for this figure.[6] Nor, indeed, is it shown that marriage in the Church of England was antithetical to the conscience of the majority of dissenters. This chapter, by contrast, looks at the actual practices of Catholics and Protestant dissenters, and the second section shows that the view that the majority complied with the requirements of the 1753 Act is well-founded.

A further aspect of non-Anglican marriage practices in the wake of the 1753 Act that has received little consideration is the treatment of Jewish and Quaker marriages. It is true that they were exempt from the requirements of the 1753 Act, but, as noted in Chapter 6, the Act codified the existing ambiguities as to their status rather than declaring such marriages to be valid. How, then, did the courts treat Jewish and Quaker marriages that were brought to their attention? In addition, how significant was the exception in terms of the number of marriages celebrated? These questions are considered in the third part of the chapter.

Since we may learn much about the way a particular law operated in practice from the terms in which debates as to possible reforms were couched, the final section traces the evolution of the Marriage Act 1836, which finally allowed all non-Anglicans to marry according to their own religious rites, and the claims made by those arguing for reform. I then briefly examine the take-up of the new modes of marrying introduced by the 1836 Act in order to ascertain what light it may cast on previous practice. While there is inevitably a danger in projecting such evidence backwards, it can at the very least be assumed that the new legal ways of marrying would not be *less* popular than non-legal ceremonies of marriage.

First, however, we must look at the extent of dissent – a necessary preliminary to show just how far and how fast the religious

[4] K. O'Donovan, *Sexual Divisions in Law* (London: Weidenfeld & Nicholson, 1985), p. 49.

[5] S. Parker, *Informal Marriage, Cohabitation and the Law, 1750–1989* (Basingstoke: Macmillan, 1990), p. 70.

[6] O. Stone, *Family Law* (London: Macmillan Press, 1977), p. 31.

context changed, and how the virtual monopoly of the Church of England came to be challenged.

THE EXTENT OF DISSENT

Il y a en Angleterre soixante sectes religieuses différentes, et une seule sauce.[7]

The later part of the eighteenth century saw increasing diversity in religious practices as a result of industrialisation and urbanisation. Methodism, for example, 'found its most promising environment in semi-industrial communities which had outstripped the capacity of paternalistic landowners and parish clergy to cater for them'.[8] The number of its followers increased rapidly: in 1767 there were just over 20,000 Wesleyan Methodists in England, but by 1835 there were over twelve times as many, to say nothing of those who preferred the new alternatives of the Methodist New Connexion, the Bible Christians, or the Primitive Methodist Church, or indeed the Calvinistic Methodists who had been inspired by Whitefield rather than Wesley.[9]

Older sects also saw an increase in numbers. Baptists and Independents adopted the recruitment strategies of 'New Dissent' and their numbers also rose rapidly.[10] Again, new factions emerged: the General Baptist New Connexion was formed in 1770 from the more orthodox Baptists who opposed the drift towards Unitarianism. By contrast, other dissenting denominations stagnated or declined. The Moravians had played an important role in the English Revival, but their numbers remained small, since they were opposed to proselytising and rejected many applicants.[11] And Quaker numbers

[7] Attributed to the Neapolitan diplomat Francesco Caracciolo (1752–99): A. Partington, *The Oxford Dictionary of Quotations*, 4th edn (Oxford University Press, 1996).

[8] P. Langford, *A Polite and Commercial People: England 1727–1783* (Oxford: Clarendon Press, 1989), p. 252.

[9] According to R. Currie, A. Gilbert, and L. Horsley, *Churches and Churchgoers: Patterns of Church Growth in the British Isles since 1700* (Oxford: Clarendon Press, 1977), Table A3, by this date the Methodist New Connexion numbered 16,737, the Bible Christians 7,804, and the Primitive Methodist Church 56,649.

[10] Congregationalists numbered 35,000 in 1800 and 127,000 by 1838: see Currie *et al.*, *Churches and Churchgoers*, Appendices 3 and 4.

[11] C. Podmore, *The Moravian Church in England, 1728–1760* (Oxford: Clarendon Press, 1998), ch. 4.

actually fell: by the start of the nineteenth century there were fewer than 20,000.[12]

The Catholic population experienced both losses and gains in this period. Within the indigenous population, numbers continued to fall after the middle of the century: it has been estimated that there was a decline of 40 per cent between 1720 and 1780.[13] One contemporary noted how the remaining population tended to cluster around elite families: '[e]xcepting in the towns, and out of Lancashire, the chief situation of Catholics is in the neighbourhood of old families of that persuasion'.[14] The dependency of the Catholic community on the small surviving Catholic elite made it vulnerable: the conversion of an elite family 'could mean the disappearance of an entire Catholic congregation'.[15] Since Catholic peers constituted 12 per cent of the peerage at the start of the eighteenth century but only 3 per cent by its close,[16] many congregations must have been lost in this way, with a consequent impact on both numbers and marriage practices.[17] Towards the end of the century, however, the numbers of Catholics were dramatically boosted by Irish immigration.[18]

But the growth of dissent should not obscure the continuing importance of the Church of England. As Rule has stressed, the idea that religious adherence stratified along class lines – Anglican ruling elite, middle-class dissenters, working-class Methodists – is too simplistic and underplays the continuing importance of the Church of England: '[i]n all social groups most people were at least nominally Church of England. Nor was there any marked trend away from this situation of a very general conformity until the last years of the century.'[19] In some cases there was considerable

[12] E.A. Wrigley and R.S. Schofield, *The Population History of England, 1541–1871: a Reconstruction* (Cambridge University Press, 1989), p. 93. This was no more than 0.21 per cent of the population.

[13] Currie *et al.*, *Churches and Churchgoers*, p. 23.

[14] J. Berington, *The State and Behaviour of English Catholics, from the Reformation to the Year 1781* (London, 1781), p. 116.

[15] Gilbert, *Religion and Society*, p. 17

[16] J. Cannon, *Aristocratic Century* (Cambridge University Press, 1984).

[17] The presence of an elite Catholic family might enable local couples to marry according to Catholic rites, since priests could take refuge within aristocratic households: see further below.

[18] J. Bossy, *The English Catholic Community, 1570–1850* (London: Darton, Longman & Todd, 1975), ch. 13.

[19] J. Rule, *Albion's People: English Society 1714–1815* (London: Longman, 1992), p. 93.

flexibility of religious practice, with individuals attending both the church and the meeting-house.[20] In Kilsby, for example, 35 per cent of those parents who brought their children to be baptised in its Independent chapel also had children baptised in the parish church.

Even more dedicated dissenters might be induced by practical considerations to take advantage of the Church of England for such services as baptism,[21] burial,[22] and – as we shall see – marriage. Wrigley and Schofield, for example, have estimated that non-conformist baptisms were only a small percentage of Anglican baptisms in this period, rising from just over 1 per cent in the 1740s to 2.05 per cent in the 1770s, 4.63 per cent in the first decade of the nineteenth century, and 6.68 per cent by the 1830s.[23] While this was clearly sufficient to distort the accuracy of the parish register, it is equally obvious that it did not match the extent of non-conformity and that attendance at chapel was not always matched by complete withdrawal from the Church of England. If dissenters conformed when this was dictated by pragmatism, one would expect levels of conformity to be still higher when it was dictated by law.

That by 1830 the Church of England 'was on the point of becoming a minority religious Establishment'[24] merely serves to emphasise that for the period under consideration it commanded the adherence of the majority. The growth of dissent was not due to a decline in the number who attended the Church of England, but rather to the appeal of other denominations to an increasingly

20 See e.g., A. Warne, *Church and Society in Eighteenth Century Devon* (Newton Abbot: David and Charles 1969), p. 109.

21 As Hair, 'Bridal Pregnancy in Rural England', 243, had noted, there were secular advantages to an Anglican baptism: 'an entry in the parish register carried great weight in the courts and was often decisive in suits affecting property and inheritance, while applicants for employment were sometimes asked to produce baptism certificates'. And in a number of cases the courts refused to accept the registers compiled by dissenters as evidence: see e.g., *Ex parte Taylor* (1820) 1 Jac. & W 483; 37 ER 452 (copy of entry of births of dissenters' children kept at Dr Williams' library); *Whittuck* v. *Waters* (1830) 4 Car. & P 375; 172 ER 747 (register of burials of Wesleyan chapel).

22 The relative paucity of non-Anglican burial grounds forced many dissenters to seek burial in churchyards, although the Anglican clergy were not always willing to accommodate them: see e.g., *Kemp* v. *Wickes* (1809) 3 Phill. Ecc. 264; 161 ER 1320; and more generally B.L. Manning, *The Protestant Dissenting Deputies* (O. Greenwood (ed.), Cambridge University Press, 1952), Part 3, ch. 2.

23 Wrigley and Schofield, *The Population History of England*, Table 4.2.

24 Gilbert, *Religion and Society*, p. 27.

large, urban, and industrialised population.[25] As Perkin has noted, migrating workers 'moved from the countryside, where the social pressures were in favour of going to Church . . . , to a small town where the social pressures were in favour of going to chapel, or to a large one where they were against going at all'.[26] Given this diversity, it is important to examine the evidence carefully, and not to draw inferences about the behaviour of one denomination from evidence relating to another.

THE EXTENT OF CONFORMITY

Dissenters marry and Papists marry in the Church of England.[27]

This, at least, was the evaluation of one eighteenth-century judge, and the evidence suggests that he was correct in his evaluation. There were, however, important differences between different sects. Those Protestant dissenting denominations that had celebrated marriages according to their own rites prior to 1754 ceased to do so. Most, of course, had not done so, and there is no evidence to suggest that they began to do so after 1754. Among non-Anglicans, Catholics were the only major group who had celebrated marriage according to their own rites but who were not exempted from the 1753 Act. After 1754, Catholic couples continued to marry according to their own rites, but supplemented these with an Anglican marriage ceremony to ensure the legal validity of their union. We shall now examine each group in more detail in turn.

Foreign Protestants and Moravians

The few registers of marriage that existed for the foreign Protestant churches prior to the Act all ended abruptly once the new Act came into force.[28] For example, the last marriage recorded in the register of the French Protestant chapel in Leicester Fields took place in

25 See e.g., Rev. M. R. Austin, 'Religion and Society in Derbyshire during the Industrial Revolution' (1973) 43 *Derbyshire Archaeological Journal* 75.

26 H. Perkin, *Origins of Modern English Society 1780–1880* (London: Routledge & Kegan Paul, 1969), p. 202.

27 *Vigevena and Silveira* v. *Alvarez* (1794) 1 Hag. Con. (App.) 8n.

28 *Report of the Commissioners appointed to inquire into the State, Custody, and Authenticity of Registers or Records of Births or Baptisms, Deaths or Burials, and Marriages, in England and Wales, other than the Parochial Registers* (1838), Appendix A.

1752,[29] while the register of Le Quarre in Little Dean Street contained no entries between the final marriage on 25 November 1753 and a baptism in 1762.[30] The registers of the French Royal Chapel in St James' and the German Lutheran chapel in Trinity Lane, London, both ended in 1754.[31]

The chances of the Moravian communities being exempted from the requirements of the 1753 Act, while never high, had been altogether dashed by the dark hints about the nature of their marriage practices published in 1753.[32] As a result of this and other anti-Moravian tracts, there was 'widespread condemnation' of the Moravians.[33] The acceptance of the Moravian church as an episcopal church came to an end, and the Moravians consequently had to accept non-conformist status. After 1754, the Moravian chapel in Bedford continued to keep a note of the marriages of its followers, but in this case the register helpfully specified the Anglican churches where these marriages took place.[34] The maverick David Taylor, whom we met in Chapter 4, appears to have flouted the law on at least one occasion, since he was expelled by the Moravians in 1765 for celebrating a clandestine marriage,[35] but once again it is the reaction of the organisation rather than the action of the individual that is of more significance in assessing the overall trend.

Presbyterians, Baptists and Independents

It has already been pointed out that the paucity of registers for Baptist, Independent, and Presbyterian congregations suggests that most did not marry according to their own rites, and that nine of the ten surviving registers pertaining to marriage ended

[29] Family Records Centre (FRC) RG4/4585. [30] FRC, RG4/4536.

[31] *Report*, Appendix A.

[32] H. Rimius, *A Candid Narrative of the Rise and Progress of the Herrnhuters, commonly called Moravians* (London, 1753), p. 54. Such accusations were not directly countered by the elliptical defence issued by Count Zinzendorf, who himself described Moravian matrimonial customs as 'somewhat odd', a phrase not calculated to allay suspicion: Nicolaus Ludwig Graf von Zinzendorf, *An Exposition, or, True State, of the Matters Objected in England to the People known by the name of Unitas Fratrum* (London, 1755), p. 23.

[33] Podmore, *The Moravian Church in England*, p. 267. [34] FRC, RG4/306.

[35] S. J. Rogal, *A Biographical Dictionary of 18th Century Methodism* (Lampeter: Edwin Mellen Press, 1999), vol. VIII, p. 27.

long before the 1753 Act.[36] The tenth, that of the Independent Chapel in West Street, Dorking, continued to record marriages until 1801, but these were marriages that had taken place elsewhere.[37] Fifteen of the twenty-one marriages recorded have been traced to a marriage in an Anglican church, but, as noted in Chapter 4, the register is not particularly well kept and one has to abandon any hope of tracing some marriages – such as that of 'Mr Stanley' to 'Mrs Ann'. Once again, the appropriate inference is that the failure to trace the remaining marriages should be attributed to a lack of information, rather than raising a suspicion that the parties did not marry according to Anglican rites.

This apart, no marriage registers relating to the period after 1754 were yielded to the 1838 Commission, and Steel's extensive survey found no marriage register for any of the Three Denominations.[38] On the rare occasions when marriages do appear in the records of any of these three after 1754, it is clear that the marriage in fact took place in the parish church. Thus, for example, six marriages are noted in the register of the Congregational Chapel in Staplehurst, Kent, between 1787 and 1793, but the marriages actually took place in All Saints church in Staplehurst.[39]

In addition to the evidence by absence – the lack of any registers of marriage for the Three Denominations – there is positive evidence of compliance with the law, as revealed by a number of studies of dissenters. Of the twenty-three couples from Llansantffraid Glyn Ceiriog who brought their children to be baptised in its Baptist chapel between 1779 (when the baptism register commences) and 1812, marriages in the Anglican church have been traced for all but two, and even these two may have married in a church in another parish.[40] An Independent chapel was built in Kilsby in the 1790s, and marriages have been traced for at least sixty-five (or 81 per cent) of the eighty couples who brought their children to be baptised there, although the true

[36] See further Chapter 4. [37] PRO RG4/3102.

[38] D. J. Steel, *National Index of Parish Registers*, vol. II, *Sources for Nonconformist Genealogy and Family History* (Chichester: Phillimore & Co. Ltd, 1973), p. 552.

[39] G. Rickard (ed.), *Staplehurst, Kent, Congregational Chapel* (1999, unpublished transcript available at Canterbury Cathedral Archives), p. 3.

[40] It should be noted that it was not even possible to trace marriages for all those baptising their children in the Anglican church: see Chapter 7.

extent of provable conformity is probably well over 90 per cent.[41] Forty-six of the inhabitants of Cardington were identified in the 1782 listing as being dissenters: of these, marriages have been traced for all but one (whose wife was unnamed in the listing).

Studies of individual dissenters show that even the most committed married in the parish church.[42] Joshua Symonds, a pastor of an Independent church in Bedford,[43] married his wife Elizabeth according to the rites of the Church of England.[44] Similarly, Francis Smith, a Baptist elder who had married his first wife in the Baptist church in 1753, celebrated his second marriage to a fellow-Baptist in the Church of England.[45]

Nor does the post-1754 requirement of marrying in the parish church appear to have generated complaint – another factor suggesting that dissenters had never enjoyed the privilege of marrying according to their own religious rites.[46] Indeed, the only complaints to the Protestant Dissenting Deputies on the subject of marriage, far from protesting against the need for conformity, revealed quite the opposite problem: that some Anglican ministers simply refused to marry unbaptised persons.[47] One Durham couple resorted to

[41] In a further seven cases there are plausible matches, but the names of the parties are too common to be sure that the couple marrying in one place is the same as that baptising a child in another. A further two mothers were explicitly described as wives in the register, but the practice of the minister was not consistent in this respect and when a tabular form was adopted in 1824 this detail was omitted entirely. In only two cases is there evidence (different surnames/mother's surname only being recorded) from which illegitimacy can be inferred.

[42] See e.g., J. Caffyn, *Sussex Believers: Baptist Marriage in the 17th and 18th Centuries* (Worthing: Churchman Publishing, 1988), pp. 100–3.

[43] H. G. Tibbutt, 'Joshua Symonds, an Eighteenth-Century Bedford Dissenting Minister' (1978) 57 *Publications of the Bedfordshire Historical Record Society* 59.

[44] The marriage took place on 3 November 1767 at St Dionis Backchurch in London. It was traced via the IGI, although without the information in Tibbutt's article, noting the bride's maiden name and her London origins, the match might have been discounted.

[45] See T. J. Budge, *Melbourne Baptists: the Story of Two Hundred Years in Melbourne, Derbyshire* (London: Carey Kingsgate Press Ltd, 1951) for details of his second spouse. The marriage itself took place in Melbourne parish church: SOG DB/REG/76917a, Smith being described as a 'staymaker, Moravian Preacher and Widower'.

[46] Although some did advance proposals for a new form of service, see e.g., J. Free, *Matrimony Made Easy; or, a New Form of Marriage, Founded on the Principles and Practice of the Holy Patriarchs, and the Laws of God, and Nature*, 2nd edn (London, 1764).

[47] *A Sketch of the History and Proceedings of the Deputies Appointed to Protect the Civil Rights of the Protestant Dissenters* (London: Samuel Burton, 1813), pp. 44–5.

marrying over the border in Scotland after such a refusal, only to be met upon their return by the incumbent's request for his fees, which he claimed were due to him wherever they had married.[48]

Methodists

The various factions within the Methodist movement ultimately split from the Anglican establishment; Whitefield's followers in 1763, Lady Huntingdon's Connexion in 1779, and the Wesleyans in the nineteenth century.[49] But for most Methodists in the eighteenth century Methodism was consistent with adherence to (and marriage in) the Church of England.[50] In George Eliot's *Adam Bede*,[51] set in 1799, the two Methodists in the village still attend their local church, and Dinah Morris, a Methodist preacher, is married to Adam Bede in the parish church. Llansantffraid Glyn Ceiriog supplies a real-world example: Thomas and Mary Evans married in the latter's parish church but had their four children baptised in Llangollen Methodist Church. And Methodists continued to marry within the Church of England even after they had formally split from the Church of England.[52]

Catholics

The position of Catholics was rather different. As Chapter 3 has shown, Catholic couples did marry according to their own rites before 1754. And numerous registers do exist of Catholic weddings that took place *after* 1754: some have been published, while others lie in county record offices or with Catholic congregations.[53] Such

[48] The case was later dropped upon the interference of the Deputies: *ibid.* p. 44.

[49] John Wesley was particularly opposed to such a separation, publishing his twelve reasons against it in 1758: see Warne, *Church and Society*, p. 106.

[50] See D. Hempton, *The Religion of the People: Methodism and Popular Religion, c. 1750–1900* (London: Routledge, 1996) p. 150, J. Walsh, 'Methodism and the Mob in the Eighteenth Century' in G. J. Cuming and D. Baker (eds.), *Popular Belief and Practice* (Cambridge University Press, 1972), and J. Stevenson, *Popular Disturbances in England, 1700–1832*, 2nd edn (London: Longman, 1992), p. 39, on the accusations levelled at Methodists.

[51] G. Eliot, *Adam Bede* (London: William Blackwood & Sons, 1859).

[52] See e.g., J. Flanders, *A Circle of Sisters: Alice Kipling, Georgiana Burne-Jones, Agnes Poynter and Louisa Baldwin* (London: Penguin Books, 2002), p. 74, which notes the marriage of a Methodist preacher in 1833.

[53] Catholic congregations declined to submit their registers to the 1838 Commission: *Report*, p. 12.

registers are usually linked to aristocratic Catholic strongholds, or the embassy chapels of ambassadors from Catholic countries.[54] But the existence of such registers is not necessarily evidence of non-compliance with the 1753 Act: the key question is whether Catholics also submitted to the legally binding Anglican rites. At first sight the very idea might appear unlikely, on the grounds that it would be incompatible with one's status as a Catholic to attend the religious services of the Church of England. But such an approach had papal sanction. Benedict XIV had considered the question of whether Catholics in Protestant countries should submit to legislation requiring them to be married by a minister of the established church, and had held that 'it was quite legitimate for Catholics to obey the civil law in this matter'.[55]

But what happened in practice? There have been some studies on the extent of compliance among Catholics. Williams, for example, suggested that a number of Catholics in Wardour, Wiltshire, married solely according to their own religious rites.[56] Similarly, Rowlands, having examined the register of Catholic marriages at Brindle in Lancashire, concluded that 'most of the Catholics of Brindle in the heart of Catholic Lancashire regarded Hardwicke's Marriage Act as something to be ignored'.[57] But a very different picture emerges from a study of ninety-five couples who married in a Catholic ceremony at the Catholic stronghold of Coughton

[54] See e.g., *The Registers of the Venetian Chapel in London* (London: Catholic Family History Society, 1996). After the 1753 Act came into force, no marriages were recorded until July 1772. Until 1784, the names of the few who married there suggest that they may have been attached to the embassy; from 1784 to 1788 there was a sudden rise in the numbers marrying there, and the names recorded tend to be Irish rather than Italian. It may be that an embassy marriage was for a short period perceived as a possible way for Catholics to evade the 1753 Act: in 1790, however, it was held that a marriage was invalid unless the parties belonged to the ambassador's household or were domiciled in the country in question (*Pertreis* v. *Tondear* (1790) 1 Hagg. CR 136; 161 ER 502).

[55] J. Bossy, 'Challoner and the Marriage Act' in E. Duffy (ed.), *Challoner and his Church: a Catholic Bishop in Georgian England* (London: Darton, Longman & Todd, 1981), p. 132.

[56] J. A. Williams, *Catholic Recusancy in Wiltshire, 1660–1791* (London: Catholic Record Society, 1968), p. 66.

[57] M. Rowlands, '1767: Religious Life' in M. Rowlands (ed.), *English Catholics of Parish and Town, 1558–1778* (Catholic Record Society, 1999), p. 272. See also Steel, *Sources for Nonconformist Genealogy and Family History*, p. 509, who suggests that many Catholics flouted the law.

Court in Warwickshire between 1758 and 1795.[58] Every single one of these couples also went through an Anglican ceremony.[59] And in most cases that ceremony took place in their parish of residence, which was not necessarily Coughton.[60] In fact, less than one-third of the couples who went through a Catholic ceremony at Coughton Court actually married in the Anglican church of the parish. This pattern explains why other researchers have underestimated the extent of compliance: the studies by Williams and Rowlands were based solely on the Anglican register of the parish where the Catholic ceremony took place and so it is unsurprising that they traced only a few marriages. The importance of the Coughton Court study therefore goes beyond the evidence of compliance at Coughton and undermines the methodology and reasoning of earlier studies. Significantly, however, these couples complied with the law on their own terms. In only five cases out of ninety-two[61] did the Anglican ceremony precede the Catholic rite, as by law it should have done. In forty-six cases the Catholic ceremony took place a day or more before the Anglican one, while in the final forty-one cases the two ceremonies were held on the same day, perhaps to obscure the order in which they were celebrated.[62]

The evidence from other parishes supports the evidence of compliance.[63] A further study of the forty Catholic marriages that were celebrated at Stonor Park in Oxfordshire between 1759 and 1799 was

[58] Warwickshire Record Office MI 163. This discussion draws on R. Probert and L. D'Arcy Brown, 'Catholics and the Clandestine Marriages Act of 1753' (2008) 80 *Local Population Studies* 78.

[59] It is clear from the occupations stated in the register that this was not a practice confined to the wealthy; cf. M. D. R. Leys, *Catholics in England, 1559–1829* (London: Longmans, Green & Co. Ltd, 1961), p. 192.

[60] In only six cases was it clear that the parties had married in a parish other than that stated in the Catholic register, while in a further five the absence of details for one or both parties made it impossible to ascertain whether the parties had married in a parish where one of them was resident or not.

[61] In three cases there are inconsistencies in the surviving records as to the exact date of one or other of the marriages, and these have not been included.

[62] This casts doubt on the claim that the Anglican ceremony usually preceded the Catholic one: see E. Burton, *The Life and Times of Bishop Challoner* (London: Longmans, Green & Co., 1909), vol. I, p. 343.

[63] See e.g., D. J. Steel and E. R. Samuel, *National Index of Parish Registers*, vol. III, *Sources for Roman Catholic and Jewish Genealogy and Family History* (Chichester: Phillimore & Co., 1974), p. 863; A. Wilcox, 'Catholics in Parish Registers: Wilcox and Wilcoxon of Maer, Staffordshire' (2003) 8 *Catholic Ancestor* 221.

carried out.[64] For all but five a corresponding Anglican ceremony has been traced, and there are reasonable grounds for believing that the failure to trace these last few is due to missing registers.[65] Similarly, Gandy found that Catholics constituted 10 per cent of the population of Culcheth in 1767 and accounted for 10 per cent of marriages celebrated in the local (Anglican) church between 1781 and 1836.[66]

Of course, the fact that all those who went through an invalid Catholic ceremony at Coughton chose to enter into a legally binding marriage by means of an Anglican wedding does not mean that all of their co-religionists would have behaved in the same way. In particular, changes in the composition of the Catholic population may have led to a change in this practice over time. By 1811 there were an estimated 250,000 Roman Catholics in England and Wales, almost four times the number there had been in 1780.[67] The increase consisted largely of Irish immigrants,[68] and in the 1830s it was suggested that such persons were far more likely than their English religious counterparts to marry according to their own rites.[69] One cannot discount prejudice against immigrants in the accounts of illegal marriages, desertion, and dependency on the poor law that pervaded these reports,[70] but the fact that such accounts came from Catholic priests[71] as well as other officials suggests there was some

[64] PRO RG4/1600.

[65] Many of the marriages took place in the neighbouring parish of Pishill, but its records are patchy and three of the Catholic marriages for which no corresponding Anglican ceremony has been traced took place within periods when the marriage register for Pishill was obviously deficient.

[66] G. N. Gandy, 'Illegitimacy in a Handloom Weaving Community: Fertility Patterns in Culcheth, Lancashire, 1781–1860' (unpublished DPhil. dissertation, University of Oxford, 1978), p. 128.

[67] Steel and Samuel, *Sources for Roman Catholic and Jewish Genealogy and Family History*, p. 837.

[68] Towards the end of the eighteenth century the Catholic population was also augmented by émigrés from Revolutionary France , but this was only temporary as most chose to return to France: see D. Stevens, *UK Asylum Law and Policy: Historical and Contemporary Perspectives* (London: Sweet & Maxwell, 2004), p. 17.

[69] *Report on the State of the Irish Poor in Great Britain* (1836) P 34, pp. 3, 23, 61–2; S. Gallagher, 'Irish Catholic Marriages in the London Lying-in Hospital Records' (1998) Catholic Ancestor 102; *Royal Commission of Inquiry into Administration and Practical Operation of Poor Laws* (1834) PP 44, p. 99; App. A. pp. 103, 105.

[70] *Report on the State of the Irish Poor*, pp. 3, 49, 62, 88.

[71] See e.g., the evidence from Rev. Joseph Kimbell, Catholic priest at St Mary's Chapel in Moorfields in the *Report from the Select Committee on Parochial Registration* (1833) PP 669, p. 70. His evidence was, however, somewhat inconclusive. Although he suggested that some of the poor Irish failed to marry in a

basis to the claims. It is worth bearing in mind, however, that these problems emerged many decades after the 1753 Act, and could not have been envisaged by even the most far-sighted of legislators.

Outside the mainstream

What of the less mainstream sects that proliferated at this period? It has been suggested by Gillis that some minor sects 'kept alive a belief in self-marriage and divorce',[72] but the examples given hardly support this argument. Gillis suggests, for example, that the Christian Israelite John Wroe 'surrounded himself with "Virgins" who were devoted to him carnally as well as spiritually'.[73] This salivating description is drawn from Harrison, whose account is much more prosaic and implies that there was scant tolerance of Wroe's behaviour: '[i]n 1830 Wroe said that he was commanded to take seven virgins to cherish and comfort him, and his immoral behaviour with some of them caused dissension among the believers. An inquiry or trial ended in a riot, and Wroe decided to leave town.'[74] Gillis' claims appear at first sight to be on stronger ground with the Buchanites, whose leader, Mrs Buchan, appears to have cohabited with the Rev. Hugh White, having left her husband and persuaded White that she was the 'woman clothed with the sun' of Revelation. According to Harrison 'the community was accused of gross sexual immorality [and] Mrs Buchan's teachings on marriage did nothing to allay such fears ... "Where the Holy Spirit of God occupies all the person, and reigns throughout the flesh, it matters not much whether they marry or not"'.[75] Yet even in this case there is little implication of self-marriage. The fact that members of the sect gave up their married status appears to be an example of self-divorce rather than self-marriage. Finally, it should be noted that the community was small (under 100 members), short-lived (under a decade), and in any case was based in Scotland, to which the 1753 Act did not apply.

legally-binding form, he also noted that 'a great number of the poor Irish do not come to us at all to be married; they go often to the Protestant Established Church'.

72 Gillis, *For Better, For Worse*, pp. 190–1.

73 Gillis, *For Better, For Worse*, p. 222.

74 J. F. C. Harrison, *The Second Coming: Popular Millenarianism 1780–1850* (London: Routledge and Kegan Paul, 1979), p. 147.

75 *Ibid.* p. 36.

Thus, far from establishing a tradition of plebeian self-marriage, the examples given indicate only that a few religious leaders behaved in unconventional ways – leaving their spouses to indulge in celibacy, cohabitation, fornication, or plural marriage. It does not establish that such practices were acceptable to the sects they led, still less that the leaders would have accepted such behaviour among their followers. Even where the leaders taught that marriage did not matter (and the only example of this appears to be Luckie Buchan) there is scant evidence that their followers adopted self-marriage as a practice. It is necessary to distinguish between the unconventional behaviour of individuals and the beliefs and practice of the sect as a whole. It is also important to be cautious when examining the claims made by opponents of new sects: circulating scurrilous stories about their sexual and marital practices was a common ploy to try to discredit them.

THE PRACTICES OF EXEMPTED GROUPS

Jewish marriages

As noted in Chapter 6, the 1753 Act did not declare that Jewish and Quaker marriages were valid, merely that they were exempt from its provisions. However, in the 1790s, when the courts were eventually called upon to determine the validity of a Jewish marriage, the fact that Jews had been exempted from the Act was seen as a strong argument in favour of the validity of their marriages.[76] Of course, such marriages had to be 'conformable to Jewish rites' in order to be valid,[77] and it was only if both parties were Jewish that the exemption applied.[78] The ecclesiastical courts therefore heard evidence on Jewish law from experts,[79] and applied it just as they

[76] *Vigevena and Silveira* v. *Alvarez* (1794) 1 Hag. Con. (App.) 8n; 161 ER 636; *Lady D'Aguilar* v. *Baron D'Aguilar* (1794) 1 Hagg. Ecc. 773; 161 ER 748; *Lindo* v. *Belisario* (1795) 1 Hag. Con. 216; 161 ER 530.

[77] *Vigevena and Silveira* v. *Alvarez* (1794) 1 Hag. Con. (App.) 8n. See also *Horn* v. *Noel* (1807) 1 Camp. 62; 170 ER 877, in which evidence of the written contract was required in addition to proof of the ceremony that took place in the synagogue.

[78] See e.g., *Jones* v. *Robinson* (1815) 2 Phill. Ecc. 285; 161 ER 1146.

[79] See e.g., *Lindo* v. *Belisario* (1795) 1 Hag. Con. 216; 161 ER 530; *Goldsmid* v. *Bromer* (1798) 1 Hag. Con. 324; 161 ER 568.

would the laws of a foreign country in determining the validity of a marriage according to the *lex loci contractus*.[80]

And exemption from the Act did not necessarily mean that Jewish couples were free from parental interference in their marriages. In *Goldsmid* v. *Bromer*,[81] which involved the marriage of a sixteen-year-old Jewish girl, the Consistory Court upheld the right of her father to challenge the marriage: 'every parent is deeply interested in the welfare of his children, as affected by such connexions; and has a right to question a matrimonial contract entered into in the minority of his child'.[82] The ceremony in that case had taken place in the Shakespeare Tavern in Covent Garden; the basis on which it was held to be invalid was that the witnesses did not fulfil the conditions of Jewish law,[83] but one suspects that it was the location of the ceremony in an ale-house rather than a synagogue that led the court to take such a strict line.[84]

In practice, of course, the exemption of Jewish couples was not particularly significant in terms of the number affected. The Jewish population of England and Wales was small (it has been suggested that it only rose above 15,000 in the 1820s)[85] and the numbers marrying according to Jewish rites were correspondingly modest. In 1838, the first year for which national statistics are available, only 135 couples did so.[86]

Quaker marriages

The position of Quakers was rather more complex. As discussed in Chapter 3, the status of a Quaker marriage had been far from clear

80 See e.g., N. Bentwich, 'Anglo-Jewish Causes Célèbres: Leading Cases in the English Courts from the Beginning of the Eighteenth Century' (1939–45) XV *Transactions of the Jewish Historical Society of England* 93, 109.

81 (1798) 1 Hag. Con. 324; 161 ER 568. 82 *Ibid.* at 327.

83 Under Jewish law, witnesses were disqualified if they were related to either of the parties or did not conform to the Jewish religion: one was said to be within the relevant degrees of relationship and the other was alleged to have profaned the Sabbath 'by riding in coaches, and snuffing lighted candles, stirring the fire and eating forbidden meats' (p. 330).

84 Note also the contemporary criticisms within the Jewish community regarding irregular marriages in this period: see Rev. A. Barnett, 'Solomon Bennett, 1761–1838: Artist, Hebraist and Controversialist' (1951–2) XVII *Transactions of the Jewish Historical Society of England* 91, 102, 106–8.

85 See T. M. Endelman, *The Jews of Georgian England, 1714–1830: Tradition and Change in a Liberal Society* (University of Michigan Press, 1999), p. 172.

86 *Returns relative to Marriages 1838–1855* (1857) Sess. 2 PP vol. XXXII.

before the 1753 Act, and this ambiguity continued long after the passage of the Act. In *Vigevena and Silveira* v. *Alvarez*,[87] for example, counsel pointed out that the validity of Quaker marriages had never been formally decided. The reasoning of Sir William Wynne in that case – that the exemption from complying with the legislation implied the validity of the exempted ceremonies – was at first sight equally applicable to Quaker marriages. There was, however, a significant difference: part of the justification for Wynne's decision that the court had jurisdiction even where the marriage had not been celebrated according to the rites of the Church of England was the fact that Jews could not be expected to marry according to such rites, being, in his words, 'Antichristian'. Since this accusation could not be levelled at Quakers, should they be expected to marry according to the rites of the Church of England?

There does not appear to have been any direct legal challenge to the status of Quaker marriages in this period, but contemporaries expressed doubts about their validity.[88] Nevertheless, their validity appears to have been assumed in *Deane* v. *Thomas* in 1829, in an action for criminal conversation. The date of the case may be significant: it occurred after *Dalrymple* v. *Dalrymple* in 1811, in which Sir William Scott had held that an exchange of consent had constituted a valid marriage in England and Wales prior to 1754.[89] Since this was the new understanding, it is unsurprising that a Quaker marriage would, when tested against the law prior to statutory intervention, be held to be valid. Even so, the court held that a Quaker register would not be conclusive proof that the marriage had taken place, and that witnesses to the ceremony would have to be produced.[90] Fortunately, the excellent record-keeping of the Quakers ensured that witnesses would be easily traceable.[91]

[87] (1794) 1 Hag. Con. (App.) 8n; 161 ER 636.

[88] See e.g., R. S. Donnison Roper, *A Treatise on the Law of Property Arising from the Relation between Husband and Wife*, 2nd edn (London: Butterworth & Son, 1826), Addenda No. 1 by E. Jacob, p. 481.

[89] See further Chapter 2.

[90] (1829) Moo. & Malk. 361; 31 Rev. Rep. 738.

[91] In Shrewsbury, for example, when Richard Reynolds married the daughter of Abraham Darby of Coalbrookdale in 1757, there were four relations and forty-five witnesses present, as identified in the register: W. Fletcher (ed.), *Shropshire Parish Registers: Nonconformist and RC Registers* (Shropshire Parish Register Society, 1922).

Just as before the 1753 Act, not all Quakers chose to marry according to their own rites; perhaps in part because of the continuing uncertainty about the status of such marriages but also because of the strictness of the Society's requirements and because the declining numbers of Quakers meant that there were fewer eligible partners within the Quaker community. These factors were interconnected: the decline in Quaker numbers has been attributed to the strictness of their procedure relating to marriage. Steel, for example, suggests that 'it is probable that failure to receive clearance to marry an outsider or relative and consequent marriage before a priest followed by disownment was one of the major causes of the decline in Quaker numbers in the eighteenth century'.[92] Indeed, such disownments actually increased in the wake of the 1753 Act:[93] in the second half of the eighteenth century over 40 per cent of the disownments by, and resignations from, the six London Monthly Meetings related to marriage before a priest.[94] Even taking into account the decline in Quaker numbers in the second half of the eighteenth century, the number of marriages celebrated according to Quaker rites was disproportionately small, and continued to decline even when the number of births and burials temporarily increased towards the end of the eighteenth century.[95] Between 1794 and 1799, for example, seventy-one marriages took place in meeting-houses in the Quarterly Meeting of London and Middlesex;[96] in the same period, ninety-one individuals were disowned or resigned for marrying before a priest.[97]

92 Steel, *Sources for Nonconformist Genealogy and Family History*, p. 655. See also J. S. Rowntree, *Quakerism, Past and Present: being an inquiry into the causes of its decline in Great Britain and Ireland* (London: Smith, Elder & Co., 1859), p. 150; R. M. Jones, *The Later Periods of Quakerism* (London: Macmillan & Co. Ltd, 1921), vol. I, pp. 189–90.

93 W. Beck and T. F. Ball, *The London Friends' Meetings* (London, 1869), p. 123 and accompanying Table.

94 *Ibid.* Similarly, disownments for marrying out accounted for fourteen of the thirty-six disownments by the Banbury Monthly Meeting between 1785 and 1789: J. V. Wood, *Some Rural Quakers: a History of Quakers and Quakerism at the Corners of the Four Shires of Oxford, Warwick, Worcester and Gloucester* (York: Ebor Press, 1991), p. 64.

95 J. S. Rowntree, *The Friends' Registers of Births, Deaths and Marriages, 1650–1900* (Leominster, 1902), p. 14.

96 Beck and Ball, *The London Friends' Meetings*, p. 90 and accompanying Table.

97 *Ibid.* Table accompanying p. 123.

Yet even so, the evidence of Quaker marriages in this period stands in sharp contrast to the lack of any equivalent evidence for other dissenting denominations. The Quaker records show that 5,487 Quaker marriages took place between 1750 and 1799, and at least a further 3,000 before the 1836 Marriage Act came into force.[98] In addition, the diaries of individual Quakers describe the weddings that took place.[99] Given that such evidence survives for such a small sect, it is implausible to imagine that other, far more numerous denominations could have celebrated their own marriages without leaving any traces in the records.

THE PROCESS OF REFORM

The evidence has demonstrated that compliance with the 1753 Act was almost universal: that virtually all Protestant dissenters, most English Catholics, and even some Quakers married according to the rites of the Church of England. One might well wonder why, if this was the case, reform was deemed to be necessary. The simple answer is that it became necessary not because non-Anglicans were failing to marry according to the 1753 Act, but because it was felt that they should not have to do so. An examination of the process of reform that culminated in the Marriage Act of 1836 illustrates a number of important points: first, that demands for reform did not emerge until well into the nineteenth century; secondly, that these were linked to changing attitudes towards dissent in this period; and thirdly, that the claims made in the course of debates reinforce the evidence discussed above regarding contemporary practice.

The process of reform was instigated by the Unitarians, who, as their name suggests, did not believe in the Trinity and as a result had not been entitled to the protection of the 1689 Toleration Act.[100] It was not until 1813 that they were even granted legal recognition,[101] but once this had been achieved they petitioned for

[98] Rowntree, *The Friends' Registers*, p. 14.

[99] See M. Dresser (ed.), *The Diary of Sarah Fox née Champion, Bristol 1745–1802* (Bristol Record Society, 2003), pp. 12, 28, 32, 40, 77, 123.

[100] Manning, *The Protestant Dissenting Deputies*, p. 3. [101] *Ibid.* ch. 5.

reform of marriage law, and a Bill to address their objections was brought before Parliament in 1819 by a Unitarian MP, William Smith.[102] The change being proposed appears modest to modern eyes – namely, that Unitarians should be able to request the omission of any mention of the Trinity from the marriage service – but even this did not win sufficient support.[103] Indeed, at least one senior churchman thought it preferable that Unitarians should marry according to their own rites than that the liturgy be changed at their insistence.[104] But a proposal that the privileges enjoyed by Jews and Quakers should be extended to all Protestant nonconformists and to Catholics failed even to secure a second reading when it was put before Parliament in 1823.[105] The Lord Chancellor, Lord Eldon, was vehemently opposed to the Bill, objecting that it 'would enable persons to open a place for the celebration of marriage in every town and village throughout England; and that, not for individuals whose religious tenets were known, but ... [for] the followers of Joanna Southcott, together with ranters, jumpers, and various other sects of whose principles they knew nothing'.[106] The increase in dissent may have created a demand for reform, but it also posed its own difficulties for reformers. While dissent had never been homogeneous, there had been an 'effervescence of fringe movements' from the 1790s.[107] Given the proliferation of sects at this time it is understandable that the Establishment might well have wanted to exercise caution about allowing new bodies to carry out marriages.[108]

102 *Hansard* (HC) 2nd Series, vol. 40, col. 864, 3 June 1819. Further petitions from Unitarians in Kendal, Sheffield, and Stockton upon Tees were presented by Brougham and Smith in 1822: *Hansard* (HC) 2nd Series, vol. 6, col. 1460, 18 January 1822.

103 *Hansard* (HC) 2nd Series, vol. 40, col. 1200, 16 June 1819. A Bill along similar lines was debated in 1822: Marriages of Unitarian Dissenters, *Hansard* (HC) 2nd Series, vol. 6, col. 1460, 18 January 1822.

104 *Hansard* (HL) 2nd Series, vol. 9, col. 970, 12 June 1823 (Archbishop of Canterbury).

105 By twenty-seven votes to twenty-one: Dissenters' Marriages Bill 1823: *Hansard* (HL) 2nd Series, vol. 9, col. 967, 12 June 1823.

106 *Hansard* (HL) 2nd Series, vol. 9, col. 967, 12 June 1823.

107 Rule, *Albion's People*, p. 156, and see generally Harrison, *The Second Coming*.

108 Even so, it is hard not to be sceptical about Eldon's opposition to the Bill, partly because he also opposed Catholic emancipation and the repeal of the Test and Corporation Acts, and partly because he had himself eloped to Scotland with Bessy Surtees back in 1772.

After this failure, the next few proposals for reform focused solely on the position of Unitarians.[109] There were two key questions that underpinned the debates. The first was whether marriage was primarily a private commitment or a public institution. Dr Lushington, for example, argued that 'individuals ought to be allowed to enter into the state of marriage in that way which best accorded with their sense of moral and religious feeling'.[110] From this point of view the commitment of marriage was so serious that it should be supported by a ceremony that had meaning for the parties themselves: 'that solemnity which should give to it, in the eyes of the parties, the most lasting and binding obligation'.[111] Opponents of reform, by contrast, stressed the public aspects of marriage, being more concerned about the potential for clandestine marriages and the issue of registration.[112] The second, broader, question concerned the role of the Church of England. Should conformity be compelled or plurality allowed? Was it necessary for the Church of England to retain a virtual monopoly over marriage? This was certainly the view of one bishop, who argued that the issue was one of civil jurisprudence rather than religious scruples.[113] Or did the current system do more harm than good? As Lord Ellenborough pointed out, the religious interests of the community were hardly advanced by requiring a one-off act of conformity by those who held alternative beliefs.[114] Even the Archbishop of Canterbury himself supported reform.[115]

This broader debate was, of course, of intense interest to all non-Anglicans. So why were dissenting denominations other than Unitarians not campaigning for reform at this time? The simple answer is that reform of the marriage laws was for many years not their top priority. The Protestant Dissenting Deputies, who

[109] Bills were debated in 1824, 1825, and 1827, and took a variety of forms. Some proposed that Unitarians should marry in the Church of England, omitting those parts of the service that offended them, others that they should celebrate their marriages in their own chapels, yet others that a civil ceremony would be the best solution.

[110] *Hansard* (HC) 2nd Series, vol. 12, col. 1239, 25 March 1825.

[111] *Hansard* (HL) 2nd Series, vol. 11, col. 75, 2 April 1824 (Marquis of Lansdowne).

[112] See e.g., *Hansard* (HL) 2nd Series, vol. 9, col. 967, 12 June 1823 (Lord Eldon LC); vol. 13, col. 1031, 3 June 1825 (Bishop of Chester).

[113] *Hansard* (HL) 2nd Series, vol. 11, col. 80, 2 April 1824.

[114] *Hansard* (HL) 2nd Series, vol. 9, col. 972, 12 June 1823.

[115] *Hansard* (HL) 2nd Series, vol. 11, col. 435, 4 May 1824.

represented Presbyterian, Independent, and Baptist congregations, welcomed the initiatives of the Unitarians but preferred to await their outcome rather than join in the campaign[116] and instead pressed for more general reform on the status of dissenters.[117]

In short, before the 1830s the issue of reform was largely driven by the ideological concerns of Unitarians.[118] There is no hint that they were flouting the law: they were asking for relief from compulsory conformity, not for recognition of existing and necessarily illegal marriages. It is apparent from the parliamentary debates that the only non-Anglicans who were thought to be flouting the law were lower-class Catholics in populous metropolitan parishes.[119] As the Bishop of Llandaff noted, there was no special form of marriage within most denominations: '[e]xcepting the Jews, the Catholics and the Quakers, no Dissenters had any peculiar marriage service of their own'.[120]

By contrast, by the 1830s the demand for reform had begun to be advanced by a broader range of supporters. With the repeal of the Test and Corporation Acts in 1828, the main grievances of Protestant dissenters had been addressed and they could turn their attention to more specific issues. Yet even then the call for reform was neither immediate nor universal. It was not until 1833 that the 'compulsory conformity to the Rites and Ceremonies prescribed by the Book of Common Prayer for the Celebration of Matrimony' headed the list of dissenters' grievances put forward by the Protestant Dissenting

116 Thus, in 1824 the Committee appointed to consider the issue of marriage resolved that 'although this Committee feel the high importance of seeking relief from the operation of the Marriage Law, as it affects Dissenters in general, and are ready zealously to direct their attention to the subject hereafter, yet, understanding that the Unitarians are now introducing a Bill suited to their particular case, this Committee think it advisable for the present to watch the result of the pending proceedings and to abstain from publicly appealing to the Legislature on the general question': Guildhall Library, Ms 03083, *Minutes of the Protestant Dissenting Deputies*, vol. 6, p. 87.

117 Until 1829 their focus was on the repeal of the Test and Corporation Acts: Manning, *The Protestant Dissenting Deputies*, p. 68.

118 See e.g., W. Fox, 'The Dissenting Marriage Question' (1833) 7 *Monthly Repository* 136.

119 See the view of the Marquis of Lansdowne expressed in the debates over the 1823 Bill. He stated that the churchwardens of such parishes were pleading for reform because of the number of illegitimate children resulting from void marriages: *Hansard* (HL) 2nd Series, vol. 9, cols. 967–8, 12 June 1823.

120 *Hansard* (HL) 2nd Series, vol. 9, col. 972, 12 June 1823.

Deputies.[121] Nor did the 'United Committee' appointed to consider these grievances even then include representatives from all dissenting denominations: the Quakers, and more significantly the Wesleyan Methodists, declined the invitation to join.[122] Reform of the marriage law was not a cause to unite all dissenters.[123] There was, in addition, a separate campaign by Catholics, taking advantage of the recent improvement in their legal position,[124] for recognition of marriages celebrated by Catholic priests.[125]

The debate on Bills introduced for the benefit of specific groups was, however, inhibited by the expectation that more wide-ranging reform would soon be enacted. The acceptance of religious pluralism had, as well as fuelling the demand for further reform by individual groups, made it more difficult for the Establishment to defend existing inequalities. The case for reform was also strengthened by the realisation that the existing system of parochial registration was inadequate and that a new system of civil registration was required – not merely for marriages, but also for births and deaths.[126] Lord John Russell was only one of the many MPs to wax eloquent on the advantages of such a system:

> It was a most important subject – important for the security of property – important to ascertain the state and condition of individuals under various circumstances – important to enable the Government to acquire a general knowledge of the state of the population of the country – that there should be a general registration of births, marriages and deaths.[127]

121 *Minutes of the Protestant Dissenting Deputies*, 15 March 1833, p. 156.

122 The Committee consisted of three representatives from each of the Protestant Dissenting Deputies, the General Body of the Protestant Dissenting Ministers of the Three Denominations, the Protestant Society, and the United Associate Presbytery of the Secession Church of Scotland: Guildhall Library, Ms 03086, *Minute Books of a Committee called the United Committee appointed to consider the Grievances under which Dissenters Now Labour*, vol. 1.

123 See Manning, *The Protestant Dissenting Deputies*, and M. J. Cullen, 'The Making of the Civil Registration Act of 1836' (1974) 25 *Journal of Ecclesiastical History* 39.

124 Catholic Relief Act 1829, 10 Geo 4. c. 7.

125 Roman Catholic Marriages Bill 1833, introduced by Lord Molyneux (*Hansard* (HC) 3rd Series, vol. 18, col. 553, 11 June 1833); Roman Catholic Marriages Bill 1834, introduced by Lord Langdale (*Hansard* (HC) 3rd Series, vol. 25, col. 1026, 7 August 1834).

126 *Report from the Select Committee on Parochial Registration*, 15 August 1833, Paper No. 669 in *Reports of Select Committees* 1801–52, vol. 14 (House of Commons, 1853), p. 9.

127 *Hansard* (HC) 3rd Series, vol. 31, col. 368, 12 February 1836. See also the *Report from the Select Committee on Parochial Registration*, p. 11.

A number of government Bills were put forward,[128] and eventually an acceptable solution was achieved in the form of the Marriage Act 1836.

While I have briefly traced the evolution of the Marriage Act of 1836 to illustrate the marriage practices of non-Anglicans in this period, the legislation should be seen as the beginning of a new era[129] rather than as the ending of longstanding problems. It was, in a number of ways, a novelty. It introduced the possibility of civil marriage, an option that had previously only been available for a very brief period during the English Commonwealth.[130] It confirmed the validity of Jewish and Quaker marriages, a point that had been uncertain despite their exemption from the 1753 Act. And, for the first time in English law, it provided for the possibility of other non-Anglicans marrying according to their own religious rites and accorded such marriages the same legal status as those celebrated in the Church of England.

Under the 1836 Act there were, therefore, a number of different routes to a binding marriage, depending on the couple's wealth or religious affiliation. A couple could marry in a purely civil ceremony[131] that was preceded by civil preliminaries[132] and registered with a new civil authority.[133] Anglican couples had the novel choice

128 See e.g., Marriage of Dissenters Bill 1834 (which proposed marriages in licensed dissenting chapels, preceded by banns or licence in the Church of England but registered by the dissenting minister: *Hansard* (HC) 3rd Series, vol. 21, col. 776, 25 February 1834; Dissenters' Marriages Bill of 1835 (which offered non-Anglicans the alternative of a civil ceremony but provided that registration would continue to be the province of the Church of England: *Hansard* (HC) 3rd Series, vol. XXVI, col. 1073, 17 March 1835).

129 Other contemporary reforms included the Reform Act of 1832 and the Poor Law Act of 1834: see generally Sir L. Woodward, *The Age of Reform, 1815–1870* (Oxford University Press, 1938).

130 See further Chapter 5.

131 See s. 21, which provided that those who objected to marriage in a registered building might 'contract and solemnize Marriage at the Office and in the Presence of the Superintendent Registrar and some Registrar of the District, and in the Presence of Two Witnesses'.

132 There were two new forms of civil preliminary, mirroring the old options of banns and licence. The civil equivalent of banns involved notice of the marriage being given to the superintendent registrar of the district where each party had resided for the previous seven days (s. 4) and the marriage notices being read out at weekly meetings of Poor Law Guardians on three successive occasions (s. 6). The more expensive licence, which cost £3 and reduced the waiting period to seven days, could be obtained from the superintendent registrar of the district (s. 14).

133 See s. 23.

of using the civil preliminaries, but retained the possibility of marrying after banns or licence as well.[134] Jews and Quakers were required to comply with the new civil preliminaries, but otherwise the solemnisation of their marriages was left to their own religious authorities.[135] Other Protestant dissenters and Catholics were also required to comply with the new civil preliminaries,[136] but were subject to greater regulation: they were required to marry in a place of worship that was licensed for marriage[137] and a civil registrar had to be present at the ceremony.[138]

But how popular were these new options? The take-up should be examined for the light that it may cast on earlier social practices. It has been suggested that civil marriage was viewed as a substitute for older forms of informal marriage,[139] but had this been the case one would expect to see an overall rise in the numbers of marriages being solemnised in 1837. Yet as Wrigley and Schofield point out, there was no 'sudden surge' in the late 1830s,[140] in sharp contrast to the increase in recorded births.[141] If civil marriage was a substitute for alternative practices, then the figures do not suggest that these alternatives had been widespread: in 1838 fewer than 3,000 couples married in a non-Anglican religious ceremony, and only 1,093 couples (just over 1 per cent of the total) married in a civil wedding.[142] And the take-up of the new options was slow.[143] The early take-up was so low that it is hardly meaningful to talk of regional variations, and the relative popularity of civil marriage in certain areas in the 1860s and 1870s can tell us little about the practices of earlier generations.[144] The most plausible explanation of the evidence is that it was only when there was a *legal* alternative to marriage in the Church of England that couples began to exercise a choice not to marry according to Anglican rites.[145]

[134] Section 1. [135] Section 2. [136] Section 4.

[137] Section 18. [138] Section 20.

[139] See e.g., Parker, *Informal Marriage*, p. 78; R. B. Outhwaite, *Clandestine Marriage in England, 1500–1850* (London: Hambledon Press, 1995), p. 140.

[140] See Wrigley and Schofield, *The Population History of England*, p. 134.

[141] *Ibid.* Table A2.3, p. 501.

[142] *Returns relative to Marriages 1838–1855* (1857) Sess. 2 PP vol. XXXII.

[143] See J. Haskey, 'Trends in Marriage and Divorce in England and Wales: 1837–1987' (1987) 48 *Population Trends* 11.

[144] Cf. Parker, *Informal Marriage*, p. 77.

[145] Other contemporary evidence supports the novelty of the options introduced by the 1836 Act. The sister of one bride who took advantage of the new provisions noted that '[a]s this is the first Dissenting marriage in the parish, it has made a

CONCLUSION

The evidence makes it clear that conformity with the Church of England ceremony was the norm, both when this was virtually the only route to a legally binding marriage and when there was a choice. The few groups that celebrated marriages according to their own rites before 1754 have left no evidence that they continued to do so afterwards. Reform only came about once English society had undergone fundamental change, driven by the increase of, and changing attitudes to, dissent, and the need for a new system of civil registration to meet the needs of a modern nation. The 1836 Act should be recognised as introducing, rather than restoring, plural modes of marriage, and the take-up of the new options if anything illustrates the continuing importance of the Church of England.

It is true that some proponents of reform had argued that their particular solution would restore the position that had prevailed prior to the 1753 Act,[146] but although this argument may have been good tactics it was certainly bad history. It was unconvincing enough when used in the context of Unitarians,[147] who had not even enjoyed legal recognition until 1813. It was particularly spurious in the context of civil marriage: as one MP riposted, that would be a return to 'the revolutionary law of Cromwell' rather than the law as it stood in 1753.[148] The fact that the old law was invoked as a precedent for very different solutions in fact indicates the confusion that existed even by the 1830s as to what the old law had actually required for a valid marriage before 1754.[149] We have already considered why and when such confusion, which has radically influenced modern scholarship on the 1753 Act, set in,[150] and will close with a few thoughts on what a proper understanding of marriage law and practice in the long eighteenth century has to offer.

little stir; indeed, nothing else is talked about': letter published in *Bradford Observer*, 17 August 1837, quoted by M. Nissel, *People Count: a History of the General Register Office* (London: HMSO, 1987), p. 16.

146 See e.g., *Hansard* (HL) 2nd Series, vol. 11, col. 438 (Marquis of Lansdowne), col. 444 (Lord Holland and the Earl of Liverpool), 4 May 1824.

147 *Hansard* (HC) 2nd Series, vol. 40, col. 864, 3 June 1819 (William Smith).

148 *Hansard* (HC) 3rd Series, vol. 17, col. 1343, 31 May 1827 (Sir C. Wetherall).

149 And note the debate between Dr Lushington and Mr Cutlar Ferguson: *Hansard* (HC) 3rd Series, vol. 26, cols. 1094 and 1098, 17 March 1835.

150 See further Chapter 2.

10

CONCLUSION

Throughout this book, my central contention has been that the marriage law and practices of the long eighteenth century have been misunderstood by modern scholars – and, indeed, ever since the judgment of Sir William Scott in *Dalrymple* in 1811. I have shown that marriage in the Church of England (if not always in the right church) was the accepted and (outside London) almost universal mode of marrying both before and after 1754. We therefore have to reject any idea of a system 'in chaos'[1] before the passage of the Clandestine Marriages Act: the Fleet certainly had its unruly elements, but it was certainly not representative of all marriages, or even all clandestine marriages. Nor was there a mass of individuals unsure of their marital status.[2] There was, of course, always the risk of a third party claiming a precontract, or indeed an actual marriage, with one's spouse, but few people could have been in doubt about what was required for a valid marriage. A contract *per verba de praesenti* should be understood as a contract, rather than a marriage, as it was understood at the time.

Similarly, we must acquit the legislators who passed the 1753 Act of being motivated purely by self-interest. No doubt some individuals did vote with an eye to their own interest, whether in exercising control over minor children or securing an heiress against parental opposition. But many must genuinely and realistically have thought that the elimination of venues such as the Fleet would be for the good of society as a whole, to the benefit of the individuals who might find themselves yoked to a stranger after

[1] Cf. L. Stone, *Road to Divorce: a History of the Making and Breaking of Marriage in England* (Oxford University Press, 1990), p. 11.

[2] Cf. *ibid.* p. 11, who claims that 'the discrepancy between canon law and popular custom was so great, that there were large numbers of persons who were quite uncertain whether or not they were properly married'.

a drunken frolic, and for the greater security of existing marriages against trumped-up evidence.

Whether the Act was particularly prejudicial to women[3] is also highly debateable. The possibility of establishing a contract of marriage to the satisfaction of the ecclesiastical courts had been difficult even prior to 1754, while those who married after the Act came into force could at least be secure that no precontract could undermine their union. In any case, there is no evidence that women were exclusively the passive victims of male perfidy in this period; women feature as the defendants in cases for the enforcement of a contract before 1754, and as plaintiffs in cases to annul their own marriages on the basis of some legal defect after that date.

One accusation that does have force, at least in part, is that of religious intolerance. But such intolerance can be attributed to society as a whole rather than Parliament alone. The exemption of Quakers alone among Protestant dissenters was clearly because they were the only such denomination to have their own marriage ceremonies. The exemption of Jewish couples also reflects their distinct status and practices; the virulent reaction to the contemporaneous Jewish Naturalisation Bill illustrates that there was perceived to be a profound difference between accepting their distinctiveness and accepting them as English citizens. And to have exempted Catholics, the only other group for which there is solid evidence of marriage according to their own rites, would probably have jeopardised the whole Bill. It would, after all, have required the repeal of existing legislation imposing penalties on Catholics, and barely eight years after the Jacobite rising of 1745 was probably not the most propitious time to try. In fact, another twenty-seven years were to elapse after the Clandestine Marriages Act before Parliament attempted to alleviate the legal position of Catholics, and even this led to riots, conflagration, and repeal.

The widespread absence of any evidence that people married by consent alone prior to 1754 requires us to reassess our view of the relationship between law and custom, and between the rulers and the ruled. If the 1753 Act had been enacted against a background of local and customary modes of marrying, then it would deserve to be ranked as part of the process whereby '[t]he legitimacy of many

[3] E. Tavor Bannet, 'The Marriage Act of 1753: "A Most Cruel Law for the Fair Sex"' (1997) 30 *Eighteenth Century Studies* 233.

popular customs and claims, most of them rooted in ancient law and practice, came to be redefined in elite discourse as usurpation, archaic ignorance, immorality, even criminality'.[4] That this was not the case does not, of course, mean that the general thesis put forward by some scholars of an opposition between law and custom in this period is erroneous, merely that it needs to be refined, and that an example of it is not to be found in the Marriage Act. Some laws may well have been enacted in opposition to popular culture; equally, an individual might be opposed to certain new laws but might observe others. A few anarchists apart, people rarely exist in a state of constant opposition to all laws. A useful distinction may be between law that *regulates* and law that *facilitates*. Eighteenth-century individuals might well have lacked respect for laws that prevented and indeed criminalised the means by which they had previously subsisted. But if they wished to achieve a particular end – to make a valid contract, will, or marriage – there would be little point in flouting the law. The distinction between law as a regulative tool and law as a facilitative tool also correlates with that between laws dealing with ongoing behaviour and laws providing for one-off events. To enter into a legally-binding marriage requires only a one-off act of compliance rather than an ongoing series of acts or a refraining from certain behaviour. (Of course, to remain in a marriage does require ongoing action, but this book has been focused on the point of entry to, not the possible exits from, marriage.) There was, moreover, no simple binary division between law and custom in the context of marriage: one could equally well describe the law as custom.

But why, it must be asked, has such a different view been advanced by other scholars? The widespread misunderstanding of the contract *per verba de praesenti* is unsurprising, given the almost constant stream of decisions asserting or assuming the correctness of the decision in *Dalrymple*, and the parallel development of common-law marriage across the Atlantic. There are, of course, sufficient indications in eighteenth-century texts and cases that should perhaps have alerted scholars to the fact that Scott had misunderstood

[4] D. Hay and N. Rogers, *Eighteenth-Century English Society* (Oxford University Press, 1997), p. 96, and see generally ch. 7, which gives the examples of the Enclosure Acts and the abolition of restrictions on apprenticeship, wages, and food prices.

the law as it stood before the Act. But to an extent we see what we are told we are seeing. If every modern text tells us explicitly that an exchange of vows of words in the present tense was a valid marriage before 1754, then every reference to consent as the essence of marriage, or to a contract *per verba de praesenti* as *ipsum matrimonium*, will be read as reinforcing this, and all the qualifying terms – marriage 'in the sight of God', or 'in conscience' – will be filtered out, the difficult-to-explain case law condemned as poor judgments, and the assertions of individuals ascribed to their confusion.

Commentators have been misled by assumptions that there was continuity between the theories articulated by medieval canon lawyers and the law as it was applied by the ecclesiastical courts of the eighteenth century, and continuity between modern cases (on the rare occasions when a court has been required to apply the law as it stood before the 1753 Act)[5] and eighteenth-century law. At the same time, much of the discussion of the Act has been influenced by what Capp has referred to as '[h]istorians' instinctive search for change'.[6] The orthodox account of the Act fits neatly with a number of easily described binary opposites: the shift from customary rites to legal rules, from an oral culture to a written one, from plurality to prescription. The fact that it put the formalities required for a valid marriage on a statutory footing for the first time has misled those who equate the absence of legislation before 1754 with an absence of regulation. Practically every modern account of the Act has stressed the novelty of its provisions, contrasting its requirements with the supposed simplicity of the exchange of vows *per verba de praesenti*. This emphasis on change is exacerbated by scholars' tendency to focus on specific historical periods: the work of historians of the 1600s provides a very different perspective on marriage rites,[7] but the implications of their work for practices in the 1700s has been largely ignored by scholars of that century. Somewhat paradoxically, both the assumption of continuity and the emphasis on change have fostered the same mistaken belief.

[5] See e.g., *Phillips* v. *Phillips* (1921) 38 TLR 150.

[6] B. Capp, *When Gossips Meet: Women, Family, and Neighbourhood in Early Modern England* (Oxford University Press, 2003), p. 375.

[7] See e.g., the excellent work of D. Cressy, *Birth, Marriage and Death: Ritual, Religion and the Life-Cycle in Tudor and Stuart England* (Oxford University Press, 1997).

And there are further reasons why scholars, not necessarily ones who have made the eighteenth-century law of marriage their special field of study, have been willing to accept a particular version of eighteenth-century practice. It is possible to perceive a tendency in scholarship over the last few decades to criticise marriage and to present modern-day alternative practices as equal or even superior;[8] apparent evidence of such alternatives in the past therefore tends to be greeted with enthusiasm. Current trends in cohabitation outside marriage may similarly encourage individuals to look for and to laud historical parallels,[9] especially those who wish to argue for the extension to cohabiting couples of certain rights currently enjoyed by spouses and civil partners.[10] My own view is that the case for reforming the law applicable to cohabiting couples is quite compelling enough without trying to make out a false case that cohabitants once enjoyed the same legal status as married couples.

And the wider popularity of ideas about supposed folk practices tells us more about modern preoccupations than it does about the past. In the increasing blandness of modern life[11] we might like to believe that peculiar customs of marriage once flourished in stable, self-contained communities that had little contact with the outside world, but such a romanticised image has scant regard for the evidence. The illicit is, moreover, usually more interesting than the regular. There is currently a whole genre of popular history that highlights the scandalous lives of certain elite women of the eighteenth century,[12] ignoring the sober, uneventful lives of the majority. In a similar vein, Tindall noted how a twenty-first-century

[8] On such tendencies, see e.g., R. Fletcher, *The Abolitionists: the Family and Marriage under Attack* (London: Routledge, 1988).

[9] See e.g., S. Parker, 'The Marriage Act 1753: a Case Study in Family Law-Making' (1987) 1 *International Journal of Law and the Family* 133, 149, who 'invites comparison between informal marriage in the past and modern cohabitation'; *Informal Marriage, Cohabitation and the Law, 1754–1989* (Basingstoke: Macmillan, 1990), p. 4.

[10] See e.g., A. Barlow, S. Duncan, G. James, and A. Park, *Cohabitation, Marriage and the Law: Social Change and Legal Reform in the 21st Century* (Oxford: Hart, 2006), p. 119, who suggest that conferring rights on cohabitants would 'effectively amount to giving common law marriage back to the people'.

[11] P. Kingsnorth, *Real England: the Battle Against the Bland* (London: Portobello Books, 2008).

[12] See e.g., A. Foreman, *Georgiana, Duchess of Devonshire* (London: HarperCollins, 1998); C. Hicks, *Improper Pursuits: the Scandalous Life of Lady Di Beauclerk* (Basingstoke: Macmillan, 2001); J. Summers, *Empress of Pleasure: the Life and Adventures of Teresa Cornelys* (London: Viking, 2003); K. Shevelow, *Charlotte: the*

campaign against a proposed office block highlighted (with questionable accuracy) that the disputed site had been a burial ground for prostitutes and paupers, commenting that '[t]he paupers and prostitutes were clearly irresistible, since that is what we currently want history to be about'.[13]

But there is a further, more practical, reason why the belief that many couples married informally has been allowed to take hold, and this is the difficulty until recently of establishing that couples did in fact marry formally. This book could not realistically have been written even ten years ago, since it has taken advantage of the increasing availability of material in electronic form. County-wide material has the potential to increase the proportion of those whose lives are reconstitutable by demographers; searchable eighteenth-century texts and legal cases allow us to put forward with confidence the hypothesis that a particular term or concept was not used at a particular time, or that it had a specific meaning. Caution must, of course, be exercised in making such claims, since current search tools are not perfect. But the apparent absence of a particular phrase does at least raise a presumption that has to be rebutted by clear evidence to the contrary.

Where do we go from here? No work of scholarship is ever final: each provides a platform from which further work can develop. I expect that some people will be unhappy with the arguments advanced in this book. To refute them, however, will require evidence rather than speculation. We must be wary of attaching too much weight to single statements, cases, and examples: it is the role of the historian to distinguish between the illustrative and the exceptional. Similarly, it would be very easy to produce a case study purporting to prove that in communities other than those I have looked at there were far lower levels of compliance either with the canon law before 1754 or with the requirements of the 1753 Act: easy, because one could simply stop looking once the most accessible resources had been consulted. Such case studies are, even with electronic search aids, highly time-consuming. An initial sift of the evidence might produce matches for, say, 70 per cent of the

True Story of Scandal and Spectacle in Georgian London (London: Bloomsbury, 2005); K. Williams, *England's Mistress: the Infamous Life of Emma Hamilton* (London: Arrow, 2007).

13 G. Tindall, *The House by the Thames and the People who Lived There* (London: Pimlico, 2007), p. 115.

sample, but tracking down the last few cases takes at least as much time again – squinting at the microfiches of original documents to detect misspellings and mistranscriptions, repeating the names of the parties over and over to try to think of different ways in which they might have been pronounced and recorded, and looking at patterns of child-bearing to make sure that the children in the baptism register have been attributed to the right couple in the marriage register. I would not claim that I have exhausted the resources available for *any* of my cohorts: family and parish documents such as wills, licences, and others might well enable some of the missing marriages to be traced, but embarking on such an undertaking would require a great investment of time for inevitably diminishing returns. I shall, of course, be delighted if future scholars manage to trace any of the missing marriages using as yet undiscovered resources.

The one point that I would stress as I come to the end of this work is the importance of approaching the evidence with an open mind. I did not embark on this project intending to show that a contract *per verba de praesenti* was not regarded in the same way as a regular marriage; indeed, it is fair to say that this book bears no resemblance to the book I initially intended to write, but I was firmly led in this direction by the evidence of the primary sources. My own journey from belief in the truth of what Scott asserted in *Dalrymple*, to doubt, scepticism, and outright disbelief has been a long one: it took a lot of primary evidence to convince me that other accounts must be mistaken, and, as noted in the Introduction, my own views have evolved over time. But just as a scientist draws a line of best fit on a graph of laboratory results, so too the task of the legal historian must be to assess the evidence as a whole, and to set individual examples and claims in context rather than seeing any one as conclusive proof of a particular practice. The thread that leads us through the labyrinth, to paraphrase Browning,[14] has to be a continuous one in order to lead us to the truth.

[14] R. Browning, 'Mr Sludge, "the Medium"' in J. Pettigrew (ed.), *Poems* (New Haven: Yale University Press, 1981).

INDEX

For EU product safety concerns, contact us at Calle de José Abascal, 56–1°, 28003 Madrid, Spain or eugpsr@cambridge.org.

www.ingramcontent.com/pod-product-compliance
Lightning Source LLC
LaVergne TN
LVHW101443200926
848483LV00001B/36
9780521516150